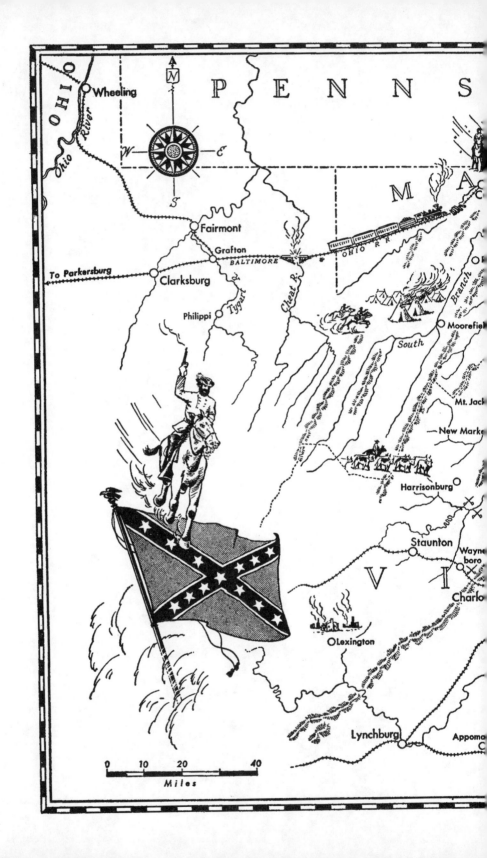

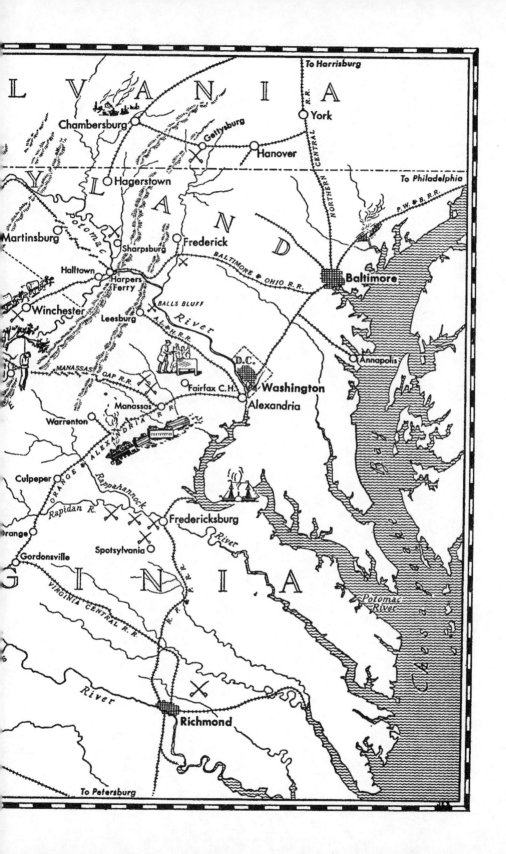

GRAY GHOSTS AND REBEL RAIDERS

Virgil Carrington Jones

WITH AN INTRODUCTION BY
Bruce Catton

GALAHAD BOOKS • NEW YORK

First Promontory Press edition published in 1995.

Promontory Press
A division of Budget Book Service, Inc.
386 Park Avenue South
New York, NY 10016

Promontory Press is a registered trademark of Budget Book Service, Inc.

Published by arrangement with Henry Holt and Company, Inc.

Library of Congress Catalog Card Number: 56-10512

ISBN: 0-88394-092-2

Printed in the United States of America.

In dedicating this book, it is my pleasure to use a toast often on the lips of all who come in contact with a certain member of Congress and former Governor of Virginia:

TO MY FRIEND, BILL TUCK

Foreword

Delving into one of the most familiar parts of the entire Civil War legend—the fabulous guerrilla warfare that spun its threads across northern Virginia, the Shenandoah Valley, and the western Virginia mountains—Virgil Carrington Jones has come up with something genuinely new and important. He has uncovered one of the principal reasons why the war did not end with a Northern victory in the summer of 1864.

The guerrillas of course had become a twice-told tale even before the war was over. From John Singleton Mosby on down, the romantic Virginians who used irregular troops and even more irregular methods to strike at the Yankee invader in the rear of Yankee armies have had more than their share of attention ever since 1861, when proper little General McClellan complained that "enemies of the United States" were carrying on "a system of hostilities prohibited by the laws of war among belligerent nations." But students of the war, almost uniformly (except for some of the Federal generals most directly concerned in the matter) have treated the whole business as a colorful, annoying, but largely unimportant side issue. The guerrillas, they contended, made a nuisance of themselves but in the long run did the Confederate cause more harm than good, both because they provoked savage reprisals by the Federals and because they funneled manpower and effort away from the regular Confederate armies in the field.

Having studied the record with vast diligence and an inquiring mind, Mr. Jones begs to differ. Guerrilla warfare in Virginia, he remarks—and he goes very far toward proving his point—was a highly effective tactic which befuddled the Federal high command, kept the invaders from getting accurate information about the strength and position of their opponents, disrupted supply and communication lines, and, by compelling the Federals to detach large contingents to protect the rear areas, went a long way to nullify the heavy advantage in numbers which the Federals possessed. From first to last the Northerners never really found an effective answer, not even when they had ruthless operators like Grant and Sheridan on the scene. Almost certainly, guerrilla warfare prolonged the war in the Eastern Theater by eight or nine months.

Perhaps the work of these irregulars is a little easier to understand nowadays, in the light of lessons learned in World War II, than it was earlier. For it becomes clear that the Virginia Confederates, generations ahead of their time, had stumbled onto one of the secrets of ultramodern war. They invented a resistance movement for occupied territory—invented it and then supported it with a great deal of vigor and ingenuity, so that while the Northerners occupied a great deal of Virginia they could hardly be said to have conquered any of it. Even late in the war, a Federal commander in Virginia was apt to find the roads behind his army just about as full of peril as the roads in his front. When the Army of the Potomac moved south in its great Wilderness-Cold Harbor campaign, it moved like a ship in the sea; the waters closed in behind it, and any line of supply that ran for more than a few miles was certain to be raveled and tattered by the attacks of the irregulars.

"Irregulars" was the word for them. Officially, the Confederate government approved of the formation of bands of Partisan warriors, giving them regular troop status and permitting them to live behind enemy lines as civilians who would blossom out at intervals as swooping, ranging squadrons of cavalry. Around the fringes, however, things got more and more out of hand. By and large, the life of a Partisan ranger tended to be a good deal more exciting and less onerous than the life of a regular soldier; chances for loot were good, and discipline was not often very strict; and what with one thing and another, a good many young men who might have been carrying muskets for Robert E. Lee slipped off to enjoy the more expansive and rewarding life of a guerrilla.

This did not always make them popular with the Confederate authorities, and Lee himself, in the latter part of the war, wrote to the Confederate Secretary of War urging that the Partisan groups be abolished, saying flatly: "I regard the whole system as an unmixed evil."

But Lee was only saying precisely what Phil Sheridan himself would have said. Sheridan, in the middle of the summer of 1864, was given the assignment of clearing out the Shenandoah Valley so that Grant's campaign against Lee could be carried to a successful conclusion. He had a powerful numerical advantage, and Grant seems to have expected that Sheridan could carry out his assignment in a month or so. Instead it took him until the spring of 1865, and the unmixed evil of guerrilla warfare was largely responsible.

Fairly early in the game, one Partisan leader defined the function of the guerrilla bands—"to hang about their [the Federal] camps and shoot down every sentinel, picket, courier and wagon driver we can find; to watch opportunities for attacking convoys and forage trains, and thus render the country so unsafe that they will not dare to move except in large bodies."

In this aim the guerrillas succeeded admirably—against Sheridan, and against Sheridan's predecessors. The powerful Federal army in the Valley was, at times, all but immobilized. On paper, Sheridan had a crushing numerical advantage over Jubal Early, who commanded the Confederate army that faced him; in actual fact he was never able to make full use of this advantage because he had to use so much of his manpower keeping the guerrillas out of his hair. Even the earlier defeat of the incompetent Franz Sigel takes on a different look when Mr. Jones' account of guerrilla activity is taken into account.

All of this, of course, led to trouble. War in the Valley took on a savage tone, and the barn-burning, looting, and general devastation committed by the Federal troops took shape, finally, as the only answer the occupying armies could make to the Partisan threat. If the Confederates had anticipated modern warfare by devising a ruthless resistance movement, the Federals countered by bringing on an equally ruthless version of total war in reprisal.

In any case, this whole business of what the irregulars did and what effect their doings had on the course of the war has long needed close examination. That examination Mr. Jones has provided. It is hardly going too far to say that one cannot fully understand the course of the Civil War in the Eastern theatre without digesting Mr. Jones' account of the guerrillas. Here, in other words, is an uncommonly interesting and important new chapter in the Civil War story.

Bruce Catton

Bethesda, Maryland
June 27, 1956

Preface

This book has been in the making many years. Soon after I began my study of the Civil War guerrillas in the spring of 1938, the impact of their activities gradually dawned on me. In time I became firmly convinced that they had done much more than they ever got credit for, and that they actually had carried on such an effective campaign of hostilities as to stymie the plans of the Union army for winding up the war.

But I was unknown as a student of the subject, as a chronicler of the events of this conflict that has earned more sustained interest than any other in history, and I realized what claim I made would bear little weight, that any of the more established writers who cared to dispute me would have an advantage I, standing alone, would find difficult to overcome. So I decided to make a trial run, a feeling-out expedition much on the order of the timid husband who first threw his hat in the front door to see whether it stayed. This testing of an idea took me to Richmond, where I laid my conclusions in the lap of that veteran historian of the War of the Sixties, the late Dr. Douglas Southall Freeman. If he would support me, I reasoned, I would be better girded to bat down unfavorable reaction of others.

It was an easy matter to arrange an appointment. I had once been employed as a newspaper reporter in Richmond, working for a short period under the same roof with Dr. Freeman, although he knew of me only through my by-line. But that slim connection got results: he invited me to come to his home in west Richmond. There I arrived promptly at the hour set, and soon was receiving some of the hospitality that in April, 1953, following the historian's appearance before the Washington Civil War Round Table, caused one of the distinguished members of his audience, Major General U. S. Grant, 3d, to remark: "Dr. Freeman is so gracious he impels you to act politely."

He was gracious to me that day, displaying a friendly interest from the very start of our conversation. But I knew he was giving me precious time from his closely scheduled writing day, so I hurried into an explanation of my visit, outlining with little preamble my theory regarding the guerrillas. "What are your reasons for such an idea?" he asked. Briefly I reviewed them while he listened patiently, without comment until I had finished, and then he said, much to my relief, "Well, I had never thought of it that way, but you are fundamentally right. Yes, I certainly agree with your conclusions."

I left Richmond jubilantly dedicated to writing a justification of Confederate independent warfare. My first book, in which I alluded to my theory minutely, was ready to go to the publishers, and I had started work on another that had little to do with the Civil War. Meanwhile, the way was now clear for me to begin, at some time or other, the volume about the irregulars. But I procrastinated over the years, writing on other subjects, and never seriously set to work on this task I had laid out for myself until Bruce Catton walked into my office one day and built a fire under me with the thought: "Why in hell doesn't someone write a history of the guerrillas?"

From that day on it was my Number 1 project. I labored diligently, covering a wide field of research, for the guerrillas of the Sixties were largely unofficial and were almost without exception ignored in contemporary reports, just as they have been in virtually all histories written since the war. That made necessary a diligent search for information, a careful screening of every reference, large or small, concerning the operations of irregular cavalry. The material was scattered throughout many different sources, in several different states. During a period of one year alone, for instance, I pored through 389 books, as well as large collections of letters and papers. When compiled and indexed, the little bits gathered fitted into a broad pattern that made possible a running story and bore out strongly the theory regarding the delay in Union plans I had felt the guerrillas caused.

The busiest part of the research and the writing of the manuscript extended over a period of nearly two and a half years. Now, in looking back to pay tribute to the kind individuals who helped me along the way, I must bow first to my wife, Peyton. As my partner in this extensive hunt for the recorded path of the irregulars, she spent many back-breaking hours of reading and copying, and I must confess that some of the choice and most important fragments of information were turned up by her patient sleuthing. An ex-society editor and newspaperwoman, she also has demonstrated over the years that she is no slouch with the blue pencil.

At the Library of Congress, a godsend to all writers who find their way to its voluminous collection of books, every person with whom I came in contact was extremely cooperative and helpful. I should like especially to pay tribute to my friend of many years, Colonel Willard Webb, chief of the Stack and Reader Division, who seems to have been born a genius. More than once when the trail of a book became dim almost to the point of hopelessness, this gentleman whom nature marked with silver hair long before it was due turned aside tolerantly from his duties to walk out and lay his hand on the volume no one else could find. "I was taught as a child," he would say in a quiet voice that drove away my impatience, "that, when you want something, there are little gremlins to rise up and get it for you."

I am indebted to many friends in Washington, especially members of the local Civil War Round Table. Among these are Dr. Francis A. Lord, an ardent student of the War of the Sixties, who kindly placed at my use many books and papers from his library; Ralph Donnelly, one of the best and most persistent researchers I know; Rex Magee, a Mississippi diplomat and a walking encyclopedia of the war; Melvin Scott, another veteran book collector, and Colonel R. H. Hannum, whose generous nature seems to make it imperative that he help others.

At Leesburg the welcome was of the plush-carpet variety. My special thanks are due Mrs. Frank Osborne, who guided me to the best sources in that area; Miss Elizabeth White, gracious granddaughter of "Lige" White, who loaned me precious books and family papers with the facetious warning that she would use her grandfather's pistol on me if they were not returned; Bruce McIntosh, president of the Peoples National Bank, whose father fought with Mosby, and Mrs. Thomas DeLashmutt, who entertained me so kindly at her beautiful and historic old home, "Oak Hill," and afforded me an opportunity to talk with that distinguished lady, Mrs. Henry Fairfax.

Nearby at Aldie, Mr. and Mrs. Henry B. Weaver were faithful friends, leading me to documents I should never have found without their help. Another who generously assisted me was Mrs. Mary McCandlish of Fairfax, a resident of one of the homes made famous by Mosby's night raid after Stoughton.

On a junket through McNeill's bailiwick I encountered many willing helpers. My task during the days I spent in this neighborhood was made easier by Ralph Haines, prosecuting attorney at Romney, West Virginia, who willingly laid aside imperative legal matters to assist me. My thanks go also to Mrs. R. E. Fisher of Moorefield, McNeill's home town, who placed her large collection of notes at my disposal and seemed not at all upset to have her household routine disrupted by my presence.

Libraries I visited on this junket were most helpful. I am indebted to Miss Mary G. Walsh of the Cumberland Free Public Library, Cumberland, Maryland, and to Verl Z. Garster, assistant curator, Mrs. Maud Wells and Mrs. Fern Gardner, all of the University of West Virginia at Morgantown, where I received treatment on a par with that of the Library of Congress.

Raymond L. McNeill of Suffolk, Virginia, formerly of Romney, a gentleman whose name indicates his interest in my project, went out of his way to be of assistance. The letters he wrote announcing my approach opened more than one door and saved me valuable time.

Generous thanks also are due Dr. Frederick Tilberg, historian of the Gettysburg National Battlefield Park, and J. Melchoir Sheads, who kindly, through the former, placed at my disposal a copy of his thesis on the Southern army's invasions of Pennsylvania.

Officials of the Baltimore and Ohio Railroad were most kind to me. Of special assistance were Lawrence W. Sagle, public relations representative, and Mrs. Virginia T. Reilly, librarian. My obligations involving Baltimore also extend to Colonel Karl S. Betts, a valued friend who not only steered me around the city but actually aided in compiling material uncovered. I am indebted further to the officials of the Pratt Library and to those of the Maryland Historical Society, all of whom were especially cooperative.

And, finally, my thanks go to the many friends, so numerous I would not attempt to mention them all by name, who constantly manifested interest in my work, goaded me to greater effort, and volunteered assistance.

V. C. JONES

Contents

PART TWO

PART THREE

GRAY GHOSTS
AND
REBEL RAIDERS

PART ONE

CHAPTER 1

May 1–10, 1861

TROUBLES IN THE CUSHION AREA

High in the black recesses of the Bull Run Mountains blue lights winked ominous signals, flashing terror to the uninitiated; while nearer Washington, in the scope of their range, a Yankee picket new to army routine, gripped his rifle and peered across the inky Potomac. Along the northern ridge of the river valley at his back, campfires of the Maryland Guard, fanned by a lively breeze, tore the darkness into tatters, casting tower-shaped pictures on the water and giving the lonely watchman a welcome sense of support. He was crouched and tense. The blue-light semaphore in the distance and a mysterious splashing that had just sounded out of the night, close at hand, were partners in his alarm. Word had reached headquarters in late afternoon that the guerrilla cavalry of Turner Ashby, Virginia blue-blood who had sounded the tocsin for Southerners trained to the saddle, was in the vicinity and hellbent for trouble wherever Federal troops could be found.

Troubles for the Union—like the threat of these Rebel signals and Partisan horsemen—were catapulting. Fresh in the picket's mind as he strained for sounds out of the blackness were visions of what had recently happened on the Baltimore and Ohio Railroad running east and west along the Potomac. It should teach a lesson: there must be more troops and better organization, especially against the menacing groups of Rebel irregulars springing up on all sides. Stories

3

published in the newspapers painted a dark picture, with no promise of pastel shadings in the near future. A dozen Secessionists from Baltimore, on their way "to join the traitors at Harpers Ferry," had held a freight train for ransom, and another burden train, laden with wheat, whisky (a great quantity of it), spades, picks, and shovels, all marked for Virginia, had been waved through unmolested.

The B. & O. was something to worry about. Actually the war was scarcely weeks old, and yet the turmoil along the winding tracks of this railway was creating more attention than that at any point short of Fort Sumter. The explanation was simple, of course: any rail line that extended through a border area in which sentiment was about equally divided, as in Maryland and western Virginia, was certain to see plenty of action. Hadn't Bradley Johnson, prominent Baltimore citizen, wearing as bright red a shirt as ever gaudied the body of a Maryland militiaman, rounded up some of his Rebel-sympathizing friends and headed for Secessionland? The pattern was set and the great procession was on, going both ways, with the area of division the B. & O. and the Potomac River, the two forming a sort of twilight zone that told who had taken which side of the great issue now tearing the country asunder.

Neither government knew exactly how to look upon the B. & O. Its board of directors had offered its facilities, valued at more than 30,000,000 dollars, to both the North and South, a neutral policy looked upon with suspicion, for it was well known that the railroad's officers, including its banker-son president, John W. Garrett, red-cheeked and in his early forties, sympathized with the slave-holding states. But there was talk now that they were planning to act contrary to their sympathies, giving their support to the national administration because they were convinced the Southern states would never be able to break away from the Union.

The splashing noise sounded again. It was nearer. The picket, heart in throat, strained to hear, wondering whether it was made by Ashby's cavalry, local guerrillas, or some energetic catfish. It more than likely came from a migrant band of zealous patriots, he suspected. Sentiment was strong south of the Potomac for a "great revenge," for the formation of a volunteer *corps d'armes* to beat back the invaders. Hundreds of impetuous spirits, confident they would be followed by large numbers, had come from Baltimore and beyond and found their way into Virginia. These men, armed with

4

shotguns and rifles, were determined to wage guerrilla warfare against the advancing Yankees.

The picket heard the noise again. It was off to the left. That would be from the direction where a scouting party, sent across the river during the afternoon, had reported peering out of the undergrowth at a body of horsemen, most of them dressed in gray uniforms, galloping madly along a country road.

He slumped closer to the ground and gripped his rifle. One more noise and he would fire, not to kill necessarily, but rather to warn the men in the tents on the ridge. Most of them would be asleep now—had been since tattoo. A fine sedative to a majority of the fellows this new life of soldiering—marching, drilling, making and breaking camp, walking post, and attending to the numerous little military routines. But a few, the stay-up-laters, among them the top officers, would be engrossed in card games and similar pastimes, and he would have to let them—and the sleepers—know they were in danger. As his thoughts turned their way, he noticed that the usual hullabaloo of the camp had died down to a low mumble and an occasional raucous laugh as some militiaman cursed his luck or uttered a remark intended to bring mirth.

He glanced toward the mountains, miles away, and seemed to be staring into a black eternity, an unbroken nothingness as limitless as time. And then all at once the blue lights flashed, supplying him with an object on which to focus. They were in a cluster and he wondered if they came from lanterns, windows, or some new device the Southerners had cooked up to outwit the North. He wondered, too, if this was a one-way proposition, or if there were answering lights flashing from some point beyond his view.

He turned his eyes away and lay close to the ground, waiting, hoping no sound would come, hoping that this splashing that had so disturbed him was after all nothing more than the myriad little noises, stealthy and mysterious, audible along any river any night when the flora and fauna were jumping to life with the rejuvenation of spring.

Seconds passed, and the noise did come, this time in a hollow, flattened gurgle that justified the alarm now causing cold shivers to run up and down his spine.

He muttered a single word under his breath: "Poling!"

Yes, poling. Nothing else could have caused that hollow gurgle,

deadened in resonance as the pole impelling a craft of some sort
came in contact with a hard object on the river bottom. He had poled
many a flat-bottom boat along the waterways around Annapolis,
and he knew. Such a sound could mean only one of two things—a
raft or some old scow commandeered from the numerous inlets dot-
ting the shore of the Potomac. But either might mean an invasion!
Yet on the other hand his fears may have been aroused by some
eager and innocent country lout snooping across the water with his
pals to learn the cause of the fires blazing on the ridge.

He eased his tension on the trigger, undecided whether to fire or
to wait until the sound came so close he could call, "Halt! Who
comes there?" as the military manual instructed, and then wait for
an answer of identity. Out in front he could distinguish nothing but
the pictures dancing on the surface of the river. If a raft or boat or
any other floating object came within the area of these reflections, he
would be able to see it. Of that he was positive, and he stared hard,
listening, trying to soften his noisy breathing.

Minutes passed, amid a silence so intense he could hear his heart
beat. But there was no further disturbance, not even the little peeps
and glucks and other odd sounds which come from the mouths of
night life, insect or animal, fowl or fish. As this silence stretched over
minutes, he was conscious of a feeling of disappointment, and also of
new alarm. What had happened to this craft, no matter what type
it be? Had it sunk? Had it reached the river bank? Or was it moored
out in the river, slowly drifting back and forth on the downstream
side of the pole by which it was anchored?

Suddenly a shot rang out on the far side of the camp, and his
blood, rushing with the shock of expectancy, brought a tingling sen-
sation to his scalp and cheeks as he stiffened in the dark. One, two,
three, in quick succession, and then a barrage, a wild uproar of explosions punctured by cries and curses. Next came a lull of a few
seconds, and then more shooting, a second outburst more terrific than
the first.

The long roll sounded from the tents. It was nervous and broken,
and in his mind the picket could visualize fat Bugler Swan as he
tried to keep his lips on the mouthpiece of his horn. A drum suddenly began rat-tat-tatting the alarm from another position in the
camp. Its signal was clearer than that of the bugle.

Everywhere now there was general confusion—men shouting,
some trying to arouse the sleepers, officers bellowing orders, orders

6

that were as inane and unnecessary under the circumstances as a lap dog at a dance. What the men needed to do was get their rifles and defend themselves, and this they could accomplish without direction from their superiors.

Except for the light from the campfires, all but one or two of the tents were in darkness. Lanterns had winked out during the first barrage of shots, not without howls in scattered instances, and the picket wondered whether the cries he heard were stimulated by pain from hot lantern globes or from hot lead.

He kept his eyes glued on the tents. In the light of the fires some of them seemed to be having the tantrums as militiamen fought to get out, either by rushing through the doors in a mad scramble or by squeezing under the sides. He saw several shelters teeter and fall over and flatten out by degrees while the men caught under them struggled to get free.

But there were some experienced soldiers in the crowd, and this was evident from the orderly firing that now opened up along the ridge, from behind tents and trees and from farther out, toward the pickets to the east and west. Enemy firing was confined to the far side of the camp, over near the area where pine and cedar poles had been nailed and lashed together to form temporary corrals for the horses.

He thought of himself and the direction to the south that was his responsibility. He must be careful; he had been so warned when first placed at the post. Secessionland lay on the other side of the river, and from that way, most likely, would come the enemy, if the enemy came. But so far his only disturbance had been the mysterious splashing. Surely, if the Rebels were going to approach the camp from the river bank, they would have made known their presence by this time.

A new outburst of firing from along the ridge and toward the corrals diverted his thoughts. He wondered if he should forsake his post and go to the aid of his comrades; but, no, that would be contrary to orders. He had been told to stay right where he lay, forsaking his post under no circumstances. And, anyway, his comrades seemed to be doing all right without him. They were still shooting from the campsite with some degree of stubbornness, indicating that they were not being driven, and he could tell by means of the gunfire and other general confusion that there was plenty of life left in them.

7

The shooting went on with rising and falling intensity. As each weapon hurled its load of lead, the flash from its barrel blazed out in a quick spurt of flame, as short-lived as the flicker of a firefly. Men dodged about like shadows, and some of them came together in little groups of two or three and dragged or toted the wounded to sheltered spots on the down side of the ridge toward the picket.

For fully half an hour the firing continued, so long that the sound became monotonous to the picket. And then all at once he realized that no answering blasts were coming from the direction of the enemy. Obviously his fellow militiamen were aware of this too, for gradually their defense efforts died to an occasional shot, stubborn and futile, like the weakened and punchless blow of a tired pugilist.

For minutes the scattered firing went on, until at last there was silence, complete and profound, as if the Marylanders had passed the word. There they lay as a team, waiting, listening, wondering if there would be a new outburst. But none came.

As dawn crept out of the east hours later, word of the attack was spread to the outside world, but it was no bombshell like Fort Sumter. Scarcely a tremor of excitement did it engender. Washington, Baltimore, and New York newspapers buried their notices of it deep in the daily columns of war news, there to remain unnoticed except by the more deliberate readers. So it was left to D. G. Duncan, confidential agent of Confederate War Secretary Leroy Pope Walker, to work up a fever over it. In a lengthy telegram from Richmond he wired the details to Montgomery, Alabama, temporary seat of the Rebel government, and for his trouble got back a curt message from Walker: "Telegraph only ascertained facts, not floating rumors, and brief them." [1]

But this was no floating rumor. The Maryland Guard had got the first taste of guerrilla warfare, the tactic that would become a rich source of horseflesh, supplies, and intelligence for the Southern army. Along the banks of the Potomac had occurred the initial outbreak of this style of fighting, based on stealth, but it would show up later in all directions. And in four years it would become an arm so effective that thousands of Union troops, even in excess of the entire number the South had in the field, would be tied up as guards and withheld from the battlefront.

These developments were for the future, and at the moment they could not be foreseen. At their camp on the banks of the Potomac the victims of the first outburst meanwhile were nursing injured pride. In rehashing their experience, the greatest gall came from an annoying recollection of the derisive, taunting echo of men laughing in unison. It had come floating over from far beyond the ridge after the Rebel firing had ceased, from out of the trees back of the spot where the first shots had sounded. That laugh, they now knew, was a parting jeer given by the invaders as they stole away in the night with dozens of horses taken out of the pine and cedar pole corrals. This war was young, and the Federals, like their opponents, had much to learn. But time would teach them one thing the boys from the South already knew—that horseflesh must be guarded next to human flesh. In the words of a soldier, "when one is 12 hours in the saddle it makes a difference what the saddle is on."

CHAPTER 2

May 11–June 15, 1861

PETITE GUERRE CLEARED FOR ACTION

One May day a military-minded man in the little rustic village of Forest Depot, Bedford County, Virginia, set down on paper an idea that was to grow like a rolling snowball. He was R. C. W. Radford, late captain of the First U. S. Dragoons, and his missile was addressed to Robert E. Lee, newly resigned from the Union army to command military and naval forces of his native Virginia. In it was an offer to raise and mount a company of a thousand active men for Ranger or irregular service if the Confederate government would arm them with long-range guns and pistols.

Captain Radford knew what he was proposing. He explained the object of such an organization would be to annoy and harass an invading army, cutting off escorts and detachments. As experience later proved, his idea was a power-laden gem, but at this early date it was to meet with an ignominious fate. Lee sent it to Colonel Jubal A. Early, organizing troops in the area in which Radford resided, and by him it was relegated to the files with a notation that the captain should be assigned to command of troops from five counties in his district.

But the idea for independent service was not to stop with a letter that wound up in Early's saddlebags. Even as Radford was writing, so was the *Dispatch* at Richmond. On the very day the Confederacy was deciding to move its seat of government from Alabama to Virginia, the newspaper in a leading editorial urged that men of the Old Dominion form themselves into companies for guerrilla warfare, using "double-barreled fowling pieces loaded with buckshot" where rifles could not be procured. This journal occasionally launched into fantasy, a privilege at times taken to extremes, as in this instance: "If the line of march of the Federal troops is made to swarm with our guerrillas, who will pick off every man and every squad that dares to leave the main body of the invading column, the very success in the field will prove ruin, for they will tempt the men further and further into the interior and involve them more and more inextricably in the meshes and snares of guerrilla warfare."

The *Dispatch* backed up this editorial three days later with another in which it stressed the importance of guerrilla warfare. It said that nothing harassed an enemy upon the march so much as the "constant hornet sting" of guerrillas, described as adversaries who could neither be caught nor avoided. "They come unexpectedly," it was explained, "drop their men here and there, are off again and on again in a moment, and cause infinite perplexity and danger." [1]

The South was ripe for this proposal. A Baltimore newspaper reported that hundreds of impetuous spirits had left the city in wagons, carriages, buggies, and other vehicles to wage guerrilla warfare against invaders from the North.[2] And already blood was shed. Fort Sumter had been fired upon, and the Sixth Massachusetts Volunteers, marching through the streets of Baltimore, were roughly handled by a mob, with fatalities to both sides. The Union guard on duty in the hillside town of Harpers Ferry fired the United States arsenal there and fled in the face of an approaching force of Virginia militia. Rebels took over, carrying drawn swords and wicked-looking muskets, and stationed loaded cannon in position to stop approaching trains so they could be searched for United States agents or soldiers.[3] At Washington the aged commander-in-chief, General Winfield Scott, severely taxed without the younger Lee to assist him, was arming the city as fast as troops arrived, and in Richmond bonfires were burned in the streets and buildings broke out in a rash of Confederate flags.

Virginia's governor, John Letcher, was faced with problems other than those of defense. Out in the mountainous area of the state to the west an element in favor of breaking away from the Old Dominion and setting up its own government was gaining strength under the leadership of Francis H. Pierpont. Letcher was notified that the people in that section would sustain him if they were given a chance to defend themselves against a Union force then organizing in Ohio. One local citizen wrote the governor: "Let us have arms as speedily as possible and the people will rise and fight." [4]

Letcher was perturbed over western Virginia, and he also was worried about the B. & O., the rail lifeline piercing the northern part of that area. Aware of the facilities it offered for arming Washington with troops from the West, he wired its president that he would take possession of the road if it were used to transport Federal soldiers.

The Union was making plans to control the B. & O. too, and it was doing so apparently without realizing that the greatest field of incubation for the guerrilla warfare advocated by Captain Radford and the Richmond *Dispatch* lay along the winding right of way of the railroad. This line stretched through a natural arena for independent action—from the Camden Street Station in Baltimore nine miles westward to Relay House, where it divided, sending one spur to Washington and another toward the west, past Harpers Ferry and Martinsburg and Cumberland and beyond, to its terminus 400 miles away at Wheeling on the Ohio River. By maintaining such an extensive transit system so near the seat of war the Federal government would be openly inviting the type of irregular fighting against which experience of centuries failed to offer an adequate defense. [5]

Time also would show that the Union, in providing such a field of incubation along the B. & O., would be supplying to the enemy's regular army an underground or fifth column that alone, through its determined and relentless activities, was to be responsible largely for the war's extension into 1865. But no one could see this at the start. A railroad over which troops and supplies might be shuttled from the West was a factor obviously entitled to a place in the overall plans for battle.

In 1861 the B. & O. was a public utility of no small stature. It was looked upon as so old that its supporters liked to say it had grown up with the nation. But it was not through sentiment that both the North and South cast covetous eyes at the B. & O. Here lay a transportation agency that would find much use in the warfare then spreading over the nation. It constituted the fastest and most direct route to the trans-Allegheny and the rich territory beyond. Over its rails would come valuable manpower and valuable stores—stores from forest, farm, and mine. The belligerent power that held claim to it, beyond question, would have a decided advantage.

At the outbreak of war the 30,000,000 dollars invested in the B. & O. made it one of the costliest roads in the country. It had 513 miles of track, not counting sidings. Ready to haul its trains were 236 locomotives, and available to make up these trains were 128 passenger and express coaches and 3451 freight cars.

Obviously no matter which side claimed it, the task of guarding the B. & O. would be tremendous. Its tracks lay through a wide variety of terrain. From Relay House where the thirty-one-mile spur branched off to Washington, the tracks wound westward, a feat of engineering. They crossed the Potomac at Harpers Ferry, at the confluence of the Potomac and Shenandoah rivers, and there connected with another auxiliary line—a thirty-two-mile spur to Winchester, this one to tap the bountiful crops of the Shenandoah Valley. For miles beyond Harpers Ferry the route extended northwestward through three Virginia counties, crossed back into Maryland, wound again into Virginia for ten miles, and then returned to Maryland to begin the ascent of the Alleghenies before swinging back into Virginia. From there on it was over some of the roughest country in America. In order to traverse it the rails had to be laid under hills, across streams, through valleys, over razorback mountains. At Grafton another line branched off to Parkersburg on the Ohio River, and this was the last. After that the Main Stem swung into the northwest until it reached the terminus at Wheeling.

Only one section of the railroad was double-tracked. This was the forty-four-mile span between Point of Rocks, twelve miles east of Harpers Ferry, and Cherry Run, thirty-two miles to the west.

Because the railroad lay exclusively in slave states, three fourths of it in Virginia, the South naturally counted it as one of its assets, especially since its president had spoken out in sympathy with the South.[6] But from the first it was realized that the problem of protecting the line might be too demanding upon the resources and manpower of the South. Its rails in the Alleghenies and beyond lay in territory that was strong in its sentiment for the North and rampant in its desire to break away from the pro-slavery Virginia government at Richmond.

Meanwhile, as the weather warmed with the arrival of May, the Federal camp at Relay House became a point of interest for the populace, male and female. Crowds flocked there daily to loiter with the soldiers or to stand off and stare at the strange doings, thus adding spice to their humdrum daily lives. Trains from Washington came out on the half-hour, and the turnpike stretching over the thirty-one miles between the two points was lively with vehicles. Some days it was estimated there were as many as 3000 persons on the grounds. Wagons filled with beer, pies, cakes, and other items of food appeared daily. Some of these, a newspaper observed, were "in charge of parties who anticipated no doubt quite a speculation in fleecing the volunteers."

Throughout all the confusion the soldiers were dividing their attention between the camp visitors and the country to the west into which disappeared the rails of the B. & O. Excitement grew and the inspection routine at Relay House became more rigid. Officers searched every train that passed. What they were looking for was armed men, guns, munitions of war, and provisions. None of these could go through. Maybe a few groceries and dry goods—except uniform cloth—for the miners in the coal fields of western Virginia, but nothing else. All other freight went back to the consignees at Baltimore. The Union meant to subjugate Maryland.

Farther west at Harpers Ferry the Rebels were up to something; that much was well known. But it was not clear just exactly what they were doing. The conductor on an eastbound train reported one day that the woods on the Maryland side were a mass of flames when he passed. Looked like the Southerners were clearing the way for fortifications, he said. The Baltimore *American and Commercial Advertiser,* seizing upon this intelligence, concluded that the first collision between the swelling military forces on each side of the Potomac might come at that point.

Troubles along the railroad increased. Here was beginning the border warfare that would continue for four years. Telegraph wires were cut almost with regularity—in widely separated places. For a time communication by rail with Washington was interrupted, and there was no indication from the ticket office as to how soon it might be resumed. This breach of train service, though temporary at most, stretched at times into such proportions that the Balimore postmaster, confronted with a growing accumulation of mail, one day sent off a dozen bags of it by light express wagon drawn by four fine animals selected for their fleetness. Once they got started the horses did all right, as equine records go, covering the distance in five hours, but there was a slight delay beforehand when the rear axle gave way.[7]

After the first excitement about the railroad was over, trains, relieved of munitions of war and other contraband before they cleared Relay House, continued to roll into the west. By May 10 word came back that the Rebels, farther along, were doing a little inspecting also; that cars were stopped at Point of Rocks, a dozen miles east of Harpers Ferry, under the supervising eye of Turner Ashby, the exciting Virginian whose dashing cavalry company was becoming such an attraction to Marylanders with Secesh proclivities.[8] Trains were brought to a halt and then they were given a careful search by none other than Captain Bradley T. Johnson, the red-shirted Baltimorean who had left home with an armed company of "Southern volunteers" back in April. Coming from the other direction, horses and beeves, bound for the East out of the West, were never permitted to pass Harpers Ferry.

On the morning of May 10 a string of cars bearing a field battery and 400 men rolled westward from Relay House—just how far was never made clear. These troops were sent out mainly for reconnaissance, on the strength of the news about the burning trees, fortified heights, and train inspections around Harpers Ferry. But they established no contact with the Rebels; they were back in a few hours, heroes all to the waiting gentry and envious fellow soldiers, and about the only subject they were unanimous in discussing was the beauty of the countryside through which they had passed.

At Richmond during early May developments gave every indication that the South planned to take possession of all western Virginia, including the B. & O., as far as the Ohio River. Orders were flashing back and forth, helter-skelter, and arrangements were made for troops in that area to rendezvous at Grafton, Kanawha, Parkersburg, and Moundsville.

Major Alonzo Loring at Wheeling, Major Francis M. Boykin at Grafton, and Captain William P. Thompson at Fetterman were authorized to muster into the service such volunteer companies as came forward and to organize them for the protection of the railroad. But the recruits were few and far between, and Boykin finally reported that sentiment in the area was so strongly Union that those men who wanted to remain true to Virginia were afraid to leave their families. Under this state of things he suggested bringing in troops from the East.

But General Lee, in charge of Virginia forces, opposed sending troops from elsewhere, claiming they might irritate rather than conciliate the population. He felt the same way about occupying Maryland.[9] So instead he dispatched Colonel George A. Porterfield of Jefferson County to Grafton to organize available manpower and to select positions at which to protect both branches of the B. & O. leading from there to the Ohio River.

Porterfield arrived at Grafton May 14 and found neither officers nor men waiting to assist him. He notified Richmond, and word came back that both arms and troops were on their way, the latter moving from Staunton and gathering strength as they advanced.

That day tension tightened along the B. & O. A train was seized at Harpers Ferry, and at eight o'clock that night all telegraph connections with the West were severed. At Annapolis, Brigadier-General Butler took matters in his own hands, occupied Baltimore, and telegraphed Washington: "Send us no more detachments till further orders." This message almost brought apoplexy to aging General Scott, who had thought all along that he was the man to say what steps the Union army should take next. Days had passed without a word from Butler, and then had come this impertinent telegram! So the general promptly snapped back by wire, "Let me hear from you," meantime planning to cool off the brigadier by sending him to Fort Monroe on the Virginia coast.

Patriotic Southerners straggled into points of concentration, in companies, in small groups of a dozen or more, in twos and threes. The West Point-trained General Cocke, commanding Rebel troops along the Potomac and only a few months separated from death by his own hand, had moved back from Alexandria to Culpeper, and now as more manpower arrived he felt his way north again to Manassas, junction point on the Orange and Alexandria Railroad for the Manassas Gap line extending into the Shenandoah Valley. There he gathered 918 men, divisible into bands of horsemen and infantry, each with a name, each short of arms and uniforms, and began to look over the country.[10] He found it favorable for defensive operations—"undulating, covered with dense forests of second-growth pines or of original oak . . . the roads very narrow (mere ditches), and everywhere such as to render artillery and cavalry of our enemy on the march of little use to him." He also found that the cover of forests, hills, and ravines made a fortress "for brave men and riflemen in which to carry on the destructive guerrilla warfare upon any marching columns."

While the tensions thus developed, the South suddenly pulled a coup along the double-tracked stretch of the B. & O. that would go down in history for its cleverness. A little-known artillery major from the Virginia Military Institute, Thomas Jonathan Jackson, commanding at Harpers Ferry, a stern-faced individual with no patience for pomp and ceremony, complained to railroad officials of the noise made by their trains, maintaining they disturbed the repose of his troops. He persisted until he got them to move all trains past that point between the hours of 11:00 A.M. and 1:00 P.M. Daily during the two-hour period almost continuous chains of cars rolled in each direction along the double track—until May 23. That day Rebel troops moved out to bottle up this concentration of traffic, drawing into their bag more than 300 cars and fifty-six locomotives, some of the latter to be horse-drawn to Southern railways by way of the Valley pike from Winchester to Strasburg.

Now the Union began moving. Eleven regiments of New York, New Jersey, and Michigan troops crossed the Potomac without opposition on May 24 and established a line that circled Washington on the Virginia side from the Leesburg road on the north to the river bank below Alexandria. It was the boldest demonstration to date and indicated conclusively that Abe Lincoln meant business. There were similar hostile developments elsewhere. General Scott had heard that two companies of Virginia troops already were at Grafton, where the B. & O. divided in its approach to the Ohio River, and he ordered General George B. McClellan, commanding the Ohio militia gathering at Cincinnati, to move there and "counteract the influence" of the Rebels. He also instructed General Patterson up in Pennsylvania to move down and threaten Harpers Ferry.

The Confederacy watched these developments with interest. Along Bull Run, a narrow stream winding on down through rolling hills to within a short distance of Manassas, Rebel reinforcements arrived and commanding officers began looking for defensible positions.

As if in retaliation for Federal encroachments, the Southerners at this time put a definite end to rail traffic along the B. & O. Faced with the approach of enemy troops from Ohio, Porterfield, who had managed to assemble a few hundred men, including the companies from Staunton, sent a detachment westward from Grafton to destroy as many bridges as possible along both branches of the railroad in that direction. Toward the east there was equally effective action. By means of extremely accurate blasting Ashby dropped upon the tracks near Point of Rocks an overhanging boulder so huge it took the Yankees until June 15 to peck it to pieces with explosives.

At Grafton, Porterfield met with growing resistance from the Union-minded citizens. Two armed men fired one night at one of his sentinels, shooting him through the ear, and the sentinel fired back and killed one of his assailants. The dead man's gun was confiscated and his body turned over to his friends, and in the confusion his name was lost to society, even though he was one of the first participants in the war to fall from an enemy bullet.

The increasing unrest along the railroad at last brought action from Ohio. McClellan, who became famous in later days for his delaying tactics, decided to wait no longer. One of the officers under his command was a stern-faced, big-chested man named Benjamin F. Kelley, colonel commanding the First West Virginia Infantry. Prudent, secretive, vigilant, and a constant churchgoer, this man, a native of New Hampshire, had left a mercantile business at Wheeling to take part in the war. His men called him "Old Ben," perhaps because of his bull-like countenance. He had a prominent chin set off by a shaggy patch of billy-goat whiskers, and extending on each side from his nose to his lower jaw was a deep wrinkle that tied in with the straight line of his mouth to form a triangle. This usually dependable leader was to see much action throughout the war and to draw the comment that he made less history for the amount of fighting he did than any other general officer in the service.[11]

It was Kelley that McClellan sent to drive Porterfield away from the railroad. "Old Ben" moved rapidly, maintaining contact with another force advancing from the east along the southern branch of the railroad from Parkersburg. The only delay was that required to build temporary bridges to replace those destroyed by the Rebels. By May 30 Kelley was at Grafton, hot after the Confederates, who had withdrawn a few miles southward to Philippi.

Early in June, Kelley made ambitious plans to surprise and capture the enemy he was trailing—600 infantry and 175 cavalry. Marching through the forested hill country, a part of the time in a driving rain and pitch-black darkness, he arranged his troops for a frontal assault to be timed with an attack from the rear. The onslaught was to come at daybreak of June 3, and so it was arranged, but the advance stumbled upon Rebel pickets and set off the alarm before the encircling movement at Philippi could be completed. Luckily warned by this turn of events, Porterfield got his men out of the trap with loss only of tents and cooking equipment, and fled toward Beverly.

Thus ended the first planned field action of the war. In terms of victory it had been won by the Federals, but their triumph narrowly escaped being costly. Among their wounded was "Old Ben" Kelley, pierced through the right breast by a bullet that might easily have been fatal.

The outcome of this fight did much to shift sentiment in the area to support of the Union. A few days later Porterfield reported: "The country to the northwest is in a state of revolution, all law-abiding citizens being driven off by the traitors, assisted by Northern troops. The private property of Secessionists, but otherwise inoffensive citizens, their cattle, young unbroken horses and colts, and the clothing of women and children, have been seized and taken off."

Though later partially exonerated by a court of inquiry, Porterfield had been placed in disrepute by the affair at Philippi. A clamor arose for his removal, and Lee soon dispatched to the area General Robert S. Garnett, an experienced West Pointer and former officer in the regular army, who had resigned to take over the duties of Adjutant General at Richmond.

The pincers began to close on Harpers Ferry. Patterson had left Philadelphia and was marching southward. General Joseph E. Johnston, who had assumed the command formerly held by Jackson, favored evacuation, citing that the Confederate force there could be much more effective in resisting the advance of the enemy if it were not retained in a fixed position but allowed to fall back and hold itself in readiness for quick movements. In this opinion he was opposed by Jefferson Davis, who placed great value on retention of the command of the Valley and Harpers Ferry.

On June 10, one week after the surprise of Porterfield at Philippi, fighting occurred at Big Bethel near the coast of Virginia, the second field action of the war, with a number killed and wounded on each side. This day Patterson cited by letter to the Secretary of

War the importance of capturing Harpers Ferry and said he could not sleep for thinking about it.[12] He was looking for the first great battle of the war to be brought on there.

Meanwhile Johnston's idea of evacuating Harpers Ferry and falling back to the interior around Winchester for a more mobile warfare gained support. Jefferson Davis finally was won over and voiced no further protest. It was obvious Maryland would be—and already had been largely—overrun by the enemy. Northwest Virginia, too, was rapidly coming under control of McClellan's advancing hordes. This left Harpers Ferry in an untenable position. The high command of the Confederacy at last seemed unanimous in choosing the surrender of that point and the destruction of the B. & O. as the path of military wisdom.

Railroad bridges, already burned east and west of Martinsburg, could be replaced within a week. That would be true of all the spans except possibly the one across the Potomac at Harpers Ferry. So the line must be destroyed in its entirety, tracks torn up, rolling stock and machinery put out of order, and everything done that would delay as long as possible the date on which this artery with the West again could be restored to military use. The task was left to T. J. Jackson.

Again the professor from V.M.I. showed ingenuity. A newspaper reporter passing along the B. & O. days later wrote that "the destruction is fearful to contemplate." He drew word pictures of what he saw: "All along the railroad were scattered cars in long lines, with the coal still burning . . . Here and there the road led above them, and looking down, we could see the inside—a mass of red hot coals. Some small bridges had been burnt with cars on them, and giving way, the cars were left piled one on another in the small streams below, all battered and bent. We counted the line of locomotives that had been burnt (41 or 42 in all), red and blistered with heat." [13]

Jackson did a thorough job. What could not be salvaged and moved to the Manassas Gap line at Strasburg was destroyed. Up in flames also went the long bridge across the Potomac at Harpers Ferry.

When the last Confederate soldier marched off southward to take up Johnston's new line around Winchester, his disappearance signified that the Union then held complete possession of the B. & O. But it would not be undisputed possession. Forces were building up to make this nearly 400-mile stretch of railroad track a constant source of trouble, at all hours and in many places, regardless of where the regular armies were and what they were doing. These forces would revert to guerrilla warfare, that style of action dating back into the ages. It was the weapon of the overrun and outnumbered, the tool that no military science known to the academies could estimate—the inexorable, taunting war of the independents, the irregulars, the Partisans, the self-centered and individualistic patriots stimulated to take up arms, and the angered farmers fighting for the peace of their firesides.

To the Confederate government at this time came an official inquiry regarding this scattered warfare. The query was from an esteemed resident of Winchester—F. A. Briscoe, Esquire. He wrote about the matter of organizing a guerrilla force, and the answer he received from Richmond within a week very definitely placed the adjutant general on record as highly in favor of the move: ". . . Such a force, when organized, armed and equipped, will be received into service and commissions issued to the officers thereof." [14]

CHAPTER 3

June 16–July 14, 1861

AS BRAVE MEN FALL

Private Allen Alonzo Kingsbury, ardent nature lover, detrained at Washington June 16 with the Chelsea Volunteers, Massachusetts First Regiment. He was from Medfield, a member of Company H, having the thrill of his life. Next day he went sight-seeing, and in the late afternoon he sat down and wrote his mother:

"I write this seated upon a sofa in the grand reception room of the White House at Washington. In the room are eight large mirrors, four sofas, 24 chairs and three large chandeliers. The sofas and chairs are covered with red velvet. I have rambled about the city to-day considerable. Ascended the dome of the Capitol, 280 feet from the ground, could see all over the city, Alexandria, Arlington Heights and Mt. Vernon. I then visited the government buildings, the Post Office, Smithsonian Institute, Treasury Building, War Department, Patent Office, and the Market. Help eat two quarts of strawberries with Corporal Jewett. Came back to the Regiment, rescued a negro from the police, had quite a time. . . . Don't think much of the city." [1]

Kingsbury, who on his third day in Washington would pass the White House and see "Honest Old Abe" and the day following be elected second cook, was exactly ten months from his death by bullet. He was disappointed with the national capital and he was dissatisfied with the food he was getting: some days, coffee and bread for breakfast, beefsteak for dinner, coffee, bread, and corned beef for supper; other days, boiled rice for breakfast, baked beans for dinner, roast beef and potatoes and lemonade for supper. But he recorded that there was "any quantity of ice cream and peddlers" around his camp.

While Allen Alonzo Kingsbury found Washington disappointing, General Winfield Scott was very well pleased with it. He was less pleased with the area under his command out toward Harpers Ferry and Cumberland. In fact, he was just at that moment drawing in his forces and trying to keep up with his generals. This was no easy task, because the men who were leading the Union forces in the field were fighting the war as they thought best and not bothering to report often to the commander-in-chief—and what telegrams some of them sent were briefed too much for the dyspeptic old officer to understand.[2]

Out in western Virginia, McClellan, affable and courteous, possessed of personal magnetism and kind to newspaper reporters, poked along in no particular hurry. At the same time busybody Patterson, at last in the vicinity of Harpers Ferry, talked of sending a detachment to Winchester and another toward Cumberland, the latter to support Indiana troops which had taken over there under the supervising eye of Colonel Lew Wallace. Scott could see no need for building up forces in that direction. "The enemy is concentrating upon Arlington and Alexandria, and this is the line first to be looked to," he wrote.[3]

Not too much was known about what the Southerners had in mind, and there were wild rumors that added to Scott's problems. For instance, the telegraph operator at Arlington Mills over on the Virginia side from Washington wired that he could see railroad bridges burning and that General Tyler, commanding at Alexandria, had gone beyond them. It took General Irvin McDowell, whose headquarters tent was set up in the yard of Lee's old home at Arlington, to put an end to this alarm. He messaged simply that there were no bridges burning, that what the telegrapher had seen was merely one of the sleepers along the Alexandria, Loudoun and Hampshire Railroad from Alexandria to Leesburg that "had been set on fire by the droppings of the locomotive."[4]

But at least one of the rumors could not be discounted. At the little railroad stop of Vienna on the A., L. & H., a short distance north of Fairfax Court House, Confederates under Colonel Maxcy Gregg of

South Carolina played havoc with a trainload of Union soldiers sent out on reconnaissance. The Rebels almost missed their chance, passing that point just a few minutes before the arrival of the train, but the locomotive whistle warned them of its approach, and they whirled about and raced back to place their two six-pounder guns on a hill overlooking the track. When the army special came jogging along at fifteen miles an hour, they cut loose with rifle and cannon fire—aiming at two passenger coaches and five platform cars, all jammed with blue-coated men, 668 rank and file and twenty-nine field and company officers, pushed by a single engine. Before the eyes of the Rebels in a matter of seconds took place one of the fastest withdrawals in history. Among the first to get away was the engineer, who unhooked the locomotive and one coach and highballed it back to Alexandria, causing much suspicion later when it was found he, too, was named Gregg. Behind him in his flight he had left a number of dead and wounded, a countryside swarming with running Federals, and much blood in the bushes.

On the scene toward western Virginia at this time came an old Indian fighter who talked in terms of Partisan and Ranger service and border war, a rare character who preferred hatchet to saber as a weapon on the battlefield.[5] He was well known to Virginians as Angus McDonald, prominent citizen of Winchester, and a man whose type even in that day was fast disappearing.[6] At Richmond he had offered his services to the Confederacy, and Jefferson Davis promptly commissioned him a colonel of cavalry and gave him a personal letter of introduction to Joe Johnston. The first week in June, Johnston welcomed the veteran at Harpers Ferry and sent him out to raise his own regiment of cavalry. It was trust well placed. McDonald soon had agents combing the country for recruits, and results were highly pleasing.[7] Among the first to join were Captain Turner Ashby and his brother Richard, both bachelors, both renowned horsemen who had done picket duty in the John Brown affair at Harpers Ferry. Shortly afterward Captain George R. Gaither arrived with a troop of Marylanders, and then appeared other volunteers, some from as far away as Alabama and Kentucky.

Angus was satisfied that among these men were "some of the very best for the peculiar services of Partisan and border war." [8] He was especially pleased with Turner Ashby. "I need not speak of his qualities," he wrote the Secretary of War, "for already he is known as one of the best Partisan leaders in the service. Himself a thorough soldier, he is eminently qualified to command." McDonald wanted him commissioned lieutenant colonel.

On the morning of June 18 [9] the old Indian fighter sat at breakfast with his family and officers of the new regiment. Mrs. McDonald never forgot the picture they made, some young, some old, all enthusiastic and buoyant with the war spirit. Of the Ashbys she wrote in after years: "I so well remember the two brothers as they sat together on my right at the breakfast table, Richard, with his handsome brown eyes and hair, his bright smile and pleasant manners, while Turner, with jet black piercing eyes, black hair and beautiful coal black beard, sat grave and quiet, but enjoying the chat." [10] This breakfast would be the brothers' last formal meal together.

Soon after they arose from the long table in the McDonald dining room, the officers rounded up their companies and prepared to ride westward. McDonald had been ordered to destroy the Cheat River viaduct on the B. & O., a combination of iron spans 320 feet long seventy-six miles beyond Cumberland. This bit of destruction General Lee had said would be "worth to us an army." [11] But Federal guards were already at that point, and it was too big a mission for a small band of cavalry to accomplish.

The second day after leaving Winchester, McDonald reached Romney and divided his command into groups for scouting duty and to secure forage and provisions. Turner Ashby took his company into camp six miles away, on the estate of George Washington, kinsman of the great George. A few mornings later he sent a party of eleven men under his brother on a scout along the railroad, and this party encountered a superior force of McClellan's Unionists and soon was in trouble. As they retreated, fighting all the while, Richard Ashby's horse fell into a cattle guard, unseating its rider. Even on foot the Partisan refused to surrender, and the enemy beat him down, puncturing his body with bullet and bayonet wounds that in seven days would cause his death.

Virginia lore tells in stirring terms of the anger of Turner when he heard of what had happened to Richard. He came charging after the Federals, overtaking them on an island in the Potomac, and there he routed them, losing two of his own men in the act and receiving a slight wound himself. Colonel Lew Wallace at Cumberland, later to earn fame with his stirring book *Ben Hur*, revealed his talent in reporting the fight, describing it as "the boldest, most desperate on record—hand to hand—with pistol, saber, bayonet and fist."

In the early days of war little things are great, even to talented writers. Thus a mere hand-to-hand combat became a full-blown fight, a saber nick a serious wound. But this was no minor skirmish to Turner Ashby, for there was personal vengeance in his blows. Folks said he was never the same after the death of his brother, that it was this experience that made him the mad, dashing, foolhardy rider he became in succeeding months, setting an example of personal daring for other Partisans to follow, and for succeeding generations to sit around their firesides and talk about.[12]

The campaign was just beginning in western Virginia. On June 21 McClellan crossed the Ohio to Parkersburg and prepared to take command in person of the troops Kelley and Wallace had led so well. Scarcely had he put foot on Virginia soil before Francis Pierpont, now sending out mail from Wheeling under the stamp of "Governor," was advising him about "evil-minded persons" who had banded together in military organizations to make war on the loyal people in that area. By the time McClellan reached Grafton June 23, he had had ample opportunity to learn what Pierpont was talking about. Everywhere he went he heard of guerrilla bands, and he began making plans to send columns of his soldiers through the mountains to put a stop to such operations. But first there must be a proclamation.

McClellan personally supervised its preparation: "To my great regret I find that enemies of the United States continue to carry on a system of hostilities prohibited by the laws of war among belligerent nations . . . Individuals and marauding parties are pursuing a guerrilla warfare, firing upon sentinels and pickets, burning bridges, insulting, injuring, and even killing citizens because of their Union sentiments, and committing many kindred acts." He then made his proclamation, to the effect that these persons, carrying on this species of warfare—"irregular in every view which can be taken of it"— would "be dealt with in their persons and property according to the severest rules of military law." [13]

A great hand for proclamations was McClellan. Two days later he issued one to his soldiers, telling them: "I have heard that there was danger here. I have come to place myself at your head and to share it with you. I fear now but one thing—that you will not find foemen worthy of your steel." Such words were well received by his men at that early stage, before they had come face to face with the grim, bloody realities of war and with one of the worst experiences of all —Virginia mud.[14]

But the proclamation McClellan made to the people of western Virginia was read by rebellious eyes. Throughout the mountainous area, where organized movement of troops was difficult and use of artillery almost impossible, warfare carried on by small bands, whether regular or irregular, seemed the only recourse. And these bands were springing up rapidly. A citizen, William Skeen, had in mind raising ten companies to fight in this style. But first he wanted to place his operations on an official basis, so he hurried to Richmond. The audience he sought at the capital brought reasonable results. The Secretary of War promised that, if Jefferson Davis concurred, this service would be ordered.

Meanwhile Bob Garnett, sent to replace Porterfield, joined his new command at Huttonsville, deep in the mountains, on the most direct line from Staunton. Matters in western Virginia had reached a crisis. A citizen of the area, himself strongly Southern in sentiment, described the situation to Secretary of War Walker: a defenseless population, erroneously regarded as wholly disloyal, separated by distance and mountains from the main strength of the South, exposed to invasion on almost every side, actually overrun by an army of 12,000 to 15,000 men, and left without sufficient support. In this citizen's opinion at least 10,000 men besides Bob Garnett's force would be absolutely necessary to put matters on more even keel.[15]

But the South was in a dilemma. It needed additional men in many other sectors. And so scarce was equipment that it could supply only a few hundred tents and blankets for the 4500 soldiers then under Garnett. Western Virginia, at this most critical period, comprised a problem beyond the power of the Confederacy to face.

The desperate plight of the Secession states, for better or worse, in no way influenced the task of the man they had sent to stop McClellan's march from the West. After taking command Garnett immediately occupied the two turnpike passes over Rich Mountain and Laurel Hill, important points because they were the gaps through which lay the main roads leading from the B. & O. He regarded them as the gates to the northwestern country, realizing that if the enemy controlled them his army would be bottled up in Cheat River Valley.[16]

McClellan meanwhile was far from sure of the Rebel strength he was facing. He thought it more than probable that there were from 1500 to 3000 Confederates at Romney, covering the approaches to Winchester. He also knew of the troops in the mountain passes, but he considered that their chief object was "to protect and furnish guerrilla parties, which are doing much damage in this region." [17] At any rate, he decided to break up this latter concentration of the enemy, after which he would move toward Staunton or some other point on the road to Richmond.

McClellan was having a minimum of trouble in storming over western Virginia. The morning of July 7 his columns started on their greatest offensive to date. They moved in two bodies, the main force, under the commanding general, closing in on Rich Mountain Pass from the west, via Buckhannon, while the other, under Brigadier General T. A. Morris of the Indiana militia, advanced noisily from Philippi to the east side of Laurel Hill and gave indications of attacking the pass there. But Morris had been told not to make an assault if he could avoid it. The major trouble for the Rebels was to come from the troops under McClellan. These would sweep from the rear, capture the Confederate supply base at Beverly on the other side of the range, take Rich Mountain, held by a force under Lieutenant Colonel John Pegram, West Pointer, and then join Morris for the attack on Laurel Hill, where Garnett was directing operations.

In the evening of July 9 McClellan's men reached Roaring Creek at the base of Rich Mountain, arriving at dusk and dropping down, tired, into the wet stubble. That night a reconnaissance was made, and in the morning another, and the findings were against a direct assault and in favor of a flanking movement.[18] The attack was led by one of McClellan's most trusted officers, Brigadier General William S. Rosecrans. It began in the middle of the afternoon—nearly 2000 Federals against 300 Rebels—and for the next three hours the fighting was fierce.[19] Twice the Union troops were driven back from the precipitous crags on the mountain crest, but for the third time they returned, and the last time was enough.

After this turn of affairs Garnett over on Laurel Hill eluded Morris and struck toward Cheat River, bivouacking the night of the twelfth at Kaler's Ford. But Union troops under Captain H. W. Benham, of the U. S. Corps of Engineers, were soon on his trail. Next morning the Confederates marched looking back over their shoulders, and some of them were called out of ranks and put to work felling trees along the way to check the pace of the Federals. The roads, made bad by recent rains and by a new downpour that started at 6:00 A.M., slowed up especially the Rebel wagon train, and it was only a short time before scouts reported the enemy close in the rear, well supported by cavalry and artillery. Out across a meadow at the side of the river at one point the First Georgia was thrown in line to check the Federals, gradually falling back to a new position and giving way to the Twenty-third Virginia, which would be directly behind it. This system of retiring upon eligible positions kept up until they reached Carrick's Ford, a deep crossing three and a half miles beyond Kaler's. There a few of the wagons foundered and the enemy got closer, cutting off some of the Georgians. The firing grew heavy, with the Rebels stubbornly protecting the ford while the Union artillery shells crashed in the trees above their heads. The rain had got heavier since nine o'clock and now was falling in torrents.

It was the Twenty-third Virginia's turn to hold the enemy in check, and this it did, falling back stubbornly. Colonel Starke, Garnett's aide, rode up and directed the regiment to make another stand at the next ford a short distance farther along. On the far side of this second ford Colonel W. B. Taliaferro, commanding the Twenty-third, met General Garnett and got orders to halt his regiment around the turn of the road, 150 yards farther on, leaving behind ten good riflemen. "This is a good place behind the driftwood to post skirmishers," said Garnett.[20]

Delegating ten men to stay with the general, Taliaferro hurried on around the bend. It was no trouble to get his soldiers to hurry; they ran in panic, falling over one another and losing some of their personal equipment in the mad race to get out of sight of the pursuing Yankees. Just as he began to throw them in line as ordered, this time with more difficulty than anywhere along the road, Colonel Starke galloped up again: General Garnett wanted the Twenty-third to hurry along until it overtook the main body.

Back at the ford, tragedy was striking at the Confederates. Garnett stood in the midst of the ten skirmishers left behind at his request. The enemy fire was furious now, rampant and hot and incessant, like the bay of dogs that have treed their prey. Garnett was a regular army man and the ten riflemen supporting him had done their best. Recognizing the situation, he directed them to fall back, and as he uttered the words he reeled suddenly, raised his arms as if to ward off a blow, staggered, and fell on his side. At the same moment a young Georgian standing beside him bowed as though trying to catch the general and gasped plaintively before pitching on his face.

Garnett died as the first general officer killed in the war, and news of his death went out to the public through John Whitelaw Reid, correspondent of the Cincinnati *Gazette*, who wrote under the by-line of "Agate." In his account of the affair the reporter was highly critical of the Southerners who had participated in the last-ditch stand. He had been riding with Captain Benham's troops in the pursuit, and thus had witnessed the tableau as the pursuers saw it. "Not a Virginian stood by him when he fell," Reid said in his report. "The whole cowardly crew had fled, and, of all that army of 4000, but one was with his general—a slight, boyish figure with scarcely the down of approaching manhood on his face, and wearing the Georgia uniform and button. Bravely he had stood by his general to the last; and when Garnett fell, he fell too. There they lay, in that wild region on the banks of the Cheat, with 'back to the field and face to the foe.' There, on that rugged bank, had come the solemn issue. They met it courageously, and fell as brave men fall." [21]

July 14 was a Sunday, and Captain Benham's soldiers slept late and afterward lingered over their breakfasts like housewives with time to waste, for it was the Lord's day and too beautiful to be spent burying the dead, Yankee or Confederate. Over Cheat River Valley had settled a strange and somewhat inconsistent quiet, the peace of heaven replacing the cruel noise and confusion of the running gunfight the day before. Further battle, for all intents and purposes, seemed far remote, for the Rebels would have fled across Cheat Mountain by this time, too well routed to make a stand. The beating, slopping rain had stopped during the night, after the soldiers had dropped on the side of the road to sleep a profound sleep, too exhausted to care, and now it was bright and clear. The few clouds in the distance were motionless and white, without a trace of darkness. Up in the trees, birds were singing their July songs, while along the river bank and up in the rocks toward the jagged precipices on the mountainside the forest denizens brave enough to steal back to their homes hid and peered and tried to understand.

For the soldiers gathered in the shade of the bullet-scarred trees along the mountain trail there should have been no worries, and yet Benham's men had something on their minds. All morning, since waking, they had shown it, each man in his own way, each over the same thing: there was the matter of the young Georgian who had died with his general. His body still lay where it had fallen, though someone had turned it over and taken a look to make sure he was dead. Dead he was, all right, drilled through by a lead slug that had torn a hole several times its own size.

Comparisons are cruel, hollow, and tantalizing, and yet these men were guilty of comparisons. They were thinking of the general and the private. They knew that, as a token of respect from a new army fighting a new war, Garnett's body would be taken to Grafton and preserved in ice until McClellan could send word to surviving relatives to come and get it. But with the brave young Georgian it would be different. He was a private, and privates were not preserved in ice. Besides, he had left no identity by which to trace his relatives, if any survived. His name and his tie with humanity had been lost in the mad chase of the day before.

But for him there would be a separate burial, a burial by soldiers, and the best that could go along with it—in James Carrick's orchard near the ford where he had fallen. These damnyankees he had fought, when they finally got moved to it, would lay him gently to rest, and in the warm July sunshine they would be silent and strangely sad as they went about shoveling the damp dirt in upon him, piling it high above the clover and the mountain grass, the witch hazel and the spicebush. That done, they would cross themselves, those who were of that faith, and then respectfully set up a simple headboard on which had been written with red-hot iron: "Name unknown. A brave fellow, who shared his general's fate, and fell fighting at his side, while his companions fled." [22]

To them he was a foeman "worthy" of their steel.

CHAPTER 4

July 15–July 22, 1861

"I WISH I WAS HOME"

The campaign in the mountains of western Virginia was one component of a huge picture rapidly centering on Washington. A day or two after his warriors buried the unidentified Georgia boy whose aptitude with a rifle had brought him immortality at the side of General Bob Garnett, McClellan congratulated them on their victory, writing jubilantly, "I am more than satisfied with you." [1] And to headquarters he wired: "Our success is complete, and secession is killed in this country . . . I shall now proceed to scour the country with small columns, unless the moral effect of our successes has sufficed to disperse the guerrilla bands." [2] His mind on this point was quickly settled, though with some inaccuracy. Next day he reported: "As far as I can now learn the effect of our operations against the larger forces has been to cause the small guerrilla bands to disappear. [3]

In this instance McClellan was gravely underestimating the unknown quantity, for the irregular bands were gathering quietly in the seclusion of forest and glen, gathering and arming and waiting their chance to pounce.

At the same time McClellan was bringing his campaign to a close, Washington was becoming more and more a madhouse. Troops had poured in by almost every train since April, and so had the following of camp parasites, gamblers, and prostitutes. Everywhere there was confusion, with soldiers sleeping in hallways and on door-steps and in the tent villages hastily springing up in the vacant lots and pastureland around the capital. This bustle and turmoil was looked upon as a necessary adjunct to war: grin and endure it, and soon the Southerners would be thrashed and driven back to their homes where they belonged.

But much of the hullabaloo in Washington could be blamed on soldiers who had nothing to do. True, Lincoln and the people of the North—the South, too, for that matter—were calling for action, but as yet most of the fighting had taken place in the mountains of western Virginia where the sound of a gunshot carried as far as the crow on the next ridge. Even the men in uniform were impatient for something more exciting than what they so far had experienced. Take Harvard-trained Henry Sanford Gansevoort. He had rushed to the capital on the Potomac in the first vanguard. New York lawyer that he was, he had had no trouble getting commissioned a second lieutenant in the regular artillery, but after that he cooled his heels, or, as he wrote home, "pendulated" between Willard's Hotel and the Capitol. To allay his boredom this young man of twenty-six soaked up all the happenings that came within the scope of his side-line observance. "Politicians haunt the streets, halls and hotels, their countenance chiseled by selfish ambition and cowardly revenge, with sharp and cold lines," he advised the folks back in Albany. "Martial music loads the still air of the morning and evening; soldiers drunk and sober, lively and grave, crowd every corner; and wagon trains are all day rumbling in slow procession to the seat of war. Affrays are of daily occurrence. Yesterday there was a fight between many soldiers. I happened to be present; and, as revolvers are carried by all, there was a general whizzing of balls. One man was fatally injured. I had a bayonet run through my sleeve while innocently passing two belligerents." [4]

And though he appeared in his writings to accept with a bored air this turbulence in an ordinarily quiet city, there was hope and expectancy underneath. He could feel that something was about to happen. One day he wrote home that "the camps are being fast vacated and regiments are crossing upon the 'sacred soil,'" and this led him to a prediction: "Next week will chronicle an advance towards the Southern Cross." [5]

The entire nation felt something was about to happen.

One day Union pickets stole out the Fairfax road, with a nervous excitement as strong as that of children playing prisoner's base.[6] Seven miles they went, and when they returned they brought with them a newly painted ambulance. Inside were a set of harness and two bags of buckwheat, and written plainly in pencil on the curtain of the vehicle was the name "John Hughes, Fairfax." This capture was an object of much curiosity around the Federal camp near Alexandria. Soldiers stood off and stared at it in awe. Because it came from the direction in which lay the enemy, they looked upon it as an omen of what might lie in store for them, this wagon designed for toting the wounded or the dead.

On the afternoon of July 16 Union troops began moving out of Washington—the first big push. Their over-all commander was Irvin McDowell, well educated, a superior conversationalist, a disciplinarian and systematic teetotaler who had no use for regimental bands and hated to see army wagons hauling liquor or beer. They went by way of the Long and Chain bridges, in winding, straggling columns, their rifles glittering in the sunlight and the officers flashing in colorful new uniforms. Others joined the advance from the camps of Arlington and Alexandria. Then they moved westward in three separate columns, each along a different route, setting up the U. S. flag at certain points to let the troops following know they were in friendly company. Cheers rent the air frequently and bands played "Yankee Doodle" as soon as they struck Virginia soil. There was skirmishing at Vienna and Fairfax as the Confederates slowly fell back, mile by mile, to Centreville and beyond, until they finally came to a stop behind the hilly slopes of the winding Bull Run, just twenty-five miles or so from the Federal capital. At Fairfax, when the advancing hordes of the Second Rhode Island Regiment swarmed in, there was riotous behavior and disorder, and several houses were burned. McDowell was on hand shortly thereafter and he made this conduct the subject of a general order warning against such foolishness: the Union army was on its way "to protect the oppressed and free the country from the domination of a hated party."[7]

On the outskirts toward Centreville, a member of the Union advance came upon some Rebels up in a peach tree and ordered them down. It might have been a college campus with an upper classman scolding a group of freshmen, for one of the boys gathering fruit yelled back for the Yankee to mind his own business. At that the Blue soldier rode up to the fence, a few yards from the tree.

"What did you say?" he called.

"I said I would shoot!" replied the Southerner.

The man from the North was fired with patriotism. "Shoot, you damned Rebel!" he shouted.

The Confederate made a record of his actions after that: "I did not hesitate . . . We dug a grave and laid the Yankee in and covered him up. I took a part of a plank from the fence and with a knife and pencil wrote:

> "A Yankee host, a mighty band,
>   Came down to take our Southern land,
> But burial in this low, barren spot
>   Was all this goddam Yankee got." [8]

That day the Rebel high command cleared the way for a maneuver that was to shape a victory. Johnston, over in the Valley looking toward Patterson's advance from Harpers Ferry and Charles Town, was instructed to elude the enemy and to bring his troops quickly by rail to Manassas to cooperate with Beauregard.

On the eighteenth there was hot fighting at Blackburn's Ford on the Bull Run, between Centreville and Manassas, the Federal advance thrusting forward and running smack into a force of stubborn Virginia troops. Winfield Scott, the Union chief, heard about this contact with the Southern army, but he was more interested in what was happening to Patterson, whom he accused in a message of "doing nothing." [9] To this leader he wired, asking if Johnston hadn't stolen a march and sent troops to Manassas. Patterson quickly replied: "The enemy has stolen no march upon me. I have kept him actively employed." [10]

But the Rebels were not as busy in his front as Patterson imagined; that night Johnston was sending off reinforcements for Beauregard and detailing two brigades to cover the movement. Patterson was nearing the end of his army career. Next day the War Department would announce that he would be "honorably discharged from the service of the United States on the 27th instant, when his tour of duty will expire." For months after that he would seek actively to explain how Johnston had managed to get away from him.

Of those interested in the fighting at Blackburn's Ford on the eighteenth, few were more concerned than Allen Alonzo Kingsbury, the Medfield boy who had come to Washington with the Chelsea Volunteers. His was an odd experience. A spent cannon ball struck him in the leg, felling him to the ground, and then he was injured internally when a wounded man fell on him. In the excitement he was taken up and lugged to the Centreville Methodist Church, converted into a hospital. But Allen was more frightened than hurt. There he lay, not in serious pain, and stared out a window at the excitement he was missing. On the twentieth he wrote home: "The Federal troops have been passing by here all day, infantry, cavalry and artillery, and one heavy gun 16 feet long, drawn by ten horses. The houses here are of the poorest kind, built of logs filled in with mud, with chimneys on the outside. The building we are in is a church, built of slate stone laid in mortar; the inside is as rough as the outside." [11]

While Kingsbury lay and stared through the window, Andrew Clement, a youth from Boston, walked the streets of Washington in search of a ride out to Centreville, where his older brother, Edward, was stationed with a Massachusetts regiment. An officer who was about to make the trip by army wagon was shaken by his story and finally agreed to take him along. Just after midnight on Sunday, the twenty-first, they started from Willard's on Pennsylvania Avenue. The moon was full and the night was lovely, and there was much excitement; everyone was talking of the battle and said it would be fought that very day.

It was quite a lark, this wholesale junket into Virginia, and much of Washington was on its way south as a part of it. On through the night, over a dusty, winding highway, rode Andrew and the officer and the teamster, a private in the army, their wagon one of a stream of vehicles. Some of the other wagons and carriages in the caravan bore citizens, many of them surrounded by baskets of food and wine, and there was much joyous laughter and singing under the full moon.

Just after daybreak, while Andrew and his companions were eating a hasty breakfast at a small tavern, they heard the first boom of a heavy cannon. They bolted the rest of their food, hurried back to their wagon, and whipped the horses to a lively pace.

When they reached Centreville, heavy firing was going on to the west, in the direction of the mountains, but no one knew exactly what it was all about; instead, everyone wanted to know what a lad like Andrew, dressed in black clothes and a straw hat, was doing so near the battlefield.

A little later in the day Andrew found his brother, and Edward immediately went into a tantrum—no sense in a boy being so close to the front where the bullets and cannon balls were flying.[12] So Andrew had to retrace his steps. It was shortly after 4:00 P.M. when he returned to Centreville. This record he later made of scenes witnessed on arrival there: "I soon found a group of sick officers who were about to dine off of boiled beef close by the army wagon in which I had come from Washington. They asked me to join them. I had just got fairly seated when the astonishing news came that our army was defeated and was retreating. I didn't believe it; but I rushed to the hilltop to see for myself. Down there on the plains, where I had been in the morning, there was certainly much dust and confusion. Just then fresh troops, the reserves, started to go down, but even to my inexperienced eye it was plain that they went in bad order and went too late."

Long years afterward people would be explaining what had happened down on the rolling hills along Bull Run. It was a new chapter in American history, with an aftermath of terror and confusion. Every Federal who ran toward Washington that night remembered the dust, and the shovels and pickaxes and boxes and barrels and other litter in the road they had to step over in order to move along. Hours of agony they spent, tired, thirsty, confused, and defeated. It began to rain just before daybreak. Gently it came at first, and slowly the dust turned into a thick paste of slippery mud. Then the storm steadily increased, until it became a downpour.

Allen Alonzo Kingsbury was among those who endured the torturous march. He had tried that morning to rejoin his regiment, but they wouldn't let him: he was wounded and there were enough Union soldiers without wounds to win this battle without calling on a man just out of the hospital. On the twenty-second he found time to write home: "Here we are in our old camp . . . The companies come straggling in . . . Everything seems sad and gloomy. The men are quiet; they are tired out, and so am I. I wish I was home."[13]

But the war was not ending, just beginning, and the fighting that had taken place around Centreville was not of a nature that invited guerrilla activity, the type that would delay the ultimate surrender. This style of warfare would come into prominence shortly, for even then Southern leaders were talking of its usefulness.[14] One officer wrote from the mountainous area of western Virginia, out amidst the spurs and crags where McClellan had so successfully routed all troops sent against him: "To me it is altogether obvious that the only way to hold this country at all is by adopting the guerrilla system, and that by this system, with ordinarily active and cheerful troops, it can be done."[15]

CHAPTER 5

July 25–August 31, 1861

RUMOR IS TRUMPET-
TONGUED

Following a routine of long standing, Mr. Sadler, undertaker at
Charles Town, went to his shop early on a July morning. He was
alert as he walked along, for of late there had been a tenseness in
the village, what with the chance of Yankee scouting parties coming down the few miles from Harpers Ferry, or the likelihood of a
new outbreak of the furor and holler left over from the hanging of
John Brown. Out in an open field on a knoll nearby still could be
seen the hole in which the gallows was set up, and that alone attracted many visitors, military and otherwise. So this day as he
neared his door, Sadler's eyes were quick to sight something that
made him push back his battered straw and cluck with surprise:
there on some boards in front of the funeral parlor lay Frank Butler, dead as a stone. Only a few hours had passed since Frank had
gone off to fight with the Southern army near Manassas, and now a
gaping hole in the side of the young villager told a part of the story.
The undertaker could surmise the rest: a comrade or comrades, conveying the body by horse or wagon, had left it during the night
where they knew it would be found at dawn.[1]

This was the aftermath farther west of the fighting along Bull
Run. In Washington the story was equally tragic and much more
confused. After the battle Winfield Scott stayed up most of the
night, trying to make sense out of the wild reports that arrived by

wire and word of mouth from his panicked army. At 1:30 A.M., just a few hours after the fighting had come almost to an abrupt stop, he wired General Nathaniel P. Banks at Baltimore to proceed to Harpers Ferry and relieve Patterson. Half an hour earlier he had telegraphed McClellan out in western Virginia to stand by, that McDowell's forces were in full retreat on the Potomac—"a most unaccountable transformation into a mob of a finely-appointed and admirably-led army." [2] A few hours later he sent another message: "Circumstances make your presence here necessary." [3]

On the twenty-fifth of July, a fair and pleasant day, there was double-barreled action in the Union high command. McClellan was formally assigned to replace the unfortunate McDowell: thus one barrel, timed to a slow fuse. The other shaped up at Harpers Ferry, where Patterson's post was taken over by cautious Nat Banks, also a slow burner. Banks was one of Abraham Lincoln's political generals. His career had started in a Massachusetts cotton factory, and then he had got ambitious, rising to the governorship, and, after that, to the Speakership of the U. S. House of Representatives. But as a soldier he was said to confine his fire-eating to his dispatches, described as "models of flamboyance and optimistic promise." Even at that, Banks looked like an improvement over do-nothing Patterson. It was Patterson who so repeatedly asked for reinforcements of artillery and troops in terms beyond the War Department's capacity to supply that Winfield Scott, forsaking austerity on one occasion, quipped: "He might as well have asked for a brigade of elephants." [4]

After the upset along Bull Run, the three-pronged Union thrust at Virginia was shorn of one of its tines. Of the two left, one was at Harpers Ferry and the other out in western Virginia, where Rosecrans had replaced McClellan and where the South still had hopes of regaining lost ground, largely by means of Partisan warfare. Meantime it would be left to McDowell's successor to rebuild the broken forces the Confederates had chased back into Washington.

Of the two Union prongs that retained their threat as military machines, the more important unquestionably was that at Harpers Ferry. There, on looking things over, Banks immediately estimated he would need 20,000 troops to hold the point securely, and this meant reinforcements. More volunteers must be had without delay. So recruiting efforts were stepped up at once, and the call met with a ready response. New fighters came from several states, some as far away as New England, and soon the heights surrounding Harpers Ferry and the adjacent meadows of Maryland were capped by long rows of tents and hastily erected huts, strange settlements that angered pro-Southern natives and gave great incentive to the guerrilla bands building up in the hinterland. With gradually increasing incidence these Partisans would be heard from, and there would be repeated correspondence with Richmond over whether or not they were an official part of the Southern army.[5]

At that moment these bands, official or otherwise, were lurking in the distance. The captain of one of them kept such a close watch on the Federals around Harpers Ferry that he was able to give Richmond a report on their strength: 10,000 men encamped at Knoxville, a few miles to the east; 2000 on Maryland Heights, 1000 in Harpers Ferry, two companies of cavalry on the Virginia side, and all "very much disorganized." [6]

Many of the young soldiers hauled down from New England, Ohio, and other places to man the heights in lower Maryland and to guard the B. & O. had no motive other than patriotism for taking up arms. Among this element was a Boston lawyer, Wilder Dwight, major of the Second Massachusetts Infantry, a unit he had helped organize. He possessed a rare ability to express himself in writing, and he had unusual ideas concerning the military profession: "I have always had a dream and theory about the virtues that are called out by war . . . The calling needs a whole man; and it exacts very much from him. Self gets thrown into the background. It straggles out of the column and is picked up, if at all, very late, by the rear guard." This he wrote about the time he was buckling on his sword to leave home.[7]

War was a pleasant experience to some men. Dwight was one of them. He saw everything, even the daily routine of camp life, in terms of romance. "The men were sent into the woods to cut brush for huts," he reported on arriving near Harpers Ferry to support Banks, "and there sprang up a camp of green leaves, as if by magic. . . . Last night we had an animated time. Just after taps one of our pickets fired, and it turned out that a man was prowling through the bushes. Soon after an excited Indiana picket fired on our men in a small thicket down the hill, and that kicked up a small bobbery. But the morning makes all quiet again. The mists are lifting from the river and hillsides, and the day is already started on its uncertain course again. The kitchen fires are smoking, the axes are ringing in the wood."

And then one of the occasional, typical, blowing Virginia rains struck in his vicinity. "If you had waked in our camp," he wrote, "you would have thought yourself in a storm at sea, with a very heavy northeaster blowing. By the rattle and creak and strain and whistle of the canvas and gale, you would have believed that the good ship was scudding before the blast. If you had shivered outside to attempt to secure your fluttering tent, you might, by a slight effort of the imagination, have thought yourself overboard. When the morning broke, after a sleepless and dreary night, expectant of disaster, you would have seen, here and there, a tent prostrate, and the wind and rain, for you could see them both, wildly making merry over the storm-driven camp." These days were unwanted days. Smoke curled from the myriad pipes of the settlements and sank despairingly to the ground. Cursing and storming, the cooks stirred fire in vain efforts to make their kettles boil, and as the rain dripped from them they appeared as disconsolate, said one soldier, "as if they would cook one more meal and die." [8]

The Union camps kept busy, preparing for war, making soldiers out of raw material. Even at this early date thought of Rebel Partisans who might come stealing out of the night bothered the Federals. "It is odd to notice how imaginative are the optics of some men in camp," observed one of them. "They are always seeing the enemy. A wagonload of rails seems a squadron of cavalry. A large Monday's wash near the horizon is an encampment. A clump of firs with two cows and a flock of sheep are as many as a thousand infantry. Their heated fancy detects a heavy cannonading or the rattle of musketry in every sound."

August came and wore along into its third week. There was no fighting and camp life developed into a routine, but, in the words of one erudite Union soldier, rumor became trumpet-tongued with reports of armies large enough to conquer the hemisphere. The nervousness that caused men to be "always seeing the enemy" extended beyond the ranks, and, before the third week was out, the high command gave orders for Harpers Ferry to be evacuated in the face of the victorious Confederates now advancing from their success near Manassas.

The march was toward Rockville in Maryland, nearer Washington, and they arrived late into camp by the riverside, after the evening had developed an autumn chill and a heavy dew. "I know of nothing more cheerless than the getting into camp late after a march," recorded one of the campers. "Every one is tired; every one is hungry; every one is cross. Everything seems to be going wrong. Yet at last all the men get their supper, or go without their supper. The last camp fire falls down into sullen coals. The last tent light fades out, and the chilly whiteness of the camp throws back the paleness of the moon. As the dawn reddens, reveille comes fresh as the lark, and soon the sunshine lights up a busy scene. The men are rested, and have forgotten their hunger in a good breakfast. The band plays gayly at guard-mounting, and a fresh life begins for the day again."

So went matters along the Potomac following the debacle on Bull Run. For the soldier in blue and the soldier in gray, each day brought a new life. Both armies were building: that on the northern side, around Washington and up in Maryland, under McClellan; that to the south, in Arlington and Fairfax and stretching toward Manassas, under Joe Johnston.

The Confederacy was beaming with confidence: the enemy Beauregard had termed by proclamation "a reckless and unprincipled tyrant," [9] had been driven beyond the Potomac. But out in western Virginia the job had not been attended to so well. The Federal invaders were still advancing, and so far all efforts of the Southerners had failed to force them back across the Ohio River.

Meantime an underground element was doing almost as much to discourage the enemy as the regular troops. Late one afternoon intelligence reached the Federals at Beverly that a small body of Rebel cavalry had collected a drove of beeves from resident Unionists a few miles away and gone into bivouac. Plans immediately were made to send out an expedition of 100 men on foot to surprise these guerrillas. The party started at nine o'clock at night. Throughout the dark hours and under a hard rain next day it toiled over the mountains, along narrow ravines, sometimes knee-deep in water, creeping along bridle paths, in single file, surrounded by trackless forests of pine and hemlock and almost constantly shut in by a dense, impenetrable growth of laurel bushes.[10] Toward dusk it waded across a stream and, just as it neared the opposite bank, a volley of musketry was poured into it from the thickets beyond, killing one man instantly and wounding three others, two mortally.

It was the third day after the fusillade before an ambulance, accompanied by a strong escort, could be got back into the mountains to a solitary log cabin where the wounded were taken. There it was found two of the three were dead and buried, and the lone survivor was ready to travel. So he was loaded aboard and the return trek begun without delay. At one point on the homeward march, in order to avoid a tedious detour, the guard left the road for a short distance while the ambulance went on alone. It seemed a safe risk: there had been no sign of the guerrillas for days. But scarcely was the escort out of sight before the vehicle was fired upon. One horse fell dead, the driver was shot through the arm, and the wounded man on the stretcher inside jumped out and went the remainder of the distance to camp on foot.

When the lone survivor appeared, one hand bound up where two fingers had been shot away, a loud clamor for revenge arose, and this time a stronger force was sent back along the trail—250 men under a major—"to beat up these outlaws in their own lair." It went eight miles farther east than its predecessor, burned the homes of several notorious Rebels, and emerged without injury from a second sudden fusillade out of the bushes. Angered by this outburst of hostility unaccompanied by a foe to shoot at, the major determined to have a try at these bushwhacking tactics himself, so he placed his fourteen best marksmen in ambush to apply a little eye-for-eye retaliation and sent the rest of his soldiers back to quarters. Two days later the sharpshooters came trudging into camp, much disgusted: not a living soul had they seen in all that time.

Seizing upon this affair, the editor of the *Intelligencer* at Wheeling made a prediction that required no great power of clairvoyance. Laying out a pattern to be followed for the next four years, he wrote that "this section of the state is to be the theater of an annoying and destructive guerrilla warfare, in which no man's life will be safe."

The hours of August were running out, and the war that was to last not over ninety days was nearing the end of its fourth month.[11] Meanwhile the armed forces of the two belligerents lay staring at each other, around Washington, along the Potomac, and out in western Virginia. As the spirit of McClellan, a good organizer, spread to his army, men got bolder. On August 28 a detachment of 250 Michiganders crossed through Arlington to Bailey's Cross Roads on the edge of Fairfax County and there stretched out quietly while Confederate pickets blazed away in noisy protest. Next day, to stop a flanking movement, the Federals answered this fire, and for the next four days the exchange continued, while the soldiers robbed nearby cornfields and, using the biggest roasting ears, tried the teacher-and-the-apple treatment upon their officers. The poultry yards of this neighborhood were unique. A Michigan lieutenant reported chickens at the surrounding farmhouses were "very aggressive," that they "attacked and bit" his men and that, naturally, his men "resented" it. During the period the Blue and Gray pickets banged away at one another at the crossroads, two of the Union corn and chicken foragers found themselves near the Rebel earthworks on Munson's Hill. They stole within forty rods of it, awaited their chance, and finally sniped at two unsuspecting Southerners, registering much personal satisfaction when their targets fell to the ground.

Troops newly arrived at Washington soon were pushed over into Virginia to set up camps along the ridges and to stare with cocked rifles at the Rebels holding forth on the next ridge. These new recruits had much to learn. The Eighty-third Pennsylvania Volunteers marched across the Potomac eight miles and, after pitching tents, ate raw pork and rye bread, something they never would have done at home.[12] All soldiers were death on gardens and fences. A five-acre field of potatoes went in short order, and it was no startling discovery to find how good a fire for cooking meals could be made from rails. And simple too: just lay them with their ends together, like the spokes of a wheel around the hub, and then shove them closer as they were consumed by the fire. Professor Lowe's balloon, an awe-inspiring sight to a generation accustomed to keeping its feet on the ground, floated overhead at times, and occasionally General McClellan rode out to look at his "brave boys" and to sympathize with their privations. Once he was heard to say, "There, those boys haven't got their pants yet. That's a shame."[13]

Much of the time was spent in drilling. As one soldier wrote home: "The first thing in the morning is drill, then drill, then drill again. Then drill, drill, a little more drill. Then drill, and lastly, drill. Between drills, we drill, and sometimes stop to eat a little and have a roll-call." At night there was spasmodic firing back and forth between the opposing ridges, just as a warning.

Thus the caldron boiled, with Yankees bushwhacked in western Virginia and Rebels and Yankees sniped at near Washington. As the summer waned, people came to look more seriously upon these little affairs making up what was turning into a real war: they might after all go on indefinitely, and that would mean the need for a large army. More men who up to this time had never bothered to enlist, thinking the neighbors already in uniform would be all the man-power their government required, took down their fowling pieces and set off for the front. Among these was a young sport from Baltimore named Harry Gilmor, a person who could not justly be accused of procrastination or a lack of patriotism. He might have come south sooner, for he was a member of the local militia and he and his family were strong in Secession sentiment. But the authorities had arrested him on suspicion of Rebel sympathies and detained him for several weeks.[14] As he crossed the Potomac, he was one of six brothers to join the Southern army, two of them to die in its ranks.[15]

Son of a farmer and descended from a prosperous shipping and mercantile family of Scottish background, young Harry, just twenty-four, was big and kind-hearted, but known to be a terror when stirred into a fight. He had been privately educated, and he had had a hand at tilling the soil in states farther west, as well as at home. His personal attraction for the opposite sex was far beyond average, and this seemed to distort his opinion of himself, for it is evident from what has gone into the records that he was convinced he was one of God's chosen few.[16]

Crossing the Potomac at the mouth of Cherry Run on the thirtieth of August, he rode in search of Turner Ashby, and the next day found him lying on the lawn of a home near Charles Town, surrounded by his rough-and-ready cavalrymen. Gilmor, never guilty of modesty, said he was a good shot with a pistol and could prove it, that he could shoot apples off friends' heads. Ashby, searching for marksmen to pick off Yankee horsemen, watched him bang away a few times at small targets and then signed him up. That night the new recruit was sent on a scouting expedition led by a slim, narrow-faced young private with high cheekbones and sleepy-looking eyes named Elijah V. White.[17]

Fellow soldiers called White "Lige" and seemed to have a lot of respect for him, both because of his scouting ability and because he came from a substantial family. He was a native of Poolesville, Maryland, and just five years earlier had crossed the Potomac and bought a large farm west of Leesburg. A ford along the river near his home bore his name—White's Ford, practicable for cavalry and infantry, but too rough for artillery and wagon trains. It was here he was married, the same year he acquired and took up residence on his land.[18] A twenty-nine-year-old six-footer with years of schooling in New York and Ohio behind him, White's military experience extended only to the slavery uprising in Kansas, where he served for some months with a Missouri company, and to the John Brown affair at Harpers Ferry, in which he took part as a corporal in a cavalry outfit from his home county. At the outbreak of war in '61 he was still a member of this cavalry company, but a change of officers induced him to transfer to the legion of Turner Ashby, who at the moment was the leader most busily engaged against the enemy.

White had ideas of his own and he talked in terms of independent warfare, of fighting along the border and of heckling the Yankees with guerrilla fighting from horseback. Gilmor, individualist that he was, had thoughts along this line, too, and the pair of them often had a communion of plans in their discussions while lying around camp.

Other minds among Southern sympathizers were following the same trend. Out in Missouri, at the head of a company of militia attached to Sterling Price's army, was a kind-hearted and industrious farmer, descended from a long line of Indian fighters, whose name in a matter of months would be a byword in the mountain stretch along the B. & O. He was gray-bearded John Hanson McNeill —"Hanse" to his friends—a father in his late forties, heavily built, a six-footer with blue eyes as keen as a falcon's. One of the most prosperous farmers in the West and a strong advocate of organized agriculture, he was nationally recognized as a breeder of livestock and as an expert on Shorthorn cattle. Though opposed to secession, he sided with the South, no doubt because of his birth and early life in Hardy County, Virginia, and with him to war went his three sons, William, George, and Jesse. He was a strenuous fighter, considerate and humane toward a prisoner, but relentless when facing an armed foe. At his side he carried a small revolver that he rarely used, for his favorite weapon was a double-barreled shotgun loaded with buckshot, an indication that he coveted close range. Late in '61 he was wounded and placed in prison at Columbia, Missouri. There he soon was permitted to roam the streets at will, under assurance from friends that he could be allowed to go anywhere and "we guarantee he will return when he promises to do so." His sojourn there soon ended and he was transferred to St. Louis, where he in time managed to make his escape.

McNeill was a fitting leader to coordinate activities with White and Gilmor. And near Washington, in the camp of the First Virginia Cavalry under command of colorful, song-singing Jeb Stuart, was another such individual. He was John Singleton Mosby, a twenty-eight-year-old lawyer. Though a private and just getting his first taste of military, he constantly dreamed of himself at the head of a fast-moving, hard-hitting band of Partisan Rangers—a roving force that would strike supply stations, capture wagon trains, cut telegraph lines, and do dozens of other things behind the enemy to slow up this attack from the North. He had been a boyhood student of Francis Marion, the Swamp Fox.

Time would bring to clearer focus the thoughts and dreams of these four men—Gilmor, White, McNeill, and Mosby, future leaders whose names one day would evoke terror. Time would bring them closer together, in a siege of guerrilla or Partisan warfare along the B. & O. and through the northern Virginia counties west of Washington that would go down in the records as one of the best organized and most effective in history.

CHAPTER 6

September 1–October 22, 1861

"The chill of the October morning has not yet yielded to the glowing brightness of the sun . . . but the leaves of autumn are falling."

—DWIGHT

For reorganizing an army the Federals scarcely could have picked a better man than McClellan. He was slow but he was thorough, and it so happened that there was no special clamor, except from the public, for him to hurry. September arrived with such a lull of action that one Union soldier concluded that "Bull Run has given McClellan the liberty to wait as long as he pleases without interference." But this observer added: "He cannot mean to lose October."[1]

In the scattered Union camps along the B. & O., on which Partisans and guerrillas were slowly focusing their attention, life became a routine, and the fascination of the great outdoors, man's spacious rumpus room, gradually paled into monotony. The pattern of this sameness spread for miles over meadowland and mountain. Long lines of clothes—pants, shirts, and drawers—flapping in the breeze. Baking ovens fashioned of mud and straw and stone drying in the sun with the flames licking from their wide mouths. The smoke of open fires casting a blue haze over the countryside and settling thickest in the valleys and creek bottoms. Bands playing on the hillside. Men drilling in the fields or busy with games in the company streets.

At night blazing campfires and bright-lighted tents, and a fire-reflected glow in the sky giving off a feeling of warmth and comfort. Over the land settled fog, sometimes a thin veil, again an impenetrable wall, bringing with it a chill. Occasionally through the still darkness the evening star looked down mildly but gave no cheer to the picket who walked post, farm boy, shoe clerk, or professional man, for in the long hours of guard duty they all glanced with the same authority at the old moon and thought to themselves that it looked almost as good in its second childhood as in its first. Soldiers off duty, always the envied, spread their beds with two blankets and a bundle of straw, and as they did so talked of the comforts back home. Inside the tents and makeshift huts, quartermaster details sat and rehearsed their exploits on the road. A teamster had beat out a horse's eye: he ought to be shot. Another had stalled the whole train by geeing instead of hawing: might as well shoot him too. The army was crazy—prescribing the four-line drive for its wagons when the one-line Pennsylvania saddle-team method was so much better. On and on it went until a late hour; how this and how that would improve things, and how the day march was better than a night march any time.

Sometimes a night was raw and bitter, with rain and chill. Tents blew down, and there was pandemonium. Dripping men huddled in the shelters of those more fortunate—or a little more adept at erecting tents. Spluttering candles flickered and died. Darkness blanketed out most of the camp. Curses and cries rent the air, louder whenever bare or slippered feet found unsuspected pools, and canvas fluttered with every gusty squall.

On the edge of camp, toward the stables and supply wagons, teamsters lolled in the midst of a Babel of mules. Off in one corner portable forges sent out sprays of sparks, for blacksmiths had to work late to keep the horses shod and ready for any emergency the bands of guerrillas or Partisans lurking in the distance might take it upon themselves to create. At their backs were barrels of flour, crackers, and hard bread, boxes of soap and bags of oats and corn. The crackers were a source of much comment. Several barrels had stamped on their sides "T. Wild & Co., Boston 1810," and one, set apart in plain view by a quartermaster with a sense of humor,

50

bore the marking, "B.C. 97." Some of the soldiers who bit into the contents believed anything they read.

At dawn it was different: each regiment to its own reveille, the "infernal reveille" for some of them, with the clang and rattle of kettle and bass drums and the shrill, cutting noise of the fife. "A little practice," stated one letter home, teaches the soldier at which point to open his eyes, when to throw back the blanket, and, at the right moment, he is in the ranks at the last ruffle of the drum, in the first glimmering of sunrise.[2]

September came, with its hot, bright, blazing days and its cold, heavy, foggy, shivering nights. While McClellan directed matters at Washington and became more and more a hero—"How we have waited for him," idolized one soldier—there were some observers who thought the Union army was still lame, that experience had to rub its lessons into the memory and habits of both officers and men before they would be able to take care of themselves on the march and in active duty—and while fending off the Partisans steadily building up their underground in Southern quarters.

As October arrived, so also did the cold. An unseasonal snowstorm covered the mountains in the dying days of September, paralyzing locomotion and driving temperatures to abnormal lows.[3] With it came discomfort, especially in the Union camps along the windswept B. & O. Federal officers warmed over pans of coals, and privates lay in their blankets at night and prayed that the Rebels might be shivering just as much as were they. The drop in temperature, some hoped, would do more than heavy artillery toward driving the Southerners from Manassas. Of an evening the sentimentalist stared at the bright gold of the western sky, the frosty silver of the evening star, and marked the cold glitter of the moonlight. To him the change in weather was ideal: "It will be glorious o' nights when we bivouac by campfires, as I hope we must soon." [4]

Talk of the next big attack gradually grew more prevalent. Some said it would not be aimed at Washington, where strong and uninviting forts were being thrown up; that the next severe blow could be looked for at a spot outside the breastworks of either army, possibly in Kentucky. And throughout all their predicting and their prognosticating, the Union privates complained of the lull and looked forward to the tempest when their deeds would give luster to the flag.

"The enemy must soon move, or we must," observed one soldier of above average intelligence, writing his "maudlin reflections" at a late hour in the "flickering twilight of a wind-troubled candle." The Confederates were talking of doing just that. Early in October, Jefferson Davis and the high command held a council of war near Fairfax and made plans to strengthen their army and take the offensive.

The South at this time got a warning that the Federals were preparing for a general advance and that it would come on October 12, most likely. The man who sent this information was J. A. Avirett, Jr., who wrote from Winchester, and he admitted his source was not very reliable. Avirett had a reputation for spreading rumors. In the same letter he said he was satisfied that some of the bullets the Yankees were firing were poisoned. He also told of a fight between the Catholic and Protestant Irish of the Union army at Baltimore, and said a young lady of South Carolina had been taken to the police station and searched by a man who took off her clothes almost to the skin.[5]

Even at this early stage the North was seriously concerned over the contraband goods, especially weapons and medicine, which were smuggled into the South under the bounteous hoop skirts of women. Kentucky's Louisville *Journal* appeared with a paragraph stating that "crinoline contains many a contraband article" and advising detectives to be on the lookout. Its pro-Southern competitor, the Louisville *Courier*, made disparaging reference to this item, and the *Journal* came back with: "Our neighbor appears to think that the only way to prevent contrabands from being smuggled under ladies' dresses is to employ great 'he creatures' to search the blustering innocents. He is a greenhorn . . . If a woman, carrying under her dress deadly weapons to be used by Rebels against our people, blushes at being examined in a private room by another woman, let her blush. Better that her blood should mount to her face than that the blood of our countrymen should be shed through her crime."

New York also was having its troubles with civilians. And surprisingly enough, the most sudden headache came from a member of a race that, by experience, should have been body and soul for the North. He was a Negro with the somewhat trite name of John Jones, and he upset tradition—and the police—by climbing to the top of a flour barrel on Thirtieth Street and preaching the Secession doctrine to a large concourse of men, women, and children. He said he wanted to get down South and help Jeff Davis whip the Yankees, and just as he was uttering such an undiplomatic bit of hogwash Patrolman Booth of the Twelfth Precinct came up and pushed him off his rather temporary perch. Newspapers reported that this sudden interruption "irritated the colored gentleman beyond endurance" and influenced him to haul off and hit the policeman full in the face. A struggle ensued that finally was settled by the officer's billy. Hauled into court, Jones declared before Alderman Chipp that he thoroughly understood the subject of slavery and could prove it if permitted to continue his harangue. The judge didn't care to hear; instead, he settled the question without further deliberation by locking up the defendant. That was the verdict, and bystanders nodded approvingly, convinced beyond a doubt that the Negro was demented.[6]

October 12, Avirett's day for action, arrived and passed without so much as a skirmish. On the eighteenth a mulatto teamster who had been hauling pickled pork from Manassas and flour from Fairfax deserted the Thirteenth Mississippi Regiment near Leesburg, crossed the Potomac and came into the headquarters of the Union Observation Corps at Poolesville, Maryland. He had been an alert man and was ready to talk. He said the Rebels were definitely alarmed, that they were not planning an offensive, but, rather, were preparing for an evacuation. They would fight at Leesburg and, if hard pressed, would fall back to the Widow Carter's mill about a mile from Aldie, retreating then, should it be necessary, to Manasses, their concentration point.

This information made sense to Charles P. Stone, brigadier general commanding the division that held this part of the Potomac, for he thought he knew what was bothering the Confederates. With October days rapidly passing, Union troops had begun to stir out of their camps along the river. As one evidence of unrest the Federal force on Harrison's Island midway of the stream near Leesburg, was strengthened, and flat-bottom boats appeared at various points, indicating a crossing might be attempted any moment. Stone communicated the mulatto teamster's intelligence to McClellan, with suggestions, and McClellan gave the nod—for a reconnaissance, not a crossing in force.[7]

Union Major General George A. McCall already was looking over the land around Dranesville. On the twentieth, he was directed to send out heavy reconnaissance in all directions. Stone was informed of this and advised to get busy too. So in the afternoon of the same day he sent reinforcements to Harrison's Island and to the two crossing points nearest Leesburg—Conrad's Ferry upstream and Edwards Ferry downstream. At the island, on his orders, a scouting party of twenty men under Captain Philbrick was ordered across to follow a little-used path in the direction of Leesburg.

About ten o'clock that night Stone got word from Philbrick. The captain had made his way along the path, unchallenged, to within twenty-five rods of a camp of about thirty tents—a camp with no pickets posted out any distance toward the river.

Stone selected Colonel Charles Devens of the Fifteenth Massachusetts Infantry to lead the next action. He was to move at once with five[8] companies under cover of night and be ready to destroy the camp at daybreak. Meanwhile two additional regiments were moved up to strengthen the forces at Conrad's Ferry and Harrison's Island.

Devens' men went across in the dark, paddling a flat-bottom boat that made innumerable trips before it got them all ashore. After landing, they crossed a narrow plateau studded with trees, after which they were faced by a steep bluff—twenty-five-degree elevations in some places, it was guessed—and this they scaled to the beginning of the path, crawling sometimes in miry clay and over rocks and fallen trees. At the top they found an open field of six acres covered with wild grass, scrub oak, and locust trees and shaped like the segment of a circle, with the outer arc surrounded by woods. Behind them as they moved out in the direction of Leesburg advanced a force of 100 infantry with orders to stand by at the top of the bluff and guard the return of the party ahead of them. And to draw attention away from Devens, plans were made at the two ferries to attempt crossings at daylight.

Shortly after dawn Devens sent back a courier with a report that brought a few chuckles: he had found on reaching the site of the enemy camp that Philbrick and his twenty scouts had been deceived by a line of trees on the brow of a slope, which, in the uncertain twilight, had appeared to be a row of tents. And furthermore, he messaged, no Rebels had been seen anywhere.

Stone was emboldened. He decided to extend this reconnaissance, to find out what the Rebels really were doing around Leesburg. A cavalry detachment and a battalion of infantry were ordered across to guard Devens' flanks while he scouted, but, for some reason, he later complained, these flankers never got where they were supposed to go.

At an early hour that morning Stone at Edwards Ferry was approached for orders by Colonel Edward D. Baker, United States senator from Oregon whose friendship for Abraham Lincoln was mutual, dating back to their younger days at Springfield, Illinois. Stone knew Baker and valued his wisdom. He had ordered him the night previous to move with the First California Regiment to Conrad's Ferry, and now, receiving a report that this order had been executed, he suddenly decided to send him to Harrison's Island to assume command and use his discretion about what he did there.

The matter of crossing the Potomac seemed no problem. Federals were going across by the boatload at several points, and firing, most of it light, could be heard as the advance proceeded. There was no evidence of organized resistance from the Confederates. Only one battery and a few companies had been heard from, and these had been driven back.

Baker caught the spirit of the moment, and the courage and initiative that had been his when he walked the floors of Congress stirred within and goaded him into what he may have considered inspired action: on reaching Harrison's Island he decided to send across his entire force—something between 1700 and 1800 bayonets —at once. His orders rang out and over they went, a boatload at a time. On the far side they pushed through the trees to the bluff, climbed it, and formed line on the river side of the field at the summit. In this position they waited. If there had been any thought of how they were to get back across the Potomac should they be repulsed, it was little in evidence. Left behind in the river to ferry them from Virginia to the island and from the island to Maryland were only seven boats—two flatboats, two ferry boats, one metallic lifeboat, and two skiffs—all capable of transporting 1080 men an hour, on a basis of one trip every ten minutes.

Noon arrived and then 1:00 P.M., and suddenly the enemy—1709 Mississippi and Virginia soldiers under Brigadier General Nathan G. (Shanks) Evans, who had helped turn the tide along Bull Run— appeared in strength in front of Devens. He fell back under Baker's wing, and the senator, wanting a fight, formed his line to await the attack. It came with great vigor at 3:00 P.M.

To the more experienced military men present, it was evident from the start that the dispositions Baker had made would bring trouble.[9] Trouble they did bring, plenty of it, and along with trouble came a hail of bullets, four of which struck down Baker at the front of his command while he was directing attention to a Rebel officer who had ridden out too bravely from the woods. Tucked in the band of the senator's hat as he fell was Stone's order of the night before, written in pencil and now stained with blood, directing Baker to move to Conrad's Ferry.[10]

With Baker's body on the way to the rear, Colonel Milton Cogswell, who had been at the head of the Forty-second New York, known as the Tammany Regiment, took command. It was his idea that the drive should be toward the left, so that a way could be cut through to join forces with Stone at Edwards Ferry. Just then a Rebel officer rode out from somewhere, dashed up in front of the Tammany boys, and beckoned for them to charge on the enemy, and it was never known just what got into the New Yorkers, whether they took it to be an order from one of their own officers or an invitation to close fighting, but at any rate they responded with a yell, charged forward, carrying with them the rest of the line, and soon drew a murderous fire at close range that cut them to pieces. That was the turning point.[11]

Cogswell gave the order to retire. It was a waste of breath, for the Federals already were retiring, running back toward the bluff, down which they scampered in mad confusion. At the water's edge, faced with inadequate means of crossing, they threw their guns and swords into the river and jumped after them. Others pushed out on logs or scattered along the bank looking for easier points of crossing. In the minutes of this panicky flight, made even more frantic by the Rebels who blazed away from the top of the bluff, occurred one of the wholesale drownings of the war. Men rushed onto the large boats so rapidly that they floundered and were virtually useless. One flatboat, hastily pushed out with wounded and fleeing aboard, sank fifteen feet from the bank, bringing a crimson tinge to the surface of the stream. The smaller boats had disappeared, no one knew where. Many men were shot as they tried to swim across or waited in uncertainty at the edge of the river; others threw up their hands in surrender, but there was no general capitulation.[12]

Soldiers arriving late at the scene of action wrote lurid descriptions. One outfit, pushing toward Conrad's Ferry "to aid in a victorious advance upon Leesburg," soon met "the faint shadows of the coming gloom" in the form of a few stragglers of the Fifteenth Massachusetts. "Our companies are all cut to pieces," babbled one of the retreating men. "Our captain is shot, our lieutenant-colonel has lost a leg, and we have all been licked." There were others, some with only a blanket or an overcoat to cover them after their cold swim of the Potomac, and all with one story: flight, death, despair. Wounded filled nearly every house along the road. Four weary soldiers came along bearing a stretcher with a dead officer on it. The lead man on the left raised his head in answer to a question from a passing column and spoke with solemn respect: "One of the Tammany boys."

Darkness brought more misery for the doomed Yankees around Harrison's Island, and before dawn a gusty rain storm blew in. In the midst of the downpour McClellan arrived and went into a hasty conference with the top officers in their quarters at Conrad's Ferry. After hearing the story his comment was brief: "Well, so far we seem to have applied a new maxim of war, always to meet the enemy with an inferior force at the point of attack." [13]

Outside in the driving rain, soldiers huddled in groups, tired and silent. Ambulances of wounded passed by. Bodies in blankets swung on poles were borne steadily to the rear with the heavy, dull tread that betokens the presence of death. Jaded stragglers, cold and half-naked, plodded along. A colonel, shivering over a small fire under an apple tree and waiting to breakfast on a single egg hard-boiling in a small tin can, hailed a bedraggled fellow clad only in an overcoat.

"Where'd you come from?"

"The river."

"What regiment?"

"Massachusetts Fifteenth."

"Did you fight?"

"Well, I guess we did some."

"How many times did you fire?"

"Thirty or forty."

"What did you do during the day?"

"Well, at first we was skirmishing along, and I got behind a tree, and I was doing first rate. I come out once, but I see a feller sightin' at me, and so I got in again suddin. Then, arter a while, the cavalry come down on us. I see there warn't no chance, and so I just dropped into a hole there was there, and stayed still. Pretty soon we retreated towards the river. We got together there, and formed a kind of a line, and then the fightin' really began. Some fellers come out near us, and says they, 'We're Colonel Baker's men.' 'Guess not,' says I. 'Yes, we are,' says they. 'I know better,' says I. 'Yes, we are,' says they. 'I know better,' says I. 'Let 'er rip, boys!' And we fired on 'em. But twarn't no use. Baker got killed, and we couldn't see the enemy, and they raked us like death. I finally come down the bank with the rest of 'em. I see Colonel Devens there. Says I, 'Colonel, what's to be done now?' 'Boys,' says he, 'you must take care of yourselves.' 'All right, Colonel,' says I, and the way my 'couterments come off was a caution. I swum the river. But I tell you there was a sight of 'em didn't."

"Do you want to go back again?"

"Well, not till I get rested."

"You're cold, aren't you?"

"I tell you, I just am."

"Want some whisky?"

The colonel proffered a flask. The soldier took it, turned it up, and gurgled loudly before handing it back. Then he expressed his thanks with a long, silent wink and walked off, his throat in contortions from the burning liquor.

CHAPTER 7

October 22–December 31, 1861

"'TIS A MISTY, MOISTY MORNING"

Legends are sometimes tantalizing fantasies; they occupy the mind and they in a manner give an outlet for the changes people would like to see made in events and things. Maybe that was the reason so many stories developed about the battlefield at Ball's Bluff. In time the Confederate officer who had ridden out in front of the Tammany Regiment and waved them to their destruction became a sinister rider on a white horse, a figure from the spirit world sent in the manner of the Pied Piper to lead these New York boys to their death. And as the weeks went by Rebel pickets in the vicinity clutched their rifles at all times, for gradually there crept into conversations strange and hair-raising stories of the "Specter Scout," a mysterious being said to haunt the woods below Leesburg. Newspapers described this phantom as "a tall, swift-moving figure," occasionally seen in the neighborhood, and linked him with several mysterious deaths of Confederate guards, shot at their posts and left without visible evidence of the source of the bullets from which they died. The North proudly hailed him as their equivalent of the sinister rider.

This was chaff to be fashioned into legend. For the record, the affair at Ball's Bluff was much worse than sinister, losses in some Union regiments running as high as 50 per cent.[1] The battle was termed by the U. S. Congress' Joint Committee on the Conduct of the War a "melancholy disaster" and by newspapers the "massacre of Ball's

Bluff." Whatever its identification, it brought a fury through the North that centered in the heart of Abraham Lincoln. It was said he sobbed openly at news of the death of his friend and compatriot of Springfield days. And the vindictive treatment that became the lot of Charles P. Stone, the officer who had given Baker permission to use his discretion, was reputed to have been directed from the White House.[2]

For the Union high command, McClellan in particular, this second major conflict between the two armies near Washington meant another definite setback. Though much had been done to strengthen the army and to wipe out the memory of the fiasco at Manassas, the outcome at Ball's Bluff was new evidence that something was wrong. One soldier who visited the Union capital at this time formed a rather desperate conclusion: "This country needs a government. Every visit I make to Washington makes me feel hopeless. Nothing is done. Not half enough doing."[3]

In the South the story was different: the battle had been a great morale-builder. And buried in Confederate reports of the affair was a new name for the pages of history, a name mentioned in the records four different times and always with praise. In their individual reports three leaders saw cause to cite "Lige" White, the independent-thinking horseman and future Partisan chief from Ashby's cavalry, whose home was only a few miles upstream from where all the fighting had taken place. One officer wrote in glowing praise: "I never witnessed more coolness and courage than this young gentleman displayed, being exposed to the heaviest fire of the enemy. He rode in front of a part of the 17th Mississippi, cheering and encouraging the men."

White had appeared on the scene at Ball's Bluff at a time when he was sorely needed. He had fox-hunted over the area many times and was thoroughly familiar with it. When he heard the opening gunfire of the battle while en route to Leesburg from his nearby home, he rushed back to get his horse and then rode rapidly to report for duty. One of the Confederate commanding officers on hand that day was Colonel Eppa Hunton of Leesburg, and Hunton immediately put the future Partisan leader to work. All day he served as a courier, and then in the closing hours of conflict was called on as a guide to lead troops into the battle. This he did by riding madly in advance and shouting, "Follow me!" And that night, when the firing ended and only a small Rebel force lay along the bluff as a guard, he led a few men down upon the last remnant of the fleeing enemy and brought about the surrender of 325 men.[4]

A few months and White would be galloping at the head of his own band, unofficially dubbed "The Comanches." In appreciation of his services at Ball's Bluff, regimental commanders drew up a recommendation that he be commissioned in the regular army. This he presented at Richmond, but was told no more commissions would be granted until a vacancy occurred. Colonel Hunton was there at the time, and suggested to the disappointed White that he apply instead for permission to organize a company for service on the border. The application met with success, and White soon began recruiting at Leesburg, at a propitious moment, for men of the neighborhood had their choice of fighting or shoveling dirt for fortifications.[5]

Also mentioned in connection with the fighting at Ball's Bluff was Turner Ashby, "Lige's" superior. Prominent residents of the counties along the Potomac urged that he be promoted to a colonelcy, a raise in rank which was claimed would enable him to organize a force of several hundred young men who would not volunteer under another colonel. These well-wishers also warned that "the condition of our border is becoming more alarming every day," that the enemy was floating coal down the C. & O. canal skirting the Potomac. As a cure for this they suggested that Ashby be made provost marshal of the area.[6]

To date, the war on two fronts in Virginia had gone well for the South—at Manassas and at Leesburg. But out in the mountainous region to the west, a sad story for Confederate arms was being written. In answer to repeated suggestions from the public General Lee finally was dispatched to the area to take command. What happened during the weeks following did little to help his career. Repeated efforts to confront and overwhelm the enemy ensconced along Cheat Mountain met with failure. This could be attributed to a combination of factors, including bad roads, rainy weather, rough terrain, and the jealousy of certain subordinates. Lee also met with obstinacy and a cool reception from General W. W. Loring, experienced Indian fighter and Mexican War veteran who seemed to resent his presence. On October 31, with the troops in western Virginia preparing to batten down for the winter, Lee returned to Richmond.

Next day, according to Federal records, McClellan formally succeeded Winfield Scott as chief of the command of Union armies. Three days later word of Scott's retirement reached the Federal camps along the B. & O., and the acclamation was general. "I did not think that the day would come when the country would welcome his loss," observed a New England officer, "but I think everyone is relieved." McClellan's fate was seen to rest on his ability to defy politicians. Even the common soldier was looking for the arrival of the "successful" general for "this righteous but blunder-blasted war." In McClellan they had a man who opposed dividing the army into corps, maintaining he should lead it alone until subordinates had proved themselves competent for higher command. It finally—and then only after the army had started moving on its first campaign—would take sharp words from Abraham Lincoln to bring this division about.[7]

The Confederates made important changes at this time too. "Stonewall" Jackson, who had bottled up the B. & O. equipment on each side of Harpers Ferry and gained fame in the desperate fighting along Bull Run, was sent on November 4 to assume command of the Valley District, with headquarters at Winchester. He was an ideal choice. Reared at Clarksburg in western Virginia, he knew the mountain country and had no fears of the task ahead of him. Arriving at his new post, he immediately suggested that he be permitted to draw to him all the troops in the area, including those of Floyd and Loring. If such a move induced the enemy to advance on Staunton, he said confidently, "it will be his ruin." [8]

Winter approached rapidly. "'Tis a misty, moisty morning, and cloudy is the weather," a soldier wrote his mother one November day.[9] Ice was in the wash basin, fingers were numb, and frost was on the breath. This warrior found something ludicrous in writing so quietly on calm, white paper while the wind whistled and shook his tent until his pen trembled. The air bit shrewdly these days, so shrewdly that divine services sometimes were dispensed with to keep the men from having to sit in "devout shiver" for an hour. Campfires were a constant problem. They led soldiers to remember that proverbs were said to be the condensed wisdom of ages and hence that there should be some reason for the saying that "where there is so much smoke there must be some fire." But so often did the smoke drive them from their tents into the shivering cold of the outdoors that they could place little faith in such a maxim. Snow fell, a thin coating of it, and it lay crisp and glistening on the ground, a blanket token of discomfort.

Then Thanksgiving arrived and the Union army made ready for

sumptuous banquets to mark the occasion. Nearly all night on the eve, cooks labored away, preparing food and roasting it in the glowing ovens of mud and straw and stone. Next day, after services and a fancy parade, each regiment consumed something like half a ton of turkey, almost as much goose and chicken, and more than half a ton of plum pudding. War could have its bright moments.

Along the B. & O. and the Potomac and in the camps branching out from Washington, there was comparative peace following the death trap at Ball's Bluff. But out in the direction of Wheeling, through the mountainous area that Virginia still claimed as a part of her domain, sounded a different story, a story unfolded in words that implied increasing trouble. The *Intelligencer,* busiest newspaper along the Ohio, was confident and closely following developments when it announced: "Accounts from different parts of West Virginia indicate that the infamous guerrilla warfare, instead of being at an end, is just commencing. There is no doubt but that the Rebels are organizing these bands daily, and sending them out to plunder and murder loyal citizens. In some of the counties where there are no military forces, there is hardly a good horse left." [10]

Thus the reputation of *petite guerre,* a much more valued arm of war as the months wore along. More important for the moment were developments concerning the major conflict, the backbone to which guerrilla operations were to be attached as ribs to the spine. Students of the war between the North and South would debate long years afterward over the question of whether the Confederates had a definitely planned campaign of action. As the commanding officers looked ahead at the close of '61 to map out the best path for the army in gray, one section of Virginia seemed clearly an objective—the rich Shenandoah Valley, often referred to as the "granary of Virginia." General Joe Johnston, commanding the Rebel forces around Manassas, admitted this in a letter to the War Department at Richmond dated on Christmas Day. He was writing in answer to a suggestion from Jackson for reinforcements with which to strike at the enemy in the mountain area and drive him back across the Ohio. Stonewall said he needed these men for other reasons too. The Confederates had broken a dam on the C. & O. canal, putting an end to the coal-hauling operations from Cumberland, and this naturally was bringing more and more pressure on the Union army to reopen the B. & O., something that he hoped to block. If efforts were made to rebuild the railroad, Jackson reasoned, the work could be protected by the Federals more easily with a force at Winchester than with troops spread along the tracks. This strength easily enough could be provided by moving Kelley from Romney and Banks from Frederick. But such a junction he was determined to prevent, a goal he was confident he could attain by cutting communications between Banks and Kelley and then threatening the latter's rear and forcing him to evacuate Romney.

Jackson wanted to strike at once, without waiting for the enemy to be reinforced, so on the last day of December he started moving. That morning the Ringgold Cavalry, recruited from Pennsylvania, moved too. They marched out the New Creek road in the direction of Greenland Gap, high in the mountains, going to the aid of two companies of loyal Virginians who had organized for the defense of their homes under the misnomer of Swamp Dragons. These fellows had been troubled by Rebel guerrillas and finally had found themselves boxed up in their log fort, soundly subdued within and completely dependent on support from without. The citizen who brought word of their plight said they soon would be faced with surrender unless reinforced.

On arrival in the vicinity of the fort, the Ringgold boys put a quick end to the emergency. They dashed up, in the manner of frontiersmen routing Indians, and drove the Rebels up the mountainside. Then they returned for their plaudits, as well as a round of handshaking and back-slapping with the Dragons. It was a joyous occasion. Both rescuers and rescued blended in a gay mood, and a boisterous time they had. The Pennsylvanians had been cooped up at Mud Creek with no more excitement than that of guarding a railroad on which no trains were running, so it was a vacation to them to take part in some action and to see new country.

Later in the day, after the excitement abated, some of the soldiers found nothing better to occupy their attention than a climb up the precipitous trail taken by the guerrillas in their flight, and somewhere in the brush on the mountainside they came upon the body of a Rebel, overlooked or forsaken by his buddies. He lay just as he had fallen, bull's-eye victim of a well-aimed bullet. The Unionists, moved by the loneliness of the spot where he had died, gathered up the gray-clad figure and took it back to camp, placing it on a bench at the side of a shed in rear of the fort. No one bothered to cover it, if there was anything to cover it with, and thus bared to a gusty gale that had kicked up from the northwest it soon froze stiff. In view of the cold and the holiday mood, burial plans were delayed, and as an expedient at nightfall some of the soldiers picked up the bench, body and all, and set it inside the shed.

When darkness filtered into the mountain gap, the men turned their thoughts to plans for the night, a serious moment, for not all of them could sleep in the fort. In this discrepancy the more unfortunate prepared to spread their blankets on the ground outside. Each of these individuals without exception, before making his couch, looked about for some object, a board or a tree branch or a log, to break the force of the wind while they slept. One of the searchers was Pat Grace, a jolly Irishman not too much given to military detail but a serious seeker of self-comfort. In his quest he roamed with abandon, assuming the wider the field he covered the better the chance of success, and in time his meanderings took him into the darkness of the shed. There he wandered blindly, endangering his shins and signaling his presence with grunts and groans as he moved about. Suddenly his fingers brushed inquisitively over the face of the dead Rebel. They lingered momentarily, torn between hope and doubt, and when finally the sense of touch messaged the true word there was a scream that caused envy in every wildcat crouching on the crags of Greenland Cap. As one Ringgolder observed, no one but an Irishman could describe the capers cut by Grace as he rushed noisily out of the shed and leapt into the arms of his companions.

CHAPTER 8

January 1–March 21, 1862

THE DEAD BEHEAD EASILY

In the spring of '62 newspapers were supplied with a bonanza of gruesome headlines like these: MOLESTED GRAVES! BURNED BODIES! BEHEADED CORPSES! SKULL-AND-BONE SOUVENIRS! And, naturally enough, the most important source of this pulse-stirring copy was the neighborhood of the first great battle of the war.

It was no lark to have to dig up the bodies of war buddies buried nearly a year. So there must have been a strained expression on the face of every man in the band that rode across the Long Bridge out of Washington the morning of March 19. It moved with purpose, fetlocks disappearing in the mud at each step, and swung westward toward Fairfax Court House. At its head, feeling important, was military-minded Governor William B. Sprague of Rhode Island.

Sprague had had a horse shot under him in the fighting along Bull Run the previous July, but that was only a minor incident. His Excellency was known to have been one of the busiest warriors on hand that day, blundering about from here to there, countermanding orders, ignoring others, and inadvertently doing about as much as anybody to see that the Yankees lost. But overlooking his faults, he was a champion of the state he headed and of all connected with it, the dead as well as the living. From the very day he led into battle near Sudley Ford his pet Second Regiment, organized under his own supervision, he planned, spurred by his allegiance, to come back and rescue for more decent burial the remains of some of its officers who had fallen. Colonel John Slocum and Major Sullivan Ballou, for instance. And perhaps others like Captain Levi Tower. Slocum and Ballou had gone down in the heat of the fighting, badly wounded, and were hauled off to a field hospital where they died. Tower's end was even more tragic, and still talked about. Falling early, he had merely requested to be turned over on his back and, this done, breathed his last without a struggle.

Long months had intervened since these men gave their lives, and soldiers from the North were becoming impatient. One of them wrote his sister: "It seems to us very slow business, this crushing out the rebellion . . . Our President is altogether too tender-hearted, too much afraid of touching the Rebels in their tender spot—their niggers . . . We must preserve the Union, but not touch slavery. Away with such nonsense, I say, and the soldiers all say so." [1]

After Ball's Bluff, the Federals lay close to Washington and continued to train and refurbish and talk of the spring offensive that could not come until the mud of the Virginia roads had dried. During this period little was heard from the enemy. Stonewall Jackson, marching his troops westward on New Year's Day, succeeded in capturing Romney, but this was rather an empty victory. Kelley already had evacuated the town before the Rebels arrived and, after they took it, there was little else for them to do. The grip of winter was the controlling factor on every hand and, though Jackson had wanted it otherwise, the high command at Richmond was willing for the forces he had left there under Loring to return eastward. Then, during the last of February, word reached Washington that the Confederates were falling back from their lines around Manassas in the direction of Richmond. [2]

As soon as he heard of the Rebels' departure, Sprague began preparing for the grave-hunting expedition. He located Josiah W. Richardson, private in the Second Rhode Island Regiment, who had stayed behind that July day to nurse the wounded. This fellow was a witness to some of the burials and thought he could lead the way to the graves. Likewise with Tristam Burgess and Private John Clark. All three got a call to stand by. Others were alerted too. When called upon, the War Department gave permission for a troop of First Rhode Island Cavalry to go along as an escort, and Walter H. Coleman, experienced in such things, was drafted to supervise the exhumings.

Seventy-one men were in the Sprague party when it left Washington. At the governor's side rode his aide, Colonel Olney Arnold, experienced and efficient, and accompanying the cavalry troop were Lieutenant Colonel Sayles, Major Anthony, Chaplain Frederic Denison, and Surgeon James B. Greeley. Sprague's private two-horse wagon and two baggage wagons loaded with forage, rations, and empty coffins rolled behind them.

It was a typical day for the season, and the countryside in Virginia was sporting a tinge of green. Near the houses forsythia shook out its golden bells, and violets pushed through the bed of tender grass. Farther off, fruit trees were dotted with a rash of buds, each so tight-lipped it permitted only a peep of color and all hanging from bursting branches bending under a driving March wind, chilly but welcome in view of its pledge of drier conditions underfoot. This promise, it might have been noted, was far from fulfillment, for the roads were still in a horrible condition and were made worse by a rain that set in before dark. In the face of such unfavorable conditions the governor's band, after coaxing its mud-spattered horses into Fairfax Court House, was quite willing to halt for the night.

Next day was still rainy and disagreeable, but Sprague was impatient. Under his goading the men saddled up and rode on, for miles, past Centreville and beyond, coming to a halt along Cub Run. Captain Samuel James Smith of Company I had met his death there during the retreat from the battlefield, and they hoped to find his grave, remembered as a rather hasty affair. But search was futile. Hours were spent walking back and forth through the bushes on both sides of the stream without finding the slightest trace of the burial spot.

On the morning of the twenty-first, with the weather still stormy and disagreeable, they covered the short distance to the stone bridge across Bull Run and found that the Confederates had blown it up before falling back from Manassas. After staring for a time at the mass of ruins and at a skeleton leaning against a tree, they turned right and rode up the east bank of the creek toward Sudley Ford. There they crossed over, barely wetting the girths of their horses. Past a barn they went, noticing seven raccoon pelts tacked to its side, something they took as an indication of the winter pastime of Rebel soldiers, and then on up to Sudley Church, used as a hospital the previous summer. At this building, its door ajar, they stopped to investigate, some of them riding their horses inside and even up to the pulpit. In a few minutes, their curiosity satisfied, they rode briskly on, past a spring at which a Negro girl was dipping water into a bucket, and at this point the governor nodded to Richardson to lead the way to the spot where the Rhode Islanders were buried.

Richardson turned off down a wooded ravine north of the battlefield, near the road leading from the church, and there pointed to two graves, the mounds of which had settled until they were nearly on a plane with the surrounding terrain.[3] They were close together, one a little higher up the slope of the ravine than the other.

"It was here we buried Colonel Slocum and Major Ballou," he said. "You won't have much trouble. I don't think you'll find the top of either coffin over two feet under ground."

With the governor and officers forming the inner rim of a circle, the horsemen gathered around the graves. Suddenly the eeriness that attaches to a graveyard at night seemed to settle over the ravine, bringing a ghostliness to the trees and the shadowy vales and causing a deep silence among the stern-faced riders. Not even the sight of a cabin on the brow of a hill near the road a short distance away helped break the spell. They stared in silence, at the mounds and at the huckleberry bushes dried to lifeless skeletons by the harsh winter, and some of them shuffled nervously and looked away, trying to divert their thoughts and relieve personal strain.

Finally Major Anthony spoke: "Get your shovels, men."

Two troopers swung from their saddles and stepped forward with the tools in their hands.

"Dig this one first," directed Coleman.

The men sank their shovels into the damp, soggy earth, one at each end. While they dug, some of the group watched a Negro girl slowly edge down from the cabin on the hill. By her gaudy dress they recognized her as the one they had seen earlier dipping water at the spring.[4]

She came to within a few feet of where the men were at work. "Y'all diggin' fo' Cunnel Slike—Cunnel Slook?" she finally nerved herself to ask, hesitating over the name.

"Colonel Slocum," corrected one of the officers.

"Yassuh, dat's it," she said. "Dat his name. Well, you ain't go' find him. Dem Georgia boys dug him up weeks ago. Dey cut his head off and carried it away and dey done burnt his body down in de hollow dere."[5]

"Where?" asked Governor Sprague in horror, shocked and striving to control the tone of his voice.

"Right down dere," she said, pointing along the ravine. "His shirt's down dere now, down in de run, an' his coffin wuz dere too, but dey got it out an' burrid a po' cullud man in it."

"Show me where you mean," suggested the governor.

Most of the group followed the girl on foot down the ravine, leaving a few of the troopers behind to hold the horses and continue the digging. Presently she pointed to a pile of ashes near the bank of the stream, some of them still gray and indicating an age of only a few weeks. Nearby lay a blanket, sodden and muddy. One of the men kicked it with the toe of his boot and it fell open, exposing several tufts of hair.

Dr. Greeley, the surgeon, stepped forward and began poking in the ashes with a stick, gradually pulling to the side several blackened objects.

"They're human bones," he announced at last. "That's a femus, or thighbone, this is some of the vertebrae, or backbone, and there are portions of the pelvis bones."

At his direction a trooper timidly gathered up the pieces in the blanket. Then the group moved a few yards farther, to a point where two shirts, one a silk and the other a striped calico, were caught in some bushes in the brook.

A trooper waded in and brought them to the bank.

"Look!" he said excitedly as he stepped out of the water. "The collars are buttoned and the sleeves are unbuttoned."

Greeley nodded knowingly. "They cut his head off," he said solemnly. "I'm certain his head wasn't burned with the rest of the body. No skull in the ashes—no teeth, or anything."

Sprague stood silently studying the shirts. "Doc," he said at last, "those aren't Slocum's shirts. I knew him well. He never wore a shirt like that. They must be Ballou's." [6]

Highly excited, they returned to the graves and found the diggers had removed no more than a foot of the dirt. The ground was so soggy it clung to the shovel and made digging extremely difficult.

"Let's try running a saber down," suggested Greeley. "If the coffin isn't buried deep, we're bound to strike it."

A saber was handed him and he pushed it into the center of the grave almost to the hilt.

"No coffin there," he pronounced.

Then he turned to the other grave and sank the saber not more than two feet before he struck a hard object. "There's one here."

The troopers swung their shovels to the second grave and began digging. In a few minutes they lifted out a coffin and opened it to find the body of the thirty-seven-year-old Slocum rolled up in a blanket.

"That's him all right," said Sprague solemnly. "I recognize him by his mustache."

Greeley nodded. "Pretty obvious what happened," he said. "The Second Regiment cut up those Georgia boys rather badly, and they were sore at Slocum, the commanding officer. They just got the wrong body." [7]

Taking with him his aide and a few others, Sprague made a round of the houses in the neighborhood to gather further evidence. A fourteen-year-old boy was a ready witness. He was questioned closely by Colonel Sayles, who had been skeptical about the burning. Answers elicited were unstudied and dogmatic. The lad was sure it was done by the Twenty-first Georgia, for he had watched. He said the Southerners put the fire out afterward because of the horrible stench created, and he added that he had known for several days in advance that they were going to behead the body.

Leaving the boy, Sprague led the way up through a grove of pine trees to a plantation house, where they were met by an old man who said his name was Newman. It was obvious he was a farmer of good reputation, well esteemed by his neighbors. He had not seen the actual burning, he told his questioners, but three or four days afterward he had gone down and viewed the ashes and the bones and the coffin. At their suggestion he accompanied them to the spot and pointed out things as they had been when he made his visit.

"It was an awful thing—barbaric," he said. "But no Virginians did it. Virginians wouldn't do such a thing. I'm sure it was the Georgians. They were terribly mad at Colonel Slocum."

At another house a white woman was the only person present to answer their questions. She had nursed the sick and wounded at Sudley Church after the battle, and she said she had witnessed the whole affair. She had begged and entreated that the dead be held sacred, she related, but the "savages" had mocked at her, so she had saved a lock of hair—a lock for friends she was confident someday would come along. Walter Coleman, remembering the quantity that had been turned up in the blanket, took it gingerly from her fingers.

Back at the graves once more, Sprague suggested they proceed to Captain Levi Tower's burial place.

Private John Clark stepped up. "Governor, I'll show you. It's in the yard of a house on the battlefield. I was lying inside wounded and watched the burial from a window."

They got into the saddle, all but a few detailed to help with the removal of Slocum's body, and trailed Clark back along the road toward the battlefield. At a cabin identified as the Matthews home they drew rein. It had been in the range of some of the heaviest fighting and its bullet-scarred walls attested to its experience. But there the day's efforts ended. Rain started falling about the time they drew up in front of it, and the nearness of twilight told them they would have to save a part of their search for the morrow.

Matthews proved a genial host. While the horses stood out in the wind and rain, seventeen men, including the governor, made their beds on the floor of the cabin, first partaking of hoecake and aromatic rye coffee offered them by their host. On the hearth at their feet while they dozed fitfully throughout the night, a log fire burned, sometimes brightening up and covering the walls with flickering shadows, at other times smoldering docilely and with little more life than the dead lying out in the shallow graves along Bull Run.

Shortly after dawn they had visits from Newman and another neighbor, Van Pelt. Each had his own story of experiences and losses and wanted to unload it. Considerable time was thus consumed.

When Sprague and party later emerged from the cabin, someone noticed the skeleton of a horse in a field nearby, and the governor, visiting the scene, recognized it as the remains of the animal killed under him during the battle. Surgeon Greeley was another who viewed the bones, giving them such a professional examination that he was able to locate the fatal bullet.

Meantime Private Clark had pointed out a large square mound at the side of the yard.

"Tower's in there," he said. "I was looking out that very window when they buried him."

Several of the troopers began digging. Soon they came to an unexploded shell and a little later to the first body. It lay face downward, apparently buried just as it had fallen in battle.

All at once there was an exclamation from one of the troopers, and he pointed to a ridge above. Gathered there, staring down like vultures from a tree, stood a disorderly band of men, in all sorts of dress, most of them clothed as farmers.

"Guerrillas!" shouted Colonel Sayles. "We'll have to watch those fellows. They'll shoot us from behind."

Some of the troopers were assigned to stand guard, and as they moved out the guerrillas disappeared.

The digging continued. Soon a second body was uncovered, and then a third and a fourth, all lying face downward, some across one another. The eighth taken out was that of Captain Tower, and there the digging was halted.[8]

"Somebody got his boots," observed Clark, staring down at Tower. "I know he had them on when he was killed."

At that moment one of the guards on the ridge fired his gun, and for a brief period the exhumings were overshadowed by other excitement.

"Just wanted to let you know those guerrillas were still hanging around," explained the sentinel when they reached him.

But the guerrillas got no nearer, and the bodies were rounded up and hauled away, along with numerous souvenirs. At the site of a Rebel cavalry camp one of the men picked up a brown paper envelope on which had been written:

"On! On! To the rescue; the vandals are coming;
Go meet them with bayonet, saber and spear,
Drive them back to the desolate land they are leaving;
Go! Trusting in God, you'll have nothing to fear."[9]

That afternoon Governor Sprague and his escort of cavalry from the First Rhode Island began the journey back to Washington. Their progress was slow, owing to the Virginia mud softened by the recent rains, and there was ample time for talk—for talk of barbaric and fiendish Southerners—really not the chivalry of the land they were supposed to be—who used skulls for drinking cups and shinbones for drumsticks. And there was talk of guerrillas, of men in farmers' overalls who haunted from the ridges like vultures from pine tops and who were said to have no scruples about shooting from the rear.

CHAPTER 9

March 21–June 6, 1862

"HE FELL GLORIOUSLY"

One of the chief inducements to guerrilla or Partisan warfare among Southern boys was the example set by Turner Ashby, the saddened, black-bearded bachelor who had swung from service with Angus McDonald to a more rigid routine as the eyes and ears of Stonewall Jackson's foot cavalry. Along the trails Ashby blazed for military history, fact and fable were so intertwined that no one bothered to try to separate them. He became a phantom, a soldier with a charmed life, a rider who appeared always at the right moment and in the right place, a knight on a charmed horse, a gladiator who found romance in war and got great fun out of toying with the Yankees who had come to invade his homeland. And always in his heart, 'twas said, he carried a will to avenge the death of his brother.

Jackson used Ashby's cavalry for outpost duty, and these riders, although occasionally censured for lack of discipline, made a great success of it. As one Union rifleman recorded by letter, "It is an interesting sight to see their line of horsemen slowly walking back and forth on a ridge, standing out full against the sky." [1] It was the screen they maintained that led Federals to far overestimate the strength of the Confederates in the Valley.

One day the Ringgold Cavalry from Pennsylvania came chasing Jackson's army southward. After a time they spied ahead of them a lone cavalryman seated atop a rail fence, the reins of his horse looped over an arm. This Rebel paid no attention to the Union horsemen as they approached; for all intents and purposes he was deeply engrossed in a newspaper spread over one knee. But when the Federals suddenly charged, thinking they had him cornered, he took to the saddle in a flash, whirled about, and raised his gun, firing twice before dashing back toward a turn in the road. The boys in blue went flying after him, and it was then his pursuers suddenly were greeted by a salute from a six-pounder cannon posted around the bend. In this manner, it is recorded, the Ringgold cavalry met Ashby, the elusive figure they saw only too often as they marched up the Valley.[2]

Always Ashby appeared to be playing a game, to be tantalizing his foes and daring them to catch him, and the outcome of it was that he and his beautiful white charger, a splendid jumper, became a symbol to the Federals. Standing alone on the brow of a hill, man and horse comprised an invitation often accepted. The Unionists rode furiously to make an important catch, and Ashby would let them approach until they were so close his capture seemed assured, at which point he would mount and canter leisurely out of sight, next showing up on the crest of a more distant hill.[3]

The dashing manner of this confident horseman stirred a responsive chord in Southerners. They heard of his feats and they pictured themselves in his saddle—more death-dealing than he, their hero—and it was not to their well-being they had such dreams, for the opportunity to put them into effect drew constantly closer. As the demand for Partisan warfare was magnified, so also the call to come help Turner drive the Yankees out of the Valley.

But not always was there sympathy with such a summons. General Joe Johnston was one who thought it a bad thing. Just before falling back from Manassas he learned that someone was passing out handbills urging his soldiers to join up for "local service" in the Valley, which it was claimed would gain for them certain special privileges. Johnston ordered these recruiters ousted from his camps, maintaining that what they were doing would produce "present discontent and future mutiny."[4]

Despite Johnston and eventually other opponents, there was no end to the demand for the so-called "local service." It was loudest around Harpers Ferry and in the counties along the B. & O. from that point to Wheeling. People whose loyalty rested with the South were resentful that Jefferson Davis would not spread his army so that it could afford them protection, and they told him so in letters. In one county 160 citizens banded together and sent the President a petition in which they described enemy depredations and said there was no time to lose.[5] Another county forwarded notice that the men of the vicinity "at last are showing signs of resistance" and added: "Last night a lady swam the Shenandoah to let us know that the enemy were being reinforced, and the first aim would be to destroy our woolen factories along the Shenandoah; also our large flouring mills." [6]

The cry grew louder. On all sides men were talking of raising their own companies—for irregular or independent service as a part of the Confederate army. There was reluctance to call them guerrillas, for the term was frowned on by the government at Richmond. In fact, contrary to the attitude in '61, Acting Secretary of War Judah P. Benjamin, in reply to queries, was sending messages saying specifically: "Guerrilla companies are not recognized as part of the military organization of the Confederate States, and cannot be authorized by this department."

Only in the West, particularly in Missouri and Kansas, were guerrillas taking the field as such at this time—and they strictly on an unofficial basis. The depredations they were committing under leaders like William Clarke Quantrill and Bill Anderson, men with criminal reputations firmly established even before the war began, were not at all complimentary. The Confederate government would have no truck with such ruthless, unscrupulous individuals, and the North was anything but tolerant toward them. Guerrillas were looked upon by the Union high command in that area as contrary to the rules of civilized warfare, and it was decreed that any prisoners so identified would be hanged as outlaws. In reply the guerrillas gave notice that, if thus treated, they would ruin the country in which they operated, burning houses and murdering loyal men.[7]

While frowning on such practice as was threatened in the West, the Confederate government did realize, through its inability to drive the enemy back across the Ohio and the many letters consequently coming into the capital, that it needed "local service" outfits. The clamor for guerrilla warfare the Richmond *Dispatch* had helped start back in May, '61, was too strongly ingrained by now to be ignored. But the government sought to avoid the onus attached to the term "guerrilla," and it was left to Virginia to lead the way in ferreting out an answer to this problem. By act of the General Assembly, Governor John Letcher was authorized to issue commissions for the organization of ten companies of Partisan Rangers. These were to be mustered into the state service but were to operate as individual units more or less on detached duty.

This act giving some formal recognition to the "local service" outfits caused a flurry of recruiting activity, particularly in the mountain counties of western Virginia. Several companies of Rangers already had been organized in that area, and arrangements were made to transfer them to more legal status. One of these was under the leadership of George Dusky, member of a family that was to bring many headaches to the Union occupation forces before the war came to an end. At the moment his father, Dan, was residing in custody of the U. S. marshal, under indictment for treason, a charge later changed more specifically to robbing the mails.

With several Partisan Ranger units already in the field, it was obvious at the start that Virginia might have to wink at its limit of ten companies. This could be handled in another way, as illustrated by Turner Ashby. When Harry Gilmor, the Baltimore volunteer, asked for permission to organize his own outfit, for irregular operations mostly in the northern part of the Valley, it was granted, but with the understanding that, while the new unit was to fight independently, it was to be listed formally as a part of Ashby's cavalry.

One March morning a Federal soldier sat in camp near Winchester writing to his mother: "Jackson and Ashby are clever men. We are slow-w-w!" Outside his tent the mules, standing in a vicious attitude of expectant kicking, gathered closely in a scourging snowstorm, their tails drawn tightly down. In a separate group the horses lay back their ears with half-closed eyes and hung their necks. At roll call soldiers stood up "in the attitude of the traveler in the spelling book, against whom the wind is striving to gain the victory of the fable." The tents in the morning's early light were darkened by the white of the ground into a cheerless and gloomy hue. Campfires smoked as men endeavored to coax a blaze from black coals and dripping wood, and kettles and mess pans were crusted with a coating of ice. Such weather in March, when it had been hoped spring would come early so that the Southerners could be more quickly brought under control!

Around Strasburg and Winchester there had been fighting between Jackson and Union General Shields, and the star of it all was Ashby. He stirred the blood of future Partisans and aroused the admiration of one Yankee soldier, who wrote: "It seems that the enterprising and clever Ashby, with his two light pieces of artillery, was amusing himself . . . He is light, active, skillful, and we are tormented by him like a bull with a gadfly."[8]

This soldier had heard directly from Jackson's camp. According to his information, Jackson was a few miles beyond Woodstock, without tents and with wagons ready to move at a moment's notice. His force was 4000 to 5000. He was reputed to have said: "My men have no uniform; they wear multiform."

In his rear, Stonewall kept Ashby with his cavalry and two pieces of artillery. The Union soldier with the facile pen formed his own convictions concerning Jackson on a basis of what he heard: "His game is a winning one even when he loses. With his small force he detains 20,000 men in the Valley . . . Vacillation is our name. We cannot take Jackson . . . My admiration and sympathy go with the gallant Ashby, and the indefatigable and resolute Jackson."

Stonewall led Shields on a merry chase. April arrived and the weather warmed. "We make life musical these hot sunny days with the screeching whir of wheels or the sharp buzz and sping of rifle balls," wrote one of the men chasing Jackson. "But the enemy keep at a respectful distance."[9] Up the Valley they went, farther from Washington, and all the time the Federals were drawing a closer bead on Ashby. Near Mount Jackson they killed his white horse.[10]

The first day of April, McClellan got aboard a transport in the Potomac and set out for Fort Monroe. He was trailing his army which for two weeks had been moving in that direction to carry out his plan of approaching Richmond from the east, from along the peninsula stretching down toward the coast. Such a move meant McClellan had had his way over Lincoln, for the President favored an advance via Manassas, along the route McDowell had failed on so completely the preceding summer. But the Administration was triumphant in one respect: McDowell's corps would be retained to guard Washington against whatever might develop in the Valley. As some folks saw it, no telling what might happen over there, the way Jackson was cutting up. Take Colonel Jonas P. Holliday, for instance. Hadn't he shot himself in the head while leading his Vermont cavalry near Strasburg? That quick. Never a word before he died. But in recent weeks he had given ample indication that he was gravely worried.[11]

General John C. Frémont, commanding the Mountain Department

in western Virginia through which ran the B. & O., had worries too. He had just learned, from letters found on Rebel prisoners, of the ten Partisan Ranger companies ordered by the Confederate government and said it represented "a systematic plan of guerrilla warfare." This meant organization, and organization meant trouble, and trouble he already had. Guerrillas entered Bulltown in Braxton County on a Saturday night, cut the telegraph wires, shot the mail carrier, swore the telegraph operator to secrecy, took all his personal effects, and decamped. Frémont thought it highly important that the Union cavalry should be armed with carbines or short Enfield rifles to inspire them with confidence and place them on an equality with the guerrillas.

The general may have been goaded into this attitude by the Wheeling *Intelligencer*, which just four days earlier published a letter to the editor that said: "In view of the increasing and devastating raids made by guerrilla bands and outlaws of every description on the peaceable citizens of the border counties of this state, it behooves the authorities conducting the affairs of the same to devise some means whereby these outrages may be checked and finally crushed out before the entire frontier of western Virginia is depopulated."

Whether goaded or not, Frémont issued a general order to commanders of posts and troops not moving in the field, directing them to use their utmost exertion to destroy the various bands of guerrillas beginning to infest the department. These guerrillas, he said, must be fought in their own style—by rapid marches, vigorous attacks, and severe measures. Moreover, sudden and frequent movements must be made, both by night and day, and the marauders must be attacked whenever possible.

Frémont was joined by Generals Banks and Kelley in his clamor for more attention to the guerrillas and for more cavalry with which to fight them. Kelley reported that refugees who had fled the western counties to join the Southern army were returning with commissions to recruit "mounted rangers" for the purpose of carrying on a system of guerrilla warfare. To help frustrate this scheme he asked for the Ringgold Cavalry, among other companies, citing that the Pennsylvanians were familiar with the rough country in which they would have to fight.

Over in the Cheat Mountain area, Brigadier General R. H. Milroy was champing at the bit. Frémont had sent him a simple order directing him to "exterminate" such guerrillas as might show themselves in his rear. As simple as that! Milroy recognized the elusiveness of the Partisans and he had a different plan. Making an obvious slur at Francis Pierpont, he suggested that, "if there is a live Governor at Wheeling," he be sent into the different counties to hold meetings and organize the civil and military powers into Union home guards for the protection of the countryside and the relief of Federal troops scattered through the area. He said that his command was greatly crippled by the assigning of details to fight the guerrillas.

But it was left to Frémont at this time to ask a question that the Federal government knew it sooner or later would have to answer: "What course shall be pursued in relation to guerrillas bearing the commission of Governor Letcher or other Confederate authority?" As evidence of his concern he reported that numerous bands were making their appearance and only waiting the coming of the leaves to go fully into their work.[12]

It was at this period that the Confederate States government, taking Virginia's example, formally entered into the business of Partisan Ranger warfare. By act of Congress and by general orders, authority was given for the formation of bands of Rangers, either as infantry or cavalry. Recruits were to be regularly received into the service, with the same pay and subject to the same regulations as other soldiers. But one section of the act extended an inducement not accorded the man in the ranks: for any arms and munitions of war the Partisans captured and turned over to the government, they were to be paid the prevailing price.

With the first year of the war coming to a close, the Confederacy also at this time extended its draft law. All white men between the ages of eighteen and thirty-five were made subject to the call of the President for military service up to three years.

But the important news from the standpoint of the Federals occupying the Shenandoah Valley and the mountain area beyond was that concerning the Partisan Rangers. Always the Union problem in this area was the movement and subsistence of the army, the enemy seeming more or less a secondary problem, to be met when time and circumstances were propitious. Partisans, on the other hand, were different. They moved quickly and they were hard to watch. Moreover, they scorned orderly battle routine, striking night or day, and always when least expected. And while military authorities in Missouri reacted promptly, dealing with a different breed of guerrilla and having no hesitancy in ordering them shot down as outlaws, matters moved more deliberately in the East, nearer the influence of the White House, even though the breed farther west cast the onus of its unsavory operations on all who might fall into the general classification.

On the last day of April, twenty-five young men who had fought with Frémont in Missouri as members of an outfit known as the Kansas Jayhawkers came into Wheeling. They were dressed in the clothes of farmers and laborers and bore the name of "Jessie Scouts," a band of Union spies who became anathema to Rebels during the summer of '62. They were the idea of General Frémont's wife, Jessie, whose name they bore.[13] Later, dressed in the uniforms of captured Confederates, they were to be found usually in the advance of the Southern army, gathering up both information and prisoners without creating great alarm.

Their leader as they came into Wheeling was a husky individual of wide experience named Captain J. Carpenter.[14] He already had had many narrow escapes, including the time he deserted John Brown's men in the engine house at Harpers Ferry by crawling through a long culvert, and there was another close shave in store for him. In telling of this later incident newspapers said it "deserves record as a bit of romance in the midst of the terrible realities of war." [15] Accordingly they related that he had been shot in the thigh while preventing the suicide of a Rebel female who had been captivated by the fame and person of the daring officer. But later all romance in the incident faded when it was found the young woman was quite a traveler and that she had a wide assortment of male acquaintances.

In a few weeks the Jessie Scouts themselves were in bad repute. The *Intelligencer* reported that "distance and the Cincinnati papers have lent an enchantment" to the small body of men, who suddenly became as unwelcome to the North as guerrillas in Missouri were to the South. Their chief sponsor, General Frémont, resigned from the army, and after that they seemed to go to pieces as an organization, some of them setting out on a wave of lawlessness and disobedience that made history. From the backs of these scouts disappeared the rough clothes of disguise, and they walked the streets adorned in the glory of velvet uniforms set off by brass buttons, red sashes, and mystic soldier straps, even though the commander of the area had ruled against such gilded emblems of distinction. Two of them got so abusive with their language on one occasion that they were placed in the Wheeling jail, famously known as The Atheneum. Another tried a novel plan for skipping from the Monroe House in that community without paying his bill. Cunningly, he mixed his baggage with that of an entertainment troupe—a traveling show-man, the proprietor of an educated monkey, and a man without arms—and thus smuggled it aboard a boat, to which he previously had sent his woman companion. But the hotel got wise and dis-patched Policeman St. Myers on the trail of the retreating lodger to relieve him of fifty dollars, which done, they marked his bill paid in full. As one newspaper said: "Leaving him to the poetic reflection that the best laid schemes of mice and men gang aft aglee."

On the second day of May the work of guerrillas brought worry to the most inner circles of the War Department in Washington. Telegraph wires were cut somewhere between Harpers Ferry and Winchester, making it impossible for contact to be maintained with Generals Banks and Shields, who were trying to hem up Stonewall Jackson in the Valley. Secretary of War Stanton went into action. He sent a message by train to Colonel John W. Geary, guarding the Manassas Gap Railroad, telling him to arrange a line of mounted couriers between Front Royal and Strasburg, messengers to leave the respective places alternately every two hours, and to establish a telegraph office at Front Royal that would remain open night and day.[16]

Geary responded to these orders quickly. He reported there were guerrillas in his vicinity too, that the entire railroad, from Manassas to Strasburg, was threatened, and that his force was too small to guard it securely.[17] Engaged in this work he had twenty-two com-panies, including fifteen of infantry, six of cavalry, and one of artil-lery.[18]

Meanwhile, in Southern circles, the fever for irregular warfare raged. The Richmond *Dispatch* published lengthy advertisements designed to attract the attention of young men. Captain John Scott of Fauquier County, bearing the requisite commission to enlist a corps of Partisan Rangers, addressed "all enterprising men," espe-cially those whose homes already were in possession of the enemy, said he planned to operate within the Federal lines, and promised an active life and a break from the tedium of camp life.[19]

In the same issue of the paper Colonel John D. Imboden, organ-izer of the Staunton Artillery, who had aided with the capture of

Harpers Ferry just a year earlier, placed a similar notice, heading it with: "Active Service in the Mountains of Virginia." He wanted "picked men," ten companies of them, all to operate west of the Blue Ridge. This "active service" he described as an arm in which "individual prowess is not swallowed up in the mere mechanism of great masses of men." His plans, he said, had the highest military and official approval in the land and, carrying them out, he would rely on great celerity of movement, sleepless vigilance, good marksmanship and plenty of old-fashioned rough fighting and bushwhacking, so as "to make the country too hot to permit a Yankee to show his head outside of his camp."

The *Dispatch* got in a word too. Giving its opinion editorially, it described Partisan warfare as "beyond doubt, the most attractive branch of the service," and predicted it would attract the attention "of all young men of daring and adventurous natures."

A report soon was circulated—and given some credence in Union military circles—that 2900 Rebel cavalry had been detached from different commands and formed into guerrilla bands. These were said to occupy the various mountain ranges and spurs bordering the Valley, where they were lying in wait for an opportunity to attack wagon trains, pickets, or foraging parties. Colonel Geary, maintaining his constant watch over the Manassas Gap line, stumbled upon one of their hide-outs in a cave five miles from Rectortown, but the enemy had flown. He estimated that there were forty men and horses and, judging from the bottles, boxes, and cans left behind, concluded they had been living quite sumptuously. He took them to be a part of the gang that had captured some of his wagons the previous week.[20] It also dawned upon him that the irregulars, aided by the increasing denseness of the foliage, were scouting and raiding with more impunity than in the past.[21]

But not all of the Rebel guerrillas were hiding in the mountains. General McDowell, whose headquarters was at Fredericksburg, in a part of Virginia where there were no towering ranges, was bothered by them also, and he so notified the War Department. Back came a furious telegram from Assistant Secretary of War P. H. Watson, a man of little consequence in the war, who said: "Like pirates and buccaneers they are the common enemies of mankind, and should be hunted and shot without challenge wherever found. Such treatment would soon put a stop to the formation of guerrilla bands and to the assassination of sentinels and other barbarities practiced by those who engage in irregular warfare."[22] As experience proved, Mr. Watson did not know whereof he wrote.

In western Virginia residents with Union proclivities became panicky as guerrilla bands were reported at numerous places. Union raiding parties went out to make circular hunts. One of these was led by General Kelley, the "Old Ben" guarding the B. & O., who found people around Parkersburg so alarmed and excited that it was impossible to obtain from them reliable information.[23] Two days later, while he was riding through a pass in the mountains, guerrillas sent a harmless hail of bullets down upon him and fled before his men could scale the mountainside on their trail.[24]

Though not as personally involved as Kelley, General Banks, who had been having his hands full with Jackson in the Valley around Strasburg, also was feeling the effects of guerrillas, expecially in his rear. The men of one of his brigades, for example, were left entirely without rations, and mostly by their own doings. Before rushing into battle they laid aside their knapsacks, to gain more freedom of movement, and foolishly piled them near a road where guerrillas were waiting to snatch them away.

Around the middle of May, Union troops under Shields at Woodstock were transferred to the line of the Orange and Alexandria Railroad nearer Washington, and Jackson saw his chance. He struck quickly at Winchester and at Front Royal, driving back Banks and Geary, and kept flying. Banks immediately began to cry for more support, and the tendency in Washington was to discount his alarm.

But Shields finally was ordered back to the Valley, and he went reluctantly. He found conditions along the Manassas Gap Railroad in a "shameful panic,"[25] with bridges burned and telegraph lines destroyed. As for the enemy that had driven back Banks and Geary, he said that from all he could learn it was inconsiderable, but conceded that "some man of energy must be sent to hold the Valley or the mountain guerrillas will take it."

For Wheeling on the Ohio River at this time there was excitement of a different variety: Mary Jane Green came back to town. Mary Jane was a virago from Braxton County and she was brought to the city in charge of a guard. On her first visit some months previous, also under guard, she had been charged merely with carrying her skirts full of letters for the Rebel army. This got her little more than a reprimand, and she was released after promising to go and sin no more. Now she was back, accused of the more serious offense of cutting telegraph lines erected by the Federal army. But this time she showed no contriteness. When her captors tried to place her in The Atheneum, an old carriage depot in which prevailed such disorders as measles, mumps, rheumatism, and occasional cases of typhoid fever and afflictions of the heart and lungs,[26] she leapt into the role of a termagant and flattened one of the soldiers with a brick. Reported the *Intelligencer:* "Mary Jane is apparently yet in her teens, but she is one of the most determined and violent Rebs that has turned up in these parts since the breaking out of the rebellion." [27]

While the month of May marked the return of Mary Jane, it also registered a temporary gap in the ranks of the irregulars. Lige White, descending Massanutten Mountain with prisoners and cornered by irate citizens who mistook his party for Yankee scouts, chose the wrong moment to raise his head above a rail fence and was clipped by a rifle bullet near the right eye. There, in the ensuing minutes until he could be rescued, he lay mentally making his will, voicing messages to be delivered to his wife, and shouting at intervals, "Tell the boys to do as I did—never surrender!" But Lige's constitution was much stronger than he may have reckoned, and his wound less serious. He would be back with his command before the end of June.[28]

June arrived with flowers in full bloom, and the weather warmed, and then the skies darkened and rains started falling in a storm that lasted several days. Floods were general. Everywhere bridges were washed away, communication lines disrupted, and there was property damage running into the millions. The Potomac reached its highest level in ten years.[29]

Despite the rain the fighting in the Valley continued in hare-and-hound fashion between Jackson and four Union armies, those under Banks, Shields, Milroy, and now Frémont, who had moved east from western Virginia. Ashby was in it all, the first to lead a charge, the last to leave a fight. One night a member of Jackson's staff, Alexander S. Pendleton—"Sandy" to his intimates—cautioned Ashby about exposing himself. It was a twenty-two-year-old cautioning a veteran of thirty-four, and the seasoned cavalryman brushed aside the warning with a light remark that his fears were not for the bullets fired directly at him, for they always missed their mark, but rather was he concerned about the random shots which always hit someone for whom they were not intended.[30]

On the sixth day of June the sobbing skies began to exhaust their supply of tears. That day Jackson's troops fell back through Harrisonburg, trailed by the enemy. Ashby was guarding the rear, and it soon looked as if he was to have one of his better days. His horsemen drew up in the woods on the road to Port Republic and got down from their saddles for a hasty morsel. But their hunger was not to be appeased. Before they could finish eating, word was brought that the Federals were entering an old field through which they had just passed, and they dropped their food and rushed out to give battle. The fighting went in their favor, pleasingly so, for among their captives was an officer who had openly expressed a desire to meet Ashby. He was Sir Percy Wyndham, a British soldier of fortune experienced in the ways of the military, having once seen service in Italy with Garibaldi.

Later there was more fighting. The Pennsylvania Bucktails, a crack outfit under Lieutenant Colonel Thomas L. Kane, pushed to the front, and in a few minutes it was evident the day was no more his than Wyndham's. Back to the Confederate rear he was taken, wounded, a prisoner. Though suffering some, his mood was one of magnanimity. This he revealed in conversation with Captain James R. Herbert of the First Maryland, one of his captors. "I have today," he said, "saved the life of one of the most gallant officers in either army—General Ashby—a man I admire as much as you do. His figure is familiar to me, for I have seen him often in our front. He was today within 50 yards of my skirmishers, sitting on his horse, unconscious of the danger he was in. I saw three of them raise their guns to fire, but I succeeded in stopping two of them and struck up the gun of the third as it went off. Ashby is too brave to die in that way." [31]

But Ashby was already dead. The bullets that had drawn ever closer finally found their mark, bringing to a horseman an ignominious death. As he led a charge in the heat of battle, a bullet killed his mount,[32] and he leapt free of the saddle, striking the ground unharmed, a darkened demon, looking more like an Arab than an American. Then on foot, in a black raincoat, he waved his troopers onward through the drizzle and fog.[33] They heard him shout and they rushed forward, and it was at that moment he staggered and fell, shot through the heart, his lips sealed without a single dying word.[34]

Strange scenes marked the road leading to the rear from where

Ashby's cavalry was fighting that day. Private Sheets was a witness to many of them. He stood among a group of Rebels watching the caravan slowly trickling back toward headquarters, and his attention was attracted to a Federal prisoner who was tall and elegantly dressed, his uniform set off by numerous decorations. Sheets wished to share what he saw: "Look yonder, boys—there's a Yankee colonel!" The words riled Sir Percy Wyndham, at whom Sheets was pointing, and he turned in his saddle and shouted with scorn, "I am not a Yankee, you damned Rebel fool!" A roar of laughter from the Southerners along the roadside followed the remark. Wyndham continued to curse and was still cursing when he went out of sight around a curve, the riotous uproar of the Confederates taunting in his ears.[35]

A short while afterward four cavalrymen riding abreast came along the road, bearing on the necks of their horses a body wrapped in a gun blanket. Tears streamed down their faces as they passed, arousing the curiosity of Captain Garber of Company A, Fifty-second Virginia Infantry. "Who is it?" he asked. "General Ashby," muttered one of the grieving horsemen, wiping at a tear.[36]

At a time of sadness and death it is sometimes the little things that remain longest in the memories of man. McHenry Howard, a Marylander assigned to staff duty, stood at brigade headquarters on the northeast side of the road toward Port Republic. For him it had been a day of great excitement—"and this I remember from several incidents," he wrote in afteryears. It seemed only a few minutes to the young soldier since he had heard firing to the rear, mad and spirited, and then had come a lull and he had watched a distinguished-looking Federal officer ride by a prisoner, fine and proud in his uniform, but dejected. Someone had said it was the Britisher, Wyndham. Later there was more firing, and finally that too had died down, as if for the night, and now the skies were clearing and the sun was sinking into shadows with a panoramic promise that the morrow would be brighter. Dusk came on rapidly. As darkness drifted through the trees, a heavy vehicle approached from the direction of the battlefield, bearing a burden once borne by four cavalrymen riding abreast. It moved slowly past McHenry Howard, its curtains drawn tight, its horses walking at a spiritless pace, and rolled on into the gloaming, leaving in its wake brave men who could bear without tears the horror and sorrow of battle, but who cried unashamedly when told of the death of Ashby.[37]

Off at a bridge across North River, Imboden, the artillerist, held fast with his battalion of Partisan Rangers, four howitzers and a Parrott gun, seriously concerned with his task of guarding Stonewall's trains against a flank movement. At ten o'clock that night a courier handed him a note from Jackson. It was written in pencil on the margin of a newspaper and it directed him to report with his command at Port Republic before daybreak. Below this message was a postscript as disarming as a funeral dirge: "Poor Ashby is dead. He fell gloriously." [38]

CHAPTER 10

INTERNATIONAL LAW
CLEARS GUERRILLAS

What to do with guerrillas? As the first year of the war ended and drew into the past, this became an important question in Federal circles, with more and more need for an answer. And while the North procrastinated in finding a solution, its armies were literally surrounded by Partisans, singly and in bands, all busily seeking to do their part in driving out the Yankee invaders. So active were they that the drama of war was partially diverted from the great events taking place along the battle fronts and shunted more toward the flanks. All mankind admires industry, and surely soldiers who staged raids in any kind of weather, over every type of terrain, at all hours of day or night, were industrious. That made it difficult to think in terms of punishment.[1]

Abraham Lincoln was as much at a loss to find a solution to the guerrilla problem as anyone else and, if anything, he was inclined to be more tolerant toward the independents than most of the high Union officials. Repeated opportunity to make up his mind was afforded him as the fighting in the Valley progressed. Out in western Virginia, a cavalry company captured Frederick W. Chewning, identified as "a notorious guerrilla," and turned him over to General Milroy, who thought it would have a good effect to try him by drumhead court-martial and hang him. Frémont so notified Secretary of War Stanton, and then asked for instructions. This he would have to do again and again before he finally got an answer, and then it was to the effect that all persons captured while operating as guerrillas should be tried by military commission at the headquarters of the nearest brigade commander, after which the proceedings in each case should be submitted for final decision to the department commander.[2]

Shortly afterward Frémont's men picked up Captains John S. Spriggs and Marshall Triplett, carrying commissions in the Ranger service from the governor of Virginia. These men, with Chewning, were to serve as guinea pigs in helping the Federal government decide officially what disposition should be made of guerrilla prisoners.

Newspapers soon announced that Spriggs and Triplett were to be hanged. This answer seemed to satisfy the North, but not Governor John Letcher. Fired to action, Virginia's chief executive promptly wrote the Confederate Secretary of War, by this time George W. Randolph, that if they were executed he thought retaliation should follow promptly. "We must let Mr. Lincoln understand," wrote His Excellency, "that for every man of this class who shall be executed we will execute in like manner one of corresponding grade selected from the prisoners in our custody."[3]

At the request of Randolph, General Lee wrote General McClellan about Spriggs and Triplett and indicated he meant business. He revealed that two men—Captain George Austin, Second Kentucky Regiment, and Captain Timothy O'Meara, New York Tammany Regiment, had been selected by drawing of lots and were held as subjects of retaliation.[4] McClellan passed the communication on to Washington. The word returned in Lincoln's handwriting was that the government had no information about the prisoners but would inquire. McClellan, desiring to stave off commencement of retaliatory executions, next replied to Lee in a tempered letter that said the two Ranger leaders, not yet tried, were held as all other captives and cautioned: "In the treatment of prisoners the United States government is controlled by principles of humanity and civilization, and I respectfully suggest to you the very great danger of violating those principles whenever retaliatory measures are based upon rumor or even upon newspaper report."[5]

Meantime Chewning had been tried by military commission, along with two other men, and all three had been sentenced to death. Soon Frémont was writing to Secretary of War Stanton to learn what to do with them, explaining that their execution had not been given final approval.[6]

Thus while the human guinea pigs were cooling their heels in prison and Washington was trying to make up its mind, individual military departments were working out their own guerrilla antidotes. In Kentucky it was directed that the irregulars be shot down on sight. Tennessee went about it a little differently. Attention in that state was focused on the citizenry, and penalties of both imprisonment and property confiscation were threatened against anyone who aided or abetted the Partisans. The department commander at Memphis, Major General U. S. Grant, also decreed that persons acting as guerrillas, without organization and without uniforms to distinguish them from private citizens, should not be treated as prisoners of war when caught. In South Carolina the department commander urged the "most rigorous and prompt" measures against guerrillas. Those caught, he directed, should be ironed heavily and sent to headquarters, with written charges accompanying them.[7] Kansas was even more heartless. There the sentence was drumhead court-martial, followed by hanging or shooting, "as no punishment can be too prompt or severe for such unnatural enemies of the human race."[8] North Carolina was overrun with Partisan Rangers, mainly on the urging of such a distinguished soldier as General D. H. Hill,[9] Stonewall Jackson's brother-in-law, but some of these bands in later months were so poorly managed that they became obnoxious to Southerners as well as Northerners. In Missouri guerrillas taken prisoner were held as criminals, and Union soldiers paroled by guerrillas were dismissed from the service.[10]

"Old Ben" Kelley meanwhile was jailing all persons under his jurisdiction who refused to take the oath of allegiance to the United States. This practice soon became like the fall roundup. Even Kelley's own brother-in-law was among those so imprisoned, and wholesale arrests went a long way toward inducing Southerners to look upon the oath as a joke. In Union ranks it soon was pointed out that Rebel officers had publicly declared the oaths voluntarily taken were not binding, that the Confederate government would guarantee to all who disregarded them the humane treatment of the usages of war if they were captured. This, it was said, made the oath a mockery and a farce, as well taken on a pack of cards, a brickbat, or an almanac as on the Bible. The *Intelligencer* reported that all the Rebels in Wirt County "will walk up in a body and take the oath every day for a week if permitted to do so. They like it. They regard it as a license to do as they please." But the best evidence of how the Secessionists felt about the oath came from an intercepted love letter a Rebel soldier in western Virginia wrote his Mary Ann. "God knows I love you more than lips can tell or words express," it began. "O, how I long for another night like the last one I spent with my dearest love in Buckhannon. These vigilant Yanks you have with you came very near trapping me, but I was willing to take the oath at any time; had taken it; would prefer taking it three times a day before eating, in preference to asking a blessing." [11]

No matter how binding, there was no thought of administering the oath to Chewning, Spriggs, or Triplett. Weeks stretched into months and the trio still were confined in prison. Then came a first-class example of passing the buck. The top authorities at Washington sent word the prisoners might be released if Pierpont so recommended.[12]

More weeks passed, and at last the Virginia House of Delegates, seeking to protect the citizens represented by this august body, addressed a resolution to the Confederate Secretary of War asking what redress the government proposed, if any, in the case of the Partisans. News had come that the Union was holding two of the trio—Spriggs and Triplett—and refusing exchange on the alleged ground that they were not Confederate soldiers but soldiers of Virginia, with which the United States had signed no cartel.[13]

This resolution brought into the picture Robert Ould, the Confederate agent of exchange. In a letter to the Union adjutant general he complained that, contrary to what McClellan had written Lee, the Partisans were not held as regular prisoners but were retained while others were exchanged. Partisan Rangers, he said, were not persons making war without authority, but were in all respects like the rest of the army except that they were not brigaded and acted generally on detached service. "They are not irregulars who come and go at pleasure," he explained, "but are organized troops whose muster rolls are returned and whose officers are commissioned as in other branches of the service. They are subject to the Articles of War and Army Regulations and are held responsible for violations of the usages of war in like manner with regular troops. So also is it with the Partisan Rangers organized under the law of Virginia." [14]

Earlier in the summer, to substantiate Ould, the Parkersburg *Ga-*

zette had published a set of instructions found upon a captured guerrilla, the last paragraph of which stated: "The commandants of companies will conduct their operations with a strict regard to the rules of civilized warfare." [15]

Soon Lee was writing again. He notified Secretary Randolph that prisoners taken by men operating under Colonel Imboden, who in May had been given authority to organize a regiment of Partisan Rangers, were sent to Richmond instead of being paroled because the enemy was holding some soldiers belonging to Imboden's command and refused to parole any of them thought to be from the Partisan corps.[16]

Comment from Washington seemed to agree with the Confederate contention. The adjutant general notified Secretary of War Stanton that Ould was right in maintaining that Partisan Rangers and independent companies, properly authorized and commissioned, should be placed on the same footing as other Rebel troops. It was pointed out that even the Union had such an outfit—the Independent Loudoun County Rangers operating around Leesburg under the captaincy of a miller-storekeeper-stationmaster named Samuel C. Means—and an investigation was promised.[17]

The adjutant general's notice in all probability was based on the outcome of a letter written by Henry Halleck, general-in-chief of the United States Army. This missile was addressed to Dr. Francis Lieber at New York City. It asked him simply for his views on the subject of guerrilla warfare, explaining: "The Rebel authorities claim the right to send men, in the garb of peaceful citizens, to waylay and attack our troops, to burn bridges and houses, and to destroy property and persons within our lines. They demand that such persons be treated as ordinary belligerents, and that when captured they have extended to them the same rights as other prisoners of war; they also threaten that if such persons be punished as marauders and spies they will retaliate by executing our prisoners of war in their possession." [18]

Lieber, a sixty-two-year-old German who in 1827 had been driven to this country by Prussian persecution brought on by his liberal opinions, was recognized internationally for his study of the usages and customs of war. He had fought in the Waterloo campaign and then with the Greek revolutionists, after which he fled to America. Here he became engaged in the field of education, founded Girard College in Philadelphia, taught for a time at the University of

South Carolina, and finally accepted a post at Columbia College in New York, where the war found him, sympathetic toward the North and ready to serve Lincoln as a trusted adviser.

His reply to Halleck began simply with the statement that "the term guerrilla is often inaccurately used" and that its whole discussion in the law of war was new.[19] He explained it was the diminutive of the Spanish word *guerra,* meaning petty war, but in this country was accepted to mean an irregular band of armed men carrying on irregular war. Its irregularity, he pointed out, consisted in its origin as a body self-constituted or constituted at the call of a single individual without resort to levy or conscription; its disconnection with army pay, provision, and movement, and its practice of disbanding and coming together again on call of the leader. But he advised that writers on international law agreed that the rising of the people to repel invasion entitled them to the full benefits of the law, and that the invader could not well inquire into the origin of the armed masses.

"This acting in separate bodies," Lieber said, "does not necessarily give them a different character. Some entire wars have been carried on by separate bands of capitaneries, such as the recent war of independence of Greece. It is true, indeed, that the question of the treatment of prisoners was not discussed in that war, because the Turkish government killed or enslaved all prisoners; but I take it that a civilized government would not have allowed the fact that the Greeks fought in detached parties and carried on mountain guerrilla to influence its conduct toward prisoners."

He advised further that it did not seem, in the case of a rising *en masse,* that the absence of a uniform could constitute a difference. The difference lay, he said, in whether the clothing worn was for purposes of stealth or disguise.

But application of the law was different, in Lieber's opinion, with reference to armed bands who formed no integrant part of the organized army, took up arms at intervals, and gave no quarter. These he identified as made up of armed prowlers, the so-called bushwhacker, or simple assassin who committed devastation, rapine, or destruction, and these were treated as outside the usages of war, as brigands and not prisoners of war.

Thus Lieber's opinion clearly gave license to Partisan or guerrilla bands so long as they operated in connection with the regular army and were enrolled as a part of it. While not mentioned as such, Partisan Rangers, the name the Confederate government had given its troops assigned to detached duty, also were recognized as within the scope of legitimate warfare, and it was not long before the Union's decision to follow the interpretation of Lieber was indicated in a brief circular: "The body of Confederate troops known by the designation of Partisan Rangers and whose officers are commissioned by the Confederate government and who are regularly in the service of the Confederate States are to be exchanged when captured." [20] Later the Union modified this provision to permit the exchange only on the recommendation of the governor of the state in which they resided, an amendment designed especially for the border states.[21]

But soldiers on both sides as this fratricidal strife stretched into its third and fourth years often decided matters for themselves. The best disciplined among them, it was recognized, would execute on the spot an armed prowler found where he could have no business as a peaceful citizen. Because they caught their foes at a disadvantage, hatreds against Partisans or guerrillas built up rapidly, and the punishment that awaited them grew severe as the contest advanced. In the end even the top Federal commanders ignored the opinions of Dr. Lieber and retaliated as their individual feelings in the matter dictated, making it a desperate affair for the irregulars. The war to them became one of extinction. Aware that their treatment rested in the will or decree of the individual leader against whom they advanced, it was with the possibility that only the direst fate awaited them as prisoners that they went out to fight for their allegiance.

CHAPTER 11

June 6–September 17, 1862

A GUERRILLA IN
EVERY PATCH

For most people the summer of '62 moved faster than any other period of the war. Things were still comparatively new, and when incidents happened they brought thrills to both the fighter and the firesider. By this time, too, even the soldier in the ranks was convinced his government was involved in no three-month affair, so the days of battling lagged less and efforts on both sides became more premeditated. The North continued to have trouble with its top brass, but it was pouring men and munitions into the effort and bolstering confidence that the Southern states could be driven back into the Union. On the other hand, the Confederates were bracing against invasion and conducting audacious warfare, a style of fighting that would be held up to military students for generations to come.

Much of this audacity centered in the Shenandoah Valley, where Jackson was parrying individual armies with major success; but now, suddenly, in the middle of June, attention focused on Richmond. The diversion of interest could be blamed on a sandy-haired little member of Jeb Stuart's staff, a man who one day knelt on the grass on the outskirts of the Rebel capital and sketched with his finger a daring plan. He was just back from a jaunt into the area occupied by the Federals closing on the city and he had seen for himself; nothing stood in the way to keep fast-moving cavalry from riding completely around McClellan's army.

This little man was John Singleton Mosby, the twenty-eight-year-old lawyer who, like White, McNeill, and Gilmor, was thinking in terms of the guerrilla or Partisan.[1] He had marched away from a growing law practice at Bristol, Virginia, with a cavalry unit from Abingdon led by William E. Jones, West Pointer and ex-regular army officer nicknamed "Grumble" because of his unending flow of profanity. Under Jones, Mosby entered with zest into a new life, a life offering him a challenge that his love of action qualified him to accept readily. No physical fear hampered him. Though he sat his saddle at only 125 pounds, his smallness was no indication of his moral courage: he once had shot and wounded a towering fellow student at the University of Virginia for slandering him, and for this breach of the peace he dutifully served a jail sentence, patiently reading law behind bars while the days of his imprisonment passed.

In the cavalry, Mosby soon was promoted to lieutenant and adjutant of the regiment, a rank he later resigned because the spring elections in the Confederate army ousted Grumble and replaced him with bearded, social-minded Fitzhugh Lee, an individual the young lawyer heartily disliked. An incident that happened while he was serving as adjutant whipped this dislike to its vertex. Jones was away and Lee was in command, and Mosby, individualist and at times avid humorist, walked up and, saluting, announced, "Cunnel, the horn has blowed for dress parade." His words fell upon the ears of a man who had no sense of humor. Lee turned livid and barked at Mosby, "Sir, if I ever hear you call that bugle a horn, I will put you under arrest."[2]

But ability was not to be denied. It was only a short time before the frail Mosby was demonstrating that he was a capable scout, so he was added to Stuart's staff, and in that capacity served his country well. And while he rode on stealthy reconnaissance, he nursed a growing desire to break away, to organize his own command of Partisan Rangers and to do the daring things he, in his present status, could only pass on to someone else.

Stuart fell in readily enough with the plan of circling McClellan's army. In a matter of hours, with General Lee's consent, he was riding out of Richmond with 1200 picked men, guided by the sandy-haired scout. Three days later, when he rode into the city from the opposite direction after a successful raid, his fame was established and that of Mosby was considerably brighter.

The *Dispatch* at Richmond saw Mosby as one of the major heroes of the daring ride, an estimate most likely encouraged by his thoughtfulness in bringing back to the editor several late Northern newspapers. This bit of public relations got him an appreciative ear, and the report published by the daily told of numerous captures made by the young lawyer. Especially did it mention a wagon laden with pistols and valuable stores, and therein was a tale to stir the blood of the venturesome. The scout was riding far in advance of the column when he came upon the vehicle, so it was told, and though he was only 300 yards from a Union cavalry camp where the Blue soldiers were drawn up in line of battle, he threatened to blow out the brains of the two men perched on the wagon's seat unless they surrendered, which they promptly did. Meanwhile, the Union cavalrymen were looking on with interest. "The Federals saw the state of things," reported the newspaper. "Their bugle blew the charge, when Lieutenant Mosby, turning in his saddle, waved his saber to an imaginary force in the rear and shouted lustily: 'Come on, boys! Come on!' Hearing which, the Federals wheeled to the rightabout, leaving the lieutenant, his prize and prisoners unmolested." No mention was made of the fact that just at that moment by coincidence, much to the surprise of the daring scout, a force of Confederates did come riding out of the woods at his rear, led by Stuart's German staff member, the huge Heros von Borcke.

Until the details were more positively known, this dash behind the Union lines was attributed to guerrilla parties. The *Dispatch* reported: "And a wholesome fear of these same parties has sprung up, and it is singular how many of them can be seen . . . According to the Yankee idea, a guerrilla band lurks behind every bush and in every patch of woodland." [3]

The hottest fighting around Richmond was divided by name into several separate battles spread over a period of seven days. Most of this time McClellan maintained fine telegraphic communication with the front. He had wires running to White House on the Pamunkey River, to Dispatch Station, eleven miles out of Richmond, and to Tunstall Station, even closer, but he soon was to learn it takes more than army intelligence to win battles. Although in sight of Richmond and happy about it, his troops began to meet reverses that were repeated too frequently for comfort. At four o'clock on an afternoon toward the end of the period, the telegrapher at White House heard a strange signal coming over the wires. He rushed to the instrument clicking on his table and was heralded by words the

Federals jokingly termed the Rebel National Anthem—"You Yankee Sonofabitch." Said the Baltimore *American:* "This was the signal given for the final evacuation." [4]

During this period of concentrated fighting near the Confederate capital Rebel irregulars rubbed shoulders with the regulars. Especially was this true in the case of White's "Comanches." They were called eastward with Ewell's troops and did stellar scouting and courier service. Once they had a chance to charge the Pennsylvania Bucktails and they did so with great success, emerging with a complete set of German silver wind instruments for a band, several prisoners, and a suit of armor that had belonged to a colonel. This armor they found to be bulletproof against all small arms except the Maynard rifle, a charge from which ripped open a hole large enough to admit a hen egg. [5]

By the second of July, McClellan's army was retreating rapidly to its boats on the James. The Southerners had done some determined last-ditch battling and they had pulled a fast move that was vastly similar to what they had done at First Bull Run: Stonewall Jackson's army, maneuvering until it could strike and defeat individually the forces of Milroy, Banks, Frémont, and Shields, suddenly and secretly had been moved out of the Valley to play an important role in driving back McClellan.

History was further repeated: Lincoln quickly gave McClellan the ax, just as he had his predecessor, McDowell, and replaced him with a man who did more to encourage guerrilla operations than any other Union leader of the war—General John Pope. Pope was a man of words, and he had fought in the West, "where we have always seen the backs of our enemies." [6] One of his first acts after taking over the command was to issue an address to the army deriding the efforts of McClellan, who had possessed the unstinted confidence of his soldiers. [7]

Pope's stated policy—"let us look before us, and not behind"— stirred the blood of every Partisan and every person in the entire South entertaining any thoughts whatever of pursuing irregular warfare. These individuals, Mosby included, mused to themselves that, while John Pope looked to the front, they would be looking to his rear.

But Pope, in addition to a formula for winning the war, had one by which he hoped to take care of Partisans. In general orders directed at the people of the Shenandoah Valley, especially those living along railroad and telegraph lines and in the rear of the Federal forces, he announced they would be held responsible for damage by guerrillas, since they themselves would share the guilt for not preventing it. Wherever the damage was done, it was decreed, citizens living within a radius of five miles should be turned out *en masse* to repair it and to pay the expenses incident thereto. If a soldier was fired upon from a house, that house was to be razed to the ground and the inhabitants arrested. Furthermore, any person detected in these guerrilla outrages "shall be shot, without awaiting civil process." [8]

Pope also followed Ben Kelley in widespread application of the oath of allegiance. In another general order he directed that all disloyal male citizens should be arrested and released only after taking the oath. If they violated it, they were to be shot and their property seized and applied to public use. [9]

The new commander introduced other innovations. He was the first of the Federal generals to order that the troops should subsist on the countryside, a policy that brought unprecedented instances of plunder and oppression. Commands were consolidated and their efforts directed at the Partisans. He also employed cavalry far more boldly than did McDowell or McClellan. By his direction the horse troops were kept well in advance of the main army and they were sent on frequent reconnaissance. One of their most important objectives was that of cutting the Virginia Central Railroad at some point between Richmond and Gordonsville, thus disrupting Lee's supply line. This duty, on the judgment of General Rufus King, commanding at Fredericksburg, was assigned to the Harris Light Cavalry. [10] The point chosen for the break was in the neighborhood of Beaver Dam Station.

The Harris Light, originally intended for the regular army and finally designated the Second New York Cavalry, set out from Fredericksburg at 7:00 P.M. July 19. It was a cool, pleasant night, and the horsemen made rapid time as they galloped through the dark. At midnight of the twentieth, one day and five hours later, King summarized their activity in a dispatch to General Pope: "They fully accomplished the object of their expedition. Arriving at Beaver Dam early this morning, they broke up the Central Railroad for many miles, burnt the depot at Beaver Dam, cut the telegraph communication, and created a general alarm in that part of the state. In the depot destroyed were 100 barrels of flour and 40,000 cartridges, besides other goods. The cavalry must have made a march of 80 miles in the 30 hours. They bring back one prisoner, a captain in the Confederate service." [11]

Though unrecognized at the time, the most important news in the dispatch was that about the prisoner. This fellow identified himself as Captain John S. Mosby, using a name that one year later would have brought cheers of elation from his captors. The Harris Light completely missed the boat in this instance. Even though he was without fame at the moment, he displayed such self-esteem it might have been evident he someday would rise above the ranks. One of the men who captured him gave this picture: "By his sprightly appearance and conversation he attracted considerable attention. He is slight, yet well formed; he has a keen blue eye and florid complexion; and displays no small amount of Southern bravado in his dress and manners. His gray plush hat is surmounted by a waving plume, which he tosses as he speaks in real Prussian style." [12]

There was no problem in his capture. Two of the Union horsemen found him dozing in the sun at the station and took him in tow before he was fully awake.[13] While he stood stolidly, offering no resistance, they searched him and found a letter that, in addition to his manner, was proof enough that he was of some importance. Addressed to Stonewall Jackson and signed by Jeb Stuart, it announced simply: "The bearer, John S. Mosby, late first lieutenant, First Virginia Cavalry, is en route to scout beyond the enemy's lines toward Manassas and Fairfax. He is bold, daring, intelligent, and discreet. The information he may obtain and transmit to you may be relied upon, and I have no doubt that he will soon give additional proofs of his value. Did you receive the volume of Napoleon and his Maxims I sent you through General Charles S. Winder's orderly?" [14]

Mosby's capture was a great disappointment to him. Since the ride around McClellan, he had been conducting an active campaign to bring about his transfer to independent service, and his efforts in this connection were noticeable in various quarters. One instance of it was a letter to the Secretary of War inquiring whether Partisan Rangers were considered a part of the Confederate army and entitled to protection. The query, given the grace of an affirmative reply, came from John B. Clarke, member of the Confederate Senate from Kentucky.[15] Mosby's wife was a Kentucky Clarke.[16]

But this letter was only one of the scout's many steps to an end. He had used it as a part of his argument to Stuart that his greatest value to the Confederacy lay in independent warfare, especially now that the Federals under General Pope were to be looking in only one direction. While they faced the front, he would become active in their rear, destroying their wagon trains, cutting their communications, capturing horses and important prisoners. Stuart saw the light. But he was preparing for an active campaign and was reluctant to give up even so many as a handful of his not too numerous horsemen, and thus he suggested that Mosby try Jackson, then collecting troops at Gordonsville to guard the Virginia Central Railroad.

So it was at the start of this mission that Mosby was made a prisoner. He was taken by his captors back to Fredericksburg and from there sent to the Old Capitol Prison in Washington. Ten days later he was exchanged—for First Lieutenant Charles A. Bayard of the Fifth Wisconsin Volunteers, a man never heard from again in official records.[17]

But Mosby's star was rising. As fast as his feet would carry him from the point of release on the James River, he went to the headquarters of the Army of Northern Virginia with the answer to a problem that was bothering Lee: Was the Federal government planning to reinforce the army that had besieged Richmond or the army under Pope nearer Washington? Mosby had learned, while waiting on the exchange boat at Fort Monroe, that numerous troop transports he could see passing were those of Burnside's army moving up from North Carolina to join Pope. This information was passed on to Lee himself, who listened intently to the newly freed prisoner as soon as he identified himself as one of those mentioned in general orders concerning Stuart's ride around McClellan, and it immediately set in motion the military cogs that were to lead to the battles of Cedar Mountain, Second Bull Run, and Antietam.

Meanwhile the little things as well as the big things that go to make a war were in progress. Newspapers carried the advertisement of some "disappointed soul" who had lost in the fighting around Richmond "a blood bay gelding 15 hands high, compactly made, and slightly sprung in the forelegs." The Sixth Virginia (Union) surprised a squad of guerrillas at a little game of "old sledge" and found, upon examining cards tossed upon the ground in the mad scramble to escape, that one poor Rebel had held high, low, jack, and the game. And up in the neighborhood where Mosby was headed at the time of his capture, General Kelley was lulled into a false sense of security. He announced the B. & O. safe and in good working order west of Harpers Ferry and, more importantly, that guerrillas were either killed, captured, or driven out of most of the counties of Northwestern Virginia. He was sustained in this viewpoint by the *Intelligencer*, which only a few weeks earlier had reported that the Sixth Virginia Cavalry was making effective forays against the irregulars: "When they have found genuine guerrillas, they generally dispatch them forthwith, and do not give them any further opportunity to violate coffins. It is, we believe, so extremely dangerous for these guerrillas that they are making themselves scarce, and the county is now almost entirely clear of them for 40 or 50 miles on each side of the Baltimore and Ohio Railroad." [18]

But the period of relative quiet applied only to the area within Kelley's range of view. In other quarters the realities of war went on unchanged. A party of Rebels rode through Luray in Page Valley near the Shenandoah shouting for Jeff Davis. Farther west, in the mountain area, numerous Federal detachments threaded the ravines and passes in search of guerrillas, causing many wild reports. Newspapers told of the death of Andy Dusky and George Downs, two of the Partisan ringleaders, and a few days later had to offer apologies and place them back on earth very much alive. With Alf Dent, another leader, it was different: he stole home one night to renew his supply of provisions, so the press said, and was nabbed by U. S. soldiers who were quietly awaiting his arrival. In another quarter the sheriff of Tucker County sent word "Secesh guerrillas are murdering our citizens and stealing our horses" and asked to be relieved of the duty of collecting taxes in such an atmosphere of obvious difficulty. Parkersburg expected a raid from guerrillas any moment.

Though his jurisdiction appeared to him quiet, "Old Ben" Kelley was keeping busy and meeting with a wide assortment of experience. One day, on a raid through Wirt and Calhoun counties, he captured a very rebellious young woman who later was identified as Sallie Dusky, daughter of Dan, the Rebel firebrand the Federals had confined to the penitentiary for robbing the mails. The general had a notion this damsel could lead him to the hiding places of the Partisans, so he questioned her at length and in complete privacy. But Sallie, used to the ways of the mountains and the trickery of mankind, clammed up tighter than a chestnut burr. Kelley tried every trick in his repertory to no avail and at last resorted to facetiousness. "Make a clean breast of it," he coaxed with a gleam in his eye, "and I'll give you a chance to pick a husband from my staff." The girl still was unmoved, so the general mentally admitted defeat and yelled for her to be taken away. A heel-clicking captain trained to promptness answered the call. Sallie was taken firmly by the arm and led to the door, but there she held back. "Look!" she whispered to the captain. "He said he might git me a husband if I would talk. Did he mean it?" The aide, suspecting the ruse, stood with solemn face and nodded emphatically: certainly the general would keep his word. Sallie took a last quick look at her recent questioner, at the stern face, the huge chest, the prominent chin and billy-goat whiskers, and then muttered in a tone loud enough to be heard by Kelley: "I'd as lief have the old man as any of you." [19]

But Kelley's worst troubles came from an informal company of Partisans who called themselves "Moccasin Rangers." Familiar with every road and path in the country, these rebel-minded natives prowled in comparative security, seizing for the Southern cause as they moved horses, hogs, and cattle, most of them from families known to be Union in their sympathies. Each and every one of them had reputation as a trickster. With few exceptions they had taken the oath of allegiance, and they gave the appearance, even in the innocent stare of their eyes when questioned, of having done so in all seriousness. The Eleventh Virginia Volunteers, a Union outfit, for example, came upon one John A. Tanner seated at breakfast at a home well up on a mountainside. Under pressure he admitted nothing and in support of his claim of innocence presented a pass duly signed by the Federal provost marshal. It was recognized as genuine, but nevertheless there was severe doubt about the purity of this calm man who had been so benignly consuming ham and eggs when interrupted. So the officers who questioned him decided to make it hard for him: they would keep his pass and he could get it by coming to their camp the next day. Tanner seemed to like the idea: "I'll be glad for you to keep it while them Rangers is about, 'cause it might get me into trouble." Thus the Eleventh Virginia rode away satisfied they would have a visitor on the morrow. But it was through the newspapers that they were to hear of the subsequent movements of one John A. Tanner. In less than three hours after they departed, the press announced, he was back with the guerrillas, riding hard and terrorizing the countryside. On a basis of this information the forfeiture of his pass was taken for granted, so it was sent to General Kelley to be used in binding John to keep the peace. "I close by saying," wrote one reporter, "I hope he may be bound with a good stout rope around his infernal throat, to see if he has meat enough on his bones to stretch his infernal neck." [20]

The Rangers read the newspapers too, and they had their retaliation for this indignity to one of their members. A few days later word was received at Wheeling that they were arresting Union men and forcing them to take an oath to support the Confederacy.[21]

They also gave Parkersburg the scare of its career. Thirty of them appeared on Tygart's Creek, sixteen miles distant, and, as a practical joke, sent a Secessionist into town to spread the word they were about to attack. This messenger did his job well: he reported that 500 guerrillas were on their way. Immediately bells of the city were tolled, quick speeches were made at the courthouse, and excitement blanketed the city and spilled over into the outskirts. The flooring of the bridge across the Little Kanawha was torn up and a cannon planted at the Parkersburg end. The city council went into most extraordinary session. Money in the local bank was spirited away to an adjoining city. Hundreds of residents headed for the neighboring hills, and telegraphic dispatches for troop support were sent to all nearby points. Meanwhile a committee of three—one Unionist and two Secessionists—stood by with flag of truce to prevail upon the Rebels not to destroy the town. This waiting was bad upon their nerves and in time the committee became impatient and decided to move out to the edge of town and stand in readiness to go into its act. As it passed through the suburbs, a company of Federal infantry stationed on regular guard duty recognized the two Secessionists and, thinking the entire trio was on its way to join the Southerners, fired several shots of protest, thereby causing a premature raising of the white flag. Then the entire alarm was discovered to be without foundation, and there was great indignation, public and private. Newspaper editors said no punishment would be too severe for the circulators of "these lying reports." But most regrettable of all, no one was positive who started them.

While Parkersburg fretted over its gullibility, the new Union commander, John Pope, a few miles to the east, rode into a large field near the crest of the Blue Ridge to review his army. One of the paraders wrote home that "the review passed off as most reviews do, terribly tiresome and tedious to the officers and men engaged, but rather a fine sight to outsiders. I was not much impressed by the appearance of our new general, but shall keep my mouth closed about him until he does something." [22] As the Second Massachusetts Infantry marched by, Pope might have noticed here and there a member with wool protruding from his ears. This was something new, an expedient to ward off one of the horrors of war newly encountered. Only a matter of hours had passed since the entire regimental camp had been awakened by a sudden and continued outburst of screams and groans. On rushing into the company streets, they discovered the noises were originating from a captain's Negro servant, found doing a tango behind a tent and yelling at the top of his voice, "Take him out! Take him out of my ear!" While the lackey tied himself in knots, a doctor came running, poured oil in the ear and gave the sufferer enough morphine to put a mule to sleep. In the morning a large black beetle poked its head up for air and was promptly seized with a pair of pincers. It was then the wool came into general use: no more bugs in ears while the Second Massachusetts slept.

And so the summer moved along. On August 9 Stonewall Jackson struck Banks at Cedar Mountain near Culpeper with a superior force, but it was just through the strong fighting example set by the leader himself that the Federal right wing was "hurled into a storm that well nigh wrecked it." [23] Harry Gilmor was there, "the rear guard of the whole army." [24] Extrovert that he was, he wanted to get closer to the battle; it was night when his unit reached position and he could see the flashes of the guns and hear the shells crashing and bursting among the trees. So, with the colonel's consent, he rode forward and in time reached Pegram's battery, just as it was being shelled by the enemy. Among its members he recognized an acquaintance—Lieutenant Mercer Featherston of Baltimore. "This is rather warm work, Mercer," commented Gilmor, preparing to move away. Just then he heard a shell come thundering through the woods and a moment later felt the wind from it as it tore off part of Featherston's head, passed through one horse, and exploded in another, flinging bits of animal flesh in all directions. The Partisan stayed long enough to see three other men beheaded and then decided maybe he had witnessed enough.

Into Confederate records at this date entered a report of special significance to the Partisans. It was a lengthy document, prepared by Secretary of War Randolph for an extra session of the Rebel Congress, and it went very seriously into discussion of the Southern army and the need for further legislation to keep it organized. The department head pointed out that many of the men had signed up for one year and, when the period of enlistment ended, either went home or, to avoid monotony, transferred to other corps or to other branches of the service. In a matter of thirty days during the spring the terms of service of 148 regiments expired, and the South had to resort to the conscript act and other measures to keep its forces together.

One by one Randolph cited the defects of the system as it then existed—depleted regiments, employment of substitutes at pleasure, promotion by seniority, and others, most of them important. With reference to the act authorizing bands of Partisan Rangers, he said the number of corps of this branch greatly exceeded the requirements of the service and seriously impeded recruiting for regiments of the line. This had been apprehended, the Secretary acknowledged, both because of the novelty of the organization and the supposed freedom from control, and the Department had adopted a rule requiring approval of the general of a department before granting authority to raise Partisans. But even that had failed to keep them within bounds, and now another method was suggested: they should be required to conform in their organization to other troops, so that it would only be necessary to brigade such of them as were needed for Partisan service to make them in fact troops of the line, although they were nominally Partisans. Randolph recommended this be authorized.

The suggested action by the Secretary of War had behind it much foundation of fact. Many conscripts and volunteers between the ages of eighteen and thirty-five were flocking to the Partisan corps. In numerous quarters irregular outfits were springing up. V. A. Witcher, major of the First Battalion of Virginia Mounted Rifles, asked to be transferred to their branch, with authority to increase his battalion, which he had raised himself, to a regiment. It already had six companies and, in thirty days, he assured, he could increase it to 1250 strong.[25]

When asked his opinion, Lee favored confining the guerrillas to their respective states.[26] At this time he was approving the organization of new Partisan units, but with the understanding that they were to be mustered for local service and to be subject to the orders of the general commanding their military departments.[27]

While the legislators, the department heads, and the high command pondered what to do with them, the guerrillas kept busy, creating a diversion in favor of the plans cooking up between Lee and Jackson. Some of their tricks they performed around Winchester, among other things teaching members of the Thirty-second Ohio Volunteers that it was better to stay within their own lines. This came about through the laxity of First Lieutenant Ulysses Westbrook, officer of the guard who one night allowed three men to pass through the pickets for a visit in the neighborhood. Subsequently there was firing in the distance, and a few minutes later two of the trio got back to relate what had happened. General Julius White, commanding, wrote Pope he thought it would have a salutary effect upon the regiment, which was shy of discipline anyway, if Westbrook were dismissed from the service without formal trial.[28] Pope passed the matter on to Halleck at Washington, where it got lost in the excitement, for the capital at the moment was about to have battles in progress almost at its outskirts.

As it developed, the three men who strayed from camp had picked the wrong time for an outing, choosing a period when guerrillas were in the vicinity in force. This became generally known on the afternoon of August 23, after a railroad train loaded with government stores had been halted and burned by an estimated fifty Rebels on horseback halfway between Winchester and Harpers Ferry. The New York *Herald* reported that "the conductor foolishly stopped it in compliance with the orders of the gang," but Ed Lucas, express messenger on board, disagreed. He was severely wounded by one of the numerous shots fired by the raiders before the train came to a stop, and he was of opinion the conductor was perhaps, if anything, a mite too slow in signaling for a halt. At any rate, the guerrillas climbed aboard and made short shrift of things. While some of them were cutting the telegraph lines beside the track, others were sacking the mail, rounding up four prisoners, and setting the train and its contents afire.

From Winchester, General White sent a mounted force in pursuit of the train-burners and then messaged Pope he didn't quite know what to make of the situation: it might be bushwhackers or it might indicate movements of the enemy down the Valley. This dispatch was followed a few hours later by another that attributed the raid to some of the late Turner Ashby's cavalry. But even of that White was not sure. Many confusing things were taking place, including brisk cannonading from what appeared to be the direction of Warrenton.

Halleck at Washington quickly became concerned. He wired Pope to ascertain if the enemy was moving into the Valley, and Pope replied that a considerable column of infantry, cavalry, and artillery had just left Culpeper and was on its way to Amissville and Luray or Front Royal. "They can be plainly seen by our lookouts, who estimate them at 20,000 . . . As soon as I ascertain certainly that they are going into the Shenandoah I will push McDowell in their rear." [29]

Thanks to the guerrillas, now occurred a different version of the shell game. Colonel D. S. Miles, in command of the Second U. S. Infantry at Harpers Ferry, assigned a company of infantry to guard each train moving from that point to Winchester. It was his belief that one company in cars ought to whip a regiment of cavalry on horseback. He also had the Eleventh Regiment of New York State Militia, whose time of service was about to expire, distributed along the railroad at four different points, but he realized this force was inadequate to keep the road open: there should be two regiments of infantry and one of cavalry.[30] While attention was thus concentrated on the Winchester line, guerrillas began to bob up elsewhere, threatening the B. & O. There the problem was much greater. No Federal troops were available to resist an attack by a large force of men anywhere between Harpers Ferry and Edwards Ferry. That meant the Potomac was open to crossing at any of the fords along that particular stretch of the river. As Miles worried over this and other matters, he received new burdens in a message of trouble from Captain Samuel C. Means, the businessman-leader of the Independent Loudoun County Rangers.

Miles confessed no pride in the operation of Means' band, the Union counterpart of the Rebel irregulars. He was aware that they committed all kinds of depredations on the inhabitants of Loudoun County, their base of operations, living on the public, taking what they pleased, and making their arrival in any community a time of dread and terror. In his last interview with Means he had warned him that, from the loose, straggling manner in which he encamped and marched, he might expect to be surprised and cut to pieces any moment.

Means was obsessed with a feeling of duty and with the importance of his command. It had been organized under a special order from the Secretary of War and mustered into the United States service at Lovettsville June 20, 1862, later becoming a part of the

Eighth Corps. To swell its ranks it moved from community to community, recruiting as it went and putting up in local churches wherever they were available. In August they set up camp at Waterford, near Means' home. Their numbers by this time had climbed to fifty.

But on the night of August 26 only twenty-three were on hand to bed down in the local church; the others were off on raids or picket duty, and Means was a short distance away at his home. Before dawn next morning Lige White, leading a band of his irregulars, officially listed on Confederate rolls as the Thirty-fifth Battalion, Virginia Cavalry, Ewell's Brigade, stole through a large cornfield, piloted by local residents, and surrounded the house of worship. He was looking especially for one of Means' men named Corbin, who was accused of vilely murdering a citizen of the neighborhood. But his surprise was not complete. A picket on duty in the wee hours heard them coming and aroused his sleeping companions in time for them to put up a stubborn resistance. The firing kept up for more than three hours, ending only after the Rebels' ammunition had begun to run short and after a young woman of the village had shown courage by bearing a flag of truce to demand an unconditional surrender. Word was sent back that the besieged would give up, but only if assured of their parole, and this White assented to except in the case of Corbin, an exception agreeable to the Federals. After paroling Means' men and rounding up fifty-six horses, White dashed into nearby Leesburg, driving before him the few Union troops stationed there. His appearance later earned him official thanks from the ladies of the town, who regaled the raiders with cake and wine, accompanied by the prayer that "the God of Battles defend and encircle you all in the arms of love." [31]

It was the affair at Waterford, another diversion like that on the railroad between Winchester and Harpers Ferry to draw attention from Lee's army, that led to Means' message to Miles: "I am attacked by at least 500 guerrillas. They will kill all if I cannot get help. Let me know." [32]

Help was sent in the form of a battalion of cavalry, but by the time it arrived the Rebels had fled, leaving behind one of their number who was too badly wounded to be moved. The information the Blue horsemen brought back relieved any fear that the Confederates were headed in force toward the Potomac east of Harpers Ferry, so Halleck had to prod anew for intelligence regarding the Gray column the Union lookouts had seen near Culpeper. In this connection Julius White tried a ruse. He dressed six of his men in citizens' clothes, armed them with shotguns, and sent them across the Blue Ridge, through Ashby's Gap. When near enough to the Rebel lines he had cavalry dash after them and chase them in among the enemy. Two days later they were back with important information: the column seen near Culpeper was not headed for the Valley. It was made up of 50,000 men, led by Stonewall Jackson, and was on its way to Manassas. They had learned other things too: Longstreet was near Salem, White's cavalry was at Middleburg, and Corbin of Means' Rangers was about to be executed.[33]

Thus came to Winchester and thence to Halleck at Washington some of the news of what was happening on the Rebel side. Jackson slipped through Thoroughfare Gap and destroyed the Union supplies at Manassas, after which he moved behind an uncompleted railroad bed a few miles from the town to give battle as the situation developed. It was the campaign of Second Bull Run, a period of fighting recognized as some of the fiercest of the war, and it resulted as August expired in a victory for the South.

While the worst of this fighting was in progress, the Union troops stationed in the neighborhood of Harpers Ferry were busy keeping an eye on the Partisans in their vicinity. In the assignment of duties between commands the Eighth Illinois Cavalry got that of watching Lige White. Its commander, Colonel B. F. Davis, was warned that the irregulars had all the advantages of fleeter horses, light equipment, and knowledge of the country, and he was reminded that it seemed to be White's business to take horses and cattle for the Rebel army. "It would be very desirable," said instructions from headquarters, "to break up his command, communications and business." [34] Another task imparted to the Eighth Illinois was guard duty on the Winchester railroad. Only one train per day, always with a company of infantry aboard, was running over the line at the moment. And in another delegation of responsibility the Maryland Cavalry unit under Captain H. A. Cole was told to join Means' Independents and scour Loudoun County for Partisans, taking care always not to confuse Davis' men with them.

Things happened fast after that. Before Davis and Cole could attend to their new assignments, Lee's army was pushing northward. Julius White got out of Winchester just in time, destroying much public property and leaving behind some valued thirty-two-pounder cannon, all of which later led to an official investigation.[35] A force under Confederate Colonel T. T. Munford, dispatched from Jeb Stuart's cavalry, attacked Means and the Maryland Cavalry at Leesburg, routing them badly. Washington got word that the B. & O. soon would be damaged again by the Southerners.[36]

Another Confederate Partisan leader appeared in the Eastern theater of the war at this time. He was "Hanse" McNeill, the bearded cattle-raiser from Missouri. After escaping in the West he hurried to Richmond and asked permission to organize an independent company in South Branch Valley, scene of his birth, and the Confederate authorities sent him to Imboden, who on September 5 authorized him officially in writing to start his band. Drawing his recruits largely from the mountain area, he organized them as McNeill's Rangers. The rank of captain he held for himself, and his son, Jesse, was named one of his lieutenants. The potential of this band rapidly increased as the months passed.

The big push of the Southern army was across the Potomac into Maryland. Lee had in mind a raid toward enemy country, and it was to aid this movement that the guerrillas were creating much of the diversion that occurred at this time. White was especially busy, for the advance was toward his birthplace and he had particular interest in what was happening. But at Frederick, pushing his irregulars alongside the regular army, he came under the eye of Jeb Stuart and was ordered back to Loudoun County. The independent refused to go, saying he was a Marylander by birth and had fought as hard as any man for the privilege of fighting upon the soil of his native state.

Stuart was cantankerous. "Do you say you have done as much as any man for the South?"

"No, sir, I did not say that. But I have done my duty to the South as a soldier, so far as my ability extends, as fully as anybody."

Stuart, a year the junior, shouted: "You did say you had done as much as any man!"

"I did not say so," disputed White.

The hassle went on, and finally Stuart, exercising his rank, ordered White back to Virginia to watch for a flanking movement by the Federal army. The latter again refused to go, saying he first would go see General Lee.

"Come on," said Stuart, "I'll go with you."

They both went to headquarters, where Stuart passed in as White was met at the door by Lee.

"I want to see you, sir," said White.

112

"Very well," Lee replied, "just wait a little and I'll see you."

In a short while Stonewall Jackson emerged and his attention was drawn to White, who paced back and forth in front of headquarters so much upset over what he considered the injustice of Stuart that he was actually crying.

Stonewall's curiosity was aroused. When White explained, Jackson remarked, "Why, I just heard General Stuart tell General Lee that you desired to be sent back, and recommended that it be done."

At this point White became so choked up that he was speechless.

Jackson remembered White from the Valley campaign. "Captain White," he said consolingly, "I think I can understand your feelings, for I was once situated just as you are now. During the Mexican War I was ordered to the rear just as a battle was about to take place, and I knew of no reason why I should be so unjustly treated, but I obeyed, and it so happened that by doing so I had an opportunity to acquire distinction that I never could have had in front. And, Captain, my advice to you is to obey orders, no matter how unjust they may be. We are poor, short-sighted creatures at best and, in the very thing that seems hardest for us to bear, Providence may have hidden a rich blessing for us. Go, Captain, and obey orders."

White remained silent.

Stuart soon emerged from headquarters, stepped off to the side, and summoned White.

"Captain White, did you say you were a Marylander?"

"Yes, sir."

"Ah, I didn't know that. General Lee wants you. Go in and see him."

When White left headquarters a few minutes later, he had orders to scout toward Harpers Ferry and to report directly to Lee. Thus diplomacy and calm settled a bad situation.[37]

The effect of Lee's movement northward was to throw Pope's army into complete confusion. Wrote that gifted penman Wilder Dwight: "We want soldiers, soldiers, and a general in command . . . Nothing surprising happened in Virginia. The force brought against us was not larger than our own, was equally fatigued, and, still more, without food. But we allowed them, impotently and with fatal blindness, to outgeneral us. We ignored what was passing under our eyes, denied the familiar maxims of military science, blustered up to the moment of defeat, and then fled back to our base."[38]

The emergency thus created brought fast action from Lincoln. He relieved Pope of the command of the Union armies and called again on McClellan, who had slowly wended his way back from the Peninsula.[39]

Following Lee, who had divided his army and sent Jackson to capture Harpers Ferry, Federal troops moved across the Potomac nearer Washington. Halleck got a message from Pleasanton, the cavalry chief, that 100,000 Rebels were on the Maryland side of the river, but the next morning McClellan warned him that this information had been derived from "the notorious" Lige White and that it was not fully reliable.[40]

During the advance north the Partisan Rangers lost one of their leaders temporarily.[41] The pistol-shooting egotist, Harry Gilmor, rode one night toward the home of a friend seven miles from Baltimore, unaware that the residence even as he approached was surrounded by Union soldiers and policemen who had come out from the city to capture some property they had been told was ready to be moved south. Thus he was captured and placed in the Western Police Station at Baltimore, where he was listed on the register as "a spy."[42] This was his first stop on the way to Fort McHenry, and there he would spend the next five months.

On September 17 there was fighting along Antietam Creek at Sharpsburg that was prominently recorded for its fierceness. This was the battle that stilled the facile pen of Wilder Dwight, shot down as he ran along the lines cheering his men. But even with death close at hand this faithful scrivener added the last link to his chain of messages home. While he lay in no-man's-land waiting for one side or the other to come and tend to his bleeding form, he wrote a note to his mother, folded it, turned it over, and, amid bloodstains, scribbled his last sentence: "All is well with those that have faith."

That day, in rear-guard skirmishing with Kilpatrick's cavalry near Leesburg, a bullet struck Lige White just under the shoulderblade and came to a stop just beneath the skin in front of his throat. This fighting young farmer had thought he was dying when wounded the preceding May; now he was sure of it. He fell behind a rock and the enemy swarmed around, and he might have been captured but for the fact that the Union horsemen were too hard pressed to bother with making prisoner a Rebel too badly shot to live long if moved.

Years afterward Lige White was horseback riding with a young granddaughter.[43] He was in his patriarchal years, a successful businessman, farmer, bank president, and Primitive Baptist preacher. Out of Leesburg they had trotted in the gloam of the evening, at a time when hearts and sentiments are mellow, and presently he drew rein.

"Do you see that rock over there?" he asked, pointing. "I once lay behind it badly wounded. The Union captain who had shot me came up and asked if there was anything he could do for me. I told him I would like some water. He gave me a drink and then muttered, 'I hope you will forgive me.'"

The old man straightened his shoulders and nudged his horse gently with his heel.

"Betsy," he said solemnly, calling the granddaughter by his pet name for her, "I thought I was going to die and, do you know, I forgave that damnyankee."

CHAPTER 12

September 17–October 4, 1862

POOR MOLLIE'S FLAG!

Anyone could see that Captain Ezra H. Bailey of the First New York Cavalry had more than ordinary appeal to Mollie Murphy. No matter how much the "bitter though sweet little Rebel" chided and kidded with other Yankee soldiers—and as belle of the little mountain village of Springfield she had plenty of opportunity—it was upon Bailey she kept her eyes. And though her allegiance lay with the South and her busy red lips did all but wave the Confederate flag, it would have been upon the captain's shoulder she would have buried her head and sobbed over her defeat—if he had wanted it that way.

Captain Ezra was one of a regiment of cavalry that had come to aid "Old Ben" Kelley in his drive to protect the B. & O. Railroad, and it was well it did. Lee's army had drifted back from Sharpsburg with most of the fight pounded out of it, but it was still stubborn and resentful, and within a week after the battle along the Antietam, to make the Rebel boys madder, Lincoln had issued a preliminary version of his Emancipation Proclamation.

While the Confederate army lay around Charles Town and the Union army around Harpers Ferry licking their wounds, for the fighting at Sharpsburg had appeared more like a draw than a defeat or a victory for either side, things were looking up for the South out in the mountains. With most of the Federals in western Virginia moved eastward to aid Pope,[1] A. G. Jenkins had swept up through the northwest and into Ohio with his Rebel cavalry, and behind him had come Loring to take over the Kanawha Valley, an area with large supplies of salt, corn, and coal oil, all important to the Confederacy. Imboden in the meantime, with his ten companies of Partisan Rangers, as many as the Secretary of War would allow, had kept Kelley moving troops up and down the B. & O. in a frantic effort to stave off the guerrillas west of Harpers Ferry. It was too late to do anything about the line from that point eastward, for the Southerners in their offensive northward had seen to the destruction of the twenty-mile stretch of the railroad in their path.

In his dilemma Kelley, with only infantry and artillery at his command, moved his men by rail, first here, then there, or wherever the threat from the Rebel irregulars happened to be strongest. What he needed, he realized, was cavalry—soldiers on horseback to chase the Gray-backed railroad wreckers along mountain paths and run them down. So his call became more urgent, and finally to his aid was sent Ezra Bailey and the New York cavalry, distinguished as the first volunteer cavalry of the war and often referred to as the Lincoln Cavalry or Saber Regiment.

These New Yorkers arrived at Old Ben's headquarters the last week in September and were immediately ordered on the trail of Imboden, said at the moment to be somewhere near Moorefield. So a part of them was divided into groups and sent to the mountains, and it was not long before one of these parties was gobbled up by John Hanson McNeill, the bearded guerrilla now actively in the field. McNeill was no ruffian, even though the people opposed to him would have it otherwise. This he displayed when the bedraggled New Yorkers were safely in tow: first thing he did was to offer their leader a drink of applejack.

But with the regimental headquarters of the First New York this was no time for gallantry. When the news straggled back that some of their best horsemen had been taken prisoner, reinforcements were sent posthaste with orders to perform a rescue. Among these supporting troops was Captain Bailey, leading a detail of two companies. He galloped with his men madly in the direction of the reported capture and, high up in the mountains, at Springfield, he brought his riders to a halt for breakfast at the hands of the community. It was then he crossed paths with Mollie Murphy.

Mollie had heard of the captures made by McNeill, at whose son,

Jesse, she sometimes flashed coquettish eyes, and she made no attempt to conceal her joy. While the hungry Yankees gulped down the breakfast reluctantly placed before them, she teased with a passion, easily explained in view of the fact that at the head of the table sat Captain Ezra. For him she had special advice: he would do well to turn back or his destination might be Libby Prison at Richmond.

"But if you persist in going on," she added, sweeping her eyes in his direction under long lashes, "I'll give you a note to Cuhnel Imboden, who is a deah friend of mine, and he'll treat you well for mah sake. I know he will."

She meant what she said, for when the captain showed interest, she immediately sat down and wrote out a note strong with the feminine touch:

"*Springfield, Va., October 4, 1862.*
"To Colonel J. D. Imboden:
"Deah Colonel: This will be handed to you by Captain Bailey, a 'Yankee,' who is not so bad as most of them, and has treated your friends kindly on several occasions. Please treat him well, and show him the Confederate flag which I gave you.
"With kind regards, I am, your friend,
"Mollie Murphy." [2]

This note Captain Ezra tucked into his pocket. Then he climbed on his horse and rode away at the head of his men while Mollie continued to prate about what a dangerous thing he was doing. "Ouah boys will get you just as suah as anything. They know these mountains and you New Yawk City slickers don't."

It was not long before Bailey's detail encountered some of Imboden's men and quickly put them to flight. The chase led toward the covered Cacapon bridge, at the far end of which was Imboden's camp, protected by two brass howitzers posted just so they could hurl shot and shell directly through the barrel-like cavern of the span. But by the time the horsemen reached that point, Blue riders were so mixed with Gray riders that the gunners were reluctant to fire for fear of striking some of their buddies.

'Twas said in the mountains in later years that the old covered span almost toppled over with the shock of the galloping squadrons. Captain Ezra's saber was flashing high that day, and it was in his favor that Colonel Imboden had set out the night before with part of his command on a bridge-burning expedition. Consequently there was virtually no resistance as the New Yorkers charged into the camp, and they came away with the contents of a wagon train that had just arrived—twenty wagons loaded with stores of all kinds and each drawn by four fine mules—as well as 150 fine horses and Imboden's private and official papers.

Back at Springfield, Mollie was eagerly waiting, but the tears came fast when she heard the news. It was then that Captain Ezra's manly appeal came into use. He calmed her and dried her eyes and then coaxed her into taking a look with him at some of her "deah" friend's "puhsonal" papers. Among them was one that drew especial attention. It was a notice to all men of fighting age and it told exactly what kind of warfare the artillery officer from Staunton had in mind.

"My purpose is to wage the most active warfare against our brutal invaders and their domestic allies," it said, "to hang about their camps and shoot down every sentinel, picket, courier, and wagon driver we can find (!); to watch opportunities for attacking convoys and forage trains, and thus render the country so unsafe that they will not dare to move except in large bodies."

After reading that part of the broadside Ezra could well understand why Mollie was so sure he was riding into danger when he left the breakfast table. Perusing further, he found other detail connected with organizing Partisan Ranger outfits, and then a paragraph that would stir even the slinking coward:

"I appeal to the men of the West to unite with me at once in the effort to deliver our native mountains from the pollution that has been brought upon them. It is only *men* I want; men who are not afraid to be shot at in such a cause; men who will pull the trigger on a Yankee with as much alacrity as they would on a mad dog (!); men whose consciences won't be disturbed by the sight of a vandal carcass (!). I don't want nervous, squeamish individuals to join me —they will be safer at home."

Colonel Imboden knew how to use words that brought out the man in men. Captain Ezra read the pronouncement over and over, much to Miss Murphy's annoyance, and then he took out a little package carefully done up in oiled silk that the girl immediately attempted to snatch away and, failing, rushed from the room in tears.

"We sent the colonel's private papers back to him," afterward recorded the official chronicler of the Saber Regiment, "but Bailey presented the flag to a young lady of Union proclivities at Flint-stone, Md., which almost killed poor Mollie Murphy."

And thereby a romance landed on the rocks, flint or otherwise, for in that day true love never was stimulated by separating a young Southern girl from her Confederate flag.

CHAPTER 13

November 28–December 31, 1862

THE TRIPLE-STUDDED
BELT OF ORION

Turnabout is fair play, even in time of war, and it was a turnabout that developed between Captain Bailey and Colonel Imboden. While the former was destroying the latter's camp, the latter was successfully carrying out the bridge-burning expedition that accounted for his absence. Under a dense fog Imboden's Partisans moved in at dawn and captured Company K of the Fifty-fourth Pennsylvania Volunteers, as large a unit as Kelley could spare to guard the Little Cacapon bridge. They next set fire to the span, after which they turned their attention to Paw Paw, where there was an important tunnel protected by the Fifty-fourth's Company B. Though not specifically intended, it was by such maneuvers that Imboden was causing Kelley to learn the hard way that not all of the irregulars had been driven from the area under his jurisdiction.

Imboden's advance on Paw Paw brought to a head a period of unrest among the membership of Company B that had been building up for weeks. It was fanned by a whispering campaign that any expert on military science would have said boded a situation that was not healthy, and it concerned chiefly the captain, John Hite, who one smug little contingent charged would refuse to fight if the chance were laid in his lap. Cruel as all backbiting is, it was said he was governed in a great measure by the second lieutenant, who happened to be his brother-in-law, H. G. Baer. At home Baer enjoyed great social position as the editor and proprietor of a newspaper that frequently lambasted and vilified the Lincoln Administration. This was a habit with Hite too. As noticed by all, he was extremely critical of the President's late proclamation concerning slaves, and he frequently abused "Old Abe" in front of his soldiers, expressing thoughts they immediately recognized as the identical sentiments of the Baer-owned journal. Moreover, Private John J. Spangler had heard the captain say in his quarters on one occasion, "I wish the Rebels would come in and take the company," and that was like a mother assigning her child to the pyre.[1]

On the day of the attack at Little Cacapon, First Assistant Surgeon Andrew W. Mathews, one member of the smug contingent, seated himself in front of his marquee. It was about six-thirty o'clock on a brisk October morning and he was prepared to enjoy the sensations of a new day, even though the beauties of the landscape were partially obscured by a dense fog. He drew the fresh mountain air into his lungs, damp as it was, and attuned his ears to the post-dawn noises of an infantry camp—cooks cursing and banging pans in the kitchen tent, privates cussing their luck for getting involved in this mess in the first place, a noisy sergeant raising hell with the water detail, and a brave warbler on the hillside above the tunnel bursting his feathered throat just for the fun of it. Suddenly from the distance staccatoed three volleys of rifle shots, separated by intervals of only a few seconds. Mathews raised his head and listened. They most certainly came from the direction of Company K over on the Little Cacapon.

Testifying at a subsequent investigation, the surgeon uttered the very obvious conclusion that he "was led to suppose the company was attacked," for it was known that Imboden was striking at the railroad whenever possible. Immediately after hearing the shooting, Mathews remarked to Lieutenant Baer, who happened to be sitting at his elbow, that a squad of men should be sent to investigate, and the only comment elicited from the editor was that "there might be a strong force."

Mathews waited a few minutes and then decided to make the investigation himself. Ordering a colored servant to saddle his mare, he rode toward the Little Cacapon. Presently he saw smoke rising from the bridge and from the camp of Company K. Because of the fog and the bushes growing in profusion on all sides, he crossed the river and rode on some distance farther, finally coming to a halt at a point he judged to be almost opposite the camp. Soon he heard a noise and saw a man run out of the thicket and plunge into the stream a little above him and swim madly in his direction.

"What's the matter?" yelled Mathews when the fellow reached the bank.

"Company K's been taken!" The swimmer seemed undisturbed by the presence of a lone horseman in uniform.

"Are there any wounded?"

"Five!"

"How many Rebels attacking?"

"Five hundred!"

With this information the surgeon hurried back to Company B. But he was a little late, for two other men already had returned with the tidings. As he galloped up, he found soldiers standing in ranks with their knapsacks packed and on their backs.

Captain Hite stood at the front of them. "Boys, will you retreat or fight?"

A roar came from the ranks: "Fight!"

The order was given, and they filed rapidly into the rifle pits excavated at strategic positions around their camp. Captain Hite went along with them. "Boys," he shouted as they made their way into the ditches, "if you fire, take good aim for the head!"

This was wasted advice. It was two or three hours before Imboden's men came into view, and then they were too far away to form a target. Half an hour passed. The Confederates gradually approached, some on foot, some on horses, and formed line down in a meadow several hundred yards distant.

"Boys, will you fight or surrender?" shouted Hite, and it was the majority opinion of those who reported on the affair later that most of the soldiers in the rifle pits yelled back, "Fight!" although a few definitely were heard to say, "Surrender!"

Then the Rebel cavalry appeared in swarms on a hill rising above the horizon, copying the perspective employed by Turner Ashby and his white horse, and the captain shouted again, "Boys, will you fight or surrender?"

"Fight!"

For minutes longer the two forces faced each other in silence, and then a Rebel horseman rode out waving a flag of truce. Hite watched him advance almost halfway and then, motioning to his lieutenants, moved to meet him.

Back in the rifle pits members of Company B were talking and cursing among themselves. This was no way to do: discussing terms of surrender even before there had been the slightest show of resistance. Here they were—ninety men armed with good Austrian rifles, each supplied with from 110 to 120 rounds of ammunition and enough bread and water to withstand a siege—just peeping over fortifications at Rebel infantrymen who by this time had moved up into small-fire range.

What targets! But not a shot!

Crouching there in the pits, they saw their officers meet the man with the flag, stop momentarily, and then go on a few yards farther for a conference with the Rebel officers. This halt, too, was brief, after which the Federal trio turned and came back. As they neared camp, Hite rose in his saddle and shouted, "Boys, get out of the pits now!"

They crawled from the ditches, muttering audibly, and Hite marched them a short distance away and told them to stack arms. This done, the officers went to their quarters and began to pack their personal items.

It was a disillusioned Company B that waited, their ears primed for any tip they could get on what was happening. But none came. Hite was heard to say, "It's a damned shame!" Nobody else said anything. Lieutenant John Cole, moving about his tent, obviously was in a bad humor, while Baer, the second looie, appeared a bulwark of silence.

And that was it—except for Private Spangler, who was sick anyway. He felt so bad, did John J., that he concluded he would not be moved from the spot. He told Hite as much: he'd be paroled or he'd be damned if he'd budge a step. They could kill him, for all he cared; he was that determined.

But when the company started marching, it looked as if John J. had changed his mind, for he trailed along 300 yards or so, and then it was that he gave evidence his over-all determination had not been shaken one whit. Beside a barn on the side of the road he flopped, as solidly stationed as a sow with twenty suckling pigs, and no amount of coaxing by his comrades would budge him. The fiery look in his eyes was that of a bridge jumper on the last ledge; he had picked a spot in which to lie, and there he would stay, do or die.

Presently Imboden came along, saw John stretched in comfort, and ordered him to join his companions. But Spangler just stared in silence, as if he hadn't even heard. The Confederate leader barked again, and then stared too, for a moment, seemingly debating in his mind what to do. The decision was told by his actions, for he turned his horse and rode away: there were too many important matters at hand to be bothered with just one stubborn Yankee. And thus it was that a private was able to bring official word of what had happened to Company B.[2]

These days, with Imboden and other Partisans busy at various points along the mountain division of the railroad, Kelley was forced to keep constantly in the saddle. On one occasion his pursuit of the Rebels took him through a village high in the hills, and there he pulled up at a home in quest of food. As his entourage was rather large and he in a hurry, he ordered two Negroes accompanying him, one his personal servant, Wilson, to go into the kitchen and assist the women of the household in preparing the meal. When the repast was ready, the general and his companions sat down at table and gorged.

Half an hour afterward, comfortably filled, Kelley walked back to his horse and there noticed the two Negroes.

"Eaten, boys?" he asked.

They shook their heads.

"Then get back there and eat. Eat all you want, but hurry."

"Thank yuh, boss," said Wilson. "But dat's all right—we got sumpin in de wagin."

A little later, riding along the road, Kelley noticed the two servants gnawing ravenously at some hard crackers and flitch.

"Wilson!" roared the general. "I thought I told you to eat back yonder!"

The Negro blew out a spray of cracker crumbs. "Well, t' tell yuh de truf, boss, dat kitchen an' dat food back dere wuz too damned dirty."[3]

But public interest at this time was not centered on "Old Ben" and his doings. It was focused instead on Confederate General Jeb Stuart, who rounded up his hard-riding cavalry and struck out for Pennsylvania after horses and military supplies. Five days' rations they carried fastened to their saddles, and on their backs so many of them wore captured Union overcoats that it was difficult to tell where their allegiance lay.[4] One farmer, fooled by the winter toggery, waved his fist in the air and swore as they corraled his horses, "I'm just as good a Union man as any of you!" And an old lady, similarly misled, listened to their stories of how they had just destroyed the Confederate army and then ran to bring out her "best brandy," something she had been saving for just such an occasion. "Some of the rascally Rebs," it was recorded, "actually filled their canteens with the devoted woman's liquor and then rode off, telling her they were 'Jeff Davis guerrillas.'" [5]

Like the ride around McClellan, the raid toward Chambersburg was much to Stuart's liking, and it was through terrain with which he was thoroughly familiar. As the Adams County weekly summarized it: "General Stuart, the Rebel horse thief who lately made such a dashing raid into this state, completely circumventing the army of McClellan and dazzling anything that any cavalry force ever attempted before, was at one time in command of Carlisle Barracks."

Horses were one object of the expedition; another was to learn the intentions of the Federal army. But Abraham Lincoln used the raid as a weapon with which to heckle some action out of McClellan, by now notoriously famous around the White House for his inactivity.

In the opening barrage of a crossfire of correspondence Lincoln held up the Rebels as an example and asked: "Are you not overcautious when you assume that you cannot do what the enemy is constantly doing?" And he followed this with an observation that completely ignored the guerrillas, now beginning to show organized activity under the leadership of White, McNeill, and others: "As I understand, you telegraphed General Halleck that you cannot subsist your army at Winchester unless the railroad from Harpers Ferry to that point be put in working order. But the enemy does now subsist his army at Winchester, at a distance nearly twice as great from railroad transportation as you would have to do, without the railroad last named." [6]

The President wanted action, and he went so far as to point out to McClellan that he was nearer the Confederate capital than was Lee's army: "His route is the arc of a circle, while yours is the chord." The general was slow to burn and he wired back simply: "I am not wedded to any particular plan of operations." [7] But then, right on the heels of that, he sent a dispatch about his "sore-tongued and fatigued horses," and that brought Lincoln up screaming: "Will you pardon me for asking what the horses of your army have done since the battle of Antietam that fatigues anything?"[8] McClellan offered a weak defense, and it was then "Old Abe" cited the activity of Stuart, waving a red flag that brought from his commanding general a lengthy recital of the unheralded feats of the Union army.

With more goading, McClellan at last announced his army was moving across the Potomac. Lee was waiting, having correctly fathomed the plans of the Union high command. He had written Jefferson Davis the enemy undoubtedly would try to get south of the James River and that it would approach by the Rappahannock rather than by the Shenandoah Valley.[9]

But McClellan had tarried too long before moving to save his career. Lincoln's patience was worn thin, and he issued an order placing General Ambrose E. Burnside in command of the Army of the Potomac, thus further burdening the army, for the new leader was to bring action, but only when it was accompanied by bad judgment and blundering. He was a modest individual with the strange idea that the speed of a job depended on how many men were doing it.[10]

After the main armies began moving southward, the blockade in northern Virginia slackened noticeably, as revealed by certain definite symptoms. One of these was the reappearance of the irregulars, who adhered to a policy of slinking out of sight when the army hordes were in their vicinity and of riding into the open with more audacity when the regulars were off campaigning elsewhere. Another was the renewed frequency with which the women blockade runners along the Potomac plied their business—not always with success. In one arrest near Chantilly at this period two prominent ladies were found to have strapped about their waists more than 100 ounces of quinine, a medicine gravely scarce in the South. A few days later six Irish women were discovered smuggling whisky through the lines in beef bladders and small bottles hidden beneath their skirts. Reported the New York *Herald:* "About 50 gallons of 'tanglefoot' were thus secured and destroyed. We regret that the law requires the intrusion of the guardians of the peace upon that hooped dominion of women that should ever be sacred." But the Irish women were outdone in other quarters. One woman riding in a carriage was relieved of twelve pairs of boots, each containing bottles of whisky or military lace, which she had strapped around her midriff. And a colored member of the bandanna tribe, ordered down from the two-wheel vehicle in which she was riding, was unable longer to conceal a five-gallon demijohn she had artfully suspended between her legs from a girdle.

Some of the spirits thus smuggled was purveyed to the Union soldiers, and always at a steep profit. Camps were not long in existence before women appeared with baskets of pies, cakes, apples, and other items for sale. It was soon commonly understood that some of these merchants, in effect, kept a part of their merchandise under the counter. Testing this rumor, officers searched one woman and found a bottle of whisky concealed in each breast and a third immediately below the waistband of her dress. On one occasion another of the peddlers was busily engaged in selling from her basket when a rough fellow slipped his hand under her skirts. She got up deliberately and, without a word of warning, drew a dirk from her waist and slashed the man across his chest. Incidents like these, reported the *Intelligencer*, relieved the monotony of camp life.

As the first week of November faded, a three-day snowstorm struck, blanketing the entire area east of the Ohio River, and Imboden, now equipped with a new supply of overcoats and blankets, employed the occasion for a raid, and so did Milroy, the Indianan who had been among the first troops to take over along the B. & O. Imboden's goal was the costly Cheat River viaduct, a target at which the Confederates had been constantly aiming since Lee the preceding year had said its destruction "would be worth to us an army." Milroy meanwhile planned to strike the Virginia Central Railroad at Staunton.

Imboden had another matter to attend to along the way. He had been told that Milroy was clamping down on the citizenry of his area in a manner reminiscent of General John Pope. Basing his action on a claim that guerrillas were robbing Union citizens under his jurisdiction, the Indianan, according to report, was demanding reparation in cash. Damages were apportioned among Secessionists, who were threatened with burned homes and death if they did not pay by a specified time. The same harsh punishment was decreed for any inhabitants living within ten or fifteen miles of the Union camps who failed to dash in and give notice whenever guerrillas approached.

Official notice of Milroy's program for checking the irregulars was brought to the attention of Imboden by Job Parsons, son of Abra-

Turner Ashby, bachelor, gentleman farmer, and *beau sabreur* of the Shenandoah Valley, whose gallant actions and silhouetted white horse in the early months of the war set a pattern followed by Confederate guerrillas. (*Library of Congress photo*)

John Singleton Mosby, frail lawyer-turned-soldier, was outstanding among the Confederate guerrillas and the one most feared in the North. He is pictured here in Richmond, surrounded by studio props, including a saber which he never carried, shortly before he was wounded and left for dead by the enemy. (*Library of Congress photo: Brady-Handy Collection*)

Elijah V. White, one of the major advocates of Partisan warfare, was noted for his fighting ability. Greatly admired by his superiors, he frequently raided on the outskirts of Washington and was in command of the famous Laurel Brigade at its surrender. (*Library of Congress photo*)

Harry Gilmor, prominent Baltimorean, was another terror along Union lines during the months when he was not a prisoner of war. This photograph was taken some years after the surrender, at a time when he was so stout his uniform coat had to be held together with a piece of twine. (*Library of Congress photo*)

Here is shown all that was left of the bridge across the Potomac at Berlin (now Brunswick), Maryland, after it was destroyed by guerrillas during the early months of the war, becoming one of the first spans to demonstrate their behind-the-lines activities. (*Library of Congress photo*)

Union soldiers march in an unbroken line across the Long Bridge leading from Washington to Virginia. This was on May 24, 1861, and was part of the advance that terminated in the first major battle of the war along Bull Run nearly two months later. (*National Archives photo*)

An artist sketches the excitement of the scene as the bridge over the Potomac was blasted by the Confederates on the evacuation of Harpers Ferry in June, 1861.

Repair work on the damaged span progressed as rapidly as conditions would permit. In the foreground can be seen the ruins of the arsenal at Harpers Ferry destroyed by the Union before the town was evacuated by them prior to the arrival of Virginia troops. (*B. & O. Railroad photo*)

Not always were the guerrillas able to escape with their captures. Here an artist pictures the din and confusion surrounding efforts by Federal troops to retake a wagon train on its way south under the guiding hands of Mosby's guerrillas. (*National Archives photo*)

Union General Benjamin F. Kelley, who commanded along the Baltimore and Ohio Railroad, battled the guerrillas from the start of the war until they finally kidnaped him from his bed shortly before the surrender. (*Library of Congress photo*)

This artist's sketch portrays the wintry scene in which tramped the lonely Union picket, expecting at any moment the stealthy bullet or knife of the guerrilla. (*National Archives photo*)

The telegraph operator was an important person in a military camp. Here the click of his magic key holds a captive audience in the flickering glow from a tallow candle. (*National Archives photo*)

Sad-eyed Ben Butler, one of the first Union leaders to feel the sting of the Confederate guerrillas during the opening weeks of the war, brought glory to his name in the Baltimore area until he irked aging General Winfield Scott and was packed off to the quieter life around Fortress Monroe, Virginia. (*National Archives photo*)

General Edwin H. Stoughton, whose star soared and then quickly sank after Mosby and a small band of his guerrillas sneaked into Fairfax Court House one snowy night and took him from his bed, was a wealthy young scion who believed in mixing frivolity with the rigors of military life. (*Library of Congress photo*)

Armored cars such as this one depicted by a *Harper's Weekly* artist were operated along the B. & O. during the war largely for the protection of bridge and track crews from the unexpected attacks of guerrillas.

Piedmont, West Virginia, was one of the busiest rail centers along the B. & O. The railroad shops shown in this photograph were several times the target of Confederate forces. McNeill's hard-riding guerrillas struck them early in '64, and a few months later they were damaged by Rebel troops under General Rosser. (*B. & O. Railroad photo*)

These Union generals—R. H. Milroy (*upper left*), George C. Crook (*upper right*), Franz Sigel (*lower left*), and David Hunter (*lower right*) —all felt the effect of Confederate guerrilla raids at different periods during the war. (*Upper left, Library of Congress photo; others, National Archives photos*)

The old Windsor Hotel, formerly the Barnum, from which General B. F. Kelley was captured by McNeill's Rangers in 1865, still stands at Cumberland, Maryland. (*Library of Congress photo*)

Near the Barnum was another hotel, the Revere House, also still standing, from which McNeill's Rangers captured General George Crook on the same night they got Kelley. The first B. & O. depot in Cumberland is shown next door. (*Library of Congress photo*)

ham, who passed along a couple of messages he had received from Captain Horace Kellogg, commanding the Federal post at St. George in Tucker County. Both of these were signed "by order of Brig.-Gen. R. H. Milroy" and they made it plain to Job that his life was in his own hands.

Parsons went to Imboden for the purpose of joining his command, the safest way to keep himself from getting killed for not paying up, he concluded, and it was while in the process of becoming a Partisan Ranger that he pulled out the papers from Kellogg. After scanning them Imboden was furious and passed them on to Jefferson Davis with this explanation: "The pretext of 'robberies of Union men by bands of guerrillas' is a falsehood. The fact is that Union men have conspired to run off each other's horses to Pennsylvania, where they are secretly sold, the owners afterward setting up a claim for reparation on the false ground that guerrillas have robbed them."

But Imboden's explanation was more or less beside the point. He mentioned the matter only as evidence of the "atrocity of General Milroy" and added: "This is only one of a thousand barbarities practiced here in these distant mountains of which I have heard for the last four months. Oh, for a day of retribution!" [11]

With Jeff Davis behind it, the matter went up the line. Robert Ould, Confederate agent of exchange, asked for assurance of the genuineness of the Kellogg papers and, when he got it from Imboden, in a letter in which the Partisan said, "Were I to report every case of outrage of this character which has come to my knowledge it would astound all Christian people," he called for action. Through Davis, General Lee was directed to ask for an official explanation and, if that were not forthcoming, to retaliate. Lee directed his inquiry to Halleck in Washington and asked simply whether "your government will tolerate the execution of an order so barbarous and so revolting to every principle of justice and humanity." [12]

Halleck immediately called for an investigation, in the meantime writing Lee that if the papers were found genuine Milroy would be notified that his conduct in issuing them was disapproved. His reply was phrased in keeping with the interpretation of legal and illegal warfare given him a few months earlier by Francis Lieber, the international authority on such matters. Halleck wrote: "The government of the United States has not only observed the modern laws and usages of war, but through the present rebellion has refrained from exercising the severer rights recognized by the codes of civilized Europe . . . Nevertheless there probably have been, as there always will be, individual acts of subordinates or irresponsible persons which can not be justified, and some of which deserve punishment. All such cases, when brought to the attention of the government, are immediately investigated and a remedy applied." [13]

The Union investigation ran into a snag. Milroy stuck by his guns, and the government at Washington sustained him. Thus rebuffed, Lee recommended that prisoners captured from Milroy's command be held as hostages for the humane treatment of Secessionists.

So, as the snow fell, it was natural that Imboden should have his mind on St. George as well as the Cheat River bridge. With 310 of his First Virginia Partisan Rangers, a part of Grumble Jones' army stationed in the Shenandoah Valley, he started from camp in Hardy County and marched over the Allegheny Mountains, expecting to reach St. George, thirty-eight miles away, the following night. But his schedule was upset by the storm, which was so great a handicap that his irregulars were forced to walk mile after mile and lead their horses, and it was not until the next day that he reached and captured St. George and the cavalry unit under Captain Kellogg.

At points along his route citizens informed Imboden of the nearness of Federal scouting parties, including Milroy's force of about 4000, reported to be moving from Beverly toward Monterey. At St. George, after rounding up all arms and supplies, the Partisan leader realized his horses were too jaded by their struggle through the snow to keep on to Rowlesburg. In addition, the storm had delayed him to such an extent that he was confident Union scouts were keeping track of his progress.

Under this state of affairs, Imboden decided to turn back. After the destruction at St. George was completed, he started marching and the next afternoon went into camp ten miles east of Beverly. It was there that a citizen rode in to inform him that Milroy's baggage train was at Camp Bartow on the Greenbrier River. This was news he had not expected, and it immediately caused him to change his plans again. He resolved to capture the train, after which he would escape through Pocahontas and Bath counties. But, despite a compass and a competent guide to keep him on a course of south thirty-five degrees east, he got so hopelessly lost that his only recourse was to retrace his steps through the snow.

Hours later, coming out of the wilderness, he learned that the Federals were trying desperately to intercept him, with three separate details galloping in various directions. Imboden listened to this and then turned his attention to a matter of major importance: he halted at a home where he got feed for his horses, the first grain they had had in days. After that he kept riding until he struck the trail of one of the three parties and, thus covering his tracks by following in the wake of the Federals and mingling the hoofprints of his mounts with theirs, he came to a gap in the mountains through which he escaped eastward.

Writing General Lee about the expedition, Imboden said he was conscious its results had been comparatively insignificant, but continued: "Our escape, under all the circumstances, without the loss of a man, is felt and acknowledged by all to be truly providential." [14] But some good had come from the raid: Milroy, hearing of the presence of Imboden and receiving an exaggerated report of his strength, abandoned his junket toward Staunton. Lee, appreciating the extraordinary difficulties encountered by Imboden and his Partisans, said the undertaking was attended with valuable results and expressed the hope that on some future occasion they would meet with the success they deserved. [15]

On his return from St. George, Imboden found an unpleasant surprise awaiting him. As at Little Cacapon, his camp had been raided and burned in his absence. This time he could thank "Old Ben" Kelley. The Yankee leader had slipped in with the First New York, Ringgold, and Washington Cavalry, Rouark's Battery, and three companies of the Twenty-third Illinois Infantry, the last in wagons. In his report he said the attack was made early in the morning. Many of the Confederates were chased to the mountains, but fifty prisoners, a quantity of arms, 350 fat hogs, and a large number of horses, cattle, and wagons were captured.

Meanwhile, Federal scouting parties, sent out over a wide area of northern Virginia, found only straggling guerrillas, [16] but the organized groups were there, though unseen. Into prominence at this time came White's irregular cavalry, newly formed into a battalion and its leader made a major. Now recognized as a part of the Second Brigade under Grumble Jones, it was engaged chiefly in detached service along the Potomac River, in Loudoun County on the Virginia side and Montgomery on the Maryland, and it was constantly active. It struck Means' revived Loudoun County Independents unexpectedly one day and routed them again, killing a lieutenant. Thus inspired, White crossed the Potomac into Maryland and captured the Federal force stationed at Poolesville, near his birthplace, riding away with sixty horses. A little later, in a running fight near Berryville, he was wounded in the thigh but managed to escape.

Other guerrillas or irregulars besides those of White also were active at this time. With alarming frequency they darted in upon the marching line of Union soldiers moving south, struck quickly, sometimes killing or capturing horses and men, and then fled to their hiding places. Captain G. A. Crocker of the Sixth New York Cavalry wrote Colonel T. C. Deven at Barbee's Cross Roads about them. He had just arrived at Markham and he was seriously concerned. "Every hill, and there are many, is infested with guerrillas," he reported.[17]

The war rolled along. Lincoln had heckled McClellan about the most direct route to Richmond, and now the new commanding general was going that way—toward Fredericksburg and the Rappahannock and the troops that Lee was amassing on the heights beyond. Everywhere in northern Virginia, Union soldiers were on the march. They crowded each road and bypath, and they swarmed in and out of Washington.

As the movement developed, certain gaps appeared in guerrilla ranks. The Federals had learned a band of irregulars were quartered at a house at Shepherdstown, near Harpers Ferry, under command of Captain Redmond Burke, one of the most ardent patriots fighting for the Confederacy. He had joined the army early in the war, some said from Texas, and soon, like Mosby, was added to Stuart's staff as a scout. Riding in the same command were three of his sons, all good soldiers. The father, a rough man but one of extraordinary courage and enterprise in action, drew praise upon himself early— at Dranesville, while falling back from Manassas, at Williamsburg, on the ride around McClellan, during the Seven Days' Campaign and elsewhere. Near Fredericksburg in August, '62, a Federal sentinel shot him in the wrist, and a few days later, at Brandy Station, he received a severe leg wound. This disabled him from active duty for some time and it was while recuperating that he gathered around him other patriots operating independently.

One night late in November, seventy-seven Union soldiers from the Twenty-seventh Indiana Infantry, led by three guides, crossed the Potomac a mile above Shepherdstown, followed a circuitous route into the town and surrounded the house in which the guerrillas were staying. Burke attempted to flee and was killed; his companions, including two of his sons, were captured.

Burke's death caused widespread lament in Rebel ranks. Among those who bemoaned him was the song-loving Jeb Stuart, who commented in a letter home: "He died as he lived, true as steel . . . His child-like devotion to me is one of those curious romances of this war which I will cherish next to my heart while I live."

As a final epitaph John Chipman Gray, a Union Twelfth Army Corps soldier stationed at Sharpsburg, wrote his friend, John Codman Ropes: "My paper is nearly out and, while waiting for a fresh supply for which I have just sent, I write on this which was found in the pocketbook of Redmond Burke, whose commission and pass I hope you have received before this." [18]

On December 3 John Chipman Gray wrote another letter to his friend, in which he said: "The great battle will be fought I think between Fredericksburg and Hanover C. H., but perhaps nearer Richmond—and it will be fought in three weeks. These are bold predictions, and I must say that I don't feel at all sure I am right, but I think I am; and if I do turn out right shall think I am considerable of a prophet." [19]

Mr. Gray was indeed "considerable of a prophet." The troops marching southward drew up at Fredericksburg and there, on December 13, was fought a battle unexcelled for ferocity at any time during the war. It began in the early morning, while fog lay along the banks of the Rappahannock, and it developed as the hours of the day advanced. That night thousands in blue lay dead and dying on the flat fields leading to Marye's Heights, for Rebel gunmen— and many of them were dead too—had found a sunken road from which to fire effectively upon the charging Federals.[20]

The days of '62 ran out fast after the battle of Fredericksburg. Snow began to fly intermittently the third week of December, and the two hostile forces—the Army of the Potomac, blocked in its crow-flight march on Richmond, and the Army of Northern Virginia, fighting with its back to the wall—lay facing each other over a wide area, from Fredericksburg to the Potomac and westward toward Wheeling. As the weather turned colder, soldiers began to bolster their covering against the elements, and it was evident that almost everybody was in favor of shacking down for the winter.

Between the two armies stretched a no-man's-land, silent except when guerrillas stole in to break up the peace or lonely watchmen fired their guns in response to strange noises out of the darkness. Up past Fairfax Court House it lay along the west bank of Cub Run, where Union regiments went out every four days to stand two days of picket duty. Along the trails they followed to their stations waited constant reminders of warfare: skeletons of horses and mules, left to rot where they fell; knapsacks, bayonet sheaths, and here and there a broken musket; human skulls and legbones bleaching in the open—ribs and torsos and teeth, bare to the sun wherever water washed away their covering, for everybody was too busy fighting a war to cover them up again. The stench in many places was unbearable, causing one soldier to comment: "Virginia is not only dead, but stinketh." [21] At Centreville, forts were so numerous that eight looked down upon one camp, all connected by rifle pits. And here and there, as taunting souvenirs, were the "quaker" guns that had kept McClellan at bay the previous winter.

The Twelfth Vermont Volunteers' turn for picket duty came December 17. Stepping briskly, they struck out from Centreville, over what seemed three miles of sharp marching across fields seamed with ditches and covered with a low vine that served to trip the pedestrian, and arrived along Cub Run at noon. The first pickets took their posts in a flurry of snow, one man to a station for the most part, but two or three at those requiring special vigilance. Beyond, out the road toward Warrenton and past the numerous little huts of logs and mud built by the Southerners before their fall-back to the Peninsula, moved a sixteen-man cavalry vedette, ready to ride hard with warning if danger approached.

The pickets, as they took their turns, had their minds divided between their fires and their dinners. If persnickety, they fried pork on a tin plate, but, if more hardened to army life, they simply cut off a slice or two and ate it raw with hard bread.

On a schedule of two hours on duty, two hours off, time passed slowly. George Benedict, junior editor of the Burlington *Free Press* in private life, had it easy during the afternoon—no excitement other than the approach of a "gaunt and yellow F.F.V." to complain about the burning of his fence rails. Downstream things were more lively. A free Negro waded across to report that a stranger in citizens' clothes had come to his house and inquired about the number and position of the Union pickets. A small detachment of men was sent out to see if they could locate this snooper and, while scouting around a farmhouse, discovered a suspicious-looking box in a barn. Inside was found a metallic casket containing a corpse, which the family living there said had been left by the Southerners the preceding March, with a promise that it would be sent for. No one supposed it ever would be.

The night settled clear and cold. Pickets were ordered to douse their fires or keep them smoldering without flame. At 10:00 P.M. Benedict came back on duty. His task was not to his liking, for as the hour grew late, time passed more slowly. He noticed the stars shone brightly, but there was little else to see. Down below he could hear the stream rippling away with constant murmur, and back of him the wind sighed and rustled through the trees. But there were only the after-dark noises until shortly before he was to go off post at midnight, and then came the report of firearms in the direction of the cavalry vedette, and shortly after that the clatter of hoofs on the frozen ground. But the sounds died away and the night returned to its nerve-wracking stillness.

Finally off duty and back in the tents occupied by the reserves, the junior editor found bright fires burning in the fireplaces and settled down to listen to a few stories and to talk about that awful battle down at Fredericksburg. All at once there was the noise of running feet, and a picket rushed up to announce that someone was moving on the opposite bank of Cub Run. Even as he blurted out his message, a musket shot sounded off to the left, and then another. Men grabbed their guns and rushed down to the ford, the most likely point for an enemy force to cross. This was an important post, where three pickets were stationed, three pickets who whispered that a small party had just come along the opposite bank, stopped at the ford, and discussed the expediency of crossing, and then, disturbed by the firing farther down, had hastily disappeared.

For a long time the Vermonters lay there clutching their muskets and staring into the dark, listening for the swish of water that would indicate someone was trying to cross. But there was no further sound, and the reserves finally returned to their seats around the fireplaces. Then a sergeant and two men, sent down the line to investigate the musket shots, returned with word that two nervous sentinels had fired at random after hearing a movement in the bushes across the run.

Two hours had passed since Benedict left his post, and now he went back on duty. But there was no further alarm that night. He wrote dutifully to his newspaper of the experience: "I saw the big dipper in the North tip up so that its contents, be they of water or milk from the milky way, must have run out over the handle. I saw the triple-studded belt of Orion pass across the sky. I saw two meteors shoot along the horizon, and that was all the shooting. I saw the old moon, wasted to a slender crescent, come up in the east. I saw the sun rise very red in the face at the thought that he had overslept himself till half past seven, on such a glorious morning. I heard a song bird or two piping sweetly from the woods; but I neither saw nor heard any Rebels." [22]

At daylight a Union cavalryman, bareheaded, on foot, his face scratched and his eyes still wide with fright, came into the lines and told of the disturbance out in the direction of the cavalry vedette during the night. He was one of the sixteen men stationed there, and it was just by the grace of God he was alive, he said. While some slept and others stood guard, White's guerrillas had charged upon them, capturing all the horses, seven or eight prisoners, and scattering the others in various directions. Touched by his story and the chattering of his teeth, someone stepped aside anl let him get to the fire.

One day over along the B. & O. from North Mountain to Cumberland, in the section of Virginia that the United States Congress had just recognized formally as the new state of West Virginia, "Old Ben" Kelley went on a tour of inspection. What he saw pleased him, for it looked as if the entire line from Wheeling to Baltimore would be in running order again by the first of January. But he was forced to admit to himself that the Rebels knew how to destroy a railroad, that they "exhibited a genius in this regard" that was most remarkable. For about twenty miles along the route every tie was partially or totally destroyed. They were torn up and piled into little log cabins and then the rails laid across them. This done, the cabins were set afire and, when the rails became hot in the middle, they were bent around trees. Only the greatest of labor could get them straight again, and that at a time when manpower was needed for the army.[23]

Kelley would have been interested in a letter the Confederate adjutant general wrote Imboden at this time.[24] It asked him to cooperate in changing his troops from Partisan to regular army service for the remainder of the war. In order to do so, it was explained, he would have to obtain the consent of his men. Within a month the necessary steps had been taken to make the transfer. The most shocking effect of this change occurred to McNeill's command, Imboden's independent arm. All but seventeen of the Rangers went into regular service, and these remaining fighters McNeill led back to Hardy County and prepared for a recruiting drive. It was not long before he was back on the trails with almost his normal strength.

The same transfer was asked of Lige White, and the squawk from his command was long and loud. Insubordination and almost open mutiny was the result, especially among members of the first two companies he had organized.[25] They claimed they had joined the Confederate service to fight on the border and under the assurance they would never be attached to any regiment or brigade. One company, made up of Marylanders, maintained that they could leave, because they owed no allegiance to the Confederacy and thus could choose as they pleased the manner in which they were to support its government. Only the firmness and coolness of their commander saved the day and kept the men from deserting in bodies. In a few weeks White was promoted to lieutenant colonel and his battalion was assigned duty under Stonewall Jackson. From then on it was an off-again-on-again proposition, with the command fighting side by side with regular units and finding only occasional opportunity to slip away to its first love—the freedom and stealth of guerrilla operations.

Imboden's departure from the ranks of the irregulars implied no letup for the Federals stationed between Washington and Wheeling. Rather were the independents at this time drawing their plans for increased operation. True, Harry Gilmor was still a prisoner of war, but he soon would be back. White was operating as a part of Grumble Jones' army in the Valley, and McNeill, wearing a high, broad-brimmed black hat with ebony plume, was doing detached service in the mountain area and reporting directly to Imboden. To their aid as '62 faded came a little man who was to set an example for the others. If there had been organized independent warfare before, it was better after his arrival. He was a rider of superhuman endurance, a leader who wouldn't tell his men to do anything he wouldn't do himself, a thinker, a serious-minded student of war and literature who came back from a day of fighting to relax around the campfire over a volume of Bryant's poems. Finally, after months of effort, John Singleton Mosby had persuaded Jeb Stuart while on a raid toward Fairfax that he should be left behind to operate as a guerrilla.

The Federals would have increasingly worse trouble with the irregulars now. It would continue to swell in significance as the war advanced, this unpredictable warfare of the guerrillas, and then there would come a general who would say, "Hang them without trial"—and do it.[26]

PART TWO

CHAPTER 1

January 1–February 28, 1863

A SCORCHED-EARTHER
STIRS THE CALDRON

An outburst of hatred in public print that completely stifled any thought of an immediate end to the internecine slaughter sweeping the nation marked the beginning of the year '63. If there had been indecision and slowness of purpose before, it was replaced now by a definite spirit of partisanship. Both governments had drawn lines that enabled the hard-to-convince to make up their minds. Lincoln's Emancipation Proclamation angered people of both faiths. This was balanced below the Potomac by a lengthy message Jefferson Davis delivered before the Confederate Congress.[1] In it he made against the North specific charges of atrocity, and in so doing used words to stir the tempers of citizens who to date had never been sufficiently aroused to show concern.

By January 5 reconstruction of the B. & O. was completed. Major General Robert C. Schenck, commanding at Baltimore, notified Lincoln that the last rail had just been laid, and said the trains would be running from that city to Wheeling on the morrow.[2]

Another letter came to Lincoln at this time. It was from John Letcher, governor of Virginia, and it asked for the release of Dan Dusky, father of Sallie, the mountain lass who would "as lief" have Kelley as any member on his staff. Letcher cited that Dusky was held on a charge of robbing the mails, while what he had done was to take "military possession" of the post office at Ripley, West Virginia, acting under commission from Richmond. As a retaliatory measure pending his release, the letter announced, Captain William Gramm of Philadelphia, soldier of the Eighth West Virginia Infantry, would be confined to hard labor. This message in a few months would bring Dan back to the mountains to carry on the guerrilla warfare he had been conducting at the time of his capture.

But much of the hatred existing among Southerners at this time, especially Virginians, was engendered by Union General Robert H. Milroy in his efforts to stop guerrilla activities by making the citizens pay damages.[3] This man's star had risen rapidly. From colonel of the Ninth Regiment of Indiana Volunteers at the start of the war he had moved up both in prominence and authority. Lawyer member of a pioneer family, he soon was placed in command of the Mountain Department, embracing West Virginia, and thereafter proceeded to give the Secessionists of that area their first severe treatment. The names of General John McNeil, charged with murdering seven prisoners of war in cold blood, and of General Benjamin F. Butler, who had so insulted the women of New Orleans that the entire South voiced resentment, were at this time on the public tongue, too, and later there would be joined with them the names of William Tecumseh Sherman and Philip Henry Sheridan. But for the moment the individual on whom the Rebels along the Potomac principally vented their wrath was Robert Milroy, admiringly referred to in the Northern press as "Old Gray Eagle." [4]

Milroy displayed great energy, and it was this energy perhaps that stimulated the greatest resentment among his enemies. He was tall and spare, with high, sloping forehead, sharp features, bristling, sandy hair and beard slightly tinged with gray. His actions were nervous and excitable, and he was usually out of patience with something or somebody. On Christmas Day of '62 he moved into Winchester from out in the New Creek area and set up a reign of terror for residents of the town that their descendants still talk about. Maintaining that he was acting on orders from Washington,[5] he took possession of private dwellings, giving the occupants only a few hours' notice and compelling them to leave their most valued possessions behind.[6] Much of the dislike Milroy drew upon himself at Winchester came from women. They resented especially his placing spies in their homes to ascertain their opinions.[7]

Among the women he met during his first days at Winchester was Cornelia McDonald, wife of the veteran Angus.[8] She was a mother-hen type, surrounded by a brood of young children, and she could defend herself and her offspring with spirit. On several occasions during the Union general's stay in the vicinity she crossed swords with him, but, though her anger at times was seriously aroused, she found that Milroy had a heart and that underneath his rough manner was a man for whom she could not suppress some degree of admiration. He had a way of laying the cards on the table with his subordinates, and he sometimes would do the same with visitors, including the irate women who confronted him.

Mrs. McDonald's first visit to his headquarters was instituted by the arrival of a large cook-stove and a detail of soldiers directed to set up a hospital in her home. It was raining and sleeting at the time, but she drew on her bonnet and wrappings and stormed off to see the commandant of these "vile Yankees." At headquarters she finally got past the guard and was ushered into a room where she found Milroy surrounded as was his custom by members of his staff and others.

"What do you want?" he asked roughly, showing surprise at the apparition she made as she stormed into his presence.

Cornelia explained, and Milroy laughed ironically, a laugh that was echoed by some of the men around him.

"Where are your natural protectors?" he inquired.

"In the Confederate army!" snapped Cornelia, puffing up proudly.

"Yes, they leave you unprotected and expect us to take care of you."

"We would not need your care if we were allowed to take care of ourselves. It is only from the army you command that we want protection."

"Isn't your husband Angus McDonald and don't you have several sons in the Confederate army?"

"Yes."

Milroy roared, "There is not a greater rebel in the South than Angus McDonald!"

"That may be, General Milroy," admitted Cornelia, "but he is fighting for what he considers the right."

Milroy paused and looked around. "There's a gentleman in my command—Captain McDonald—who is a relative of your husband, I believe."

A tall, red-faced man arose.

The woman looked at him. "Where is Captain McDonald from?" "From Indiana."

"Oh, no!" she said. "Oh, no. He can be no relative of ours, for we never had any in Indiana. Besides, my husband had only one brother, and they were children of Major McDonald of the U. S. army who lost his life in active service during the War of 1812. He was the only son of his father, who fled from Scotland after the rebellion of 1745, the last effort in the cause of the Pretender. So you see, General Milroy, rebellion, if it is rebellion, is in the blood of the race."

"Ah," said he, "my ancestors came from Scotland, too, at the same time and for the same reason."

"Then," said Cornelia, recognizing her moment, "have you no sympathy for us, our ancestors having suffered in the same cause?"

Milroy turned away and spoke to Captain McDonald: "Go with her and see what can be done."

Homeward through the rain and sleet strutted Cornelia, the captain strolling along at her side and shielding her from the storm with an umbrella. "So elated was I at my success," the woman recorded in her diary, "that I never felt the effect of the multitude of eyes looking through the windows as I passed, and looking wonder, too, at the unwonted spectacle of so stout-hearted a rebel as I, walking with a Yankee in a fine uniform."

At her home the cook-stove and the detail of soldiers were quickly cleared away, and as the captain prepared to leave he confided that his name was Isaiah. Whereupon Mrs. McDonald concluded that he definitely was no relative of her family, "for who ever heard of a fierce Highlander named Isaiah?"

Milroy's transfer to Winchester, where he operated for a period under the command of Kelley, was for the purpose of watching the Rebel forces in the Shenandoah Valley and to protect the B. & O. It was a mere post of observation, or, as the military termed it, a post in the air. His immediate foe was Grumble Jones' troops, scattered from Strasburg to Staunton and variously estimated at from 5000 to 6000 men, and Imboden's command in Cacapon Valley, placed at 1500.[9] Against these, in addition to Milroy's force, were paired Kelley's units, based at Harpers Ferry, and four regiments scattered on outpost duty along the railroad to protect tunnels and bridges.

At the very start of '63 Jones staged a raid on Moorefield, farming-center village of 1500 surrounded by mountains skirting South

Branch Valley, and caused the Federals there to destroy a church filled with supplies. McNeill's Partisan Rangers went along in close support and made valuable captures, including men and horses.[10] This town, as seen by the Union, was a Rebel stronghold, surrounded by guerrillas and bushwhackers. Milroy wanted them broken up and, on one occasion, when notified of the capture of a most notorious individual of the neighborhood, wired back: "Good! Stick him in jail and keep him there till you catch a horde of them that are about there, and then send them, with descriptions of their crimes, to Major Darr at Wheeling." [11]

One result of the Jones raid was to cause additional Union troops to be moved into West Virginia, among them the One-hundred-sixteenth Ohio Infantry Regiment. This unit was stationed at Romney, recognized as the key to New Creek, Cumberland, and the railroad as far east as the Little Cacapon, and shortly after its arrival it was greeted by the guerrillas, who made off with a four-day batch of its mail. Regimental records described the incident as "a most disgraceful piece of carelessness on the part of a cavalry escort." [12]

The One-hundred-sixteenth remained at Romney two months, during the worst period of the winter, and the weather and the isolated surroundings soon caused despondency to set in among its members. No boon to their patriotism was it to be squatting in camp in the heart of the mountains in subfreezing weather and trying to keep warm over inadequate fires. Besides, the men had many hours to idle away, and thus came the opportunity to think of ruses and mischief and ways of avoiding the hectic army life into which fate had shoved them. Gradually their officers awakened to the fact that the Rebels in that part of West Virginia were helping them flee from their loneliness, in so doing making use of a shrewd method of depleting the Union army. In increasing numbers as the winter wore along soldiers appeared with paroles signed by guerrilla chiefs, indicating they had been captured and released. Thus compromised, they on their own responsibility would either go home or refuse to do duty. Again and again this happened. Finally suspicion was aroused when McNeill, preparing to capture a forage train of twenty-seven wagons five miles from Romney, yelled out as he surrounded the vehicles: "I don't want to hurt you. Throw down your arms and I'll parole every devil of you and you can go home." This was apparently what the infantrymen riding atop the loads of hay wanted to do, for they threw down their weapons without firing even one shot at the Rebel raiders. So quickly was the capture made that the cavalry escort, which had galloped on ahead, dashed back to find the hay cargo in flames and their fellow Ohioans missing. Comparisons verged on the ridiculous: McNeill had appeared with twenty-four men and fled with seventy-two prisoners and 106 horses. Thus it was that someone smelled a rat and called for an investigation, and in this way it was found that the parole business had become quite a lucrative activity. Local residents kept supplies of blanks on hand, all authentically signed by McNeill or some other guerrilla leader, and issued them in trade for such rare items as coffee and sugar.[13]

Imboden reported McNeill's raid on the wagon train to Lee, who passed the news on to Jefferson Davis with the comment: "These successes show the vigilance of the cavalry and do credit to their officers." Two days later the raid was mentioned in general orders, with fitting praise for McNeill.[14]

Now a rhubarb between Imboden and Milroy commanded the public attention. Imboden had sent a detail of soldiers to bring in Sheriff Trayhorn of Barbour County. Next morning part of a company of Union soldiers went in pursuit, and a little later two of the Confederates involved in the arrest of the sheriff were found dead in the road. Imboden wrote Milroy they had been murdered, and threatened retaliation. Milroy replied that he knew of nobody who had been "murdered" except in battle. He also used in his letter a few flowery phrases about the "superior humanity of the Federal government" and then concluded: "I notice that the Confederate government is about to offer $100,000 for my head. Had you better not come down to Winchester and go into the speculation?" [15] Imboden ignored the jest.

Early in February, Milroy got word that Grumble Jones was at Strasburg and sent troops to intercept him. These came back empty-handed, for they had found no one at Strasburg. But they learned that Jones was at Mount Jackson, busily conscripting, and that his strength was only about 2000. Milroy messaged Kelley with confidence: "I can take him easily." [16]

But Jones had no idea of getting himself into a trap. He was on an important foraging expedition aimed at tapping the rich Shenandoah Valley for supplies of cattle and other meat, a step in preparation for the spring offensive.

Over east of the Blue Ridge much of the attention was drawn to

Mosby. Housewife Barbara Broun, writing of the Yankees in her diary, said: "They charged through Middleburg one day last week after Captain Mosby who had taken 38 of their horses and some eight or 10 men. He pays them a visit every few days to their camp and brings up twice as many Yanks as he has men of his own. It really looks funny to see probably three or four of our men bringing up a dozen Yanks." [17]

Before February was half gone, Milroy was fretting over his forced inactivity.[18] A handful of guerrillas captured the stagecoach running between Martinsburg and Winchester and carried off, among other prisoners, Captain Charles W. Dietrich, assistant adjutant general, and Lieutenant William Burchard, aide-de-camp of General Cluseret. By quick action Milroy managed to rescue them. Then a deserter came into his camp and told him that Imboden had been made a brigadier general, was assigned to command of the country east of the Shenandoah Mountains, and was preparing for a campaign in West Virginia. "I respectfully ask," he wrote Schenck at Baltimore, going over the head of Kelley, "to be permitted to interfere with this arrangement. If General Moor will advance on Imboden by way of Huntersville and Warm Springs, and Mulligan will advance from New Creek by way of Petersburg, to Franklin, and I move on him up the Valley, by Staunton (brushing Jones out of the way), his forces can all be gobbled up, the base of guerrillaism and raids into West Virginia effectually cut off, and permanent peace given to that region." [19] It was the plea of a man suffering from claustrophobia. If the clamp on his movements were not removed soon, he said, he would be forced to resign. No longer could he keep to himself his disgust at Kelley's pacifism. "I would much prefer being a private in an active fighting army," he added, "to being kept in command of the stationary advance of a railroad guard under a brigadier-general not of a very hostile or pugnacious disposition toward traitors."

Milroy believed the United States government the best in the world and he had little sympathy for those he thought were trying to destroy it. His scouts captured, in the act of conscripting, a Rebel lieutenant who had a reputation as a bushwhacker, horse thief, and murderer. "What shall I do with him?" Milroy wired Schenck. "I would like to hang him if Jefferson Davis and Halleck did not make too big a fuss about it." [20]

This general who preferred the scorched-earth method of fighting was venomous toward the Baltimore and Ohio Railroad.[21] He said it was costing the government 50,000 dollars per day to operate it, and yet it was employing traitors and gutting every Unionist engaged in its defense. He charged that it extorted four or five prices for the fare of sending a dead soldier's body home, and cited the particular case of a member of the One-hundred-twenty-second Ohio Regiment who had to bury his brother at Winchester because he could not pay the exorbitant sum asked to convey the body to the Ohio River. "This Augean stable needs cleaning out badly," Milroy advised Schenck. "I reported a lot of these traitor employees to General Kelley several weeks ago, but the general is one of those good-natured, kind-hearted gentlemen who would much rather at any time meet a traitor with a stick of candy than the sword, and excused them." [22]

But General Milroy was to stew longer in his own inactivity, for the Union high command was not yet ready to turn him loose on an offensive in the face of an accumulation of uncertainties. Afloat were too many wild rumors about what Lee was planning. And further, there was evidence the Rebels were not as inert as Milroy might consider them. Some nights, even though no enemy had been seen in the area, blue lights flashed in the passes and along almost every ridge of the Bull Run and other ranges of mountains west of Washington, and from this it was known that the friends of Secession were still quite busy.[23]

CHAPTER 2

March 1–8, 1863

THE NORTH LOSES A
GENERAL—AND HORSES

Since the first week of December, Fairfax Court House had been under the command of a young brigadier general who loved wine and women and made sure his appetite for both was generally satisfied. People may have wondered how Edwin H. Stoughton, at twenty-five,[1] could have risen so rapidly in rank, and if they took the trouble to investigate they found many things responsible. As "a soldier by education," [2] he led the Fourth Vermont Infantry into action at the siege of Yorktown in the spring of '62 and a few weeks later took part in the Seven Days' Campaign around Richmond, compiling a record for his part in the fighting that drew laudatory comment in official records.[3] Added to that, he was a member of a wealthy Vermont family, and he had social status and personal attraction.[4]

When ordered to Casey's Division of the Washington defenses as a Part of the Twenty-second Army Corps under command of Major General Samuel P. Heintzelman, young Stoughton was assigned to command the Second Brigade. This unit was on guard out in the Fairfax area, and, on assuming command there, Stoughton set himself up like a lord, with all the trimmings. He was fifteen miles from his government's capital, from the high brass that could frown on his doings—fifteen long miles, traversed by rough roads difficult to travel over, especially in the dead of winter. So there was virtually no power, military or otherwise, to keep the new general from living pretty much as he desired, and his way of living was elaborate.

Official orders decreed that the brigadiers along the chain of outposts around Washington could establish their headquarters "at the points most convenient to their commands." [5] Stoughton chose to set up his at the courthouse proper, in the comfortable, two-story brick residence of Dr. William Presley Gunnell, in the very heart of the village.[6] Around him, quartered in other homes of the community, were his staff, aides, couriers, and a guard of about 200 men. All the conveniences allowed an outpost officer were his. There were fine horses, carriages, servants, as well as rich viands and other stores to compete with those of Moses Sweetser, sutler, who had set up shop in a building directly in front of the courthouse.

Thus the town of Fairfax was Ed Stoughton's bailiwick, to be run just as Ed Stoughton wanted it run; his superiors were elsewhere and the bulk of the troops under his command were stationed miles away. On top of that his provost marshal, L. L. O'Connor, was reputed to be drunk most of the time and was quick to wink at things that were not exactly proper.[7] The regiments for which he was directly responsible were so far away that their direction, in a day of slow communication, would seem to have been by remote control. Off to the north, toward Vienna, was his main cavalry camp, with parts of the brigade on outpost duty at Centreville, Chantilly, Dranesville, and Occoquan. This arm had been strengthened slightly after Jeb Stuart's raid toward Dumfries, and its commanding officer was quartered only a few yards away from the residence of the brigadier. A man of broad experience, this cavalry leader was none other than Sir Percy Wyndham, the British soldier of fortune and ex-veteran under Garibaldi. He had been exchanged following his capture by the Confederates on the very day of Turner Ashby's death.

In another direction, four miles away at Fairfax Station, lay the principal camp of the infantry, Vermonters all. Such an arrangement quite naturally became a sore subject with the soldiers. The commanding general should reside closer to his charges, according to their way of thinking, and the nearer his way of life to theirs the better. A picket walking post in the snowy cold of a wintry night could not help turning his thoughts occasionally to the general snuggled up in a warm bed at the courthouse—possibly with a companion. The privates knew what was going on. They had shared in the rumor making the rounds of the camps and they were well aware that their young brigadier had a guest, a special guest, billeted by herself in a well-guarded tent not far from his headquarters. She was a twenty-year-old truant from Cambridge, Massachusetts, a girl with many male friends, constantly showered with favors in return for her illicit love. That they knew, did the soldiers.

They knew that when she slept by herself a picket walked post outside her tent. She had joined the Army of the Potomac just about the time Stoughton was rising to the command of a brigade, and it was only a short time until she was a part of his headquarters, secretly sharing herself with him and sometimes with members of his staff. At her service were horses, orderlies, escorts, sentinels, and quarter rations, for on her shoulders were the straps of a major, a notation of rank that entitled her to all these privileges. It was the partition of her love, sometimes extended even to take in the Rebel army, that one day would lead to her arrest and expulsion, all at the hands of a jealous high-ranker. After all, the entertainment that earned for her bed and board was of a nature considered highly unofficial and frowned on by quite a few. Moved to comment on it in later days, one responsible official said: "The condition of morals among officers who found congenial companionship in the society of such women is apparent and needs no coloring from pen or pencil." [8]

But Stoughton was not bothered seriously by morals and he cared not what the soldiers thought. He was living the life of Riley, and of this life he made the most, allowing nothing within his own control to interfere. Each morning and evening the brigade band marched out in front of his headquarters and serenaded him with "soul-stirring, harmonious and patriotic music." [9] Gay was the life of the brigadier, and the parties he gave were lavish and frequent.

In his social life around the courthouse Stoughton knew he could expect only trouble from the natives. He once made this the subject of a letter to headquarters.[10] In it he advised that "the women and other irresponsible persons" in the neighborhood should be compelled to take the oath or go outside the lines. "I cannot fix upon any one person or persons who are culpable, yet I am perfectly satisfied that there are those here who, by means known to themselves, keep the enemy informed of all our movements." He told that Rebel soldiers had paid their families in the vicinity visits for a week at a time without being discovered. "There in our midst," he added, "men who are on their parole, who have large families (mostly women) who are rampant Secessionists, and disguise it on no occasion. They are themselves constantly informed of their friends in the rebel service, and, I have no doubt, are in constant communication with them."

One of the women the young brigadier had in mind when he wrote this letter was a pretty lass of his own age named Antonia Ford, daughter of a local merchant. Her home was one of the largest in town, and there the newcomers and occasional wayfarers found lodging. At times Generals McDowell, McClellan, Pope, and others had made it their headquarters.[11] Several of Stoughton's officers were quartered there, and this in itself was a threat to Union security. The girl had a way about her that made men quickly take her into their confidence. She was of striking appearance, with light hair and brown eyes, and she was a witty and entertaining conversationalist. One Federal official described her as "a young and decidedly good-looking woman, with pleasing, insinuating manners." [12]

If Stoughton had had positive knowledge of what she was doing, he most certainly should have banished her from the lines immediately. She was an avowed Southerner, and so were her father, Edward R., and brother, Charles, the latter first sergeant in Jeb Stuart's artillery under the amazing young John Pelham. Her love for the South was almost an obsession. Before the first battle of Bull Run she rode with an aunt twenty miles or more to tell Stuart she had overheard Union officers in her home say they were going to use a Confederate flag in a ruse to turn the Rebel army's flank. That deed, plus her later friendship with the cavalry leader, had brought her, all in fun, a commission as his honorary aide-de-camp, with rank of major, to be "obeyed, respected and admired by all the lovers of a noble nature." And now, with Fairfax Court House under the command of a lively young brigadier general who was livening it up with more social life than it had enjoyed at any time during the war, she was having a heyday as a spy, especially with the new guerrilla leader, Mosby, only a few miles away in the woods toward Aldie. This elusive individual, heard from with increasing frequency as the winter advanced, had been on picket duty as a private while quartered near her home during the first winter of the war.

Mosby's eye was on Fairfax from the beginning of his irregular operations. One of the principal reasons for this was the Britisher, Percy Wyndham. The Partisan leader's dashes on the Union camps in Fairfax had caused Wyndham untold anxiety, forcing him to drive his cavalry hard over the winter roads in an effort to capture the Little Rebel. One day several paroled Federals returned to camp with a verbal message from the Confederate guerrilla that, unless the Union horsemen were better armed and equipped, it wouldn't pay to capture them.[13] The veteran who once had obeyed the commands of Garibaldi had no use for independent warfare, and he especially disliked Mosby. Each longed to capture the other.

Aided by Antonia, it was her boast, Mosby became thoroughly familiar with the military establishment in and around Fairfax. She made it her duty to find out the number of Union troops stationed in the vicinity, the location of their camps, the places where officers were quartered, the precise points where pickets were stationed, the strength of outposts, the names of those in command, the nature of general orders, and similar information, all of which she said she passed on to the guerrilla leader. For three days and nights he remained at her home, disguised as a citizen. It was a preoccupation with the two of them, this undercover work, and they made great sport of their deceit, according to her story. On one occasion, while horseback riding with a member of Stoughton's staff, she came upon Mosby cantering along the road, still in citizens' clothes, and they saluted each other smartly as they passed.[14]

Early in February, on a basis of the information thus gathered, Mosby wrote Stuart, who had urged Wyndham's capture, that the cavalry in Fairfax was so isolated from the rest of the command that to gobble it up would be easy.[15] He added that he had harassed it so much its pickets were kept within half a mile of camp.

Later in the month something happened that focused Mosby's attention more sharply on Fairfax. With twenty-six men he captured an outpost of forty Federals and horses between Chantilly and Centreville. This so infuriated Wyndham that he tabbed Mosby publicly as a horse thief, a harsh accusation in that day of four-legged transportation; and for what it was worth, Mosby came back with a reply that all the horses he had stolen had had riders and each rider had had a saber and two pistols. Washington soon got a rumor, later denied, that Wyndham had been captured.[16]

By March 1 Stoughton was aware he was being spied upon. He wrote a letter to headquarters on that date to call attention to a gap in the picket line in the direction of Dranesville and wound up with an unexpected bit of information: "Last night, about 9 o'clock, while I was at headquarters, at the station [Fairfax Station], a man, undoubtedly a spy, was at the courthouse, dressed as a captain. He interrogated all my servants minutely respecting the troops in the vicinity, asking if I kept my horse saddled in the night, and other suspicious questions." [17]

Three days later A. H. Bliss, Union telegraph operator at Centreville, sent notice of a gap of about three miles in the picket line between that place and Chantilly. This message was wired to General Heintzelman and was referred to Colonel R. Butler Pierce, who was responsible for the cavalry south of the Potomac. [18]

That same day a soldier stationed at Fairfax Court House, wrote a friend in Vermont a letter with the following information: "General Stoughton, who commands the Second Vermont Brigade, has his headquarters in the village, although his brigade is five or six miles away. What he could or would do in case of an attack, I don't know, but it seems to me that a general should be with his men. If he is so fancy that he can't put up with them, the government had better put him out. There is a woman living in the town by the name of Ford, not married, who has been of great service to General Stuart in giving information, etc.—so much so that Stuart has conferred on her the rank of major in the Rebel army. She belongs to his staff. Why our people do not send her beyond the lines is another question. I understand that she and Stoughton are very intimate. If he gets picked up some night he may thank her for it. Her father lives here, and is known to harbor and give all the aid he can to the Rebs, and this in the little hole of Fairfax, under the nose of the provost-marshal, who is always full of bad whiskey. So things go, and it is all right. No wonder we don't get along faster." [19]

Early in March a reconnaissance of 200 men was sent toward Middleburg. It was a cold and dark night through which they rode, and in the eerie hours before dawn some of the soldiers began passing the bottle, an act that became too frequent and too general, because in time they encountered other Union troops and were panicked into a mad flight across country toward Centreville. Some of the men, a bit clearer-headed than the others, cautiously rode ahead until they could identify as friends the soldiers advancing toward them, after which they all gathered around a mill at Aldie to feed their horses. In the groups thus combined were fifty-nine men, [20] and it was then, while they were on foot and their animals were unbridled, that Mosby, with seventeen of his raiders, charged from behind an elevation at the western end of the village and routed them, capturing nineteen officers and privates and twenty-three horses.

The *Star* in Washington, when it heard of this incident, took occasion to do some preaching: "Another bungle has taken place on our front . . . What is imperatively necessary here is some cavalry commander who can enforce such discipline among his men as to keep them always in the state of caution as will prevent his pickets from being gobbled up through the careless and gross negligence of the officers he sends out in command of detachments." [21]

There was unrest along the picket lines. Rebel cavalry was reported at Manassas. Other bodies were said to be assembling at Wolf Run Shoals and elsewhere on the Orange and Alexandria Railroad. At Union Mills two Michigan cavalrymen were boldly captured within reach of their own artillery. So it went; and thus in the face of an accumulating threat of trouble a notice to be on the alert was sent all commanding officers along the ring of outposts.

This warning reached Stoughton, but it in no way interfered with his plans for a party. He had in mind a headquarters soiree, complete with champagne. There would be dancing and gaiety and great fun, augmented by the presence of all the feminine beauty they could round up for the occasion.

The night of March 8, a Sunday and usually rather a dead period of the week, was selected as the time for this gathering. During the day Stoughton's mother and sister, who had come down from Vermont for a visit and were staying in Georgetown, arrived in Fairfax Court House by carriage and were put up at the Ford home, only a few yards from where he was to entertain.

As the hour of levity approached, all went well except the weather. A melting snow lay on the ground, and in the late afternoon rain began falling and turned the earth's covering into a slush. But such weather was not a paralyzing influence. Rather, it added coziness to an indoor party and served as a magnet to draw people together, encouraging fraternization as a means of diverting attention from the dreariness blanketing the landscape and blotting out the buds that soon would be bursting forth with the song of spring. Succeeding generations had passed along the habit of taking the elements in stride. Ladies hoisted their sweeping skirts and tiptoed through the mud if the emergency demanded, or, if convenient, fell willingly into the arms of their male companions to be toted from carriage to doorstep. Thus the scene in front of the Gunnell home as twilight deepened and darkness began to sharpen the mellow light shining from the windows.

While the hours ticked by in an atmosphere of laughter and song, the uproar emanating from the Gunnell home grew louder. Soon the rolling hills of Fairfax echoed with the sounds of merriment. They reached out toward the billets of the soldiers in the headquarters guard and around the courthouse to the tents of Telegrapher Robert Weitbrecht and his orderly. Pickets on duty in the village listened and wondered as they walked post, thinking of the frivolity that was theirs back home and of the day when perhaps they, too, would be wearing braid on their sleeves and maybe stars on their collars, and hence would be entitled to take part in such affairs.

Virtually all the officers stationed in the vicinity were on hand. Percy Wyndham was the exception, and this time luck seemed to be on his side. During the afternoon he was called to Washington unexpectedly, but his guest, Austrian Baron R. B. Wardener, was there, and so were Colonel Robert Johnstone, commanding the post, and Captain Barker, Lieutenant Prentiss, and others. Stoughton had had parties before, but this was one of his best.

Midnight approached. The champagne continued to sparkle in the glasses. The gaiety grew louder and the guests more oblivious of the war and weather conditions outside. After all, concluded those whose minds were not too befogged with wine, the nearest Rebel forces involving any threat to their safety were at Warrenton, roughly twenty-five miles away, and, furthermore, as a barrier to prevent any sudden dash upon headquarters, there was the line of outposts, which only a few persons in authority realized were broken by gaps. But more important, this was no weather for military offensives. The roads were still bottomless in places, and the Virginia mud was so thick as to make logistics out of the question.

In the drizzling darkness a new day dawned, without salute from the revelers, and then a little later some of the older women of the group began to conceal their yawns and to suggest that maybe all this fun should come to an end for the time being. The idea got around and was accepted, and slowly the group dispersed, peals of girlish mirth ringing out at the front door as the men, some a bit unsteady, struggled to help the ladies into the vehicles. Then a slap of the reins, and a giddap or two, and away into the night rolled the coaches and the carriages and the buggies.

Some time after the crowd had gone, the lights winked out at the

Gunnell home one by one. Lieutenant Prentiss, headquarters staffer, was attending to these chores, for the brigadier already had taken to his bed, smelling strongly of champagne, as attested by the empty bottles on a table close at hand.

Then the village folded up and those who were on the night watch settled down to wait out the chilling hours until dawn. Operator Weitbrecht snuggled near his telegraph key, nodding, yet awake to the fact that no one could tell when some important message might come clicking out from Washington. An oil lamp burned dimly on a cracker box in the background, and a few yards away at the street intersection, in a window of the hotel converted into a hospital, burned another. This latter illumination spread in a dim semicircle, out across the mud and mire toward the courthouse, and now and then it caught the gleam of a picket's rifle as he walked post.

The hour of 1:30 A.M. passed, proving beyond doubt that every last one of the revelers had found their couches. Another half-hour ticked by, and then there was the noise of cavalry coming from the direction of Fairfax Station, splashing in on the soupy road that everyone knew led only to the camp of the Vermont infantry. The picket in front of the hospital heard it and continued to walk his beat. That would be Yankee horsemen: no Rebel troops could be within miles, maybe fifteen or twenty, way out beyond Aldie where Mosby was said to have his men scattered over the countryside.[22]

The cavalrymen drew nearer and divided, and some of them went toward the faint light in the telegraph operator's tent, while others came directly down the street to the point where the picket continued his tiresome tread. He was concerned but not alarmed. It could be only Union cavalry: no need for a challenge. And then in the drizzly faintness of the lamp he found himself staring at the cold steel of hostile revolvers, big Colt six-shooters, the tone of whose owners conveyed a warning they were in no mood for foolishness.

After that things developed fast. The horsemen divided into small groups and went about their business with the precision of well-planned and well-informed scheming—some toward the home in which was supposed to be sleeping the Britisher, Percy Wyndham, some toward other dwellings in which officers were quartered, and some toward the stables in which were standing the fine, sleek horses of the high brass. One band remained at Operator Weitbrecht's tent, grilling him with hasty but thorough questions, after which it moved on toward the brick residence in which slept the ambitious Stoughton. By daylight it would have been seen that there were only thirty of these night riders, all acting on the instructions of a small, wiry leader with a black plume in his hat and all of them garbed in heavy raincoats to protect them from the weather.

Lieutenant Prentiss, awakened by shouts that there were dispatches outside for the brigadier, was gullible enough to open the Gunnell door to the raiders. Six men walked in, but it was the smallest of them, the wiry one with the plume in his hat, who stuck a gun in the aide's ribs while he stood in the hallway in shirt and drawers holding high a smoking oil lamp.

Upstairs the beplumed intruder walked into the bedroom of Stoughton and pulled down the covers. The brigadier was lying on his side, snoring, but he roused up stupidly when Mosby lifted his nightshirt and slapped him on the behind.

"Get up, General, and come with me!"

The sound of a voice brought Stoughton more fully awake and, when he realized the man bending over him was a stranger, he roared: "What is this! Do you know who I am, sir?"

"I reckon I do, General. Did you ever hear of Mosby?"

"Yes, have you caught him?"

"No, but he has caught you." [23]

"What's this all about?" Stoughton roared again.

"It means, General, that Stuart's cavalry have taken over Fairfax and General Jackson is at Centreville."

"Is Fitz Lee here?"

"Yes," lied Mosby.

"Then take me to him. I knew him at West Point." [24]

When the raiders left Fairfax an hour after they had entered, they took with them, besides Stoughton, two captains, thirty privates, and fifty-eight horses.[25] Baron Wardener was in the group, and so were Captain Barker and Lieutenant Prentiss. Provost Marshal O'Connor had escaped only because, ten minutes before the Rebels arrived, he had gone out the Vienna road, drunk or sober, to visit an outpost. Colonel Johnstone, post commander, escaped, too, but under less fortunate circumstances. He was awakened by the sound of horses in the street and bounded out of bed in deshabille to raise a window and shout: "Halt! The horses need rest! I will not allow them to be taken out! What the devil is the matter?" No one answered, so he yelled again: "I am commander of the cavalry here and this must be stopped!" [26] It was then he realized the riders at whom he was shouting were hostile and that the method they would employ to carry out his instructions would not be to his liking. So he turned and fled, as nude as he was, to hide beneath an outhouse behind the home at which he was staying.[27]

Half an hour after the fast-moving raiders trotted out of town on the same road they had entered, the alcoholic-loving O'Connor got off the first report of what had happened. His message was telegraphed to Heintzelman in Washington at 3:30 A.M., and in it the provost marshal did a masterful job of briefing:

"Captain Mosby, with his command, entered this town this morning at 2 A.M. They captured my patrols, horses, etc. They took Brigadier-General Stoughton and horses, and all his men detached from his brigade. They took every horse that could be found, public and private, and the commanding officer of the post, Colonel Johnstone, of the Fifth New York Cavalry, made his escape from them in a nude state by accident. They searched for me in every direction, but being on the Vienna road, visiting outposts, I made my escape."

Then he had an afterthought, which was added in postscript: "All our available cavalry forces are in pursuit of them." [28]

But Mosby had escaped, and all that was left to the Federals was to get their records straight. When Abraham Lincoln was informed of the major items of loss—a brigadier general and fifty-eight horses —he scratched in his chin whiskers and slowly remarked: "Well, I'm sorry for that. I can make new brigadier generals, but I can't make horses." [29]

Study immediately was focused on the entire incident. The Secret Service, under the direction of Secretary of War Stanton and headed by General Lafayette C. Baker, soon came to the conclusion that the success of the raid had stemmed from information supplied by a Rebel spy in Fairfax Court House. This secret agent the finger of suspicion pointed toward was Antonia Ford, and in a matter of hours a female detective was on the way to see what she could find out. This woman, posing as a Secessionist en route to pass through the lines at Warrenton, stopped at the Ford home and there was welcomed. Antonia accepted her as a sister of the same allegiance, and in no time at all the two were conferring confidentially in an upstairs bedroom. Between whispered secrets the girl proudly pulled from beneath the mattresses of her bed the honorary commission signed by Jeb Stuart.

The girl's arrest followed four days after the raid. On a basis of what she had told the woman detective, she was taken into custody by a Secret Service officer and placed in prison in Washington. With her went the commission, as well as a number of private letters from officers and others in the Rebel service and eighty-seven dollars in Southern bank bills and Confederate notes found upon her person. Also seized from hiding places in the home were money and evidences of debt amounting to 5765 dollars.

Other prominent residents of Fairfax, all men, also were arrested, among them Antonia's father. These were released in a short time, but the girl was held in Old Capitol Prison, much to the anger and resentment of her friends and the Confederacy. Immediately a campaign was started to bring about her release. Even Moses Sweetser, the local sutler, was moved to write a letter in her defense. Identifying himself as a Union man from the North, he pointed her out as "a young lady of refinement, education and great modesty," a defenseless female "as pure and chaste as the 'morning sunbeam.'" [30]

Confederate authorities also came to her defense. Jeb Stuart wrote Mosby: "I wish you would send me whatever evidence you may be able to furnish of Miss Ford's innocence of the charges of having guided you in your exploits at Fairfax so that I can insist upon her unconditional release." [31]

Antonia spent months behind bars. When she was released and sent to Richmond, after a diet that consisted principally of rice and bad meat, she met her friend, John Esten Cooke, who was so touched by her appearance that he later recorded in his book, *Wearing of the Gray*, that "she was as thin and white as a ghost—the mere shadow of her former self."

But Antonia, in words uttered subsequently by Mosby himself, "got her revenge." One of the Union officers quartered at her home during the early part of the war was a Major Joseph C. Willard, cofounder of the Willard Hotel in Washington and for a time provost marshal of Fairfax, and it was he who was largely responsible for effecting her release. Years her senior, they were married in Washington March 10, 1864, a year and a day after the raid that brought about her imprisonment. Seven years later she was dead, her friends claimed because of the diet she was forced to subsist on while in confinement.[32]

An even more tragic fate awaited Stoughton. As he had requested when aroused from his post-party sleep, he was taken to Warrenton by Mosby and placed in the care of Fitzhugh Lee. His release in May was followed shortly by his resignation from the army, and he soon was practicing law in New York City.[33] On Christmas Day of 1868, he died in Boston, Massachusetts. His demise, had it occurred in the neighborhood of Fairfax, would have been big news, but in this New England city it almost went unnoticed. At most the mention it received was insignificant, certainly for one of such social—and at one time important military—standing. Buried deep in the list of deaths in the Boston *Transcript*, midway of column six on page two, was this notice: "25 inst., Edwin H. Stoughton of the city of New York, 30."

It was thirty for Stoughton in years and thirty for Stoughton in life.

CHAPTER 3

March 9–May 1, 1863

THE GREAT RACE TO
CATCH MOSBY

While the two armies lay in winter quarters, approaching spring swelled the buds and warmed the air, over highland as well as lowland, and the objective that had led Imboden to beat his way to the northwest during the fall of '62 came once more into focus, this time accentuated by the failures of the past. Cheat River bridge, major key to interruption of traffic on the B. & O., still spanned the gorge that made its existence necessary, and Confederate leaders most responsible for its continued presence were constantly haunted by the classic words of Robert E. Lee that its destruction would be "worth to us an army." Thus there were always plans of a sort under way in Rebel circles to tear down the lofty structure.

The scheme mapped out as the weather relaxed came from a master planner. "Hanse" McNeill, the cattle expert, had a notion he could traverse his native mountains and destroy the span, aided largely by stealth, and he outlined his idea to Imboden. It made sense as the guerrilla chieftain described it. Given authority and 600 men, he would slip in quietly and quickly and do what thousands had failed to do before. Imboden approved and sent the Partisan leader in person to sell the plan to Secretary of War Seddon.

Seddon saw logic in the proposal too. He looked upon McNeill as "a very brave and enterprising Partisan officer." [1] Moreover, he had been of opinion all along that the best way to accomplish destruction of the bridge would be by a sudden and unexpected dash of a small force.² Thus he was on the verge of approving the project when he realized it would perhaps be wiser administratively to leave the final sanction to Major General Sam Jones, commanding the Department of West Virginia, in whose jurisdiction the effort would be attempted. So he wrote to Jones and entrusted the letter to McNeill for delivery.

In this one move may have rested blame for the ultimate failure of the undertaking. Had Seddon given his blessing to the plan as originally presented, and sent McNeill back to the mountains to put it into effect, it might have been a success, largely through its brashness and its element of surprise. As matters developed under the War Department's manner of handling the proposal, however, delay developed and with it came complications.

Sam Jones agreed with the idea of entrusting the raid to a cavalry force of 600 or 700 men. His answer was prompt, given the same day McNeill arrived at his headquarters with Seddon's letter, and he furthered the proposition by supplying the Partisan with an engineer officer and ten mechanics, specialists equipped with the skill and tools for such work, to make sure complete destruction of the bridge and trestle would be accomplished. But he added at the same time the first complication: he proposed that the expedition be extended to include an attack on the small force at Beverly, estimated at 400 men, and that Jenkins' cavalry be sent through the lower Kanawha Valley to capture beef cattle from Ohio, if nothing else.

As the next leg of the development unfolded, McNeill handed Grumble Jones a letter from Seddon asking him to supply a portion of the force necessary to make the raid. The project, it was explained, "has long engaged the attention and special interest of the President." ³

At the same time General Lee, who had been informed of the move by letter, answered that he approved of the undertaking, but would be unable to supply any part of the troops because he was expecting Hooker's army to move against him as soon as the roads would permit. He suggested instead that the men be obtained from Sam Jones, and wrote immediately to encourage this.

Sam Jones now gave the growing snowball another push. He directed Colonel John McCausland, commanding at Princeton, to strike toward Fayetteville, and General John Echols, at Narrows, to send a part of his cavalry toward Raleigh Court House, both as diversions to protect Jenkins. The plan of a stealthy, lightning stroke against Cheat bridge was moving thus farther and farther into the background.

Soon there was evidence of further confusion on the part of Sam Jones. He had received a letter from Imboden discussing a raid and he assumed the reference was to McNeill's, for he could scarcely believe that there would be two expeditions starting from and for the same points. So he assumed whatever undertaking was agreed upon would be under Imboden's direction, and he cautioned this cavalry leader to be sure there was no apprehension between himself, Grumble Jones, and McNeill.

Sam Jones was thoroughly confused, it developed, and he revealed this to Grumble, explaining that Imboden apparently was planning an expedition that would embrace McNeill's. But he warned that there must necessarily be some delay and some misapprehension, because Imboden could not start as quickly as McNeill, who would be ready to move on March 22.

While confusion of plans increased, General Lee wrote Imboden that the season was at hand when the expedition should be executed and that, as soon as roads and streams would permit, it should begin. He added if all desired could not be accomplished at least the wooden bridges on the B. & O. at Oakland and Rowlesburg could be destroyed and cattle, horses, and men obtained from the region.

Next came word from Jefferson Davis. In an indorsement to one of Lee's messages, he wrote tersely that "now is the time to destroy . . . the Cheat River bridge, if possible." [4]

But snow- and rainstorms struck in the dying days of March, pushing streams out of their banks, and little meandering rivulets in the mountains bulged into angry torrents. As another setback the engineer officer Sam Jones had supplied to wreck Cheat bridge became ill with fever and a substitute had to be provided.

By this time Sam Jones was putting other thoughts together. He wrote Lee he would cooperate in any way possible with Imboden's plan of operations, now thus identified rather than in the name of McNeill, but he still thought he could, a little later in the season, make an expedition against the railroad that would bring better results. He estimated that, because of the lateness of spring and the need for grass to feed the horses, this could not take place before May 1.

But plans for an earlier raid continued. By the first week of April the starting date definitely was fixed for the fifteenth, and it was announced officially that Imboden would be in command.

Meanwhile Grumble Jones put his shoulder to the snowball and gave it an extra shove, pushing it farther away from the original goal of effectively blocking traffic on the B. & O. He proposed to General Lee that he also make a raid on the railroad, moving simultaneously with Imboden. Lee agreed: two blows at the same time would certainly increase the probabilities of success, provided both movements were "expeditious and bold" and carried out with the utmost secrecy. He also made it known that he considered the collection of cattle, horses, and provisions as important, or more so under certain contingencies, than destruction of the railroad.

Thus the move against the B. & O. went into additional tangents, loosely tied together by two common purposes. Under the new plan Jones was to take charge of the expedition against Oakland and Rowlesburg and Imboden of that against Beverly and Grafton. The major objective would be one of foraging rather than destruction, hinting that Lee, even at that early date, had in mind supplying the Confederate army so it would be in position to act offensively, and he may even then have been thinking of a trek in the direction of Gettysburg.

So McNeill's initial idea—the surprise-tinted strike of fast-moving horsemen—was abandoned for a multipronged invasion intended primarily to bring back food and horses for the hungry Rebels.

The last orders went out and the hordes of gray-clad fighters got ready to move—on the fifteenth. Then, the day before the expedition was to begin, Lee upset the schedule by wiring Grumble Jones that Union cavalry was moving on him from the east. This temporarily put a stop to plans, until Jeb Stuart could block the Federals near Culpeper.

Finally, on the twentieth of April, two months after McNeill first had voiced his proposal, the raid into West Virginia got under way. Instead of 600 dashing horsemen, it was executed by better than 7000 infantry and cavalry troops, weighted down by wagons and other factors necessary to the moving of a large force.

By the middle of May the campaign had ended and both Jones and Imboden were back. They had had remarkable success foraging, but the Cheat River bridge still towered on its stanchions, ready to convey the trains of the B. & O. across the giant gorge it spanned. And that was what it was doing the day after the raiders returned, for the damage to the railroad was immediately repaired.[5] Work crews followed close on the heels of the Rebels, throwing up in a matter of hours spans that in peacetime would have kept builders busy for weeks or months.

The march performed during this raid, which stretched over the period of a month, was an example of human endurance. Jones, for instance, moved his troops in thirty days over 700 miles of rough and sterile country, most of the time on half-rations. During fourteen of the first twenty days rain fell, and the roads became so deep in mud it took nine hours to traverse two miles. On Cheat Mountain, snow was eighteen to twenty inches deep, and there the men had to face a pelting sleet storm.

As they marched into the northwest, they forced the enemy to destroy stores and flee from Beverly, Buckhannon, Weston, Bulltown, Suttonsville, and Big Birch. On reaching the railroad at Fairmont, Jones moved to the east and Imboden to the west, burning and blasting and foraging. Along the miles of track between Oakland and a point thirty miles beyond Fairmont, they destroyed every bridge of any importance except two. Jones, summarizing his efforts, reported that he set fire to sixteen railroad bridges, 150,000 barrels of oil, and a large number of boats, tanks, and barrels, and wrecked many locomotives and a tunnel. One span demolished was 600 feet long. It had taken two years to build, at a cost of half a million dollars. Also burned was the library of West Virginia's governor, Francis Pierpont, "in retaliation for a like act on the part of the ambitious little man." [6]

Of this vast destruction the part best remembered by the soldiers in afteryears was the burning of the kerosene oil, which some of them in letters home spelled "caracene." Jasper Hawse, a Virginia cavalryman, termed the scene "beyond description." [7] He remembered the great noises as the oil drums exploded, and likened them to those of the heaviest artillery. "The river was soon covered with oil and the maddened flames leaped from boat to boat until for miles it was indeed a river of fire," he said. ". . . As the darkness settled, the scene became more awfully grand, for by this time the wooden barrels, boats and first tanks containing the oil had burned away, and the flames had spread until the very elements seemed one vast sheet of flames, the mighty roaring of which could be heard for miles, resembling the roar of distant thunder or the rushing of mighty winds or water in the distance."

But the bridge over Cheat River, during this time, never felt the tremor of even a blasting cap. Blame lay with Jones and his subordinates. Grumble divided his command and made attacks on the span from two directions, but each was poorly executed and futile, and he hesitated to renew them "without the hope of surprise," the element McNeill had counted on heaviest to make his grand idea a success.

Back with them Jones and Imboden brought more than 700 prisoners, 3000 head of cattle, and 1200 horses, some of the animals acquired at a total price of 300,000 dollars less than they would have cost inside Confederate lines. There were wagons, arms, grain, and flour. Two mills had been impressed by Imboden and run day and night.

In accomplishing the raid they had lost between them forty-six men, killed, wounded, and sick. Rare was the undertaking of such proportions that had so few casualties.

McNeill cooperated throughout the entire campaign, and so did Lige White. Both led their commands on successful components of the expedition, yet only as a part of a major, over-all raid that strived to do by force what McNeill had wanted to do by stealth.

The whipping boy on the Union side for this expedition was Robert C. Schenck, commanding at Baltimore. Nesting in his desk after it was all over was a caustic message from Halleck: "The enemy's raid is variously estimated at from 1,500 to 4,000. You have 45,000 under your command. If you cannot concentrate enough to meet the enemy, it does not argue well for your military dispositions."[8]

Jones and Imboden brought their raiders back toward their old camps to find that activities closer to Washington had been at a peak. A great battle had been fought in the dense growth around Chancellorsville, and Mosby, the guerrilla leader, was cutting wide swaths, building his reputation as an independent, increasing his fame.

After Mosby's capture of Stoughton a concerted effort was made to catch him, a goal that was to be sought for the remainder of the war. Scarcely had the youthful brigadier general been snaked away from Fairfax before the Yankees were setting traps to snare the Rebel Ranger. In executing what appeared to be the major of these, they sent out wagons on an expedition that was to have all the earmarks of a simple foraging roundup. Trotting along with them went an escort of cavalry, just small enough to invite attack by the Partisans, for hiding in each vehicle was a squad of the

Pennsylvania Bucktails, all armed with powerful rifles. But the trick failed to work, because the guerrillas, in chasing the cavalry back upon the caravan a short while after it started out, became suspicious and retreated before they got too close. Foraging was usually done in open wagons, they knew.[9]

At this period Mosby's activities were confined to Fairfax County. One pleasant March night he struck at Herndon Station—with the aid of citizens, the Federals charged—and carried off twenty-five prisoners, including a major, captain, and two lieutenants. Before the week was out, he and his growing band appeared suddenly at Chantilly, were chased into a patch of woods, and there turned upon the enemy with complete success, routing their pursuers, killing and wounding a number and capturing thirty-six men. A few days later, near Dranesville, the Rangers were surprised at a farm where they had spent the night, and again, in a spirited fight, the tide was turned in their favor. They killed and wounded twenty-five, including three officers, and captured eighty-two, with horses, arms, and equipment.

The effect of these stinging affairs along the Union outposts was to draw more and more attention to Mosby. Scouts frequently were sent in various directions to capture him.[10] Officers most responsible for Mosby's successes were threatened with court-martial. And the clamor grew louder for the raiders to be driven out of the neighborhood. In desperation the Federals at last turned their vengeance upon the private citizen. Since the Partisan subsisted his men on the countryside, scattering them between fights and calling them together by prearranged signal, people living in the neighborhood of his operations were blamed generally for enabling the Rangers to elude capture. At one period punishment meted out to families at Middleburg was so drastic that they petitioned Mosby to move elsewhere. But this sentiment soon changed, for the damage he was inflicting upon the enemy in time became obvious and he developed into quite a favorite among Southern sympathizers.[11] He wrote Stuart about the changed sentiment and added that he thought it "the universal desire here for me to remain."[12]

Because of his constant hammering and his repeated success, more and more praise was heaped upon Mosby in Confederate circles. Lee was lavish in commending him in correspondence with Jefferson Davis, and urged that he be promoted. Shortly afterward Jeb Stuart was able to notify the Partisan that his promotion at last had come through and that he was now a major. In the same letter he instructed the raider to organize his command and to avoid calling his men Partisan Rangers, explaining that this term was in bad repute, but it was advice that Mosby ignored completely.[13] He liked the term himself. It had attraction to the average soldier, and he knew it would draw him recruits faster than would "Mosby's Regulars," the substitute Stuart suggested.

The guerrillas now were facing their two busiest years. The last great offensive of the Confederate army, desperation personified, was in the making, and badly needed was the help of the little independent bands. It was known in the Rebel high command that the Federals had reopened the Orange and Alexandria Railroad as far as Warrenton Junction, but it had not been learned for what purpose, so Stuart appealed to Mosby. He asked him to wreck a train, thus interrupting operation of the line, and to find out if possible whether Hooker, who had succeeded Burnside, was moving troops in the direction of Centreville.

Mosby made his plans accordingly, and on an early May morning he trotted with his band into Warrenton. There he drew rein but only to stop briefly, for he was headed toward the railroad.

That day to the east, around Chancellorsville, there was activity, and the graveyard whistle of heavy guns was in the air. For days the movement among Federal troops in the Washington area had been toward Fredericksburg and the big battle "Fightin' Joe" Hooker, he of florid complexion, was said to be getting ready to launch. All day in sun or rain they marched, and at night when they came to rivers too deep to wade, they went across on thick planks laid from pier to pier, and in so doing made an imposing scene. Men slogged down muddy roads and paths leading to the streams, and at their banks they walked gingerly along boards laid end to end, moved out, steadied and balanced, with now and then an exception, and then, closing up the gaps made by these mishaps, they kept on in an endless chain, their figures ghostly apparitions in the flickering lights of blazing pine knots. These torches were placed where they would throw the broadest reflection over the great caravan of humanity moving in their orbit, over men whose shoulders were stooped with heavy packs and over the boiling, seething water rushing wildly along in gurgling turmoil among the rocks below. And finally came the battle, another of fearful carnage, of endless firing, of wood fires at night, of baked bodies sought out by burial parties busily turning them over to see if some unburned rag beneath might identify the army with which they had fought.

One person on hand as a witness to what was happening within a few miles of Washington at this time was George Grenville Benedict, junior editor of the Burlington *Free Press,* he who had written so religiously to his newspaper of experiences on guard duty around Centreville.[14] The Twelfth Vermont Volunteers, the regiment whose activities George was most interested in recording, was ordered to guard the Orange & Alexandria at Warrenton Junction, and on the fateful morning of May 3, at a time when Stonewall Jackson, shot mistakenly by his own men, lay dying at Chancellorsville, the young editor climbed aboard the engine of a supply train at Union Mills and set out to pay the Vermonters a visit. Past the fields of Manassas, cross-lined with rifle pits and dotted by earthworks, moved the train, picking its way over rails torn up and bent by the Rebels the previous summer and now "straightened after a fashion" and relaid. On each side of the tracks was strewn the destruction of war—burned remains of freight cars and battered, shot-riddled hulks of powerful locomotives, lying as still as dead buffaloes.

It was an experience for Benedict. Past Bristoe the engine on which he was riding rocked and swayed, facing into the open country toward Warrenton Junction, and then all at once those aboard it saw a figure on horseback galloping madly toward them along the tracks. The engineer applied his brakes and waited for the approach of this rider who obviously had motive for his speed. He was almost upon them before he drew rein, babbling excitedly, and it was with some difficulty they were able to make out from his jumbled words that he was the telegraph operator from the Junction, now in the hands of Rebel cavalry, he said.

Everybody except the telegraph operator got aboard and the train rocked on to Catlett's, where there was a different story. People there reported Rebel cavalry had attacked at the Junction, but Federal troops soon rushed in and drove them away. Thus reassured, the engineer was waved ahead.

A few minutes later, as the train neared Warrenton Junction, those aboard could see several soldiers in blue uniforms gathered around the lone building at that point, and scattered over the surrounding area were the bodies of a dozen or more horses. Leaping from the train, Benedict ran toward the assemblage, but he had taken scarcely twenty steps before he came upon the body of a dead

Confederate, stretched out, face upward, in coat of rusty brown and pantaloons of butternut. A few minutes later he was shown papers taken from the Rebel's pocket. Some of them were signed by General Lee, and they identified the victim as Templeton, one of Stonewall Jackson's best scouts, and revealed he had been in Washington within the last two days.[15] Nearer the building, the editor saw seventeen wounded Southerners of all ages. They lay in their own blood, some with bullet wounds, some with saber cuts, for the skirmish had taken place only a short while earlier and there had not been time to attend to them. Off to one side, well guarded, was a small group of prisoners.

Benedict walked toward the building, passing the body of a Federal cavalryman covered by a blanket. Inside on the floor of the house lay other wounded, receiving treatment from a surgeon.

It was a story easily told. Mosby, as planned, had attacked and surprised the Union guard stationed at Warrenton Junction and driven them into the building. When they refused to surrender, he turned to an unusual ruse, smoking them out by burning hay at the lower windows, and just as they hung out the white flag to keep from suffocating, the Fifth New York Cavalry, camped nearby, rushed up to investigate the disturbance and caught the Rangers at a disadvantage. The result was one of the worst repulses of Mosby's career.

Stonewall Jackson's death was not alone the aftermath of the great battle at Chancellorsville, another Confederate victory. Days following were like the closing moments of a horrible dream. Wounded men by the boatload were brought into Washington, followed by the prisoners and eventually the bodies of some of the dead. Among the captives was J. C. Birdson of Company B, Twelfth Virginia Infantry. He arrived the Sunday after his capture and was marched from the wharf to a police station. There he stood in line to be enrolled by name, regiment, and company. Directly behind him were three strangers who said they were from Company H of the Thirteenth Virginia Cavalry. Birdson had relatives in that company and he had visited them so often he was positive he could identify just about every person in it. But not these three. He waited his chance and finally drew a member of the trio to the side.

"Look," said Birdson, cautiously lowering his voice, "you're not from Company H of the 13th."

"Why do you say that?"

"Because I could identify every person in that company. Where're you from?"

The man looked around to make sure he would not be overheard. Then he whispered: "Mosby, but we can't let the Yankees know it. They'd skin us alive." [16]

Almost all at once, as the fear of these prisoners indicated, the Union army had a new game: catch Mosby. Up and down the line, after the attack at Warrenton Junction, this ambition spread. Catch Mosby, dead or alive! Blue cavalrymen barricaded in the building at the station had had a chance to watch the little raider, his plume waving wickedly as he dashed about directing the Rangers, and they told what he looked like. Milroy especially wanted the independent leader out of the way, for, alarmist that he was, he had heard of Stoughton's fate and he didn't want such an ignominious capture happening to himself. And while those playing this game were at it, 'twas agreed, they might as well capture White and McNeill, thereby setting themselves up for promotion. Gilmor, the other Partisan chief the North heard most about, was again on the loose, an exchanged prisoner, and now was down in Richmond talking about organizing a new command for independent service. [17] In time he could become an object of search also.

Inspired by this campaign to wipe out the guerrilla leaders, two ambitious lieutenants of the Sixty-seventh Pennsylvania came up with an idea they were confident would bring one member of this foursome into the bag. Mosby had been seen of late in the neighborhood of Upperville, and there they would set their trap. Several companies, both cavalry and infantry, were assigned for their use, and off they went. At Berry's Ferry the foot soldiers crossed the Shenandoah River by skiff, and then they all headed for Upperville, the plan well worked out in their minds: ahead would ride the cavalry to invite pursuit by the Rebel irregulars, who would be drawn back along the road to a point where the infantrymen lying in concealment could pour a heavy fire upon them from ambush.

The scheme seemed to work well at the start. Near Upperville, Confederate guerrillas began to appear out of the bushes, and before long there were enough on hand to organize a pursuit. It started back along the road, and as it began one of the Union horsemen dashed on ahead to give the Federal infantry notice to get into the bushes.

Quickly the stage was set. Into the undergrowth disappeared the riflemen, their hearts in their throats, for wild tales were being told about the horrors awaiting the Yankees captured by these Rebel ruffians they were lying in wait to murder. They swallowed hard and gripped their rifles and, before long, they could hear the horsemen coming. There was noise and confusion and shooting on the highway, the thunder of many hoofs, and the cries of pursuers and pursued. The ambushers nearest the front peeped out and saw great clouds of dust, and they waited no longer to pull their triggers. The first shots brought a barrage, and the slaughter was sufficient to go in the records. The only trouble was that the riders the riflemen were killing were their own cavalry, for the pursuers were not creating the particular clouds of dust into which the bullets were poured.

It was a massacre. Some of the Blue cavalry were dead on the scene. Some died the next day. "That more were not killed," wrote William H. Beach, scribe for the First New York Cavalry, "was due to the wild, excited firing of the infantry." [18]

Among the wounded were the two ambitious lieutenants. They recovered, but one of the last victims to die was James I. Gleeson of Company B, a general favorite. He was buried two days later with impressive ceremony, and it was recorded that his good mare Bess followed her dead master to his grave, seeming to mourn as sincerely as his comrades.

CHAPTER 4

May 1–July 5, 1863

YANKEES CAN
BUSHWHACK TOO

As May advanced, Milroy sent a message to Schenck at Baltimore that was highly significant. One sentence of it read: "I can hear nothing that is going on east, west, or south." Other Union leaders might have wired the same statement with as much reason, for the plans of the Confederacy were thickly shrouded in mystery. Everyone suspected that "Marse Robert," the aggressive Rebel leader, was building up for an offensive, yet there was great uncertainty as to where the action would come now that Hooker had been set back on his heels at Chancellorsville.

Whether Milroy knew it or not, things were happening in widely scattered areas, all of more or less importance, and, when officially reported, the next step would be to determine whether they were for screening purposes or otherwise. The Jones-Imboden raid in West Virginia posed many questions, and nearer Washington, Mosby was spreading woe in broken doses. One day he burned two bridges on the Orange and Alexandria Railroad, took some prisoners, and tore up the track, causing a train to derail. To the Federals this was plain, cussed guerrilla warfare, and by official report John Singleton was set down as a rascal of the first order. From headquarters came word that no punches were to be pulled in getting rid of these "bushwhackers . . . who operate on the right of and within our

172

lines," all of whom were to be "put out of the way—no matter how, so they are gotten rid of." [1]

Stung and embarrassed by this enemy depredation so close to the Union capital, there was accordingly greater concentration on the idea of catching the Partisans. In a few days Schenck was able to notify the news-seeking Milroy that Mosby was in Loudoun County plundering and impressing citizens, and directed that a force be ordered out from Berryville to intercept the Rebels. Promptly a detachment from the First New York Cavalry, under the veteran William H. Boyd, much experienced at chasing guerrillas, was dispatched to the area. Near Upperville, Boyd spied a force of Rangers in the distance and tried a flanking movement that failed. Then he charged, with no better success, for the raiders turned tail and fled. And as the chase developed into a full-fledged affair, one of the Confederates, mounted on a gray horse whose speed seemed miraculous to the New Yorkers, stayed far behind the others to get a few shots at the pursuers. Several times he repeated this daring act, killing a sergeant's horse and wounding Private Patrick Donnelly of Company C so badly that he had to be left at a nearby home. And in the next few days, after his companies had returned to camp, Donnelly was visited by Mosby and treated with such kindness that the convalescent took up residence in the neighborhood after the war.

The experience growing out of the chase near Upperville that spring day convinced the Federals under Boyd's command that Mosby was a dangerous man in the field. One who acquired that opinion was William H. Beach, later to chronicle the army days of the New York regiment, and it was a conviction he never changed, though he did at a later date alter his estimate of the irregular leader as a private citizen. This came about when he met Mosby as an invited guest at a banquet given by the Wisconsin Commandery of the Loyal Legion and was surprised to find him "a quiet, mild-mannered gentleman." [2]

Depredations of guerrillas continued. Near the end of May the Federals were led to believe that the Confederates were concentrating cavalry at Culpeper, presumably for the purpose of a raid into Maryland, but that was as much as they knew. Mosby at the time was known to have established pickets near Catlett Station, and Union infantry on duty there reported hearing a continual sound as of wagons or artillery moving toward Bristoe. Of further concern was a message from Lee urging Imboden in the mountains of the northwest to move his command east by easy marches and to have it ready for active operations as soon as possible.

One day Mosby struck and destroyed a train at Catlett Station, using a piece of artillery in the attack. This was a type of weapon not customarily employed by fighters whose success depended on their ability to strike and flee. But no matter how illogical it might sound, it very definitely was true: the gun was the proof, for it had been captured.

The incident was a live topic at Fairfax Court House the following day. There, while soldiers talked, the sun glistened on the artillery piece. It was a brass mountain howitzer—a twelve pounder, and it had been taken by the Rebels at Ball's Bluff in '61. Now it was back in Union hands! When brought in from Catlett's, it was placed with its limber directly in front of the cavalry headquarters of Federal General Julius Stahel, a personable Frenchman whose favorite pastime was talking with the ladies about mutual acquaintances in Paris. This officer was praised officially for recapture of the gun, a feat expected to be followed by "yet more gratifying achievements." [3]

There was discussion of the gun at Fairfax, and there was even more of it around the camp of the Seventh Michigan Cavalry, guarding the bridge across Kettle Run two miles north of the spot where the raid had taken place. One of those most interested was E. R. Havens.[4] It was his lot to have had a hand in developments the night before the gun's capture that indicated something was about to happen. As sergeant of the camp guard he had gone on duty at twilight, posted his last picket, and was on his way to the reserve when he heard a shot from the sentinel just stationed. He hastened back to investigate and was informed that two men on horseback had approached and, on being hailed, had ridden away, drawing the fire. While this information still was being poured into his ears, another shot sounded from the next picket. Havens rushed that way and was told the same story, and before this explanation was completed a third shot rang out. The sergeant hurried on to the scene of this newest alarm. There the picket said he had wounded one of the men, was positive of it, because he had seen the victim carried away on the saddle of his companion.

At 1:00 A.M. the sergeant was relieved, slept a few hours, and came back on duty at dawn. While posting pickets around 7:30 A.M., the telegraph line running south was cut, but this was not known to him until later.[5] So far as it was his knowledge at the moment, there had been no aftermath from the visit by the horsemen who had heckled his pickets. But he was both worried and puzzled. Why should two horsemen advance upon sentinels around a camp—except to gain information? And for what purpose? He was determined to find out.

Carefully he went over the ground, searching for tracks left by the intruders. He was thus engaged shortly afterward when he was pleased to see the regular track patrol coming. Sight of this precautionary detail calmed the sergeant's fears, for he knew it would as usual examine every foot of the rails for evidence of tampering. But he continued with his own search, realizing there may have been other reasons beside damage to the railroad that lured the intruders.

Within an hour a train whistled in the distance. In a few minutes it rolled into view, an engine pulling ten cars loaded with supplies and headed for Bealeton and the Federal troops along the Rappahannock. Havens was still looking for tracks when the locomotive rumbled past and chugged away southward, but, bowing to temptation, he straightened and watched the picturesque scene it made as it rolled along in the morning sun, moving downgrade toward a patch of woods a mile or so to the south. The time was closing on nine o'clock.

The sergeant kept watching, fascinated by the roaring giant of the rails. He was still staring when it entered the woods, its stream of smoke dropping lower and spreading out and enveloping the top of the string of cars, and then he saw the locomotive swerve sharply and the entire train lose its regularity and come to a halt in jumbled confusion. A spurt of smoke burst from the trees at the side, and the roar of a heavy gun echoed over the countryside. It was the prelude to an evacuation. Like ants from a hill, men poured out of the cars and took to the undergrowth and trees, among them Lieutenant Hartshorne and the thirty men from the Fifteenth Vermont Regiment stationed on board as a guard. The sergeant made mental note of what a stirring scene it was to witness, a scene both gripping and terrifying, and it took on a tone of helplessness for the Michiganders at Kettle Run shortly afterward when flames began to rise from the loaded cars and they realized they could not reach them in time to prevent complete destruction.

Of those on board the ten-car special, only the fireman got advance warning they were rushing into trouble. A wire stretching into the trees from a rail caught his attention just as the train entered the woods, and a moment later he saw the wire become taut and the rail jerk out of position, an action that would cause historians to say the rail was "adroitly displaced." But the locomotive was so close upon it by then that there was no chance to warn the engineer. A moment later the fireman was lying in the wreckage badly injured.

Scarcely had the train come to a standstill before a great noise sounded from the trees and a ball from the little mountain howitzer plowed through the boiler of the engine. It was then that the guard and other men on board fled to the woods on the opposite side, there to stare in panic while the Rebels picked over the rich stores intended for the Union army before setting fire to the lot, train and all. After that they rode away, dragging their little gun and spilling fresh shad and sole leather from their saddles, and behind them Federal troops in the neighborhood—from the Fifth New York, First Vermont, and Seventh Michigan—galloped hard in pursuit. They assumed Mosby had 200 men, but this estimate he later derided, maintaining he had but forty.[6]

The pursuit ended at the head of a lane bordered by a high fence. There the raiders whirled the howitzer about and fired a charge of grape. It went into the ranks of the Fifth New York and was followed by hand-to-hand fighting, and then came charges and countercharges, with men falling on each side. As the advantage passed back and forth along the lane, the artillery piece spat out additional loads of death until its limber was empty. By this time Union reinforcements had appeared, and when they rode into view, Mosby blew a shrill blast on a little whistle he carried for that purpose, and the Rangers scattered in all directions as was their custom when overpowered. Behind them they left several of their best fighters, some wounded, some dead, among the latter Bradford Smith Hoskins, a British devotee to the profession of arms, former captain in the Forty-fourth Royal Infantry and holder of the Crimean Medal. He had carried the indorsement of Jeb Stuart.

Four days later the Gettysburg campaign got under way, and the clouds of dust rising above the highways told Union scouts positively that Lee was advancing north. Soon both armies were in motion along parallel lines, the Confederates west of the Blue Ridge, the Federals east of it. Hooker's army was inside the arc formed by the route Lee had chosen and thus had the shorter distance to travel, consequently finding it easy to pace the enemy. It came up by way of Fairfax and Centreville, and near the latter place it passed over the area along the Bull Run that had served as a stage for two great battles. Plenty of evidence of the terrible conflicts was still visible. Unexploded shells, solid shot, broken muskets, remains of gun carriages, graves, and bones of unburied heroes told their stories. Somewhere amidst the marching column a human skull came into play and was kicked along by the horses. "No one seems to care much about it," recorded one of the eyewitnesses, "for worse sights have so often been seen before." [7] And worse sights would be seen at the little Pennsylvania town toward which they were heading.

Action now spread to many areas, and there was alarm along the Washington outposts. A detail from the Federal reserve on the Frying Pan Road was called out to relieve the picket line. It was 3:00 A.M. As it rode through the dark, its members, half-awake and yawning stupidly, were overtaken by other horsemen—in blue, it was assumed. No one seemed in a hurry; no one was alarmed; no one was belligerent. There was no hail, no challenge, no suspicion by the Unionists. Everybody forged along, bent over their horses, and before the Federals were conscious of what it was all about they were prisoners of Mosby. At Fairfax Court House at dawn the incident was reported to Stahel, and he galloped madly to the scene, there to stop and sit and stare as though he expected his reservists to spring free out of the ground.

Miles away in West Virginia, McNeill's Rangers came together for a spurt of activity designed as a protective screen for the Confederate left flank. They drove a Federal force out of Romney, western gateway to the Valley via Winchester, and held it for more than a week until forced by the enemy in superior numbers to take to the mountains.

But most of the attention attracted to the independents at this time was drawn by the activity of Mosby. Villain that he was to the North, he seemed to be raiding around the clock, creating diversions of all sorts, obviously to help Lee's army get across the Potomac. White was helping, too, fighting as a regular and leading his "Comanches" under their official indentification as the Thirty-fifth Battalion of Virginia Cavalry. At the battle of Brandy Station

177

his command fought as a part of Stuart's troops, fought well and lost ninety men, and then it was transferred to Ewell's Second Corps, pushing toward Pennsylvania. Harry Gilmor also was with Ewell. Promoted major and given authority at Richmond to organize a new battalion for independent service, he was back in trim now, riding hard and bothered by the memory of the gallant young John Pelham, artillerist *par excellence,* whose end he had helped bring by dropping him, wounded, over the neck of a horse where accelerated bleeding speeded his death.[8]

June days are lovely days in Virginia, more attuned to love-making and play on the lawn, to swimming-hole frolics and siestas beside the fishing tackle, than to anything approaching war. They mark the beginning of the season when minds turn to the lighter side of life, when dreams are of the sweet-tasting roasting ears and the luscious melons, which come in midsummer from the gardens. This was the atmosphere to which many of the men fighting in Lee's army were accustomed, Mosby's Rangers included. And the Partisans, like others as the trek northward swung into full speed, laid aside these memories and turned to the more serious art of armed defense.

Without letup Mosby was jumping about from here to there. One day he attacked a wagon train moving from Winchester and carried off men and horses. Another, he skirmished, so reports said, with the First New York Cavalry at Salem,[9] and lost his private saddle horse. But there was more to the story than appeared in official records, and "skirmished" was not exactly the word for what had taken place.[10] The indefatigable Captain William H. Boyd, it developed, had been on Mosby's trail again. This time he was called out after news of the wagon-train attack reached headquarters, and he was told to take a scouting party and find the guerrilla leader heckling Federal operations. As advised, the captain started on a meandering course that extended over a wide area, and there was much door-knocking and disturbance of private citizens as he went along. At Salem the trail got hot. Folks said the Partisan was staying at the James H. Hathaway home a few miles from town and that his wife was there with him.[11]

This information was obtained by Boyd late one evening. He and his party had been riding hard all day, but fatigue was not allowed to dictate in this instance. He immediately set out for the Hathaway home, wending his way recklessly through the dark and arriving after midnight. Surrounding the place, his soldiers searched every room, but the best they could find was a warm bed, parts of the raider's uniform, and his wife, very much distressed. Further search availed nothing, and the Unionists finally rode away, taking with them the proprietor of the dwelling, an aged man, and one of the Partisan leader's favorite horses, which they promptly christened "Lady Mosby." Some time after they had gone, the little cavalryman, wearing boots and underwear, swung in from the limb of a tree near a window of his bedchamber and felt again for his warm couch.[12]

On another day Mosby had a rendezvous with Stuart, and the following morning he brought his men together at Rector's Cross Roads.[13] There he organized them into the Forty-third Battalion of Partisan Rangers. When the voice vote for officers was over, a formality at best, for Mosby previously had chosen the candidates and let it be known he wanted them elected, he headed toward Maryland to surprise two Union companies stationed at Seneca.

The Federals got numerous reports of Mosby's junket across the Potomac. He had intended to attack at night, but his guide got lost and delayed the arrival until morning. Even at that it was successful. The camp was routed and burned.

Hooker heard of the raid, and so did official Washington, and the wires were kept busy sending messages about the best way to intercept the Rangers on their return. Hooker wanted the entire country beyond the Bull Run Mountains toward Middleburg scouted and watched. In compliance, Stahel at Fairfax sent out three different parties to scour the area, and they rode night and day, with orders to search all houses for arms and ammunition, to arrest all men known to be disloyal, and to take all horses that might be used by guerrillas. Back at headquarters two days later, they were able to tell that Mosby had disbanded at a certain hour and at a certain place; furthermore, that he had taken no artillery with him across the Potomac. But that was it; they had been unable to overtake or intercept him. And in their many miles of riding over the countryside only a few prisoners had been rounded up. One of these was captured while he awaited his turn in a Middleburg barbershop, and it was not learned until later that he was Captain James William Foster, Mosby's top-ranking officer, just elected, and that the white horse standing at the tie rack in front of the tonsorial establishment was his reward for bravery displayed at Seneca.

In a message to headquarters Alfred Pleasanton, Union cavalry leader, suddenly came forward with a new idea for disposing of Mosby. His plan was embraced in an inquiry as to how much of a bribe Hooker could stand to get the raider's services. "There is a chance for him," explained Pleasanton, "and just now he could do valuable service in the way of information as well as humbugging the enemy." [14]

Just where the cavalry general got his idea that Mosby could be bribed was not recorded in a manner to be understood by posterity. At any rate, the reply he got was that he should not hesitate as to the matter of money, but should use his own judgment and do precisely what he thought best for the public interest. So far as recorded history is concerned, there the matter seems to have ended. It was never made clear, either in Union or Confederate records, how far Pleasanton proceeded with his plan of bribing Mosby and with what reaction it was received by the Partisans, even if he was ever approached. Twelve days after the bribe first was proposed, Pleasanton wrote headquarters: "I shall try Mosby tomorrow." No explanation followed, and it is thus questionable whether "try" in this instance referred to an attempt to bribe or to a planned attack on Mosby. The raider had recently returned from his raid on the camp at Seneca and was in the general vicinity of Middleburg, while Pleasanton was a short distance away at Aldie.

For the sake of the record it would not have seemed a good time to broach such a matter to Mosby, if there was ever such a time. At the moment his star was rising. Almost at will he rode in and out of Hooker's army, gaining information that he daily passed on to the Confederates. One evening at a private residence near Aldie he happened upon a staff officer bearing dispatches from Hooker to Pleasanton and captured him. The messages thus intercepted disclosed that Hooker was looking to the gap through the mountains at Aldie with solicitude, that Pleasanton was occupying the place, and that a reconnaissance in force toward Warrenton and Culpeper was planned. They also listed the entire number of Union divisions, thus enabling the Rebels to estimate the strength of the army marching against them. On the basis of this information Stuart abandoned an attack on Aldie with cavalry alone and was able to warn Wade Hampton at Warrenton in time for him to break up the proposed Federal reconnaissance.

When Stuart later prepared to head northward out of Virginia,

Mosby made a further contribution to history. He proposed that the Rebel cavalry chief lead his troopers on a circuit and advance into Maryland between Hooker's army and Washington, thus causing great consternation among the Union high command. Like the ride around McClellan near Richmond the preceding summer, it was an idea that appealed to Stuart. It had initiative and daring, and there was a possibility it would bring new fame to his dusty horsemen. But the bold plan backfired, providing students of the war in later generations with one of their juiciest subjects of discussion. This turn came when Stuart delayed long enough to capture a supply train and thus was late arriving at Gettysburg, depriving Lee of the services of his cavalry at a time when they were sorely needed.[15]

As troubled as he was with the major problems of directing the Fifth Corps, dignified Major General George G. Meade, in a few days to take over as commander of the Army of the Potomac, was as anxious as anyone on the Federal side to intercept Mosby. "I came near catching our friend Mosby this morning," he wrote General O. O. Howard, Eleventh Corps chief, as they neared the Potomac. He explained that he had gained reliable intelligence that the Partisan would pass a certain place at sunrise and that he sent forty men on horses and 100 on foot to ambush him. The outcome Meade succinctly recounted in his letter: "Sure enough, Mr. Mosby, together with 30 of his followers, made their appearance before sunrise, but, I regret to say, their exit also, from what I can learn, through the fault both of foot and horse. It appears Mosby saw the cavalry, and immediately charged them. They ran (that is, my horses) toward the infantry, posted behind a fence. The infantry, instead of rising and deliberately delivering their fire, fired lying on the ground; did not hit a Rebel, who immediately scattered and dispersed, and thus the prettiest chance in the world to dispose of Mr. Mosby was lost." [16]

Guerrillas seemed to be everywhere as the Blue troops moved north, and official reports made ample note of it. Hooker wired General Dan Tyler the empty promise that he would "take this guerrilla cavalry in hand shortly." [17] Much more upset over their activities, Major General Daniel Butterfield, chief of staff for the Army of the Potomac, prescribed a drastic formula for their treatment, one that took no heed of the interpretation of international warfare supplied by Dr. Francis Lieber. "Catch and kill guerrillas, then try them, will be a good method of treating them," he wrote the commanding officer of the Fifth Corps.[18]

Flaunting this prescription, some of Mosby's men captured General Howard's aide-de-camp and an orderly. The two Unionists had started for headquarters from their camp at two o'clock one afternoon, and Howard wired Butterfield next day that they hadn't been heard from since. Negroes living in Loudoun Valley were able to reveal what had happened to them, though, in passing on the information, they somehow got the idea that the pair were carrying dispatches from Hooker instead of Howard.

As Ewell's corps moved northward, White's battalion was permitted to take the lead, shifting its operations back into the category of border warfare, at a time when it was riding through country with which it was thoroughly familiar. One night it attacked simultaneously Means' Loudoun Rangers at Point of Rocks and Cole's cavalry at Catoctin Station and then lay in wait for a supply train. Its luck was of the best. In a few minutes a locomotive could be heard chugging along from Harpers Ferry, headed for Baltimore with twenty-two cars, most of them loaded with produce in transit away from the path of the Rebel army. White's troopers acted speedily. After flagging down the engineer they dumped into each car shovelfuls of red-hot coals from a furnace at Point of Rocks, and in short order the entire train was a burning ruin.

White was to play a prominent role in this newest campaign of the Confederates. His battalion was the first to ride into Hanover. It also was the first to reach Gettysburg, after it had driven off the Twenty-sixth Pennsylvania Militia. And when Lee's defeated army turned back toward Virginia, it formed the rear guard and fought repeatedly against scattered Federal forces that tried to overtake the Rebels.

Out in the mountainous area to the west, McNeill's Rangers were doing their part for the South, too, and in a more practical way. Confederate General Bradley Johnson, reporting to Seddon the capture of Milroy's order book, in which he said there were orders to burn property and kill citizens, also announced that his men had seen McNeill passing down the Valley road with 740 head of sheep, 160 head of cattle, and forty horses he had taken on a junket into Pennsylvania. Back home once more, the Partisan leader destroyed the water station, blacksmith shop, woodhouse, sandhouse, and supervisor's office at Sir John's Run, the water stations at Rockwell's and Willett's Run, the trestling over the Great Cacapon River, and a number of tool houses and hand and truck cars.[19]

The report about Milroy's order book was one chapter in a saga of rough handling for its owner. In the advance on Gettysburg, Milroy was chased out of Winchester. That was after he had been advised to act with caution and to fall back "when forced." And he had spiked his guns and destroyed stores and fled in the dark hours of early morning, only to have his demoralized army shelled later in the day as it scurried toward Harpers Ferry, leaving better than a third of it along the way. That meant curtains for Milroy, the general whom the women of Winchester had so violently disliked. Scarcely had he reached a haven from the arrogant Rebels on his heels before Halleck was wiring Schenck: "Do not give General Milroy any command at Harpers Ferry. We have had enough of that sort of military genius." [20]

Perhaps fate was harsh in its treatment of Milroy: the Confederates had cut the wires between Winchester and Martinsburg just as his telegraph operator was beginning to receive an order for him to fall back at once.

In her diary Cornelia McDonald, the housewife who occasionally crossed swords with Milroy at Winchester, ignored an opportunity to rejoice. Reporting his departure, she wrote simply: "Milroy evacuated the fort during the night and stole away leaving the flag flying . . . [He] escaped alone by a byroad. Our men threaten to hang him if they catch him on account of his treatment of the people of the town." [21]

A few days later Hooker was on his way out. His separation from the command of the Army of the Potomac marked the end of a chain of curt telegrams between Lincoln and himself. At the start of the campaign the President advised his general not to be trapped by Lee, where he would take the risk of being entangled upon the Rappahannock River, "like an ox jumped half over a fence and liable to be torn by dogs front and rear, without a fair chance to gore one way or kick the other." [22] And then the soldier had been told by the citizen in the White House to follow Lee and to "fret him and fret him." [23] Four days later Lincoln sent another barb: "If the head of Lee's army is at Martinsburg and the tail of it on the Plank road between Fredericksburg and Chancellorsville, the animal must be very slim somewhere." [24] And to continue the wreck of good relations he questioned Hooker about a report that he had been in Washington on a particular night. That was enough for the military man. Next day he messaged Halleck that he "earnestly" requested to be relieved from his position. Almost within the hour his request was granted and Meade, courteous, gentlemanly, reserved but lacking personal magnetism, was named as his successor.

The Confederate army came back from Pennsylvania in the hot, dry days of July with a future that promised nothing. The great sally into the North had ended on a ridge where a horde of charging Virginians drove until Union cannon shot them to pieces. From the start it had been a successful move. Lee planned the offensive to draw Hooker's army away from the Fredericksburg area, where it was in an almost impregnable position, and that it did. But in Pennsylvania the Rebel concentration was slow and initiative was lacking, resulting in back-breaking defeat for the Southerners.

As the butternut troopers retraced their steps from beyond the Potomac, they left behind proof of one point that was generally unrecognized at the time: that the North when invaded would turn to irregular warfare also. This was revealed by General D. N. Couch, commanding the Department of the Susquehanna, made up largely of native militia. He told of unexpected strength—5000 men from the counties bordering the Juniata, who filled the passes leading to their homes and threw up military works. These, he said, "were an army of bushwhackers, commanded by ex-officers." [25]

CHAPTER 5

July 6–September 2, 1863

FIRE AND SWORD

THE ONLY WAY

After the fall-back from Gettysburg, the First New York Cavalry settled down for a time at Sharpsburg, Maryland, two miles from the Potomac and directly across the river from Shepherdstown, held by the Confederates. Days were hot and sultry, the lethargic, soul-sapping period of mid-July when the slightest exertion brings on a rash of sweat; so everybody in that area seemed willing, after the long jog to and from Pennsylvania, to take it easy. In this spirit the nearness of Sharpsburg and Shepherdstown made no difference, and intercourse between the two towns in time developed from a distant hail to a picket-line jamboree. Sentinels on horseback, gradually building up confidence, moved out closer to each other until they met in midstream, there to talk calmly, man to man, to swap coffee and whisky and tobacco, and maybe to exchange a newspaper or two. No one cared especially about fighting. There had been enough of that on the trek northward, and now it was time for a breather.

And so things went between the Yankees at Sharpsburg and the Rebels at Shepherdstown, all under arms, and yet behaving as peacefully as folks in a Quaker settlement. No belligerence, no shooting, no killing. Only their clothing, equipment, and habits were proof a war was in progress. So far as their politics or a division of sentiment was concerned, the Potomac alone denoted a cleft, and even that was no barrier, not even to commissioned officers. One morning it was told to incredulous Yankee listeners that Guerrilla Chief Harry Gilmor, known to carry with him on raids a blood-hound and a thick, baggy English robe so he could sleep in the woods, had swum across at the invitation of an officer friend and, before returning, had swapped yarns in relaxed conversation for nearly an hour.

In such atmosphere it was much easier for Union officers at Sharpsburg to take hold of a particular problem that gradually worked toward the forefront of their consciences. At Shepherdstown lay many Federal wounded, assembled there during the hostilities of the Gettysburg advance and now cared for by an enemy deprived of vital necessities by the North's crippling blockade. No doubt these helpless men were starving and dying from lack of proper medical attention. Why not send them aid? But first someone must go across with flag of truce and get permission from the proper Confederate officer for this to be done—for a surgeon and nurses to come with supplies of medicines and provisions. This preliminary chore finally was assigned to Captain James Hunter Stevenson, a worthy selection. He had the advantage of experience, the self-assurance of a thirty-year-old Irishman of good breeding and edu-cation, and a background of years in the army along the American frontier. Arrived in this country in 1847, he had joined the United States Dragoons and Mounted Rifles and had fought with them un-til wounded by the Indians around Jefferson Barracks, Missouri. After that the army granted him a pension, and now he was back in service, recovered and repaying the government for its kindness.

Stevenson took his assignment at Sharpsburg seriously. It was to him a mission of great responsibility, one of compassion and still one of considerable formality, in the performance of which he would go out as the official emissary of a great nation. And so, be-fore starting, he dressed himself in full regalia, a spanking-clean uniform, complete with sash, side arms, and spurs. Then, so attired, he strutted down to the river bank, a fine broth of a boy, and sat upright while two men rowed him across in a small boat. *Erin go brath!* A great day it was for the Irish.

On nearing the opposite shore with flag held high, the business-like hail of a Rebel sentinel, faithful to his post, came harshly to the Irishman's ears: "What's your business on this side?" In his best brogue Stevenson proclaimed loudly the purpose of his visit: to forward a message to the commander of the troops in the vicinity of Shepherdstown.

The burrs were plentiful in his speech, a factor that may have accounted for the picket's ensuing silence.

Stevenson spoke more deliberately: "Who's in command here?"

"There he is yonder," replied the picket, pointing to an approaching horseman.

"Who is he?"

"That's Major Gilmor."

The major rode up and dismounted on the bank directly above where the boat by this time had landed. He stood for a moment, listening to the picket's explanation, and then beckoned for the visitor to approach.

Stevenson was uncomfortable. Such a marked contrast in their dress was noticeable that he wished he had not been so particular about his own personal appearance.[1]

As the Irishman approached, Gilmor waited, right hand on the pommel of his saddle, left on the hilt of a long cavalry saber. He was dressed in gray pants, tucked into the tops of cavalry boots, a gray flannel shirt, with rolling collar, black neck scarf with flowing ends, and a light felt hat set off by a black, drooping feather. Stevenson took him to be five feet ten or more and his weight 170 to 180 pounds. His hair was light and well trimmed, and he wore a mustache of just the right size for his face and stature. Fair of skin, with color in his cheeks, the only marring feature in his countenance appeared to be a slight cast in one of his large blue eyes. "Altogether," concluded Stevenson, "I thought the horse and man, just as they stood there, would have made a spirited picture to place at the head of an account of the Confederate Partisans, or guerrillas, of the Shenandoah Valley."

When Stevenson explained the purpose of his visit, Gilmor voiced pleasure at meeting a member of the "gallant First New York Cavalry," a regiment he identified as having a good name in the Valley, and he added that he would be pleased to do any favor that lay within his power. As for the doctor and nurses, he gave his permission for them to come across, but stressed that they would not be permitted to return until after the Confederates had departed from Shepherdstown.

The Union officer, assenting to this condition, saluted and turned to re-enter the boat.

"I'd like to see the end of this war," Gilmor pleasantly threw after him as the craft pushed out into the water. "I wish it would come to a close soon and in a manner satisfactory to all. If any man says war to me after that, I'll knock him down."

Stevenson laughed his accord and waved a friendly farewell as the boat slowly swung about and headed for Maryland. The Potomac at the moment was far quieter than it had been for years.

But matters were less serene a few miles south of the river. Lee's army backed toward the Rapidan, and the Federals followed, assembling around Warrenton, where they spread out, fan-shaped, and waited to see what Lee would try next. In this situation the problem for the Northern command was to feed a horde of 100,000 men and 8000 horses, spread over an area seriously deprived of foodstuffs. In terms of logistics this meant bringing in supplies of food and feed in hundreds of carloads, on train after train, some of them lugging as much as 1200 tons. Faced with such a problem, the Union decided to abandon the Shenandoah Valley to the Rebels and to concentrate on keeping open the Orange and Alexandria Railroad south to the Rappahannock and the Manassas Gap Railroad from Manassas to White Plains.[2] This decision provided a new avenue of activity for the guerrillas.

Since returning from Gettysburg the irregulars had been more in force than ever in the past. They were constantly active, heckling and capturing supplies and interrupting communications, and their interests were scattered over a wide area, especially along the O. & A. and the B. & O. In West Virginia, McNeill had increased his force and was pooling ideas with Lee on the best methods by which to slow up the Federals in his direction. White, after Gettysburg, was permitted to remain behind on detached duty and was ready to strike along the Potomac in the territory that was familiar to him by birth. At Shepherdstown, Gilmor was busy rounding up recruits for his new command and determined to get back in the forefront of Partisan operations, and Mosby, in his glory with the broad arena between Washington and the Rappahannock as a field for his daily activities, was taking on new strength and expanding his reputation.

These leaders were relentless in their drive to worry the enemy now occupying most of northern Virginia, and their little bands bobbed up here and there in a helter-skelter pattern that no Union commander could foresee or fathom. Federal camps were raided almost nightly. One unit was gobbled up after the Partisans lay in the brush until they overheard the countersign and then, using it, relieved every picket before dashing in in force.[3] As a soldier affected by these ruses observed: "Many a man has fallen without seeing when the bullet sped; and many a party has disappeared without leaving any tidings of his fate." The way this participant saw it, the independents had things their own way, for "the almost universal sympathy of the inhabitants in their favor made every citizen their courier and every house their signal tower." [4]

George Armstrong Custer, the golden-curled officer who had been so fanatically confident of the ability of McClellan, was bothered by the guerrillas, and so was General Howard. Halleck felt their peskiness too. For five days he was unable to get word from the new chief of the Army of the Potomac, so angering him that he wanted to drive out every guerrilla and disloyal man between the Potomac, Rappahannock, and Blue Ridge.[5]

But the first problem in exterminating the guerrillas was to find them. For their purposes the countryside in which they operated was ideal, and they could complain of no want of support. On all sides, with men and women alike, was noticed an attitude of rebellion, of resentment against the Northern invasion. Even in the hills of West Virginia, by comparison a fairly peaceful area since the Jones-Imboden raid in the spring, there was turmoil. One day it was brought on by a young lass named Maggie Reed. She was found to have waded a river up to her armpits to give information to a band of Confederate guerrillas, enabling them to capture the town of Buckhannon, and her arrest followed immediately thereafter. Once in custody, she was confined under guard at the local hotel, there for a stay that she herself made temporary by spitting at passing Yankee officers from a second-floor window. In a matter of hours, because of such obnoxious behavior, she was transferred to The Atheneum at Wheeling, and on arriving at this bastille she developed into so determined a little rebel that Jailer Jones lost his patience and had her cowhided. To him and to others war brought many problems.[6]

In developing plans for reopening the Manassas Gap line, idle since the preceding year, Meade notified Quartermaster General M. C. Meigs that he wanted the railroad rebuilt from Manassas to

White Plains as soon as practicable. Next day the West Point-trained Herman Haupt, engineer in charge of military railways for the Union, made an exploratory trip over the road and found it in bad condition from grass and weeds.[7]

The following morning Haupt made another trip over the line, and this time there was trouble of a different nature. Guerrillas fired into the train and removed rails in several places, leaving numerous horse tracks along the right of way. Then and there Engineer Haupt made up his mind about certain factors, and so reported: to operate the road with security the country must be patrolled and cavalry pickets must be stationed at important points. Moreover, every citizen of suitable age for draft not in the army should be regarded with suspicion and closely watched, for, he added, "I am told that many men have been exempted from draft on condition of joining Mosby's band, who are guerrillas at night and farmers by day." [8] He decreed that trains should be run as much as possible by daylight and with guards on board, but admitted that heavy business would require some night operation, at a time when guards could afford little protection.

The O. & A. was just such a problem. One morning Train Number 1 out of Washington rolled into a trap set for it on a curve a mile and a half from Burke's Station. A rail had been taken out and horseshoes dropped over several of those left in place. When the train plowed into this obstruction and came to a halt, twelve men in uniforms variously mixed between blue and gray jumped out of the bushes and opened fire. But before their bullets could do serious damage, a detachment of the Fourth Delaware, riding on board as a guard, blazed away from the windows and, after a few shots, jumped off the train and engaged in a foot race through the woods, chuckling as they ran at the antics of one fat Rebel who "particularly distinguished himself in getting out of sight." J. H. Devereux, assistant to Haupt, summed up the outcome of the attack thusly: "The guard saved the train and its convoy, and Providence saved a smashup, which for some time would have prevented the Army of the Potomac from receiving supplies." [9] It was noted meanwhile that the Rebels themselves had "saved" a wreck by removing a rail on the inside rather than the outside of the curve, a chance selection that kept the train from rolling down a twelve-foot embankment and ending in a serious pile-up.

But minor as was this wreck, it brought a chorus of protests.

Devereux was the most concerned, observing: "It is pitiful that a handful of Rebels can be allowed the chance of so retarding the progress of our army in such a measure as an accident like this might cause." Haupt also voiced complaint, explaining that as long as these attempts to throw off trains continued there could be no security to Federal communications. He recommended that the gaps of the Blue Ridge be occupied, that the fords of streams be guarded, the country patrolled and inhabitants warned. He also had in mind searching houses and seizing arms, an extreme measure, he admitted, but added that "those who appear to be farmers during the day are the parties who injure us at night." [10]

His suggestions brought prompt action. In a matter of hours Halleck sent out notice that the numerous depredations along the O. & A. called for "prompt and exemplary" punishment.[11] Officers were ordered to arrest and confine, or put beyond Union lines, every citizen against whom there was evidence of disloyalty. People living within ten miles of the railroad also were notified that they would be held responsible in their persons and property for any damage to the road and would be impressed as laborers to repair it. "If these measures should not stop such depredations," warned Halleck, "the entire inhabitants of the district of country along the railroad will be put across the lines and their property taken for government uses."

Union Cavalry Chief Pleasanton, ordering out scouting parties in various directions, instructed them to shoot "on the spot" armed citizens found with guerrillas.[12] Headquarters circulated word that "no mercy need be shown to bushwhackers. These guerrillas must be destroyed." [13] And the Washington *Star* announced that some of "Mosby's pests," described as "citizens when in the power of our troops and thieves and secret murderers when opportunities occur," were held as prisoners and probably would be tied on cowcatchers of railroad engines "to be the first and surest sufferers in case of accidents from obstructions placed on the rails."

Early in August, Mosby appeared in the vicinity of Fairfax and Annandale, rounding up prisoners and telegraph operators and sutlers' wagons. Some of the sutlers were paroled, after which they rushed back into Washington to tell of their experiences:

They had been taken into a deep ravine, about half a mile from the road. There, surrounding them, were what seemed like sixty Partisans, all splendidly mounted and most of them uniformed in dark jackets and gray pantaloons, the latter set off by a yellow cord down the seam. They also wore gray felt hats, one side turned up and fastened with a rosette, the other crowned by a black feather. With rare exception the raiders were neat and heavily armed, and there was plenty of evidence they had been busy. Scattered about their hideaway were the remains of wagons, trunks, boxes, and other remnants of raids. They made it plain, did these guerrillas, that they meant business; so impressed of this was one sutler that he voluntarily gave up to them 1700 dollars in currency.

Disregarding the danger implied by the presence of Rebel irregulars in the neighborhood, a wagon train pulled out of Alexandria and took the Little River turnpike toward Fairfax. Near Annandale the proprietor of Gooding's Tavern, a citizen widely known as James Coyle, taunted the drivers, telling them they would not get through safely and then parrying with smugness their questions as to the source of his information. A short distance down the road, true to his prediction, the lead wagons were attacked, but Union cavalry in the neighborhood rescued them and, in consequence, an evil fate befell Mr. Coyle. The drivers of the last wagons to roll by the tavern could see his corpse lying on the floor of his own house, where he had been shot dead by vengeful teamsters who had doubled back from the intercepted vehicles.[14]

To quell this Rebel terror on the outskirts of Washington, Union scouting parties came out in profusion, beating the trails and lying in wait to ambush, but these were efforts wasted. A Federal observer at Fairfax Station soon gave word that Mosby had left, that he had departed after gaining all the information desired of the positive strength of the forces guarding the railroads.

This spree in which Mosby terrorized unguarded points in Fairfax, causing even Union officials to assume that he originally had intended raiding along the railroad and had changed his plans after encountering the sutlers, brought caustic comment from General Lee. The sage leader complimented the Partisan's boldness and good management, but berated him for using so few men and for centering his attention on wagons rather than on the enemy's communications and outposts. Damage to the railroad was what the Confederate commander wanted, and he added that the Union threat of punishing citizens on the line must be met by meting similar treatment to Federal soldiers when captured.

Lee had another complaint. Recent newspaper announcements

bared a thirty-odd-thousand-dollar sale of Yankee plunder by Mosby's men behind the lines at Charlottesville. Such details had better be attended to by someone other than the Rangers themselves, Lee advised.

His criticism went no further. Within a few days the War Department at Richmond was preparing to send Mosby a supply of percussion torpedoes for use on the O. & A. In this Jeb Stuart concurred, but with the suggestion that someone acquainted with the employment of such explosives be sent with them.

Whether Lee's comments reached Mosby or whether he ignored them, the Partisan was back in the neighborhood of Fairfax the latter part of August, this time primarily to scout along the railroad, as he revealed in his own report. But again the traffic along the highways diverted his attention. Captain Ned Gillingham of the Thirteenth New York Cavalry was one of the unfortunate Yankees who came within his net. It was the captain's lot to be sent out from Centreville with a pocketful of dispatches for Washington, and he went trailed by an escort of eight sergeants, each of whom had been granted a few hours' leave in the capital they were defending. He rode without fear, for his route lay well within Union lines and, so far as he knew, no Rebel threat had existed since Mosby's departure earlier in the month. As he galloped toward Annandale, a detachment of the Second Massachusetts Cavalry rode into view ahead of him, and he and his guard drew up for a salute and to watch the New Englanders pass.

The leader of the Massachusetts troops was not as confident as Gillingham. "Do we need fear any danger?" he asked.

"So far we have not met with any obstructions," the New Yorker consoled, making a statement very definitely beyond contradiction.

But scarcely had he proceeded 400 yards farther before a party of Mosby's horsemen fired on him and ordered a halt.

Captain Ned was a brave but naïve individual. To him gray meant Rebel and blue meant friends, and there were pieces of blue uniform visible among the men firing at him, so it was to these garments his confusion could be traced. "Hold up firing!" he shouted. "You fools, you're firing on Government troops!"

The reply made no sense to Gilly: "Surrender, you Yankee bastard!"

And it was no warning to him either, for he was a man who had to be floored with evidence before he would believe. "I can't see the joke!" he screamed and, turning to two members of his escort, ordered them to draw their sabers and follow him. In the ensuing melee, blades and pistols were freely used, and the dispatch bearers from the Thirteenth New York went to pieces before superior numbers. Their rout was most complete. For the sake of the record only by good fortune did Captain G. manage to escape, shot through the arm, and the same was true with one of the sergeants, who bore a bullet in his hip as he fled. For the moment, beyond question, Gilly's naïveté was badly shaken.[15]

Next morning Mosby left all but three of his men in the woods and went off on a scout along the railroad in search of unguarded bridges. He found three, and these he planned to burn after dark. But until then there would be nothing to do but lie in concealment. So he hurried back to his waiting command and just by chance happened to arrive at a bad moment, for it was not long before a drove of 100 enemy horses, escorted by half as many soldiers, trotted into view along the road, dangling a temptation that was too much for the wily Partisan. Ignoring the wishes of Lee, he reverted again to the capture of prizes rather than to the destruction of communications. And his action may have been justified. Here were a hundred sturdy mounts from the stables in Alexandria trotting along the open road, where it would take only a little finesse and spark-and-dangle fighting to add them to the Rebel string.

He made his dispositions quickly. Half the Rangers would dash ahead on a circuitous route and attack from the front, while he with the other half closed from the rear. Off they went, bent over their horses with excitement. Near Gooding's Tavern the enemy party was overtaken, and there in the dust and heat of late afternoon the Rebels brought new terror to half a hundred Unionists entrusted with thousands of dollars' worth of horseflesh. The rout was immediate. Soldiers in blue forsook their trust and ran to cover, there to fire at anything and anybody, and with telltale success, for the pressure on them suddenly relaxed. This came about when Mosby reeled in his saddle, steadied himself, sat momentarily as though stunned, and then turned his horse and rode out of the combat, blood pouring from his side and thigh. That was all it took to end the fight. His Rangers saw him leave, and they mistook the significance of his action and followed him, permitting all but twelve of the Federals to escape.

Word of Mosby's injury spread rapidly. It swept through the camps around Washington, and hastily organized scouting parties set out anew in quest of the reward that would be theirs if the guerrilla chief were brought in dead or alive. They rode hard while rumors gained momentum, and in a matter of hours it looked as though what they might find would be a body instead of a dangerous raider. Newspapers positively announced Mosby's death, even to details, and filled their columns with reviews of his colorful career.

Rejoicing was universal in Union ranks. At the camp near Washington of the Second Massachusetts Cavalry Volunteers, Chaplain Charles A. Humphreys conducted a morning funeral service for Private John McCarthy, one of the victims of the fight at Gooding's Tavern. The dead man's company, for some reason given the misnomer of the California Hundred, trailed behind his casket, and so did field and staff officers, all equally solemn. As the minister saw things, by such requiems was higher morale maintained. "This recognition of valor always tells for good with the men and makes them more brave in danger and more faithful in every duty," he explained.[16] Such thoughts were not a part of the service as conducted at the graveside of Private McCarthy. Words uttered were concerned with the life everlasting, but minds churning in bowed heads were picturing another open grave, possibly in the shade-spattered depth of some forest glen, accepting into its cavity the blanket-wrapped body of a sandy-haired guerrilla chieftain.

But somehow, in the days following, stories of Mosby's death failed to rest peacefully in trash baskets and other receptacles for cast-off newspapers. Like the ghost of the unrestful dead, they continued to haunt, to be disturbed by denials and counterdenials. From somewhere bobbed up the unwelcome rumor that he was not dead, that he was still alive and gamely fighting for his life. The more this tale was repeated, the more it seemed to be substantiated. It was said he had been taken through Middleburg on a stretcher. A woman traveler rushed to the *Star* in Washington with still more current news: she had actually seen the Partisan at Upperville. He lay in an open wagon supported by pillows and shielded by umbrellas, his face showing plainly the ghastly hue of death. Around the vehicle circled nine horsemen and farther back were fifty or sixty others, straggling along the road. And then the newspapers were left on a limb with the undisputed announcement that the raider had been taken via Culpeper to the home of his parents near Lynchburg.

So for a time rested the matter of Mosby, and suddenly for friends of the South closely following the war attention was turned from him to the ridge-running terrain through which galloped the guerrilla band of Hanse McNeill. The North was venomous, cowardly, and backhanded, said these stanch individuals, in its efforts to curb the ex-cattle breeder. Capture and punish him and his men, yes, but not his family. And the latter was what had been done. Confederate Exchange Agent Robert Ould became much concerned. To his Union counterpart he wrote a strong letter. Mrs. McNeill, her daughter, and four-year-old son, he reminded, were prisoners at Camp Chase, sent there after they had been arrested while on a visit to West Virginia from Chillicothe, Ohio, and in his opinion this was not right. How could the Federals complain of the detention of inoffensive men sympathizing with the Union, he asked, "when helpless women and children, meditating no wrong to you, are sent to your prisons?" [17]

It was another phase of a pattern of punishment for the guerrillas that was becoming more and more confused. Nothing the Federals tried seemed to be slowing down in the slightest the brazen episodes troubling the Union command from its top brass to its bottom private. Extensive searching parties availed nothing; threats to shoot on sight were ignored, and now even the incarceration of peaceful citizens failed to supply a safeguard against Partisan attacks. One night Colonel Horace Binney Sargent, clear-thinking officer of the First Massachusetts Cavalry, sat down to write out a routine report, and his thoughts got away from him and caused him to extend his account into extra pages. Several of them were devoted to his theory on the best and only way to get rid of the pesky Rebel raiders.

Binney believed "a policy of extermination," that and that alone, would achieve the expected end. "Tonight I might, perhaps, report that there is not an armed Rebel within the circuit of country that the colonel commanding expects me to clear," he said. "Tomorrow the woods may be full of them." [18] It was his idea that every man and horse would have to be sent within the lines, every house destroyed, every tree girdled and set on fire, "before we can approach security against the secret combination of a sudden force within musket range of our outposts," and he admitted that this method was not original, that it first had been adopted by Attila, King of the Huns.

"The people here," he explained, "all have sons or brothers in the cavalry. The mountains are full of men whose statements are fair, and whom nothing but infantry can capture and the Dry Tortugas control. Regiments of the line can do nothing with this furtive population, soldiers today, farmers tomorrow, acquainted with every woodpath, and finding a friend in every house."

Colonel Sargent had made up his mind about the situation: "I can clear this country with fire and sword, and no mortal can do it in any other way."

CHAPTER 6

September 2–December 31, 1863

"MOSBY'S MEN'LL CUT
YOUR THROAT"

Union soldiers who went to sleep on Cemetery Hill the night of September 10, all members of the First West Virginia Infantry, had no way of knowing most of them would be dead or prisoners by dawn. Nor was there an oracle on hand to tell them that the spot they had chosen for their camp, restful and secluded and high above the floor of South Branch Valley, would in a few months receive into its bosom the body of the man most responsible for their unforeseen fate—Hanse McNeill.

As they crawled into their low shelters, two men to a tent, they could see less than a mile away below them the faint lights of the little West Virginia village of Moorefield, seat of Hardy County. Only a few hours had passed since some of them looked upon this community for the first time, and now, here they were, satisfactorily bedded on one of the highest spots in the neighborhood, where they could stare down on any enemy who approached in the style of regular warfare. But as they saw it, they had no real reason to fear anyone; fully fifty pickets were stationed out in all directions, to lie in the dark and listen and watch for the approach of hostile forces.

And when dawn came they expected to hear the faint sound of firing in the direction of a patch of woods on Howard's Lick Road, just four miles away. Arrangements for this had been made before they took to their blankets. It was the work of Colonel J. A. Mulligan, commanding the Fifth Brigade. Shortly before dusk a courier came in from his headquarters at Petersburg, thirteen miles to the southwest, bringing a message that directed Major Edward W. Stephens, Jr., top officer on Cemetery Hill, to send one of his six companies of infantry and his only company of cavalry to cooperate in an attack on a band of Rebels said to be in those woods.[1] Around 9:00 P.M. the men selected for this raid moved quietly down the hill, and shortly afterward a stillness settled over the camp and lights went out to the last one, even those in the two A tents at the end of the street occupied by Stephens and the other officers.

Thus, in perfect confidence, Federals laid their plans for the elimination of an outpost that Imboden, before returning eastward some days earlier, had set up to watch the movements of the enemy in South Branch Valley—seventy men led by two captains. But the dark hours brought developments that would swing the balance in favor of the Rebels. As twilight faded and a late-summer moon stole quietly above the mountains beyond Cemetery Hill, a band of eighty dusty riders, newly from the Shenandoah Valley, followed Hanse McNeill to the patch of woods on Howard's Lick Road. This was home country to him and he moved with ease, picking abandoned paths and avoiding the highways, always spurring his horse along at a killing pace, for the plan he had in mind would bear no delay.

After Hanse went into a huddle with the two captains deep in the woods, the moon rose higher over the valley, deepening the shadows and shortening their stature, and in the dead of night the countryside grew deeply quiet. No sound carried to the camp on Cemetery Hill after Moorefield residents went to bed, and the lonely pickets nodded and gazed blindly at the moon and entertained serious thoughts about why guards were needed. Everywhere, so far as the atmosphere about them was concerned, there was peace, the deep, lonely quietude that comes to the mountains. Fresh on the night air was the sweet odor of pine and hemlock, hallmarks of the hills, and off along the ridges leaves were browning and taking on a crispness that signaled the approach of fall and frosty weather. Soon the silence would be broken by the seasonal scamper of squirrels hunting nuts; and denizens of the forest would prowl in the dark after lairs to afford them protection from the biting wintry winds. This was no theater for war; it was God and nature crying out for mates to come together and to settle down in their wilderness homes, and for babies to be born. No enemies in force could be close enough to warrant such a heavy picket. The Union had taken over South Branch Valley, lock, stock, and barrel, and meant to hold it. To this end at that very moment the two companies were marching, making their way through the dark for the attack at dawn on the handful of Rebels near Howard's Lick Road.

Midnight passed, and the three hours following, and still there was no sound that came to the ears of the pickets, not even the noise of 150 horses moving in their direction with a quiet which comes from practice. Onward these steeds were spurred, inexorable under the guidance of steady reins, and a mile from town, unseen and unheard, they were tethered in a group. Fifteen men stayed behind to guard them, while away on foot stole the remainder of the band, moving at a snaillike pace. Up front leading the way was Hanse McNeill, buoyed by a new spirit as he traversed terrain he had memorized as a boy.

Slowly, quietly, holding to one another at times and not daring to speak above a whisper, they approached Cemetery Hill. Much of the distance they crawled on hands and knees, hugging the ground, afraid to rise for fear of attracting the attention of a picket. But Hanse knew where to go, and he led them through the line of sentinels and halted at a point halfway between the picket posts and the camp. There they straightened up and walked two by two toward the line of white tents now dimly visible in the moonlight. As they trod carefully over the earth, their minds now freed of the strain of crawling, they noticed the customary signals of approaching dawn: in far-off barnyards chanticleers distended their throats and sent out into the night air a message that has meaning to man and fowl alike. And down below, winding in a path of beauty along the valley floor, was the silver ribbon that marked the shimmering waters of South Branch, northward bound to join its mate and form the Potomac.

As the raiders approached the eastern side of the camp, McNeill motioned to his men in the moonlight. They understood, for the signal had been prearranged, and to the last man they stepped out singly until they stretched hand to hand abreast of the entire line of tents.

Thoughts approached unanimity as they waited tensely: here before them lay a village of sleeping soldiers; not a challenge had been given. And on the other side of camp, along the crest of the hill, barely visible in the moonlight, stretched a series of rifle pits. Some of the Rangers, riding with McNeill for the first time, stood there and wondered if they were walking into a trap, if those pits were filled with the men who were supposed to be asleep in the tents, men who were veterans of Kernstown, Port Republic, and Second Manassas, who were waiting in nervous anticipation, guns cocked and ready, waiting to mow down the stealthy enemy who had so naïvely stolen into their trap.[2]

But there was little time for wonder. Earlier McNeill had broadcast an order for no one to fire until he signaled with a volley, a devil-rousing blast from the double-barreled shotgun he carried as his favorite weapon. And all at once a gun was discharged. It was not the shotgun and it was not in the hands of the enemy, and the Rebels, taking it as the signal, sent an indiscriminate volley into the camp and then dashed in among the tents.

In the flash of seconds Cemetery Hill's crest was turned into a bedlam of confusion. Shouts of "Halt!" "Surrender!" and "Rally, boys, rally!" rang out in the moonlight. Occasional shots were fired. Tents were ripped from their supports. Men dashed about in all directions, some clothed, some in their underwear, some pursuing, some pursued. And from the end of the camp street, where the horses were corraled, came a chorus of snorts and neighs and clanging chains.

Some of the Federals ran toward a patch of young pines near the rifle pits, but most just lay there in surprise and dismay when their shelter was torn from above them. One Ranger jerked away a tent and, to the two men lying there side by side, shouted, "Surrender! You're my prisoners!", and he was terribly surprised when one of the Union soldiers sat up and replied in a sleepy voice, "Well, don't get so excited about it."

A McNeill man, a six-foot Georgian, called on a Federal officer to give up his arms and was shocked to get for an answer, "I am an officer and will only surrender to an officer." But the Southern boy had his own opinions about such a thing, and he raised his gun and barked, "We'll see! At this moment we are on equality, sir, officer or no officer!" Without further remark the Unionist submitted.

Near the rifle pits the Federals who had managed to flee into the young pines were bothered by the cries of "Rally, boys, rally!" later claimed to have come from the Rebels. These yells seemed to imply a test of manhood, of personal bravery, serving as a taunt to the consciences of the men in the low trees, and they at last formed behind an adjutant and lieutenant and dashed back to the support of their comrades, staging a daring exhibition of loyalty that brought them into the arms of the waiting Confederates.

One of these men from the pines got separated from his companions and rushed in alone, bent over, running blindly, gun poised for a bayonet thrust. As he dashed through the hazy moonlight, a dozen guns were trained on him, but not a trigger was pulled. Instead, a clubbed rifle spelled his doom and brought him groaning to the ground.

When the excitement died down, 146 Federals stood in a group as prisoners, among them three captains, five lieutenants, and some of the pickets who had rushed into camp to find out what the confusion was all about. Missing was Major Stephens, an escapee by right of knowing when to flee. About the camp were scattered thirty Union soldiers, dead or too badly wounded to be moved. And over under a tree stretched the forty-eight-year-old McNeill, overcome by the strain and exertion of the long ride from the Shenandoah Valley and the tenseness of the night attack. But his trouble was temporary and in a few minutes he was back on his feet.

As dawn broke, the Rangers rounded up their captures and prepared to leave. Booty was voluminous—wagons, ambulances, horses, harness, guns, ammunition, camp supplies. In their possession also as they rode away was the order brought by the courier from Mulligan the night before. And had they read it carefully, they would not have passed through Moorefield and taken the South Fork Road, for ahead of them waited the Union detail that was supposed to have attacked the Rebel camp on Howard's Lick Road at dawn.

During scattered fighting that followed along this route, some of the prisoners and one ambulance were lost. Miraculously, not one of the Rangers was killed or wounded in the ambush set for them, but their escape from a tragic blow was of the hairbreadth variety: a bullet passed so closely beneath McNeill's nose that it abraded the skin and drew blood.[3]

In attacking the Federal camp on Cemetery Hill, the cattle breeder had accomplished one of his greatest feats, and he deserved better reward than he got. At the moment a request he had forwarded to headquarters through a legislator in Richmond was meeting with rejection at the hands of General Lee. It was a petition for authority to increase his command and to act independently of Imboden. The plea arrived at a time when Lee was receiving complaints, later denied, of depredations by some of the bands of Partisans and, in view of these and a growing conviction that this branch of the service was a waste of manpower, he gently but firmly refused. His reasoning was that it was better for McNeill to continue reporting to Imboden because, to do otherwise, would be to place two officers in command in the same district and divide the forces required for its defense.

While McNeill's Rangers were taking their prisoners and plunder out of South Branch Valley, miles to the east Captain Walter S. Newhall was on his way back to camp from a raid toward Middleburg. Mosby was reported in the neighborhood, recuperating from his wound, and the captain had been ordered out with four regiments of cavalry and four pieces of artillery. His mission was unsuccessful, and as he retraced his route his thoughts wandered. He glanced back over the long line of horsemen and the guns under his command and was forced to laugh at a comparison that to him seemed ridiculous. He had caught glimpses of the little bands of guerrillas haunting the countryside. Never more than a handful. Always moving. Always gadding from here to there, bent on mischief. And he concluded that to be hunting them with such a force as the one stretched out behind him was like shooting mosquitoes with a rifle —"very smashing to the little insect if you hit him." [4]

Elsewhere along the Federal lines matters were far from quiet. Guerrillas were especially hard on Colonel Judson Kilpatrick's orderlies, killing one of them at noon of a September day and capturing four others an hour later. General Howard, in official report to headquarters, commented that "the peculiar manner of the citizens in this quarter, the lurking of spies and guerrillas in the neighborhood, and the extreme quiet of the enemy have excited my suspicion that a raid or larger movement of the enemy is contemplated." He sent out scouting parties in several directions and they came back with word that the only thing they had seen had been small groups of irregulars. One of these passed through Hopewell Gap with two Union prisoners, another came down from the Bull Run Mountains and advanced toward Centreville, and a third skirmished with the First Indiana Cavalry at White Plains. Still another party was reported by a telegraph operator to be lurking beyond Watery Mountain signal station and to be very active in watching Union movements around Warrenton.

Howard was daily becoming more rabid about the guerrillas. His

Eleventh Corps was entrusted with the protection of the O. & A. and he was finding it a problem growing in intensity. He had a brigade and battery at Bristoe, another of each at Rappahonnock Station, two regiments at Manassas, and guards stationed every quarter-mile along the railroad, with reserves at appropriate points for their relief. These last dispositions he considered especially important because of the guerrillas, and he said it would not do to abandon them.[5]

One party of scouts sent out after guerrillas at this time was under command of Major Henry Cole of the Potomac Home Brigade of Maryland Cavalry. He was an ambitious individual, and the Baltimore *American* took due note of his activity, commenting that he "is of the same value to us that White and Mosby are to the Rebels."[6] After a wide sweep of the area along the Potomac he came back thoroughly convinced that Mosby was once more in the saddle. He had come upon the Partisan and four of his men, he related, leading two stolen horses along a road near Harpers Ferry and had given chase. In this effort he was encouraged by the positive identity of the Rebel chieftain, based on a description by the citizenry, and he eventually got so close to the raider that he forced him to abandon his horse and clamber up among the rocks on a mountainside.

Other than Cole's report there was no confirmation of the mountain climber's identity as Mosby, but it was definitely known that the Partisan had returned to his command. He had come back after a trip to Richmond, where he visited Lee and other officials and was given a supply of torpedoes to be used on the railroad. It was only a few days afterward that there was positive evidence that he was moving along the enemy's line of communication. The New York *Herald* reported his return and a visit by him to Warrenton, solely for information and without thought of plunder.[7]

Lee's worry at this time was a recurrent report that Meade was detaching troops and sending them by rail to Burnside, operating against Joe Johnston's army farther south. Gilmor sent word that 5000 soldiers were moved over the B. & O. every night. As other evidence General Howard, leading one of the two units said to be in motion, was seen to take the cars at Catlett's Station, and the other corps, the twelfth, was reported to be marching toward the rail head at Manassas.

In a desperate move to block this transfer of strength Lee broadcast a call for a unified effort to put the railroads out of commission, and the Washington *Star* took note of the action by reporting that the guerrillas had been ordered to draw in closer to the main army.[8] But this defense was only partially successful. Imboden took a look at the B. & O. and said it was too strongly guarded to attack, an assumption Gilmor found to be true by actual experience. Along the O. & A., on the other hand, the story was slightly different. Even though billets of Union soldiers were stationed every fourth of a mile, transportation on this line was interrupted for one entire day, and Lee notified Jeff Davis that it "may have been owing to the operations of Mosby or White, to whom I sent instructions to that effect." [9]

Mosby was raiding along the O. & A. at this time. In one attack he destroyed the bridge over Cameron's Run while the guns of two forts frowned down upon him, and then he dashed on into Alexandria and captured Colonel D. H. Dulaney, aide to Governor Pierpont, from a home on the outskirts of the city. This incident was so prized by the guerrilla chieftain that he wrote his wife about it.[10] He told that he was led on the expedition by Dulaney's own son, who happened to be one of his Rangers, a member of Company A, and he took great delight in describing the scene that took place between the two.[11] Just as they were about to leave, he related, the father sarcastically remarked to the son that there were an old pair of shoes around the house that he had better take with him, "as he reckoned they were darned scarce in the Confederacy, whereupon the son, holding up his leg, which was encased in a fine pair of cavalry boots just captured from a sutler, asked the old man what he thought of that."

But efforts to block the railroad completely were not successful, so Lee turned to another plan, aiming to keep the Federals facing him so busy that they would be unable to detach additional troops. He started crossing his forces over the Rapidan early in October, and most of the month thus was taken up with wholesale skirmishing over a wide area extending along the entire Union line. As Lee moved, the Partisans moved also. Striking with perfect timing, they rose up at the back of the enemy camps and went through their repertoire of tricks. Supplies were destroyed. Telegraph wires were cut. Couriers disappeared. Pickets were captured or died at their posts. A long train of supplies moving from Gainesville to Warrenton bogged down around New Baltimore, and it was some time before the guard in front and rear discovered what had happened. Finally they learned that guerrillas, posing as the thirteenth New York Cavalry, had unhitched 145 horses and mules in the middle of the train and fled with them.

Operations of the irregulars were widespread. Colonel Henry S. Gansevoort, commanding New York State volunteer cavalry near Washington, returned from the capital, where he had gone to procure Sharp's carbines for his men, to find everything in confusion. Officers and privates had gone two nights without sleep. Seven sergeants and two privates among them had been captured. More embarrassing was the revelation that his pickets had allowed what they thought was a cow to wander through their lines unmolested, later discovering the visit was from a Rebel on a horse with a cowbell tied around its neck. Henry was despondent when he sat down to correspond with the folks back home: "Mosby still troubles us . . . I lost two men last week, fine fellows they were too. In the dark the enemy crawled upon them when they were on post as pickets, and shot them through the body. We buried them a day or two ago with all honors. Thus it goes: I lose about, on the average, a man a day, by death, capture or discharge."

In the face of Lee's push and the threat from the guerrillas at his rear, Meade backed upon Fairfax and Washington, and there stopped while the high command in the Union capital fretted. He was frank to admit he did not know what the Confederates planned to do, and this brought out the wiseacre in Halleck, who wired: "When King Joseph wrote to Napoleon that he could not ascertain the position and strength of the enemy's army the Emperor replied: 'Attack him and you will soon find out.'" This was all it took to fire the famous Meade temper and he quickly flared back: "If you have any orders to give me, I am prepared to receive and obey them, but I must insist on being spared the infliction of such truisms in the guise of opinions as you have recently honored me with . . . I take this occasion to repeat what I have before stated, that if my course, based on my own judgment, does not meet with approval, I ought to be, and I desire to be, relieved from command." [12]

But the barb between the desk-chair general in Washington and the commander in the field went no further. After a campaign of skirmishing the Confederates backed across the Rapidan and quiet settled once more between the two armies.

By November things were so peaceful that Meade again moved out toward the Rappahannock, and sutlers were allowed to reopen trade with the army, to a limited extent, via the O. & A. But the guard could never be dropped, as the Sixth Corps learned the hard way. It moved into Warrenton and there barely escaped a serious loss at the hands of guerrillas. "Last night a daring attempt was made to carry off General Sedgwick," one of its members wrote home. "I shudder to think of the possibilities of success in such an expedition, but it was unsuccessful last night." [13]

Off in the West Virginia mountains, McNeill was still busy with his share of the guerrilla depredations. Early one morning he secreted his men along a road, part of them in an old house, and attacked a train of eighty wagons loaded with quartermaster and commissary stores moving from the rail head at New Creek to General Averell's troops at Petersburg. The surprise was successful and resulted in the capture of 245 horses and twenty-five prisoners. Hundreds of Federals were ordered out to intercept him, but were unable to keep on his trail in the dense hill country.

Late in November, Meade displayed threats of moving across the Rappahannock. Lee recognized these and immediately turned to the guerrillas for help. He counted on Mosby to keep the O. & A. out of operation and, to this end, suggested to Imboden that he send a force, possibly Gilmor's command, east of the Blue Ridge to assist him.

Mosby promptly intensified his activities along the railroad, and the Union guard stiffened in response. Additional troops moved in, some of them badly in need of rest after arduous front-line duty. In one detachment of these was John Chester White of the Fifteenth Pennsylvania Cavalry, such a chronic victim of diarrhea that he was unable to get his required hours of sleep. One night he sat around a campfire, delaying his repose because of his condition. Only a few hours had passed since his ailment, coming upon him while he was trying to catch a nap squeezed in for warmth between two camp buddies, had attacked him with such violence that he was unable to wriggle free in time and, as a result, had to take a predawn bath in the freezing waters of the creek. As he stared into the fire and shuddered at thought of that unpleasant experience, the cries of an infant, as lifelike and pathetic as those identified with a nursery, sounded from the woods at his back. He listened while they several times were repeated, and at last his curiosity drove thoughts of self-preservation from his mind: he got to his feet and started on a trip of exploration. "Don't," advised an old sergeant seated across the blazing logs. "Walk out there in them woods and Mosby's men'll cut your throat." [14]

So it went, from week to week, the guerrillas using every ruse of stealth and surprise to accomplish their object and the Federals forced to keep constantly on the alert, knowing the moment they dropped their guard might be their last. December arrived and its days were unchanged from those of the month previous. From Washington to Wheeling the story was the same: with tantalizing irregularity the Partisans struck, raiding wagon trains, capturing couriers, cutting telegraph lines, storming isolated outposts, sniping at pickets. Under this strain upon the Unionists it was no wonder Christmas was celebrated by many of them in a manner that for just a few hours would make them forget. The observance at the camp on Kettle Run along the O. & A. seems to have been typical in many instances. John Chester White described it in his diary:

"Here we had snow, and Christmas Day was beautiful and bright, while 'only man was vile.' Camp kettles of commissary whisky, mixed with canned milk and styled milk punch, and others full of beer, had been sent by the officers to their respective companies, and a number of the former, as well as the men, proceeded to get beastly drunk, after a double cordon of sentries had been thrown around the camp." [15]

But for some of the soldiers guarding the Union there was no let-up in routine. A dispatch came in at headquarters of the Army of the Potomac telling of a frolic that Mosby and his principal officers were to hold at Salem. Accordingly, orders went out, and they reported that the festivity was to be held at the homes of Dr. Bispham, second on the right entering the village from Warrenton, and of Mrs. Murray, who lived about midway of the street in a large white house. Out from Warrenton moved the Third Pennsylvania and the First New Jersey Cavalry, 250 men strong, under command of Major Janeway, "a smart and competent officer." [16] They rode without halting and burst in upon the village with clank of spur and saber, only to find that the Rangers, apprised of approaching danger, had brought their merrymaking to a sudden close just ten minutes earlier and had departed.

Lieutenant Rawle Brooke, one of the 250, recorded the aftermath of this dash upon Salem: "All day long the cackling of hens has proved that if last night's expedition did not frighten away the Salem guerrillas, it did clear out the Salem poultry." [17]

CHAPTER 7

January 1–March 11, 1864

WAR IS WAR, EVEN
AT TEN BELOW

The first day of '64 was one of the coldest of the war, and it may have been an omen of the intensity that would be brought into the conflict before the calendar was turned to another year. On this day a freezing rain changed to snow, and then there was utter frigidity, with no wind.

In such weather, extreme enough to freeze solid both hoof track and camp bucket, soldiers might have been expected to stick closely to their billets, with fires blazing and blankets heaped high. But not so the Partisans. General Averell, who had just returned from a raid upon the railroad below Staunton, found parts of White's and Gilmor's battalions, with detachments of regular troops, assembled near Winchester, and it was this discovery that caused Union soldiers to be hurried down the B. & O. from Wheeling, forcing upon them an experience they never forgot. All night long they lay in open gondola cars, covered only by their overcoats, and their suffering was intense. Also sharing in the misery brought by the elements at this time was the Fifteenth Pennsylvania Cavalry, ordered away from Kettle Run to Alexandria. At their new post they settled down in an open field, a part of which had been set aside as a cemetery, and therein lay a problem that they solved by taking the easiest way out. When they tried to establish camp, they found it almost impossible to drive stakes into the frozen ground, so they forsook alignment and sank the pegs wherever they could, in some instances winding up with graves inside their tents.

At the start of the new year the plight of Lee's army was alarming. Many of the soldiers were without shoes, the cavalry was worn down by its pursuit of Averell, and food was dreadfully scarce. Even after each man was limited to a quarter of a pound of salt meat per day, there was never enough of a reserve on hand to insure feeding the troops for more than three days at a time. To help in this emergency General Early was sent to the border counties of West Virginia after cattle reported within the enemy's lines.

In some instances, due to delivery interruptions by the guerrillas, Union rations were short too. This was true with Meade's army at the beginning of '64, and it became so severe at times that on one occasion, as the general rode past, the soldiers manifested their discontent by shouting after him, "Hardtack! Hardtack!" It was an affront that caused the Meade temper to flare to extremes, and the entire camp, innocent as well as guilty, was punished with two hours of drill under loaded knapsack.

The snow got deeper and the weather colder, and military activity, thus stymied, dropped to a minimum. Jubal Early alone seemed to be busy, and he simply because of the grave food problem. As he moved westward, aided by Imboden and Gilmor and McNeill, alarms went up and down the ice-covered wires along the B. & O. Rolling stock beyond Cumberland was moved toward the Ohio River and, to make things more difficult for the Confederates, the people of New Creek and Piedmont were forbidden to use lights in their homes at night. Despite this caution a Federal wagon train on its way from that point to Petersburg was captured intact with the exception of one span of mules that a Negro teamster, through some foresight and much godly fear of Rebel prisons, unhitched and drove madly into the mountain fastnesses. Another train rolled past Moorefield while McNeill's Rangers sat still and looked on, and the Wheeling *Intelligencer* said this was because discretion induced them to hug their campfires. Making much use of mixed metaphor, the newspaper added: "The grapes were beyond their reach, and consequently were sour, and they returned to their corn bread with about the same relish with which a man would enjoy the parings after having disposed of the apple, or kiss a lady's gloved hand after feasting upon the rosebud lips of a blond." [1]

Early's raid was not the success Lee hoped it would be, and yet it was not altogether a failure. Gilmor's command alone, left to hold a gap between Moorefield and Petersburg, captured 3000 pounds of bacon and quantities of hard bread, horseshoes, and nails. The Union reported Early so hampered by icy roads he could not move his artillery across the mountains. At any rate, it seems to have been the weather and not the enemy that kept "Old Jube" from returning with more animals and wagons than he did. Even at that he brought back some relief, though the food problem of the Southern army still remained a major worry.

While the early January cold gripped the Eastern theater of war, a reporter for a Northern newspaper sat in a tent on Loudoun Heights, overlooking Harpers Ferry, and wrote with more feeling in his heart than in his fingers. Words poured out through his pen, running freely onto the sheet of foolscap spread across a cracker box, and haunting him as he scribbled, stirring his thoughts in a manner that even a "faithful chronicler of events" found it painful to record, was a voice that had cried out in the night, in the bleak, miserable hours before dawn: "Give the damn Yankees no quarter, but secure the arms and horses!" That was four hours ago, and now the man from whose lips that cry was said to have come lay only a few feet away, wrapped in its white winding sheet of snow. Papers in his pocket identified him as Captain William R. Smith of Mosby's terrible guerrillas.[2]

A gust of wind whistled briskly through the trees, whipping a tent flap and giving the journalist a broader view of the arena on which had taken place the events he was describing. Here was death, with its attendant pathos and misery and sadness for the folks back home! Scarcely an hour earlier the sun had come up on a scene laid in darkness, amid the roar of gunfire and the scream of men crazed by passion or panicked by fear. Prints of bare feet spotted the snow; bloodstains were scattered in a broad pattern, and bodies of half-naked men lay starkly still, mute witnesses to what had happened. All this in a camp—the camp of Coles' Potomac Home Brigade Cavalry—laid out on heights considered high enough above the plain to be judged safe from attack. It had come only two weeks after the site first had been occupied, two weeks of looking down on the suspension bridge across the Shenandoah River that was the reason for its being there.

But no one could tell when or where Mosby would strike!

In that day there could be no voice-recording of the cruel, heart-

less cry attributed to Smith, no way to repeat in evidence that which
had been oral. But Federals against whom it was raised would stake
their lives to a man that they had heard it rise above the din of
confusion. "Horses," they would swear, was the last word uttered by
this still form, lying face up in its shroud of snow, a dark smear over
its chest marking the trail of a heart-piercing bullet. Corporal Henry
Tritch, upset by sight of the dead, was out in the street, at that
very moment, proclaiming his conviction in a loud, excited, irrational
voice.

Near Henry lay another body, centered in a pool of frozen blood.
A few words scribbled by someone on July 27, 1863, across a strip
of paper taken from his uniform, revealed the identity: "Guards and
pickets will pass Lieutenant Colson, Major Trimble's staff, in and
out at pleasure." No good this strip, now. Colson of Baltimore! You
never could tell who was fighting with Mosby.

Other objects marred the whiteness of the camp street. Near a
tent stake a photograph lost from an overcoat pocket in the heat of
battle, of victory or defeat, waited to be found. A Union soldier with
sharp eyes eventually would pick it up, turn it over, look down on
the face of a beautiful lady and read her fine, evenly formed handwriting: "For Brother Willie, from Florence."

The reporter in the tent made note. Farther over, near each other
on the edge of camp, still and rapidly freezing, stretched the bodies
of three dead Rebels, no strip of paper tucked in their pockets to
reveal name or rank, if it mattered.

Prone in tents up the street line, silent most of the time and some
of them waiting for death, rested nearly a dozen wounded prisoners.
One of them, soon to be bemoaned by Mosby and Stuart alike, would
talk without prodding. He was Lieutenant William Thomas Turner
of Baltimore, he said, and his uncle was Captain Turner, recently
in command of the United States war vessel *Ironsides* at Charleston. On his honor, repeated the dying man over and over, Smith
never uttered that cry. Smith was human. Smith was a nice fellow.
Smith was . . . the victim's words gradually faded to a whisper,
dry and toneless, and at last he stopped talking, closed his eyes, and
prepared to meet a stranger who shakes hands only once.

Other wounded and other dead were scattered over the countryside, close by, some of them, and others miles out. Union troops sent
in pursuit found blood all along the line of retreat.

Hours later, farther down in Virginia, Mosby prepared his report of the affair. He didn't know what had happened, he wrote, but things had gone wrong. Quietly through the night they had stolen, cold and miserable, led by Stuart's veteran scout, Frank Stringfellow. They had avoided the pickets and made their way into the camp by scaling a path up the face of a cliff. Near the row of tents Stringfellow and ten men went off to capture Major Cole in his headquarters some yards to the side, and it was with this party that something seemed to have gone amiss.[3] While Mosby was getting his column of nearly 100 Rangers together, Stringfellow and the others came charging back, yelling and shooting, and evidence of what followed still smeared the snow in the streets of the camp.

The Day after Cole buried his dead, a message arrived from Mosby under flag of truce. Could he send for the bodies of Captain Smith and the two lieutenants? Cole was ready with an answer: yes, he could send, but, if he really wanted them, he'd better try again to surprise the camp on Loudoun Heights.[4]

By the middle of January more snow fell, bringing with it warmer weather, and suddenly the bottom fell out of Virginia roads and traffic was brought to a halt by the sticky mud. Young General Rosser, West Pointer fighting under Early, took the occasion to fire a blast at the numerous bands of irregular troops trying to help the cause of the Confederacy. He had been miffed by their activities for months, and an exchange that flared up between McNeill and him during the food-raising expedition to West Virginia had rather served to clinch his convictions. Rosser had his own ideas about what the Rangers should do, and McNeill, the ex-rancher who respected horseflesh and knew when and when not it was humane to force animals over icy roads, was slow to execute them. No matter how much the young brigadier argued, the tall, bearded Partisan leader remained silently stubborn, monotonously shaking his head.

So Rosser came back with his mind made up to write a letter, to denounce the Partisans in specific terms—all Partisans. And that letter he wrote to General Lee. In terming the irregulars an evil to the service Rosser claimed he was moved by a desire to serve his country. He described members of the independent bands as thieves, guilty of stealing, pillaging, plundering, and doing every manner of mischief and crime, "a terror to the citizens and an injury to the cause." And flashing back on his experience with McNeill, he said they never fought and couldn't be made to fight. Then he enumerated the effects of their presence upon members of the regular army. Only Mosby was mentioned by name, and he was given credit for keeping the Yankee army from straggling.[5]

Now the Partisan service got its test. Rosser's letter moved up the line. Jeb Stuart, in his indorsement of it, admitted such organizations were as a rule detrimental to the best interests of the army, but he did so after citing Mosby's command as "the only efficient band of Rangers I know of." Lee also concurred in the justice of Rosser's charges and recommended that the law authorizing the Partisan corps be abolished. This was done by the Confederate Congress within the next few weeks, and soon there was a general movement to have the independent bands merged with regular commands. But it was a matter for the records only. Since Gettysburg the South had been fighting with its back to the wall, and the struggle ahead was too desperate for much attention to be given to such minor details. And so, though abolished on paper, the Partisans continued to operate as they had in the past.

While the South was adopting legislation to end guerrilla bands, the North was bothered with a different matter. Too many Rebels were appearing in blue uniforms, so at last word went out from the Army of the Potomac in General Order Number 6 that no person, regardless of the clothing he wore, should be permitted to approach within rifleshot until he had been identified. In the future, it was warned, an attack or surprise would not be excused merely because it was conducted by individuals in friendly garb. The time to put an end to this practice was now, and that was what the Union meant to do. Guerrillas or others found so clothed were to be hanged on the spot.[6]

Late in January the weather warmed and the skies clouded, and there was mist and a little rain in most places and a thunderstorm east of the Blue Ridge. Lee's army was still hungry, pursuing a hand-to-mouth existence, so he took advantage of the break to send Early back across the mountains after cattle, first advising him he was positive there were many head in Hampshire and Hardy counties undiscovered on the previous raid. "Old Jube" started with two brigades, four pieces of artillery, and Gilmor's, McNeill's, and White's Partisan Rangers. At Moorefield his forces were divided, one brigade taking the right bank of South Branch and the other, under General Rosser, traveling along the opposite bank.

In following his route Rosser, supported by the Partisans, topped a mountain range to spy a train of ninety-odd wagons, each drawn by six mules. It was advancing along the New Creek road toward Petersburg, and dispositions immediately were made for an attack. The artillery was rolled to the front, fuses ready, and the first shells routed the 800-man Union guard. In a matter of minutes the entire train was captured, except for the animals from nearly half the wagons. These were unhitched hastily by the drivers and whipped and stoned into the mountains. Left behind in the vehicles were rations that rarely got through the blockade—bacon, rice, coffee, sugar, brandied cherries, pickled oysters, boned turkey, Boston gingerbread, and Goshen cheese.

After destroying the wagons from which the animals had been unhitched, Rosser advanced on Petersburg. There he found the garrison had fled, leaving behind stores, forage, and 13,000 cartridges.

McNeill meantime was sent across the mountain to round up cattle, and he went only after another run-in with the young brigadier general whom he looked upon as no more than a boy.[7] Gilmor's and White's commands were kept behind by Rosser to lead the advance toward Patterson's Creek. This mission was successful. The railroad bridge over the stream, the water station, engine house, and several hundred yards of track were destroyed and the telegraph wires cut. Then, marching northward along the railroad, the Confederates burned the bridge over the north branch of the Potomac six miles east of Cumberland.

Gilmor came back from the raid on the railroad with a feeling that he was riding on borrowed time. In his left breast pocket, beneath two coats, nestled a deck of cards that had been almost completely penetrated by a rifle ball. Only one card had escaped defacement, and that the one nearest his skin, which he was surprised to find was the ace of spades. Thereafter, whenever the Partisan met Rosser, a standing question was tossed at him by the brigadier: "Major, are spades trumps?" [8]

But Gilmor was soon ready to make a new test of his luck. C. W. Lowe, surgeon of the Fifth West Virginia Cavalry, stationed at Martinsburg, made this reference to it in a little black diary he carried in his pocket: "1½ A.M. Train on B. & O. R. R. going west thrown off the track and passengers robbed. Damn such luck."

That, in short, was the story. Jeb Stuart had sent Gilmor a message to cut the B. & O. as a means of barring the arrival of troops from the West, and the guerrilla leader immediately made a quick dash from the Shenandoah Valley to accomplish the objective.[9]

Traveling only by night, supported by twenty-eight men, the first day he spent in a barn near Strasburg and the second in a patch of pines along the Opequon. In the dark hours before dawn of the third day out he and his band arrived at Brown's Shop, at the east end of Quincy's Siding, eight miles from Martinsburg, and there lay in wait after placing obstructions on the track—fence rails to check the speed of the locomotive and a heavier barricade farther along to cause derailment.[10] The first train to come along was an express that had left Baltimore at six o'clock the previous evening. On board were convalescent soldiers from the hospitals around Alexandria, as well as a few notables, including members of the Maryland legislature and ex-United States Senator Jesse D. Bright of Indiana, former president of the upper chamber of Congress and active member until expelled for disloyalty early in '62.

The Rangers made quick work aboard the flyer after it came to a halt, and good they did, because just as they prepared to leave a loaded troop train rolled up from the west. This created an unexpected emergency, and the raiders reacted promptly. Even as they could see Union infantrymen pouring from the cars, they paroled their prisoners and fled back in the direction of the Valley.

Gilmor might have received high praise for this raid had he been more discreet. Once on board the train, he first hurriedly searched for the express agent, hoping to get the keys to the safe, but this individual had disappeared.[11] "I then went back to see how the men were getting on," the Partisan leader naïvely related, "and was told some of them had been robbing the prisoners and passengers. This was against my positive orders, and I threatened to shoot any one caught in the act."[12]

Later testimony revealed that Gilmor had given orders the evening before that no citizens, especially women, be molested.[13] The Partisan chief said he took only about 900 dollars in greenbacks from the mailbags, but that was not the story spread by the newspapers. It was reported "on good authority" that the trainmen and all passengers were robbed. Each person was told to "stand and deliver" his valuables. "The work is said to have been done most thoroughly, with all the grace and sang froid of experienced highwaymen," reported the Baltimore *American*. "Even their pocket knives and toothpicks did not escape the plunderers. Those who did the robbing were accompanied by pistol holders, who thrust the muzzles under the noses of their victims whilst they were being plundered." It was alleged the raiders took away with them 100,-000 dollars in greenbacks, nine gold watches, two silver watches, fifty to sixty hats, thirty overcoats, a hundred fine revolvers, a large lot of sabers, and a number of carpetbags.

It was this robbery of passengers, strongly attested to by innumerable witnesses, that brought Gilmor official censure. General Lee, when he heard of it, wrote Secretary of War Seddon: "Such conduct is unauthorized and discreditable. Should any of that battalion be captured the enemy might claim to treat them as highway robbers. What would be our course? I have ordered an investigation of the matter and hope the report may be untrue." [14]

But a greater furor arose over an incident that happened near Strasburg during the raiders' return. There seven Confederates, identified by subsequent testimony as members of Gilmor's party, interrupted a Jewish caravan of wagons on its way to Maryland to stock up on merchandise for resale at Richmond. One of the merchants, after rough handling, gave up two money belts containing 6000 dollars in gold, chiefly in twenty-dollar pieces, a silver watch, and a greatcoat of invisible green with yellow silk sleeve linings, a fur collar, and a small Hebrew prayer book. One of the Jews was the son of a prominent businessman in the Confederate capital, and it was largely through him that an effort was made to identify the guilty persons. In a short time two detectives were sent to the Valley to investigate and they ran across a confusing trail. After a Negro had piloted them for six miles, for instance, they happened to search him and find in his pockets one of the watches taken from the merchants. Furthermore, there was evidence that Gilmor, while under the influence of liquor, had boasted of arranging the whole affair, though he said he had not taken part personally in the actual robbery.

For a time Gilmor's future in the Confederate army was uncertain, and it was only the great excitement attached to the war that kept more attention from being drawn to him. Northern newspapers made such an outcry against him that the Confederacy finally called a court-martial at Staunton. Made up of members of the Seventh Virginia Cavalry, it sat for a week, interviewing witnesses and compiling evidence. But the verdict finally was for acquittal, based largely on Gilmor's denial that he knew of the robberies and excuse of his Rangers that they took the men passengers to be military people in citizens' clothes. They denied all knowledge of any looting of women.

Winter life, with its boredom and sameness in days when cold weather made roads difficult to traverse, was hectic for soldiers, especially for the Union cavalry stationed in the area most preyed upon by guerrillas. They had little to do but lie about their camps, whiling away hours that seemed longer with each successive tick of the clock; and it was quite natural that their thoughts should turn tauntingly to the freedom enjoyed by the Rebel independents, the abandon with which they rode the country and brought back prizes in the way of loot, food, and even money. Perhaps that was what led William E. "Pony" Ormsby to steal away from the camp of the Second Massachusetts Cavalry under cover of darkness.

But social behavior would find it difficult to explain what induced "Pony," aided by only eight of Mosby's men, to attack the rear guard of a scouting party from his own regiment when it passed through Aldie shortly afterward. In this one-sided fighting the deserter was captured, taken back to camp, and his fate decided by a drumhead court-martial.

Men who were witnesses set down in diary and letter the details of the chilly, cloudy winter's day on which "Pony" died as a warning to others who might have in mind escaping the boredom of camp life by fleeing to the Rebel irregulars. It was an occasion engraven upon their memories. By unit, soldiers of the thirteenth and sixteenth New York Cavalry and of Ormsby's own regiment were marched into an open field near their camp at Vienna, led by the youthful Colonel Charles R. Lowell, kinsman of the great American poet, James Russell Lowell. The young colonel alone was enough to convince the private in the ranks that the decision handed down by their emergency court would be identical with the verdict of any court, no matter how great its dignity. Lowell was a graduate of Harvard, with the face of a boy, but he had served in the Sixth United States Cavalry, part time as captain, and he had the bearing of a soldier and the courage of a hero.

Under his watchful eyes the men marched out into the field, each solemn-faced and visualizing himself in the shoes of poor Ormsby. By long practice they formed a hollow square—double lines on three sides, the fourth left open as the objective point of operations. Then came the regimental band, moving slowly and playing a dirge as it paraded in front of the brigade. Behind the musicians rolled an ambulance, drawn by members of the firing squad and bearing a crude coffin on which sat the condemned man. To the center of the square the vehicle was rolled, and there "Pony" jumped to the ground and helped unload the heavy box.

The band brought the dirge to a close and instruments were lowered, and then the regimental adjutant marched stiffly to the center of the square and read the findings of the court. There was dead silence after his last words faded out, a tense period of waiting as if someone were expected to give a reply. The seconds ticked off slowly, painfully, with the breathless slowness of minutes, in a quietude so deep that the click of a trigger would have violated the lull with the sharpness of a rifle blast. Men in ranks, their cheek muscles as still as marble, swallowed hard. Good old "Pony," a lovable guy, a real pal. Comrade Mortimer, his bunkie, had been saying that all morning.

A voice cracked on the air, a sergeant barking orders; and like automatons members of the firing squad swung about, stepped forward, and split into two platoons of ten men each. Somewhere among their twenty guns was a blank cartridge.

Lowell now spoke in a manner that belied his youthful face, his words coming in a tone marked for its solemnity and calmness: "William E. Ormsby, do you have anything to say to your fellow soldiers at this moment of your last stay on earth?"

It was then that "Pony" showed courage that might have brought him medals if properly applied. He bent over and rapped on the coffin, striking it three sharp blows with his bare knuckles. The soldiers standing there in ranks counted each one of them. Then he straightened, smartly erect, as if at attention, and a wry grin wrinkled the smoothness of his face. "That box is mighty hard, men. Hope you put some shavings or something inside." The remark fell flat, greeted only by deep silence, and he changed his attitude in mute apology. Speaking slowly, voice steady, he recounted the deed for which he had been tried, admitted his error, and justified his punishment, pointing by way of demonstration to the paper heart pinned to his coat as a bull's-eye. "Farewell, comrades!" he concluded, and bowed his head while a chaplain muttered a prayer. That ended, he took a seat upon the coffin, unassisted, folded his arms behind him, and gave the order to fire.

A ragged blast shook the earth and echoed across the field. Smoke jerked from the guns, lost its suddenness, and spread out in a common cloud, thinning rapidly to a veil. Above the sharp reverberations now slapping back and forth between the soldiers and a background of saplings in the distance sounded the clergical tones of the chaplain, spoken as he bent over the bleeding form draped across the coffin: "May God have mercy on your soul!"

Those who cared noted that it was four minutes past noon.[15]

CHAPTER 8

A GUERRILLA BOWS
TO CUPID

Guerrilla George Dusky, brother of Sallie, was in love. His affections, West Virginia was surprised to learn, were in some way captured by Mrs. Mary J. Briggs, thirty-year-old widow who eked out a living by pedaling a sewing machine in Anderson's Boot and Shoe Establishment near Wheeling's suspension bridge.

Love is an admirable thing, commonly agreed, and from the beginning of time folks in all walks of life have watched its development, the old because it brings back memories, the young because it stimulates their dreams. But love can be galling if there are elements about it that do not conform to the pattern—as when a hardened guerrilla, cruel, bloodthirsty, and fearless, pens moonstruck notes showing he has completely surrendered to a meek little imp named Dan Cupid.

George was brought to Wheeling from Parkersburg. There, he was embarrassed to admit, he had been cornered in enemy territory at a moment when he was unable to offer his usual resistance.

At Wheeling, Jailer Jones locked him up in The Atheneum, following a routine of long standing, and a few hours later picked up the *Intelligencer* of current issue to read that his new prisoner had spent the last three years of his life "in shooting Federal soldiers and looking through the iron bars in different prisons."[1] This information may have been responsible thereafter for the caution with which the keeper of the keys listened to noises around the jail.

One day not long after George became an inmate of The Atheneum, Mary Briggs strolled up for the sole purpose of making a social call, so she said, flaunting her hips in a manner that made Jailer Jones wonder. But he let her in, after a modest bit of frisking and a stern warning about smuggling in objects of forbidden character.

Next day she was back again, as gay as a queen's seamstress, and, if anything, her stay was a little longer. This became a routine over the weeks, these visits of hers, and then, on one of her appearances, at a time when Jailer Jones was supposed to be looking the other way, she was caught slipping an item through the cell door that in all probability would have led to a prison break.

That was the end. On future occasions even the outer door was barred to the Widow Briggs, and no amount of shouting and stomping and cursing and thumping would open it.

There matters stood, with Mary's love for George unshaken and amazingly strong.

One balmy night Jones sat at a window on the south side of the jail listening to the sounds of spring. Out of the darkness came the chorus of weird noises that is the finest music in the world to the nature lover. It is a confusion of insect melody, a signal that the slow-moving vernal equinox has edged farther into the background and that a new growing season is at hand.

For a man who must spend his hours within a barred building surrounded by a high brick wall, the cadence was as pleasing as the emotional notes of Beethoven. So Jailer Jones attuned his ear to its faintest offering, reveling in this peace that contrasted so violently with the rabble sound that usually blared forth from the wildcat element under his care. He closed his eyes, and gradually his features took on a smoothness and a blend of harmony that signified serenity at its peak.

But this rhapsody was not of long duration. Suddenly in the midst of his captivation the jailer stiffened. His eyes flew open and his facial expression lost its calm. Somewhere there was discord! Somewhere the human element had taken over from nature, and the symphony had become a concerto.

The jailer jerked his feet down from their point of elevation. A burning candle was at his elbow, and he took this and set off uncertainly on a junket of investigation. His ears had pointed him toward the south wall.

Through the heavy front door and down the stairs to the yard he hurried, holding high the candle. As he neared the spot from which the discord had seemed to come, he heard an object strike the ground, and this stopped him in his tracks. There, braced for an emergency, he looked around and, in the faint candlelight, his eyes spotted a small parcel rolling on the grass. With action that belied his years he pounced upon it. And that was when the confusion started.

Like a wildcat hurtling from a limb, a woman landed on the jailer's back from the top of the wall and snatched the packet from his hand. It was Mrs. Briggs.

For a moment there was a mad scramble, above which the widow could be heard screaming, "I'll die before you get it!" She fought desperately, scratching and kicking and biting, even though the leap from the wall had broken her leg just above the ankle. As she struggled, somewhere in the folds of her voluminous dress a small bottle of nitric acid was smashed and its contents spilled upon the combatants, burning both. That, combined with the pain of her leg injury, was enough to take the fight out of the woman, and she sank to the ground, her spirit gone.

From then on Jones had complete control of the situation. He got Mary into the jail and summoned medical attention, and then he settled down to examine the parcel. Inside he found a bottle of chloroform, another of nitric acid, a chisel, a box of steel pens, two love letters, and two copies of late newspapers—"a harmonious lot of stuff certainly, to say the least of it," observed the *Intelligencer*. Further investigation revealed that the package had been tied to the end of a long pole, with which Mrs. Briggs was attempting to reach the window of the cell in which lodged her lover.

The entire incident was reported by the *Intelligencer* a day or two later. And the newspaper also published one of the two love letters, thus revealing that Mary, whom George affectionately referred to as Mollie, had a sense of humor, for she had addressed the missile to "Captain George Dusky, C. S. A., confined in A. Lincoln bastile in Wheeling, via the Southern express."

The "express" at the moment was lying in The Atheneum with a cast on her leg. This was trouble on top of trouble, for in her letter she told George that she was not feeling well, that she had a high fever and could scarcely breathe. But she made it plain there was nothing wrong with her his company couldn't cure. And then came endearing language that somehow grated on the senses of the readers who knew the reputation of the hardened Guerrilla Dusky: "Indeed I need your loving arms around me, and your lips pressed to my loving ones. Oh come, love, and take me in your arms; it will cure me; it requires but that to make me well. Will you send the garter tonight? I would rather you would keep it till you could come with it, and put it where it belongs."

The newspaper wound up its account with a report that Mrs. Briggs was in much pain from her fractured limb, and added: "She is . . . rather stoutly built and, although by no means an unattractive woman, she is a most uncompromising Rebel."

A day or two later, in the yard adjoining the jail, was found a reply in George's handwriting. On the front he had written: "Will you carry this to the one it is directed to? It contains nothing of any consequence to any except the above named lady . . . I hope the finder will have a nobler principle than to betray a lady on her sick bed."

But the finder failed to live up to this hope, and again the public was treated to a printed declaration of love. George wrote with "a heart overflowing with wretchedness." If he had 50,000 dollars, he said, he would give it freely to restore "you as you was last Friday eve." Then he turned his wrath upon the *Intelligencer:* "That vile scoundrel, the editor, has enlarged, or else some of his accomplices, but I entertain a different opinion to what is expressed by him, that you are not attractive; you are attractive; your very nobleness of heart makes you so if nothing else, but there is many other things . . ."

The editor had an answer, published directly beneath the letter: "Mr. Dusky is mistaken if he supposes the *Intelligencer* said the lady to whom this letter is addressed was not attractive."

Days went by, and then the public was informed that five prisoners, "among them George Dusky of Briggs-Dusky notoriety," had attempted to break jail by catching Jones off guard. The effort was futile. Loud cries of the jailer brought his wife and daughter, two husky women, and "right nobly did they assist him," soon restoring quiet to The Atheneum.

Some time later a careful examination of the jail revealed a broken screen over George's cell window. When questioned, he admitted he was to blame, explaining that he had torn it loose so he could place a little mirror in such position to "see the green foliage upon the trees and the verdure upon the hillside south of the city."

His interrogators seemed unconvinced, and the guerrilla finally changed his story, confessing that he had removed the screen in order to communicate by letter "with persons outside."

He had more to say. Reported the newspaper: "While conversing upon the subject, Dusky spoke very darkly and mysteriously about certain old scores which he had to settle with certain persons when he got out of jail."[2]

Two other times he tried to escape. One day a woman from Ohio—a relative of the Duskys, she said—dropped by with an armful of books "of a highly moral character" for the guerrilla. Jones was dubious, and his suspicions were well founded. Behind a false back of one of them he found an implement that might have returned to Partisan warfare one of its formerly active members.

George was a constant problem. His separation from the Widow Briggs made him "as ill-natured as a bear with a sore head," the *Intelligencer* reported, and there was growing concern about what should be done with him. This the opposing governments finally would decide.

The day came when George was released at Fort Monroe, in exchange for a Federal officer, and that was a great day for Jailer Jones. His words were in no way qualified when he said he had had more trouble with this love-letter-writing prisoner than with any six it had been his responsibility to guard.

PART THREE

CHAPTER 1

March 12–May 15, 1864

"I FIGHTS MIT SIGEL"

The North's grand strategy as the weather opened in the spring of '64 called for a relentless, unremitting employment of strength. It would be applied in a combined movement, eight different armies stepping off simultaneously and crushing by unanimous drive the Rebel forces of Lee and Johnstone and whoever else was left on the side of the Confederacy. With overwhelming numbers pitted against dwindling ranks, and well-fed troops facing lean and hungry soldiers, some of them existing on wild onions and unsalted corn bread, results could favor but one adversary.[1] Combined and thrown into concerted effort would be everything the Union could get together to bring to a close an impossible war that already had dragged over three weary years.

This strategy was the strategy of Ulysses S. Grant. He was a man new to the councils held in the presence of Abraham Lincoln, a West Pointer who had fought his way to prominence in the West, a cigar-smoking individual known even in Washington for his bottle-raising. But he believed in getting results, no matter how much matériel and how many casualties were required along the way, and results were what the Federal government wanted. Promotion to lieutenant general had preceded by only one day his appointment as commander-in-chief of United States armies.

In putting the new strategy into effect, Grant proposed to move out and drive hard against the South until the last Confederate was forced to surrender. The movement would be executed by twenty-one army corps of 533,000 officers and men, striking along the entire battle line from the Atlantic to the Rio Grande. In the West, Banks would move up the Red River toward Texas. Farther east, Sherman, with three combined armies, would storm Atlanta and then push on to the sea. Around Richmond the drive would come from various directions: Butler up the James from the coast, Meade down the Rappahannock, Crook from West Virginia, Sigel up the Valley, to keep the enemy in that area busy, a move later changed to provide for him to advance all the way to Charlottesville or Staunton and then to move toward the Rebel capital. And as Meade's army got under way, Burnside would come down with the Ninth Corps from Annapolis to guard the line of the Orange and Alexandria Railroad and protect Washington.

It was grand strategy, grand in the sense that it was all-engaging; it was simple strategy in that it called for force and unanimity of action, something no Union commander had accomplished in the past. If there was a time factor, it was not spelled out, but Grant gave every indication that he expected to be in Richmond before the summer ended.

Grant was a man of performance and he wanted around him subordinates of the same caliber. For that reason one of his first steps was to look over the corps and division leaders and to replace them where he thought replacements were needed. Faces familiar to Washington and along the B. & O. disappeared. Out went, among others, General Alfred Pleasanton, veteran leader of Union cavalry and a host who entertained with six-course dinners,[2] and in his place came a little-known general of doubtful capacity, Phil Sheridan, a 115-pounder who had grown a mustache and beard solely to hide his youth. One surprising appointment was that of General Franz Sigel, a forty-year-old German-American who loved to sit and talk about music, who was named to head the Department of West Virginia. He had fought in the revolutions in Germany, leading an army of 80,000 and gaining a reputation as one of the most accomplished artillerists in Europe.[3] But he had shortcomings, both in strategy and tactics, and he was accustomed to fighting in the grand manner, surrounded by flashy aides and a cavalry escort. It was also noticeable that he lacked the ability for organization that would be required to take an army through a hostile country teeming with guerrillas.[4] In his choice by Grant some people saw politics, the influence of Lincoln to cage the German vote for the fall elections. Citizens feared Sigel would be too partial in his selection of officers of Teutonic extraction.[5] But he took over command with some degree of popular acclaim, for in a short time "I goes to fight mit Sigel" was a familiar saying up and down the Valley.[6]

Some biographers of Grant have claimed he had a basilisk's gaze, that he could sit and whittle and smoke and look off beyond the immediate scene, and that what he was looking at was likely to come down in blood and ashes and crashing sound a little later.[7] As the new commander-in-chief laid his plans, he no doubt whittled and chewed his cigars and looked westward from trains running back and forth between Washington and Culpeper, but it is doubtful that his gaze went far enough. His eyes failed to see blue lights winking out of the darkness of the mountains, scattered campfires adding mystery to the night-blackened countryside, curious figures on horseback in the daytime staring patiently down from the hills, or the strange little bands of riders who lurked always on the trail of Union forces threading the area. These things were portents of importance beyond the vision of the basilisk. And they conveyed unwholesome news for grand strategy: out there was the guerrilla, the unknown factor, the warrior who followed no fixed schedule, no orthodox method of warfare. He it was who would upset the timing of the Union army.

Grant was culpable. Even from the beginning he took steps indicating he ignored this element, proved by the record to be made up of some of the best-organized Partisan bands in history. In one of his gravest omissions he took no action to protect the B. & O. —and therein he was leaving bare the Union's Achilles heel.

The first of the steps Grant took without respect for the guerrillas concerned Sigel's department. Soon after the German moved out along the B. & O. to take charge, announcing his presence through an advertisement in the newspapers, he sent an account to headquarters of what was involved in his command. He had 22,397 soldiers and 128 pieces of artillery. These were scattered along the entire line of the railroad, in squads, companies, and regiments. For the protection of small details guarding trestles and bridges, blockhouses had been and were being built. But not one point on the railway, with the possible exception of Harpers Ferry, was considered adequately defended. Even Cumberland with its 8000 inhabitants, the most important city between Baltimore and Wheeling—and the community where the new department chief would have his headquarters—was without satisfactory protection. New Creek, harboring immense military storehouses, was in the same predicament. And the condition of the troops, who had been lying still for so long a time, was poor.

At the same time Sigel was preparing his report, Grant was writing him from the field at Culpeper, sending an order that would diminish further the inadequate guard along the B. & O. Out of the Department of West Virginia, to aid in the move southward, must come everything "except a small force judiciously distributed for the protection of the most important bridges." [8] Of the 22,000-odd soldiers under Sigel's command, no fewer than 8000 infantry, three batteries of artillery, and 1500 cavalry were directed to be assembled at Beverly, there to await further directions on when to start the grand advance.

As Grant proceeded with his plans, Lee's scouts watched. Foremost among these was Mosby, operating constantly in the rear and on the flanks of the enemy. At one time a Union scouting party under the ambitious young Charles R. Lowell was sent through Loudoun County in search of the sandy-haired Partisan. The Union troopers stole carefully about the country, but their stealth was wasted. From families of Northern faith along the roadside they got messages of regard from Mosby: while they searched for him, he was reconnoitering them. [9]

Scouts Lee sent out to learn Grant's plans brought confusing intelligence at first. Bodies of troops and numbers of wagons were seen moving by rail toward Washington from the Rappahannock, in an opposite direction from the Confederates. This made no sense at the start, but it was later traced to the Union leader's determination to weed out all deadwood from his army before starting on the windup campaign.

One day amid all the confusion around Washington, pretty Elizabeth Bacon, bride for little more than two months of the fabulous young General George A. Custer, toast of most families north of the Potomac, wrote her parents something she had heard at a dinner party: "A story was told at table of one of Mosby's gang—it might have been himself—meeting a girl near the city and giving her a lock of his hair to give Lincoln with his compliments, and he would take dinner with him within 10 days." [10] This note revealed that Elizabeth was not a reader of the newspapers, for the Union capital's own daily, the *Star*, within the week had published the story, with certain variations. It told that the hair had definitely come from the head of Mosby and that he had entrusted it to the wife of a refugee whom he had encountered in the upper part of Fairfax County. And with the lock were sent two messages: one to Lincoln and the other to Governor Pierpont in Alexandria, and each to the effect that the guerrilla chieftain would soon visit them to make their acquaintance.

Lincoln never heard further from the threatened visit of Mosby, although if anything the guard on Chain Bridge was strengthened and more planks than usual were taken up at night. But Pierpont narrowly escaped. Only a rupture of the Rebel Partisan's plans prevented the promised visit. Mosby actually made a reconnaissance in front of the governor's quarters, concealed in a wagon loaded with hay, but further action was abandoned when he learned that the Union guard had been informed by citizens that his command was hiding on the outskirts of town.[11]

By late April the pieces in the jigsaw puzzle Grant was mapping began falling into place. The sick and the disabled and the parasites were moved away and the armies made ready. Captain Lemuel Abijah Abbott, stationed in the Union capital with the Tenth Vermont Infantry, wrote in his diary on the twenty-seventh: "It has been a pleasant spring day. Burnside's corps passing through Washington." [12]

Next day Burnside's troops were seen at Centreville, and Mosby was there watching them.[13] He had just come from a dash along the O. & A., an incident General Grant later recorded in his memoirs: "While my headquarters were at Culpeper, from the 26th of March to the 4th of May, I generally visited Washington once a week to confer with the Secretary of War and President. On the last occasion, a few days before moving, a circumstance occurred which came near postponing my part in the campaign altogether. Colonel John S. Mosby had for a long time been commanding a Partisan corps, or regiment, which operated in the rear of the Army of the Potomac. On my return to the field on this occasion, as the train approached Warrenton Junction, a heavy cloud of dust was seen to the east of the road as if made by a body of cavalry on a charge. Arriving at the junction the train was stopped and inquiries made as to the cause of the dust. There was but one man at the station, and he informed us that Mosby had crossed a few minutes before at full speed in pursuit of Federal cavalry. Had he seen our train coming, no doubt he would have let his prisoners escape to capture the train. I was on a special train, if I remember correctly, without any guard." [14]

General Grant was making the understatement of the week when he assumed that "Mosby would have let his prisoners escape to capture the train." On board that day, in addition to the commander-in-chief of the Union armies, was the fiery young George A. Custer, soon to take prominence as one of Mosby's most virulent enemies. [15]

The day after the raid along the railroad Mosby reported that Burnside had gone into camp at Bristoe, with an estimated 10,000 troops, and warned: "You may rely on it that the Yankees will try very hard to make the impression that a heavy column will advance up the Peninsula. Their papers announced on Tuesday that Burnside had gone to Fortress Monroe." [16]

The grand advance of all the eight separate armies was scheduled by Grant for May 4, but days ahead Sigel's troops began concentrating. [17] By April 28 they were gathered at Martinsburg and by May 2 at Strasburg, with a cavalry force trotting westward to spread false rumors as to their strength and intended movement. [18] That day Imboden, commanding Confederate forces in the Valley, rode out from Mount Jackson to meet him.

Imboden's troops at the moment numbered 1592 men, including 100 scouts on duty either in front or at the rear of the enemy, as well as the Partisan bands of McNeill and Gilmor. [19] The Rebel leader was under the impression that there were about 11,000 Federals in front of him, and he hurried off a plea for reinforcements. But Lee replied that he was sorely pressed by Grant and could not spare any of his strength at the moment, that Imboden should delay Sigel as much as possible until aid could be sent.

As Sigel advanced, the guerrillas moved in, striking relentlessly in many sections, like bees by day and night hawks by night. Mosby was extremely active. He went into Martinsburg while it was still swarming with Sigel's troops, moved about under cover of darkness, and brought off a number of horses and prisoners. Intercepting a wagon train near Bunker Hill, he added more animals and men to his bag, after which he divided his command into three sections and scattered them in different directions, leading one of them himself toward Grant's communications along the Rappahannock.[20]

Sigel flashed a frantic dispatch for no trains to be moved without a strong escort. Important messages were directed to be sent in cipher and to be forwarded by cavalrymen stationed at various points. But it made no difference: messengers were unable to get through anyway.

Back in April, Lee had tried to organize an attack against the B. & O., urging Imboden with the support of Mosby to make a raid in that direction, but streams flooded by spring rains prevented the action. As Sigel moved away from the railroad, McNeill's Rangers were detached and sent off to accomplish this objective, both to worry the Federals and to prevent new troops from coming in out of the West.

McNeill left with mixed feelings. Only a few weeks had passed since he was made to withstand the embarrassment of a court-martial at Staunton called by none other than Imboden. The charge concerned some deserters from the regular service the Partisan had permitted to join his command and had refused to release when directed. His guilt was indisputable, but his intentions seemed honorable. In the end his notable war record, coupled with the positive assurance that he had meant no wrong, brought about his acquittal.[21] If he carried hatred or resentment in his heart as he rode into the northwest, it was not reflected in what he accomplished.

Hours after he set out from Imboden's headquarters, McNeill drew up at Indian Old Field, in Hardy County, near his former home at Moorefield, for a bit of refurbishing,[22] and the information he acquired while at this point was highly encouraging. Unionists along the B. & O. were complaining of the exposed condition in which the railroad was left. Troops had been congregated at New Creek, Cumberland, Martinsburg, and other key points on the line, but these were moved away during April, as the date for Sigel's drive up the Valley neared, and no others had appeared in their place. It was said these were to come from Ohio and were to consist of 100-days men, recruits who had signed up for the period it was estimated it would take Grant to reach Richmond.

After nightfall on May 3 McNeill moved away from Moorefield and struck northward, accompanied by sixty men. A few hours before he resumed his trek, Union Secretary of War Stanton wired

Governor John Brough of Ohio an inquiry about the troops to protect the railroad, and the answer he got back was that seventeen regiments were ready to move as soon as they got rifles and blankets.

McNeill's Rangers rode throughout the night, slept in the woods next day, and climbed back into their saddles at dark for more hours of riding. At four o'clock next morning an early-rising citizen heard horsemen on the road near his home up along the sweep of the Alleghenies and learned they were the Partisans on their way to Piedmont. In great patriotic fervor he saddled his own steed and dashed away in the predawn darkness, facing a four-mile ride to carry a message to New Creek. It was 5:00 A.M. when he drew up in the town, his mount foaming and he sputtering, but no one connected with the military would pay him any mind. A guerrilla band was on its way, he shouted, and then looked up supplicatingly to the heavens when uniformed men merely hunched their shoulders and walked away asking, "So what?" To which the citizen waved his arms excitedly and cried anew: Piedmont was five miles to the west, a point of great importance for working the railroad, where there were machine shops and vast equipment stores—and few troops.[23]

But the rider was beating the air in vain. Only employees of the railroad would listen to him, and they had no manpower to send to Piedmont. But they did get an engine and five cars connected up as a train and brought them out near the main line, ready to convey troops if needed. Even these efforts were wasted. When great columns of smoke began rising above the horizon to the west some two hours later, a seventy-five-man detail with one howitzer was started in that direction—on foot, on a march that took an hour and a half when it could have been covered by rail in fifteen minutes.[24]

While the patriotic citizen was making his dash toward New Creek, McNeill led his Rangers along the route toward Bloomington bridge, a thirteen-year-old span across the Potomac at a point where the B. & O. began the ascent of the Allegheny Mountains. It was "daydawn," according to the Partisan leader, when they got there, but their wait was of short duration.[25] In a few minutes a freight train going east drifted downgrade and was flagged to a stop. Acting quickly, the Partisan put part of his raiders aboard, left behind a ten-man detail under Captain John T. Peerce, on detached service for the Confederate army, and ordered the remainder to follow in the wake of the train as it rolled toward Piedmont, bringing with them the horses of those on board.

The locomotive, operated by an engineer with a revolver near his ear, rocked slowly over the mile and a half to Piedmont. Along the way trees grew in close proximity to the tracks, leaving a tunnel-like lane for the train to pass through, while behind it came the Rangers on horseback and the riderless steeds. Thus, with the freight as a screen, the Partisans were able to get inside the important rail center before their presence was discovered by the small garrison on duty there, and the capture of the town was accomplished almost without a shot.

One of the first acts of the Rangers after they had taken over the place was to cut the telegraph wires, but they were unable to do this before an alert operator had sent a message of warning to New Creek and beyond. President John W. Garrett of the B. & O. was one of those who received it, and he spread it even unto the borders of Ohio. "Blankets and arms are on the way," he soon was wiring Governor Brough.[26]

Goaded by the telegraph operator's message, the military at New Creek sent off the seventy-five-man party and the howitzer. Shortly after they left, an unidentified man dashed away in the same direction on horseback, and forty-five minutes later people standing on the heights above Piedmont saw him come galloping up the New Creek road at full speed.[27] Far below them he appeared, a tiny automaton on a foam-flecked carrier. They watched him stop at a tiny speck on the green countryside, identified as McNeill's outer picket; then he and the speck moved together to a second speck, there for another brief halt, after which all three passed into the town.

Things happened fast after that. Smoke mounting up from the burning railroad property that made Piedmont important increased in volume. There were explosions and great flashes of flame, and a pandemonium of noise. Then out in the suburbs, westward toward Bloomington, McNeill's men could be seen assembling, and in a few minutes they rode away, long before the Union detail from New Creek made its appearance.

Behind them the Rangers left destruction that would go down in the records for completeness, an accomplishment that no doubt revived in their leader's mind thoughts of what might have happened to Cheat River bridge the previous year had he been permitted to carry out the raid he projected. They had set fire to the Georges Creek Railroad [28] bridge across the Potomac and had burned seven large buildings, some of them filled with machinery, engines, and cars. Included in the group were the machine and paint shops, and the sand, oil, engine, and roundhouses. They tore up 2000 feet of track, destroyed nine locomotives and seventy-five or eighty freight cars standing in the open, and sent six locomotives under a full head of steam toward New Creek.

Out at Bloomington as they fled westward, they found Peerce and his ten-man detail had not been idle. Three trains, a mail express, and two freights made up of eighteen cars laden with commissary stores, all captured without a shot, were rapidly becoming smoldering ruins, a part of them on the arch of the railroad bridge.[29] On board the express, consisting of the locomotive and a baggage, mail and four passenger cars, were 104 soldiers returning to their posts around Baltimore and Washington. A citizen had warned that they were coming, and they were quickly taken prisoner by a massive display of bluff, capped by a minute little individual from Baltimore named Charley Wilkins, who mounted the rear platform of the train and repeatedly yelled to an imaginary command to send up companies F and G.[30] Also among the passengers were the wife of General Lew Wallace, commanding the Middle Department at Baltimore, and the daughters of General Schenck, ex-departmental commander in the Union army and now back in his old seat in Congress. But no indignity was accorded the ladies. Peerce, hat in hand, rode to the windows of the car in which they sat and informed them that their train had been captured by Southern troops —"men who were gentlemen before they were soldiers." [31]

While the Rangers loitered at Bloomington, the Union force from New Creek appeared on the scene and halted to swing the howitzer into action. The few shots fired made no contribution to the Union's success in the war, for the raiders fled in advance of the heavy shells, and the Federal pursuit soon swung about for the return to base.

One purpose of the Rebel raid had been to make Sigel detach some of his troops for the protection of the B. & O. This action came on the day after the dash on Piedmont was accomplished. A force of 450 men from the Twenty-second Pennsylvania Cavalry was sent westward, and the following afternoon they came up with McNeill's band resting on a mountainside near Moorefield. High on the slope lay the Rebels, reading the mail they had taken from the express at Bloomington bridge, and they continued to loll there, undisturbed and peacefully scanning love letters and other missiles, until the Federals climbed to within a short distance of them. Then they swung into their saddles and skedaddled in a mass movement across the back of the mountain.

Washington yelled loud over this attack on the railroad. Even while his wife waited with other women for transportation away from Bloomington, Lew Wallace wired a fellow officer: "The raid on the road at Piedmont must wake us up. The destruction of property there was enormous, considering that it was accomplished by but 75 guerrillas. Such a thing must not happen to us." [32] There would be other repercussions, one of which would penalize the 100-days men from Ohio: instead of going into comfortable quarters for guard duty at Washington and Baltimore as originally planned, all but two of their regiments would be assigned to blockhouses and other lonesome outposts along the B. & O.

But the over-all effect of this blow at Sigel's back was greater than appeared on paper. He moved his army up the Valley thoroughly beset with troubles, most of them brought on by guerrillas. In front of him waited Imboden with a small force, the size of which the Federal commander knew, but out behind the rolling hills, down in the gullies of the Valley and up along the recesses of the mountain slopes rising on each side were the guerrillas, strength unknown. The New York *Herald* at this time kindly announced that Mosby and White were in the army's rear, but this told Sigel nothing he didn't already know. He had learned by hard experience that McNeill was there, and soon to come his way were reports that Gilmor was back in action. On arriving at Staunton, so the rumor went, General John C. Breckinridge, distinguished politician and soldier, dispatched to the Valley to aid Imboden, had reviewed the court-martial against the Partisan, including all the evidence of his robbing the Jews, and had decided that he would do the South more good in the saddle than in jail.

Guerrillas were reported over a broad area. Mosby was said to be in Loudoun, in Berryville, throughout the mountains along the Shenandoah, up and down the B. & O., and even toward Fredericksburg in the rear of Grant's army, where he was accused of attacking an unguarded ambulance train.[33] But some of this was due partly to the fact that Mosby's name was the name most familiar to the tongues of Federal privates. When the irregulars struck, the cry up and down the line was identical: "Mosby!"

No matter who was to blame, depredations went on without letup. Couriers disappeared. So did wagons and horses, and sometimes vehicles were found standing in the road minus horses, a maze of hoofprints pointing accusingly toward the mountains. Supplies became so scarce at times, due to interruptions, that Sigel is reputed to have said on one occasion, "A biscuit is worth yust now more den a bayonet." [34] The garrison at Harpers Ferry asked for more cavalry to use against the guerrillas. [35] Martinsburg, from which Sigel's army was being supplied, was in a panic. Horses were taken from two sutler's wagons on its outskirts, and suspicious persons could be seen on the hills staring down at the town with a spyglass. [36] General Kelley, commanding troops guarding the B. & O., was screaming too. He was exceedingly anxious to get some good cavalry, and he had no scruples about wiring: "We must kill, capture or drive McNeill out of the country before we can expect quiet or safety along line of road." [37]

Scouting parties of from 200 to 600 cavalry were sent in various directions, with orders to follow the guerrillas as far as they could. But it made no difference how far or fast they rode, results were negligible. The Rebel Partisans knew the country and the best hiding places.

At last Sigel was driven by circumstances, or so he thought, to divide his force. It was a desperate move, questionable beyond a doubt: dividing an army variously fixed at 7000 horsemen and foot soldiers to cope with known Rebel regular strength of fewer than 1600. A Confederate signal station on top of Massanutten Mountain, overlooking Strasburg, was soon wigwagging intelligence of what was in progress—two bodies of cavalry of about 1000 each were riding out from the flank of Sigel's army, one westward on the Moorefield road, the other eastward through Front Royal. Imboden, when he received the message, surmised that this was being done, before the march up the Valley was continued, to determine whether the enemy was in greater force within striking distance on either flank. [38]

Imboden was correct in his surmise. The flanking parties were dispatched to learn what was happening on the outskirts, beyond the nearest mountain barriers, the one moving eastward into Luray

Valley having as its main objective protection of the Federal troops against Mosby.[39]

At four o'clock that afternoon, a Sunday, Imboden rode westward from his camp at Woodstock with a part of his force, including McNeill's Rangers. He was headed for "Devil's Hole" Pass in the North Mountain, and rumors circulated in the neighborhood told that he was going only a short distance in search of better grazing for the horses. While he faced the setting sun, Harry Gilmor's little-revived band swung out toward the east, unnoticed against the larger movement, and trotted toward Luray.

Next evening Kelley passed on the bad news to Sigel: "Rumor says that your cavalry were attacked this A.M. near Wardensville by a superior force, under Imboden and McNeill, and were totally routed . . ."[40] A few hours later he was forwarding the additional information that the Union force had burned its wagon train and fled through Romney and across the Potomac.

There was other bad news in store. Rain began to pour, and from down Fredericksburg way a stubborn Grant, amazed by an equally stubborn Lee in six days of heavy fighting, sent word that he was proposing "to fight it out on this line if it takes all summer."[41] A wagon train swinging southward from Martinsburg was attacked by some of Mosby's men and several members of its guard were killed or captured. As Sigel pushed on to Woodstock, one of his division wagon masters was handed a note bearing the signature of the chief quartermaster. It ordered the vehicles to be swung about, sutlers' wagons and all, and to go to the rear. The wagoner reread the message in the dripping weather. It made no sense, so little in fact that he studied the handwriting carefully and was suspicious to the point of conviction. A good thing he was: waiting back there with gloating eyes was a band of guerrillas.[42]

Then came the staggering blow. Sigel's flanking party that had gone toward the east had been headed by the veteran William H. Boyd, now a colonel, the same energetic leader who had driven Mosby to the limb of a tree in his nightdress the preceding summer. Boyd took his time in the rain, unmolested and unaware that a band of Rebel Partisans was riding on his trail. Gilmor was waiting at Mount Jackson when Imboden's victorious troopers returned from the west, and now their attention was turned toward the Blue Ridge. Next day about sunset, Boyd led his blue-clad horsemen, all from the Fifteenth New York and Cole's Maryland Cavalry, into a trap. Imboden wired results to Breckinridge, who by this time had gathered up a force of about 3000, including reserves and the Virginia Military Institute cadet corps, and had got down the Valley to Harrisonburg: "We pitched into him [Boyd], cut him off from the roads, and drove him into the Massanutten Mountain. Numbers have been captured, together with about half of all their horses. They are wandering in the mountain tonight cut off . . . Colonel Boyd was wounded." [43]

Sigel's flanking parties, sent out chiefly to guard against guerrillas, had each met with a sad fate, and the delay they caused would bring the same lot to the main force marching up the Valley. The irregulars daily were striking at the wagon trains, intercepting communications, capturing horses, and snatching up stragglers. Much of this period was spent in scouting, in a futile effort to capture or drive off the guerrillas.[44] And now Breckinridge, with 2500 hardened soldiers and 500 not-so-hardened reserves and V.M.I. cadets, was ready to join forces with Imboden.

Imboden spent the intervening time quietly at New Market. On the afternoon of May 14 Sigel's troops began to appear along the Valley pike from the northeast, and drew up north of the town. The remainder of the day was spent in an artillery duel, and that night the soldiers lay down in the rain to sleep.

Two hours before daylight Imboden was aroused by the rays of a tin lantern shining in his face as a camp guard shook him to announce that General Breckinridge had arrived. Soon the Confederates were taking position, and daylight brought cavalry skirmishing around the town. The battle grew hotter as the day advanced. At last the strain became so heavy upon the Rebels that the V.M.I. cadets were called into action—225 boys ranging in age from sixteen to eighteen—and behind them on the field as casualties they left nearly a fourth of their number. But they had helped turn the tide, a tide that was capped by a master stroke of flanking by Imboden, the old artillerist from Staunton.

At seven o'clock that night Breckinridge sent headquarters a brief summary of the day's happenings: "This morning two miles above New Market, my command met the enemy, under General Sigel, advancing up the Valley, and defeated him with heavy loss. The action has just closed at Shenandoah River. Enemy fled across North Fork of the Shenandoah, burning the bridge behind him." [45]

Theories on the cause of Sigel's defeat were tossed around for weeks as Grant tried to correct this upset to his combined movement, but the soundest explanation seemed to point to the guerrillas. Sigel had under his command, in addition to artillery, eight regiments of infantry, four regiments of cavalry, and detachments from three others, but he was able to bring only six regiments of foot soldiers into battle, along with his cavalry and artillery.[46] His other troops were scattered along the road to the rear, guarding his wagon train against the Partisan horsemen who had been heckling him constantly from the moment he started up the Valley.[47]

CHAPTER 2

May 16–June 19, 1864

GUERRILLAS BLOCK
THE AMMUNITION

Slow tidings of bad news serve to postpone the misery. So it was that Washington was spared for nearly forty-eight hours the shock of what happened at New Market. The day immediately following the upset went in the records as another in which the Lord's blessings favored the cause of the Union. A succession of heavy rains swelled the streams, preventing pursuit.

But on the seventeenth of May the Lord seemed to waver in His allegiance. That was the day word arrived that the Army of the Shenandoah had been defeated. Sigel tried to cushion the blow, reporting to Kelley that he "had to withdraw" behind Cedar Creek because he was greatly outnumbered, "as Breckinridge has evidently thrown his principal forces against me." [1] This intelligence was passed on to Halleck, and it reached him at a bad time. Grant had just forwarded a suggestion that Sigel keep on up the Valley to Staunton, [2] and in reply the Chief of Staff was forced to answer: "I have sent the substance of your dispatch to General Sigel. Instead of advancing on Staunton he is already in full retreat on Strasburg. If you expect anything from him you will be mistaken. He will do nothing but run. He never did anything else. The Secretary of War proposes to put General Hunter in his place." [3]

Hunter it was. Grant was having trouble with Lee and he could not be obstinate about who was to take over direction of the only segment in his eight-army attack against the Confederacy that seemed to be failing. Sharp on the heels of Halleck's original message came a note to the effect that Lincoln would name Hunter to the command of the Department of West Virginia "if you desire it." [4] Grant had too many other problems to be bothered, so he hastily wired back: "By all means I would say appoint General Hunter, or anyone else, to the command of West Virginia." [5]

David Hunter, son of a Virginia minister, was no prize. [6] An opportunist friend of Lincoln who posed as a Moses to lead the nation out of its troubles, he had never shown ability as a field commander. From his native New Jersey he went to West Point, and then he developed through the years, both in and out of service, into what was described as "an honest, anti-slavery paymaster, with a dyed mustache and a dark-brown wig." He fought in the Mexican War and afterward was stationed at Fort Leavenworth, Kansas. It was there he heard Southern officers in the garrison say Lincoln, or no other Abolitionist President for that matter, would ever take office, and this information he passed on to Abe, building up an acquaintance that led to his choice as one of four officers to accompany the President-elect from Illinois to Washington. After the inauguration he was ordered by General Scott to take charge of the White House, and the ex-paymaster was on his way. When war came, he was appointed colonel of a cavalry regiment and then a brigade, and in the first battle of Bull Run he was wounded. Recovered, he was assigned to the Department of the West and, after some months, to the Department of the South. He was the first to issue an order freeing slaves and he was the first to organize a regiment of freedmen for military duty, actions that earned him tremendous hatred throughout Dixie. His Virginia cousins detested him. Nearing his sixty-second birthday, he had just returned to Washington from the Red River campaign when he was picked to succeed Sigel.

This change of command was not altogether to the liking of the private soldier in the Army of the Shenandoah. Sigel had been considered a good officer, kind to his men. But Hunter had the appearance of being quite different. One soldier wrote of him in a diary: "Dark complexion, black moustache, stern looking. We don't like his looks." [7]

Hunter left Washington by special train at noon of the twentieth. As he rolled westward along the B. & O., there were significant troubles in the area he was to command. Near Strasburg a wagon train swung southward with supplies for his army, and suddenly, in brazen contempt for the 600 infantry and 100 cavalry guarding it, a small band of Mosby's guerrillas struck with death to both sides. The Partisans were driven off, but not without strong hint that the Army of the Shenandoah would have to detach a heavy force to guard its communications. After the attack only one train went up the Valley to Hunter's troops, a highly important development in view of what was to happen at Lynchburg.

This one train that got through to him was a disappointment and drew sharp orders from the new commanding general. Thirty of its wagons were loaded with forage and a number of others with superfluous clothing, something the moving army didn't need, so Hunter directed that only ammunition—and not one pound of any kind of stores—should be conveyed to him in the future.

But Hunter need not have worried about the future: the guerrillas saw to it that this one train brought him his last supplies.[8]

Once at his post the new commander quickly took charge. Before many hours passed he was wiring Washington that he had directed Crook to move immediately on Staunton, where they could combine their forces and push directly east via Charlottesville and Gordonsville. That night, while he worked over his plans, he could see rockets from Rebel hands soaring through distant darkness. They zoomed upward and disappeared, their duty performed, leaving behind for the enemy silent messages of annoyance, mystery, and contempt.

Waiting for Hunter's approval at his new post was a proposal by General Max Weber, commanding at Harpers Ferry, that the First New York Veteran Cavalry should be sent through Jefferson and Loudoun counties to clear out the guerrillas. The suggestion got a quick rejection: "This regiment cannot be spared from operations in the field." [9]

Kelley meanwhile was more seriously concerned over the Rebel Partisans, especially McNeill. At about the same hour Hunter was wiring Washington of his plans to meet Crook, "Old Ben" was ordering a detail of 150 men in the direction of Moorefield. Its leader was Captain James P. Hart, a man well familiar with the area, and Kelley gave him no minute instructions. "I will simply say," he ordered, "I want McNeill killed, captured, or driven out of the Valley." [10] This was a fond hope Kelley was to voice several times before the Partisan was in his grave.

At Moorefield, Hart's contact must have been solely with friends of Hanse McNeill, for everyone he talked with said the independent had gone to the Valley. So the captain at last accepted this as the truth and retraced his steps, unaware that the man he was looking for lurked with his band in the hills only a short distance away. When he heard that Hart had been duped, Kelley was furious and quickly ordered him back to the area, on another futile junket, this time almost to his destruction. [11]

Hunter, in organizing his command for the march up the Valley, made certain significant changes. To guard the railroad he would leave at his rear, and from which he hoped to draw ammunition and supplies when needed, he assigned Sigel, the officer he had succeeded. This appointment was made at the direction of the authorities at Washington. [12] Sigel was to have complete charge of the guard along the B. & O., with Kelley and Weber as his subordinates, each assigned to a particular section of the line.

Looking over the men comprising his army, Hunter found them in good shape except for the cavalry. That arm, he wired Halleck, needed a new commander because it "is utterly demoralized from frequent defeats by inferior forces and retreats without fighting." [13]

Developing his plans, he made conscious—and revolutionary—effort to improve the efficiency of the fighting force. "We are contending against an enemy who is in earnest, and if we expect success, we too must be in earnest," he wrote in general orders. [14] After this preamble he proceeded to lay down specific instructions. There was to be no dawdling, no foraging, and no looting along the way. The army was to be streamlined, even to the contents of wagons: ammunition, camp kettles, tools, and mess pans. And only one wagon to a regiment. Soldiers were restricted to the clothes on their backs, an extra pair of shoes and socks, 100 rounds of ammunition, four pounds of hard bread, and 10 rations of coffee, sugar, and salt. Commands were to be supplied from the country. "Cattle, sheep and hogs, and if necessary horses and mules, must be taken and slaughtered," he decreed. The army was to march and camp in order of battle, the infantry in front, cavalry in rear, and artillery and trains in the center. [15]

Up the Valley waiting for these orders to be carried out were the guerrillas, poised to enter into their peculiar operations. The task before them would be difficult and hazardous, but results would be concentrated: every time they captured a wagon they would be depriving an entire regiment of its reserve ammunition.

In utter defiance of the threat from the Rebel irregulars, Hunter became parsimonious in meting out the strength of train escorts. Colonel William P. Maulsby, commanding at Martinsburg, asked 400 men to a train, and Hunter replied that this seemed three or four times too many, except for those of special and urgent value.[16]

Maulsby thus was placed in an impossible position. Denied extra troops as train escorts, he was forced to make the best of a bad situation. His first test of this nature came on May 23, the day Hunter had chosen to commence the march southward. From Harpers Ferry he was notified that 150 of Mosby's men had crossed into his neighborhood and immediately he flashed a warning: "Send no trains out unless very well guarded, as they will surely be attacked." [17]

Hunter was delayed in getting his army under way. Difficulties magnified. Guerrillas struck at Martinsburg, at Berlin, Maryland, at scattered points closer to headquarters, and blockhouses along the weakly guarded B. & O. mysteriously went up in flames. A lengthy proclamation was distributed to prominent Secessionist citizens over the name of the commanding general. It shifted the burden of penalty for the Partisan attacks upon the populace, just as Pope and Milroy and others had done in previous years: for every train fired upon or soldier of the Union wounded or assassinated, the houses and other property of every Secession sympathizer within a circuit of five miles from the place of the outrage would be destroyed by fire. Furthermore, for each piece of public property jayhawked by the marauders, an assessment of five times the value would be made upon the citizens of Southern allegiance within a circuit of ten miles, all to be held in custody until payments had been made.[18]

Little things and big things happened simultaneously. While Hunter warned the public, Andrew T. Leopole, a guerrilla of long experience, went to death on the scaffold in the presence of General Lew Wallace and staff.[19] And at Grafton, West Virginia, the gun of Dan Dusky, a massive fifteen-pound weapon with a five-eighth-inch bore, was placed on display as U. S. government property.[20]

At 10:30 A.M. May 26 Hunter's army began moving.[21] It had been told it might have to eat quite a bit of horsemeat before it returned.

Swinging southward in a long line went 8500 men, while in the opposite direction, empty, rolled a string of wagons.[22] Somewhere en route Rebels concealed in houses took potshots at the teamsters of these wagons and, in compliance with Hunter's orders, the buildings in which they hid were burned.

That night the army went into camp at Fisher's Hill, worried by Confederates lurking in the distance ahead. A halt was called, both in caution and to await arrival of a supply of shoes. For the next two days scouting parties were sent in all directions, some in Rebel gray, to make sure Hunter was not marching into a trap.

At 4:30 A.M. on the twenty-ninth the advance was resumed. Shoes had been obtained, and Hunter notified Halleck he was ready, destination Lynchburg.[23] He was much pleased with the infantry, though worried over a shortage of knapsacks, a disparity that made it necessary to convey by vehicle some of the ammunition ration of 100 rounds per man.[24]

There was worry aplenty.[25] Hunter expected important dispatches to come to him via a line of communications set up through Edenburg and Woodstock. How uneasy his feelings, then, when he was notified McNeill's Rangers had changed position and were operating along that route!

As Hunter marched south from Winchester, on the trail of the army rolled sixteen wagons guarded by eighty-three men from the Fifteenth New York Cavalry under Lieutenant A. I. Root. Late in the afternoon it reached the little village of Newtown, so new it had scarcely a dozen houses. Soon after the train had cleared the community, Partisans under the dashing Harry Gilmor, carrying love letters and proposals of marriage among his papers, attacked and captured it.[26] The affair was of short duration. Panicked, the guard fled, leaving behind a captain dead, nine soldiers wounded, and nine captured.

That night was sleepless for the Newtownites. They threw their efforts into the emergency gallantly, bringing the wounded into their village and giving them all the attention and medical care possible, but they went about these activities with terror in their hearts. Out on the Valley pike within walking distance smoldered the remains of a dozen wagons, all of those left behind by the guerrillas, and fresh in their thoughts was the proclamation issued by Hunter.

When Gilmor rode back into Newtown a few hours later, he found only strained countenances. "We shall be homeless before tomorrow night," the villagers told him. The Partisan leader was moved by their fears. Ripping out pen and paper, he dashed off a note of dire threat. He held thirty-five men and six officers as prisoners, he said. These he would take to a secure place in the Blue Ridge and, upon learning that Newtown had been burned, would kill them and send their bodies to the Valley. Then he rode into the night, leaving the villagers to their fate.

Next day, the thirtieth, was a day of anxiety but not of burning. No Federal troops appeared at Newtown, and the residents, suffering under the suspense, proceeded with their care of the wounded. As they suspected, developments of a retaliatory nature were under way. The First New York Cavalry got orders: a detail of 200 was to move next morning at three o'clock to burn every house, store, and outbuilding in Newtown except the churches and the residences of people known to be loyal citizens of the United States.

This unpleasant chore was assigned Major Joseph K. Stearns, who by some chance was a friend of Gilmor. He led his detail, one of whose officers was Captain Ezra Bailey of Mollie Murphy adoration, into Newtown in the early dawn. There waiting for him were the villagers, still sleepless, prominent among them the young and the aged. They brought letters to prove their husbands and brothers and fathers were fighting with Lee's army and not among Gilmor's Partisans. That on their word of honor. They stood in communal groups and wrung their hands while tears flowed freely. And they told over and over that they had spent tireless hours caring for those nine wounded Union soldiers they had hauled in from the scene of the burned wagons.

Stearns and his companions listened, and murmurings of disapproval over their orders were heard. The major was so touched that he preferred facing a firing squad to destroying the homes of helpless people. His fellow officers shared his defiance. So, after long deliberation, back to his command he rode, taking the note of threat from Gilmor, and three days later he went in person to report his decision to Hunter. There, to the surprise of many, the matter ended.

Hunter's army marched on. The weather was hot and muggy and

the men at night, unable to sleep, sat up late and watched the Signal Corps members as they experimented with rockets from Roman candles. Even the private was told to keep a sharp lookout for guerrillas, another reason for their lack of sleep.

Harrisonburg came into view. Many of the men were barefooted. In two regiments alone, 387 were without shoes.[27] And rations were running low, so low that soldiers took to foraging, in direct violation of Hunter's efficiency orders. Some of them were caught and taken before the commanding general. In his fiercest manner he prescribed blanket punishment: all noncommissioned officers to be reduced to the ranks, all privates to carry a heavy fence rail over the shoulder while walking a beat for four hours. One lonely trooper made a special recording of the incident in his diary: "The lack of rations and seeing the boys undergoing a severe punishment made a gloomy time for us . . . We are 70 miles from our base of supplies, which must be brought to us in wagons under a strong guard. Cavalry must do that duty. Reported that they have much trouble from the guerrillas under Mosby and others. They keep concealed in the woods along the pike. From the hills they can be seen far up and down the Valley."[28]

Up to this period of the campaign Hunter had been bothered only by guerrillas, which was bother enough in view of the fact he could never make sure what they were doing. McNeill was said to be preparing for an attack on the B. & O. Closer at hand, Mosby was assembling his men at Berryville, 400 to 600 of them, according to reports, and it could not be determined what he was planning, whether a raid on the railroad or an attack on the next wagon train that tried to move up the Valley. But all intelligence concerning him was confusing. He was seen at Upperville, and again, on the same day, at Berry's Ferry. Rumor even said he had attempted to sneak into Alexandria and kidnap Governor Pierpont. All of it made a puzzling picture.

But for that matter Hunter knew no more about the Confederate regulars than he did about the guerrillas. Through Harrisonburg and on southward he pushed, wondering what was in his way. At a little village on the Valley pike known as Piedmont, on June 5, he got some indication. There in front of him appeared a small army of Confederates, mostly cavalry, rounded up and rushed from below Lynchburg by Grumble Jones, the leader under whom Mosby had fought at the beginning of the war. For ten hours that day severe fighting rocked the little village and then, as darkness settled, the Rebels fled southward, completely routed, their commander shot through the head.

Next morning two ambulances and a squad of three men led by Major Charles T. O'Ferrall, one day to be governor of Virginia, appeared in front of Hunter's advance waving a flag of truce. Its function was to gather up the bodies of Jones and two colonels killed in the fighting at Piedmont and, in doing so, to delay the enemy's progress if possible until the routed army could escape through a gap in the mountains. Greetings between the opposing forces were friendly and mutual, and a courier was hurried off to Hunter. An hour and a half passed before a reply was returned. It was not satisfactory: Hunter refused to see O'Ferrall. The Confederate officer was insistent, more to cause delay than to recover the bodies. So a second courier was dispatched, and this time the Union leader sent back a curt note that the Rebel dead had been decently buried. O'Ferrall picked up his flag of truce after this assurance and departed, his mission largely fulfilled.[29]

That day Hunter got specific instructions from Grant. Sheridan was on his way up from Richmond to destroy the railroad around Charlottesville, and the commander-in-chief wanted the army in the Valley to move toward Lynchburg and begin destruction from that direction.

But Hunter had a problem: his ammunition was becoming dangerously short, especially in view of the amount used in the ten-hour fighting at Piedmont. Replenishments from the nearest rail head, the B. & O., were blocked by guerrillas. It was an emergency that called for immediate action. Among the less seriously wounded of the Federals after the fight with Grumble Jones was Major General Julius Stahel, a brave and energetic officer. Unfit for further field duty at the moment, he was directed to return to Martinsburg, to assemble all the troops available, and to escort up the Valley a wagon train loaded with ammunition.

Stahel started back on his mission. The area in which he must organize the train was anything but peaceful. General Lew Wallace had just notified Halleck that the B. & O. neighborhood was infested with bands of guerrillas, "not strong enough to fight, but numerous enough to commit all kinds of depredations, such as breaking into toll-houses, stealing horses, etc." [30] And Gilmor was said to be organizing for a raid somewhere between Martinsburg and Harpers Ferry.[31]

Meanwhile Hunter reached Staunton, bothered by increasing reports of guerrilla activity. A new Partisan leader, Mudwall Jackson, was said to dominate that section, and Federals wondered if his name had been confused with that of Stonewall Jackson, long in his grave.[32] On the second day there, Crook arrived from West Virginia after a successful raid along the Virginia and Tennessee Railroad. The combined forces—18,000 men—now moved southward, destroying railroads, Rebel supplies, and manufacturing establishments.

At Lexington, where it was thought the V.M.I. cadets and Confederate horsemen under General John McCausland were waiting to give battle, batteries were run forward and a bombardment started. This was kept up for several hours and then, at noon of June 12, the town was entered without resistance. The next few hours were infamous to the residents. Hungry soldiers looted at random. Somewhere they found Captain Matthew X. White of the First Virginia Cavalry, there to see his mother, and took him off in the woods and shot him, leaving his body to be watched over that night by three young girls. An aged citizen, prominent in the community, resented the intrusion in such strong language that someone struck him over the head with a saber, inflicting a mortal wound. In rapid succession, mills and warehouses, the home of Governor John Letcher, who had just issued a proclamation urging the people to adopt guerrilla warfare against the invaders, and the buildings of V.M.I., including the professors' houses, went up in flames.

It was cold and calculated destruction. As one Union soldier wrote: "Many of the women look sad and do much weeping over the destruction that is going on. We feel that the South brought on the war and the State of Virginia is paying dear for her part." [33]

Hunter left Lexington in flames and kept on southward. And now there was someone else moving to get in his way. Sheridan's projected movement to destroy the railroad around Charlottesville had failed. At Trevilian Station on the Virginia Central Railroad sixty miles or so west of Richmond, Confederate cavalry under General Wade Hampton blocked his path, sending him on a wide circuit north and east in order to get back into the Union lines. This left the way open for Lee to dispatch troops after Hunter, and picturesque old Jubal Early, grizzled tobacco-chewing artist who loved fighting next to whisky-guzzling, was sent toward Lynchburg to do his best.

Early moved with two objects in mind: the first was to destroy Hunter, and the second, he wired General Breckinridge at Lynchburg, "is not prudent to trust to telegraph."[34] His progress was rapid—Louisa Court House one night, Charlottesville, nearly thirty miles away, the next. He covered ground like a conquering hero, messaging for cars to be sent to convey his troops, cussing at every count, instilling confidence in his men. He and Lee had had an extended conference before he left the lines around Richmond, and he knew what he was about.[35]

Matters were not so pleasing to the Federals. Sigel had got word from Hunter about sending ammunition and was prepared to do so in a train of forty to fifty wagons guarded by 500 infantry and 300 cavalry. Then Stahel arrived on the scene fresh from Hunter with talk about a larger train, and plans were changed. The hours following comprised a period of severe tension. Grant's only apprehension about Hunter was that he would run out of ammunition.[36] Halleck was worried about this too, and on top of that he was pessimistic about the possibilities that any train could get through to the army around Lynchburg.[37] He knew, from reports coming into Washington, that guerrillas were waiting in force to intercept the next wagons rolling up the Valley.

Hunter's march became desperate and problems mounted. Orders were given for all wagons that broke down to be burned, for all horses that gave out on the road to be shot. Wagons without horses were put to the torch also. Nothing must impede the army's progress; it must get to Lynchburg and capture the Confederate stores reputed to have been assembled there.

The morning of the seventeenth, Federal troops made their appearance on the northern outskirts of Lynchburg. They delayed action, waiting for the remainder of the army to arrive, and at one o'clock in the afternoon there was loud cheering from the heart of the city: Jubal Early had stormed in, cussing and spitting, to join the V.M.I. cadets and McCausland's cavalry and other forces assembled there by Lee's orders. At intervals for the next twenty-four hours more such cheering was heard as trains brought in additional troops, swelling the defenders of the city to 10,000 infantry and 2000 cavalry.[38] Union soldiers lay on the skirmish line that night knowing they would face stiff resistance on the morrow, for there was hammering and chopping all night. They wondered why their own forces were idle, but concluded that their cavalry was flanking the city.[39]

Next day there was rugged fighting for a brief period, and then Hunter began moving back. "We did not think such a thing possible," wrote a Federal soldier. "We must and would take Lynchburg at all hazards; rations we must have and we could get them only in Lynchburg. We could never retreat, that was impossible; if we were not all captured we should certainly starve." [40]

But Hunter was retreating, as impossible as it might seem. He was moving by a roundabout way toward West Virginia, taking the route Averell, the guitar-twanging Union cavalryman, had followed when he made his dash on the railroad the preceding fall. It was a circuit that would take him far out of the battle area along the Shenandoah and bring him back into the picture weeks later at Martinsburg. Hunter's trail, some historians would say, was like that of Xenophon when he moved from Cunaxa to the Black Sea in 401 B.C. Hard on it came young Henry Kyd Douglas of Jackson's staff, for this was the Stonewall Brigade Early was leading, and the youthful soldier wrote vividly of what he saw: "It was a scene of desolation. Ransacked houses, crying women, clothes from the bed chambers and wardrobes of ladies, carried along on the bayonets and dragged in the road, the garments of little children, and here and there a burning house marked the track of Hunter's retreat. I had never seen anything like this before and for the first time in the war I felt that vengeance ought not to be left entirely to the Lord." [41]

To the surprise of everyone, including the Wheeling *Intelligencer,* one of the newspapers that scored him unmercifully, Hunter reported his expedition had been "extremely successful." [42] He said he deemed it best to withdraw because he was running short of ammunition and supplies in the presence of an enemy he believed superior in numbers. Writing of it later in life, General John B. Gordon, Early's capable lieutenant, said: "If I were asked for an opinion as to this utterly causeless fright and flight, I should be tempted to say that conscience, the inward monitor which 'makes cowards of us all,' was harrowing General Hunter." [43]

For long years to come there would be discussion and theories as to why on his retreat Hunter had chosen to go out into West

Virginia instead of retracing his steps through the Valley. The decision had been left up to him by Grant.[44] One reason for his choice may have been assurance from Crook that supplies were waiting along the route that he himself had just followed in coming east. But it is obvious Hunter remembered the guerrilla bands lurking along the roadside to upset his progress if he backtracked. They would see to it that no supply trains from as far down as the B. & O. got to him, and that would mean starvation, for his men had stripped the country on their way to Lynchburg and the Southerners had hidden what little food remained.

Along the B. & O. while Hunter retreated westward, Stahel worked frantically to ready the ammunition train that had been his obsession since early June. On the twenty-fourth it was ready to move, but by that time no one knew the whereabouts of the army for which it was intended. Stahel advanced cautiously, uncertain whether to go southward or westward, and in that dilemma his progress was slow until an order finally came, while he still was only a few miles out, for him to swing the train about and return to Martinsburg.

This order saved ammunition for the Union army, and it no doubt prevented casualties to both sides. While Stahel was getting his important train under way, Mosby was at Berryville gathering troops to attack it as soon as it got far enough away from its base.[45]

June 20–July 30, 1864

"NOTHING BUT THE DEEPEST SHAME"

Judging from the great test to which he was subjected, Henry Halleck obviously was immune to high-blood pressure. The bloaty-faced chief of staff, serving from behind his desk in Washington as a liaison between all the armies Grant was trying to move simul-taneously, had problems and frustrations that were many. One of his greatest difficulties was lack of information. When guerrillas weren't busy cutting the telegraph wires leading into the Union capital, they were rounding up Union couriers, and sometimes they did both. That was the reason largely that a period of two weeks went by without Halleck hearing directly from Hunter. He knew that Stahel had been sent back to organize a column for the protec-tion of an ammunition train, a train he very much doubted would get through the screen of irregulars operating in Hunter's rear, but that was the extent of his knowledge of the Valley campaign.

Actually, the operations of Hunter, as well as those of officers directing the other armies, were the problem of Grant, the com-mander-in-chief, and Halleck was willing enough to let them drop in his lap. It was his own responsibility to tie up the loose ends and dispatch troops and supplies where they were most needed. And therein was involved a matter of making decisions that was much more complicated than the one of putting little potatoes in one basket and big potatoes in another. Out in Kentucky, for example,

Rosecrans and Sam Curtis were asking for 20,000 troops to oppose 2000 guerrillas.[1] They not only were asking; they were trying to stimulate action by stampeding members of Congress with telegrams. It didn't make sense, and the chief of staff wrote Grant about it, more to let off steam than with any hope of attracting sympathy.

Though unrecognized by Halleck, and apparently by Grant, a more urgent matter was working its way to the fore as rapidly as the guerrilla-stymied communications of the Union army would permit: Hunter's disappearance into West Virginia had left the Shenandoah Valley wide open and Jubal Early was on his way northward, on as beautiful an end run as ever upset the populace of an anti-slavery nation. He was putting into execution that other object that was "not prudent to trust to telegraph."

Halleck eventually got word of this new threat, but in the meantime troubles bobbed up nearer the Union capital. A four-man patrol of the Sixteenth New York Cavalry was fired on near Annandale one night, and two of the number escaped to spread the alarm. There was quick response. A detail of forty heavily armed troops rode out under the command of a lieutenant to investigate. They threaded their way doggedly through the night, past dawn, and into the morning without stopping. An hour or so before noon, on the road between Centreville and Chantilly, they came upon a field of new-mown hay and there they called a halt to feed their horses. In the shortest time thereafter they were transformed from war to peace, some curling up in the hay to sleep, others climbing into cherry trees beckoning from the other side of the road. But, at most, their intermission from the rigors of scouting duty was brief, for it was in this situation that Mosby dashed upon them with a band of his Rangers, carrying off almost the entire group.

News of the surprise so near the capital brought added confusion to the chief of staff. A woman had just appeared at Harpers Ferry with information that Mosby, with about fifty men, was lying in the vicinity of Berryville. Next day Washington got word that the Partisan was elsewhere, that he was raiding near Upperville in an effort to round up 1000 artillery horses. Then came new worry: it was telegraphed that McNeill had left Moorefield on a scout. Kelley was especially alarmed over this intelligence, for he had a notion Hanse might be after government horses quartered on a farm he owned out in that general direction.

Reports on McNeill's activities soon were at hand and they were not pleasing. Instead of raiding the government corral, he had pulled a coup similar to the one Mosby applied against the cherry-eaters. While 100 members of the crack Sixth West Virginia Cavalry, enjoying the pleasant warmth of a June day, splashed in the nude in South Branch River near the little village of Springfield, Hanse dashed down with ninety Rangers, captured sixty of the embarrassed bathers and carried them away, along with 104 horses. There was only enough of a fight to result in the killing of five Federals and the wounding of two of McNeill's mounts. Kelley immediately dispatched an officer to investigate, wiring headquarters he feared it would turn out "a great disgraceful affair." [2]

The guerrillas seemed on a rampage. Next day Mosby was seen in an area far from the field of new-mown hay. General Weber found him at Charles Town and quietly wired headquarters to cooperate in setting a trap for the raider. So far as official records were concerned after that, the remaining daylight hours passed quietly, and then at seven o'clock that night President Garrett of the B. & O. sent a telegram indicating all was not calm. He informed Weber the mail train east had passed Sir John's Run at one o'clock in the afternoon, but had not arrived at Harpers Ferry at seven. He also heard an enemy force had appeared at Duffield's Station, eight miles beyond Charles Town.

Weber already suspected trouble. The telegraph wires between Harpers Ferry and Martinsburg had been cut between one and two o'clock, and fifty cavalry and 300 infantry were sent to investigate. These troops came upon Duffield's to find it almost a deserted village. At two o'clock, an eyewitness told them, one of Mosby's Rangers appeared under flag of truce and demanded an unconditional surrender, the strongest term of capitulation, and that was what he got. Behind him, at proper signal, came a large force of the guerrillas, drawing two pieces of artillery, and in short order the station was reduced to a shambles. The camp and all papers of the two companies of the First Maryland Brigade stationed there were burned. The lone store in the neighborhood was looted of about 2000 dollars' worth of dry goods, groceries, boots, and shoes, and a government warehouse pillaged to a damage of about 4000 dollars. But the mail train escaped; it was late, and warning was spread in time to stop all rail traffic at Martinsburg and Sandy Hook until next morning.

But these frustrating attacks by the guerrillas were a minor disaster. Grant was still beset with his problem of taking Richmond. The summer was nearly half gone and he as yet had not attained his objective. Lee's stubborn resistance had forced him to move his army south of the James River, and there it hammered away each day with little change in results. As for the over-all progress of his eight-army campaign, matters in each sector except the Shenandoah Valley were developing satisfactorily. It was the exception that called for serious planning. The Union commander-in-chief, a strange leader, slow to excite, was unaware that Early was pushing down the Valley. Reports had been confusing, and Grant was confident that the Confederates sent to block Hunter had been called back into the lines at Petersburg. With such assurance he wired Halleck as the beautiful June days neared a close: "I wish you would put General Hunter in a good place to rest, and as soon as possible start him to Charlottesville to destroy the road there effectually." [3]

Rest would do Hunter no good; his days were over. In time he would bring his bedraggled troops back to Harpers Ferry, but it would be in an aura of disrepute, for the public had lost faith. The Wheeling *Intelligencer* kissed him off with such comment as this: "General Hunter's brief authority in the Kanawha Valley has nigh damned him in the estimates of all good officers, and with the soldiers and citizens he has entirely 'played out.' The unbridled license given the soldiers had not exalted him in their minds one particle; and the wanton and indiscriminate destruction of property, and the utter disregard of the true Union sentiment has awakened the scorn and contempt of every honorable man and woman, and brought forth the hisses of the home traitors and contemptible sympathizers. The interest of this military department demands a commander of some propriety, prudence and manliness." [4]

Early's march down the Valley was a masterpiece. So rapidly was it done that it was left to a loving husband to give the Yankees along the B. & O. their first notice the Rebels were coming. This love-starved Rebel soldier got word to his wife to be in Martinsburg by the night of July 2, estimating he certainly would arrive there the following day at the latest. Such joyful information was more than the spouse could keep to herself and she let it leak to the military authorities at Frederick. Soon it was making the rounds.⁵

So far as Halleck was concerned, this tip from the husband only made his problem more complex. The telegraph lines west of Harpers Ferry had been down for days, due to guerrilla raids, and he knew little of what was going on in the Valley area. He notified Grant he had heard conflicting reports that Breckinridge and Pickett were following Confederate cavalry toward the railroad, while others said they were not in the Valley at all. But he acknowledged the enemy would be wise to strike into Maryland and Pennsylvania while Hunter was out in West Virginia.⁶

Some parts of what Halleck had heard were true. Gilmor's band of independents were riding in advance of Early's army and it was largely due to their activities that intelligence from west of Harpers Ferry had been blocked.⁷

Washington was alive with reports at this time, and many of them concerned the embarrassing activities of the guerrillas. Union operations in the Valley, as far back as the days of Stonewall Jackson, had been something of which the high command was ashamed. Now they were no better. An army of 18,000 had marched all the way to Lynchburg and there, because of supply shortages brought on by the Rebel guerrillas, had been forced completely out of the field of action for weeks. It was time something was done about this annoyance, so Congress acted. Even as Gilmor was cutting telegraph wires the legislators were considering a bill to give field or department commanders power to execute sentences against guerrillas, and on July 2 this was approved. It was intended to result in quicker punishment for the irregulars, a step its proponents claimed would be the effective measure sought all along to check the Partisans.⁸

By the second day of July, Sigel along the B. & O. knew there was a general advance of Rebels down the Valley, but apparently he alone had the knowledge, for, as late as 5:00 P.M. of the third, Grant was assuring Halleck from Petersburg that Early's corps was in his front and that only remnants of Grumble Jones' troops, and possibly Breckinridge's, could be threatening Hunter's department.⁹ Three days later Halleck was still trying to guess what was happening, with estimates forwarded to him of Rebel strength en route down the Valley ranging from 7000 to 30,000.¹⁰

Early by this time was moving into Maryland. He had driven

out the Federals at Martinsburg, captured the large army stores accumulated there, and was destroying the railroad.[11]

These July days constituted an active period for the guerrillas. Early had let it be known he wanted their cooperation, and he was getting it from various directions. Gilmor was forming the advance, riding ahead with his independents and sending back word from time to time of what the army of regulars in his rear could expect. Out in West Virginia, McNeill had enlarged his force and was prepared to make repeated raids along the B. & O., tearing up track and burning bridges. Nearer Washington, Mosby scooted across the Potomac with a twelve-pounder gun and destroyed stores and other property at Point of Rocks.[12] The pattern was developing, all of it part of a coordinated plan to create a diversion and to distract attention from Early.

Activity of the guerrillas caused considerable concern from Washington westward along the B. & O. Secretary of War Stanton, sizing up the Rebel threat, said, "Thus far it seems to be a raiding expedition by some of the Partisan robbers that infest that region, and who have joined together."[13] But Brigadier General E. B. Tyler, commanding at Monocacy Junction, was a less temperate man. Sight of individuals in citizens' clothing patrolling the Potomac, men who were supposed to belong to "Mosby's gang of outlaws" and who captured or shot Union soldiers whenever they separated from their commands, infuriated him. He wired General Wallace at Baltimore: "I have instructed my command not to bring any of them to my headquarters except for interment . . ."[14]

On the Fourth, a day of celebration, 150 men from the Second Massachusetts and Thirteenth New York Cavalry rode out to scour the country for Mosby. It was led by twenty-four-year-old Major William H. Forbes, second tenor of the Harvard Glee Club; and riding with him was the club's first bass, Chaplain Charles A. Humphreys. But there was no time for singing on this junket; these men knew they were in guerrilla country and they moved in a compact group, making as little noise as possible. They went by way of Aldie and drew up the next day at Leesburg, where they heard of the attack on Point of Rocks and that Mosby was hauling back plunder by the wagonload. Forbes decided to waylay the Rebels on their return and backtracked to Aldie, stopping near a little church that had been the site of Mosby's first rendezvous in January, '63.[15] It was late afternoon of the sixth before he got there, and his men had barely crawled from their saddles when pickets came rushing in with news that Mosby's band was approaching with a twelve-pounder Napoleon.

The gallant young Colonel Charles R. Lowell of the Second Massachusetts Cavalry summed up in a report to headquarters the action that followed: "I have only to report a perfect rout and a chase for five to seven miles." [16]

It was the Federals who were chased. Mosby's men had dashed into the field where the Union horsemen were lined in orderly rank and had used their handy pistols so effectively the Blue cavalry fled after letting loose only a single volley from their more cumbersome carbines. Fifty-seven prisoners were rounded up, among them Major Forbes and later Chaplain Humphreys.[17] Among the dead were a captain and a lieutenant, and scattered over the field were thirty-seven wounded, ten of them too severely to move. Mosby had lost one killed and six disabled, narrowly escaping injury himself when Forbes came upon him in combat and plunged a saber through his coat.

Halleck was seriously worried. News of the rout a day's jog on horseback from the Union capital was no laughing matter, and he urged caution. This advice was heeded, for weeks passed before another party went through the area searching for Mosby.[18] One of the next meetings with the guerrilla leader occurred in Snicker's Gap, when some of the Ringgold Cavalry from Pennsylvania, first of the Union horsemen to sign up for three years of service, were surprised and a number killed and wounded. A member of the regiment recorded: "If the Ringgold Cavalry had caught John S. Mosby any time after the Snicker's Gap affair, all he would have been worth to his country or to his people would have been his insurance policy. Then and there his doom was for once sealed, the only man by them thus doomed during the war." [19]

But the day Mosby captured Forbes was not without some cheering news for Halleck. Grant wired that he was sending the Sixth Corps to Washington and that he would like it returned "as soon as you deem it perfectly safe to do so." And again he pointed out the importance "to our success here" of a raid up the Valley similar to the one Sigel and Hunter had attempted.[20]

Halleck's concern increased. Early had crossed the Potomac and was pillaging in Maryland, and some of his cavalry under McCausland got 20,000 dollars from Hagerstown as ransom to keep the town from being burned. Then Early was paid ten times that much to prevent his destroying Frederick.

Suspense spread over the Maryland and northern Virginia countryside, and in the midst of all this terror of an invasion was reported a romantic little episode that shone like a diamond among a handful of clinkers. The *Star* was the first to broadcast it, announcing that a group of Washington men and women had gone on a picnic to Falls Church, just seven miles away from the White House, "and in the midst of their pleasures they were surprised at the appearance of about twenty-five of Mosby's men, who told them not to be afraid, and danced a set with the ladies, after which they went to the wagons and devoured the cream and edibles provided for the occasion." Then they dashed away, roguish and gallant fellows all, leaving behind an air of excitement and more than one fluttering heart.[21]

On the ninth the worried Halleck got more cheerful news. The telegraph wires brought in word that Wallace was in front of Early at Monocacy Junction, fighting desperately and giving more time for the troops from Grant to arrive. These, it now was announced, would consist of the Sixth and the Nineteenth Corps, the latter freshly in from New Orleans.

By the tenth it was known that Gilmor's irregulars were on their way to destroy the railroad north of Baltimore. Residents of that city sent screaming telegrams to Lincoln, demanding military protection, and the President calmly replied that every soldier available was disposed "for the best protection of all," after which he advised, "Let us be vigilant, but keep cool." [22]

Next day Early's troops were on the edge of Washington, but their appearance had been delayed by Wallace just long enough to save the capital. Even as the Confederates were extending their lines and preparing for attack, the first brigades of the Sixth Corps from below Richmond began marching down the gangplanks of transports along the Potomac. On the twelfth, there was fighting in which most of the capital's male population, including the President, took part, but the Rebels were driven away.

Gilmor in the meantime was having quite an experience. He had been asked by Early at Sharpsburg to break the rail connections with the North, thus preventing or delaying the arrival or reinforcements from that direction. Such a junket would take the Partisan leader into familiar country, in the neighborhood of his old home, so he made a joyous affair of it, stopping at various points en route to drink toasts with friends and to enjoy the companionship of the ladies. He also stopped for a visit with his family and then he went on to Magnolia Station a few miles north of Baltimore, riding hard and giving the 130 men in his detail no time for sleep. Reaching the railroad, he lay in wait, taking his time, undisturbed by enemy resistance. After a while two passenger trains came along, only forty minutes apart, and he burned them both, one after it had been run out on the wooden bridge across the Gunpowder River. Passengers were shown the utmost kindness. Their baggage was piled at the side of the track under guard and was distributed to each by claim check.[23]

Among these passengers was a man dressed in citizens' clothes who was pointed out to Gilmor as Major General William B. Franklin, corps commander formerly assigned to Banks' Red River campaign. The guerrilla leader went himself to investigate and found the identity correct. Franklin admitted he was en route home to recuperate from his arduous experiences in the field. Because of his condition and in respect to his rank, a carriage in the vicinity was commandeered and he was placed in it, with three men riding at the side of the vehicle as a guard.

Turning away from the Gunpowder bridge, Gilmor struck toward Towsontown, stopping along the way to quaff a bit of ale with friends. Night came on and with it the real test. It had been hours since the Partisans had slept, and after nightfall most of them nodded in their saddles, some falling fast asleep and dropping in a stupor to the ground. The combination of alcohol and lack of rest was too much for their endurance.

Gilmor himself was among those who napped while riding, and it was perhaps a pull he unconsciously gave the reins that caused his mount to wander from the path. At any rate he was aroused sometime later by a sudden cry of "Halt!" The horse stopped so quickly it almost threw the guerrilla leader from the saddle, and then came the cry again, "Halt!"

The Partisan shook himself awake. "A friend!" he called.

"Friend to whom?"

"Friend to the Union. I belong to the First Virginia Cavalry and my company has been out in Harford County on a scout after Gilmor's raiders. My captain sent me ahead to tell you he was coming so that you would not fire on him."

"All right," said the voice out of the dark.

Gilmor swung his horse about. "I'll go back and tell him to come on." [24]

The Partisan's familiarity with the country now was of great benefit to him. He recognized his whereabouts under the light of a quarter-moon and in time got back on the trail of his men. Only a short ride later he came upon the carriage in which Franklin had been riding. It was empty, and lying in the road beside it, all sound asleep, were the three men assigned as a guard. "Right glad am I," Gilmor later observed, "that my pious friends were not there to hear me when I found that Franklin had indeed escaped." [25] The prisoner had fled into the night, leaving behind a valise in which were personal items, including a prayer book presented by his sister, some photographs, and a silver snuffbox inlaid with gold. These articles later were returned to him.

As Early fell back from Washington, the Union made hurried efforts to overtake him. Major General H. G. Wright, leading the veteran Sixth Corps that had arrived just in time to save the capital, was placed in supreme command of all the troops assigned to the pursuit.

Wright left Washington with a rising howl in his ears. The Confederates had burned the Silver Spring, Maryland, home of Postmaster General Montgomery Blair, and now the Cabinet officer was making a wholesale condemnation of the officers in command at the capital. He said they were poltroons, that not more than 500 Rebels had been in his community, while the North had 1,000,000 men in arms. It was the cry of a sorrowful, dejected victim, but it brought a quick response from Halleck: Did such a denouncement have the sanction of the President? If so, the name of the accused officers should be stricken from the rolls; if not, the slanderer should be dismissed from the Cabinet. There the matter dropped. The immediate problem was to catch Early and check the guerrillas, not to make a furor over the angry words of a homeless man.

On the fourteenth Grant, who apparently still was under delusion as to just how far Hunter had been driven out of the picture, sent word that he should follow Early "as rapidly as the jaded condition of his men will admit." [26] Washington at the moment had no idea where Hunter was.[27] He had last been heard from at Parkersburg, West Virginia, and there, so far as official reports went, had ended the flight that began June 19.

But Grant had work for Hunter to do. He wanted him to push after Early with "veterans, militiamen, men on horseback, and everything that can be got to follow to eat out Virginia clear and clean as far as they go, so that crows flying over it for the balance of this season will have to carry their provender with them."[28] He directed him to come up the Valley to Gordonsville and Charlottesville and to destroy the railroad between these two places. Wright, in the meantime, should be sent back to Petersburg with the Sixth and Nineteenth Corps.

At Washington the situation grew more intricate. Guerrillas bobbed up on the outskirts of the city. They were reported at Georgetown, in Arlington, at Alexandria. Mosby was among them and was said to have with him three pieces of artillery, thus making of him more than just a hit-and-run foe. The Thirteenth New York Cavalry ran into him near Falls Church and lost thirty men and two officers.[29] Its commanding officer, Henry Sanford Gansevoort, sent a warning that "he is continually around us." On the strength of this, several scouting parties were sent out, one scouring the country for fifteen miles below Alexandria, but they were unable to find him.

By July 15 Hunter was back at Harpers Ferry, and there he waited while criticisms were heaped upon him. It was said officially that he had had a rather active campaign against the newspapers of West Virginia, whose reports he resented, and that his command was so badly cut up and demoralized that he had horse-whipped a soldier with his own hands.[30] Grant, of all his superiors, was inclined to be lenient with him. As was so often done in judging the outcome and fixing blame associated with a campaign, success and failure were discussed only in terms of the regular army. No mention was made in official correspondence of the guerrillas who had cut Hunter's line of communications and prevented his wagon trains from bringing the ammunition he needed. These men were the fleeting irregulars, the patriotic individuals who fought today and tomorrow for a sudden and immediate end, who appeared out of nowhere and fled in the same direction, having no representation present at councils held by the academy-trained military leaders. But the records would show that it was the Partisan and not the soldier of the line who was fighting at Hunter's rear.

No one in Union circles was happy over what had taken place up and down the Shenandoah Valley since the Lynchburg campaign.

Sigel had been defeated, Hunter blocked, and now Early had brought a threatening handful of Confederates to the very edges of Washington, causing great fright. It was taken for granted he would escape. Assistant Secretary of War C. A. Dana said Early would get away with all his plunder and recruits, "leaving us nothing but the deepest shame that has yet befallen us." [31]

Now the ax began to fall on certain heads of the Union army. Sigel and his cavalry chief, Major General Julius Stahel, were ousted and Brigadier General George C. Crook was placed in command of the Department of West Virginia. Hunter meanwhile was burned up over the appointment of Wright, a junior of his own rank, and he was writing letters to the War Department asking that he might be relieved by some officer "more enjoying the confidence of the President." [32] He also was trying to exonerate himself, blaming the failure of the Lynchburg campaign on "the stupidity and conceit of that fellow Averell." [33]

There was much wrangling among the Federal high command at this time, carried on in an atmosphere troubled by announcement that the guerrillas were rendezvousing at Culpeper, possibly with the intention of attacking near Washington or Alexandria.[34] Grant, directing affairs remotely from below Richmond, continued to hound Halleck to send Hunter toward Gordonsville and Charlottesville, taking care that the army should not be squeezed out into West Virginia again. If such a raid was not possible, then he wanted the commander in the Shenandoah to make all the valleys south of the B. & O. "a desert as high up as possible, removing every particle of provisions and stock, but not burning houses." [35] Halleck accordingly instructed Wright to pursue Early until he was positively in retreat toward Richmond and then to return with the Sixth and Nineteenth Corps to Washington, leaving Hunter to continue the pursuit.

A few hours later Grant sent another message. In this he suggested that the Departments of the Susquehanna, West Virginia, and Washington be merged into one, with an over-all commander. The officer he recommended for this responsibility was General Franklin, the captive who had fled so precipitately while Gilmor's men lay asleep in the road.

Hunter, conscience-stricken and dejected, was in a fury. An engineer on the B. & O. visited him at Harpers Ferry to discuss track repairs, and learned he was burning private residences and planned to burn the entire village of Charles Town if he found guerrillas there.[36] Halleck heard of the threat and cautioned against it. If this course is pursued, he said, "such retaliation will follow as will largely add to the losses and sufferings of our border."

The chief of staff also at this time called Grant's attention to a situation that might be dangerous. The Union army lay south of the James River, and that meant it was not as near the Federal capital as Lee's troops. Any moment the Rebel leader might send a detachment dashing up the way Early had done, and that would make both Washington and Baltimore vulnerable, especially since Hunter's army was too small to guard West Virginia and the B. & O. and at the same time resist any considerable Rebel raid north of the Potomac. In answer Grant urged Lincoln to call for 300,000 new recruits to be put in the field in the shortest possible time, advising: "The greatest number of men we have, the shorter and less sanguinary will be the war." [37]

By July 19 Early had retreated so far up the Valley that Wright determined it was time to return to Washington with the Sixth and Nineteenth Corps, leaving Crook with the Eighth to pursue the Confederates. As he started moving back on the twenty-second, stationing cavalry under Colonel Lowell on the front, flanks, and rear to guard against guerrillas, scouts from Mosby's band, busy at the heels of the moving column, hurried the news to Jubal.

At this point Lincoln stepped into the picture. He had read every dispatch received at the War Department and he had his doubts about the wisdom of sending away the Sixth Corps. Because of his indecision he had Halleck wire Grant on the twenty-third that he, Ulysses S. Grant, and he alone, must decide the question. Early that morning the President telegraphed Hunter to ask if he could take care of the situation in case Early turned back, which it was assumed he would do as soon as he learned Wright had left. The answer received was discouraging.

Despite Lincoln's fears for the safety of Washington, Grant insisted that at least a part of the Nineteenth Corps should be returned to Petersburg. He made this decision under the conviction that Early would rejoin Lee, so troops could be detached and sent to help fight Sherman in Georgia. Apparently unaware that Federal troops were moving back, Wright and Hunter, he said, should be permitted to keep on to Charlottesville and Gordonsville.

The Sixth Corps returned to Washington on the eve of the

twenty-third, and Halleck notified Grant that it probably would embark for Petersburg the following night. By this time, however, Grant's mind was more firmly made up and he telegraphed Halleck to send the Sixth, but to retain Wright and the Nineteenth. "I would prefer a complete smashup of the enemy's roads about Gordonsville and Charlottesville to having the same force here," he advised.[38]

But it was too late for this plan to be followed. Wright already had moved back, and Early had whirled about and again was marching into Maryland, harvesting crops as he went. One Union official at Washington described the pursuit of the Confederates, on the whole, as "an egregious blunder." [39]

At a time of stress, trouble seems to come in broken doses. So it happened now for the Union. Rumors began somewhere that Longstreet had been sent to the Valley to support Early, a report that became a monomania, a bugbear continually haunting the Federals during the latter half of '64. In a few hours it was said even Lee himself was in the Valley, a bit of news that taxed the credulity. But not much time was spent in digesting it, for a more shocking development was in store: from the operator at Martinsburg suddenly came clicking over the telegraph a message that Crook had met with disaster.

The wires buzzed. Soon the report about Crook was confirmed over and over. It was announced that he had been flanked by Early at Winchester and his entire force put to flight.

And that was the story. After routing Crook in a spirited battle, the Southerners spread out and began destroying. The B. & O., restored to running order since its destruction in early July, was torn up again. Guerrillas showed up in some places along its line, the regular army in others. Breckinridge was said to be making a raid toward Wheeling. Kelley revealed that McNeill was doing "a great deal of damage" and that no Union cavalry was available to follow him. Mosby was located at Adamstown where he had destroyed the wires and taken possession of the railroad. Longstreet's corps was reported on its way to threaten Washington. And then came news that the Rebels were burning the town of Chambersburg, Pennsylvania, in retaliation for the torch applied by Hunter on his march up the Valley. Carlisle, it was flashed over the wires, would be next.

All this at a time when Halleck was informing Grant that the weather was so hot that marches would be very slow! And with reason. For Halleck was getting messages from Hunter that the dust was so deep the infantry was suffering dreadfully, six men having fallen dead in one of the smaller brigades.

The troops that converged on Chambersburg were led by General John McCausland, who had fled from Lexington to escape Hunter. Supported by Bradley Johnson and Harry Gilmor, his troops swarmed onto the fairgrounds in the outskirts before dawn and, as daylight arrived, they pushed in, along streets and alleys, to the courthouse and there announced terms. They were in writing, signed by Jubal Early: 100,000 dollars in gold or 500,000 dollars in currency—that and that alone—would prevent the burning of the town.

The reaction was scattered and stubborn. One councilman immediately flared that not five cents would be paid to the Rebels. Another replied that there was not 50,000 dollars in gold or currency in the community. But no one took the lead and made an effort to raise the money. McCausland allowed time for deliberation and, when he was satisfied the ransom was not forthcoming, gave Gilmor the signal to start burning. Fifty fires in various parts of the downtown section seemed to flare up at once, spreading rapidly over a twenty-block area.

At Lexington some of the finest dwellings, including that of Governor Letcher, had been put to the torch. Remembering this, McCausland gave Gilmor "peremptory orders to make a thorough work of it" and especially to destroy all fine dwellings.[40]

While the independent leader stood watching flames envelop the heart of town, he suddenly spied a fine brick mansion situated on an eminence to the northwest. A few minutes later, accompanied by two men, he dismounted in front of its door and knocked.

A woman swung back the portal. She stood erect, facing him with a poise and dignity that attracted his admiration. Bowing, hat in hand, he informed her with embarrassment that he was there, much to his regret, to perform the extremely unpleasant task of burning her home, a measure the South was obliged to resort to in order to prevent or check the terrible devastation that such men as Hunter were committing below the Potomac.

She stared at him silently, and his embarrassment increased. He reminded her that Confederate soldiers had been seen at Chambersburg twice before and that in each instance their behavior had been spoken of in the highest terms, some residents saying the Rebels behaved better than the Union troops.

Suddenly the woman began weeping, bowing her head and sobbing brokenly, but she acknowledged in the midst of her tears the truth of his remarks. Blame for allowing such horrible acts of cruelty to go unpunished, she said, lay with the Administration in Washington.

Tears ran in streams down her cheeks as she spoke. But there was no bitterness or resentment in her voice and not one time did she ask that her home be spared. Her only request was that she might have time to remove some articles of particular value and a few pieces of clothing. Gilmor consented.

As she turned away, she pointed toward the dining room. "Breakfast is on the table," she said. "Won't you have something to eat while I am getting my things together?"

Gilmor and his companions entered. A wine decanter on the sideboard caught their attention and they poured a glass around before taking a seat. Then they began gorging themselves and, as their stomachs filled, the bitterness and hatreds of war softened. Balanced against the blazing background of the town were the peaceful surroundings of this home and the soft voice of the woman, and for once the temptation to disobey orders was strong.

When she returned, her arms full, they were still eating.

"I'm ready," she announced.

Gilmor got to his feet, pushing back his chair. "What's your name, madam?"

"My husband is Colonel Boyd of the Union army."

"What!" Gilmor exclaimed in disbelief. "Colonel William H. Boyd of the First New York Cavalry?"

"Yes."

"Then, madam, your house shall not be destroyed. I have fought against your husband in the Valley of Virginia for two years and I know he is kind and lenient to the citizens, warring only against men in arms."

So Gilmor rode away, leaving his companions behind as a guard to make sure no torch touched the home of the man who on one occasion had chased Mosby to the limb of a tree in his nightclothes.

270

CHAPTER 4

July 31–August 22, 1864

BUT NO PRISONERS

Sheridan! In high Union circles the name meant little to anyone except General Grant and his cavalry chief, the man to whom it belonged. Yet all of a sudden it rose up out of semi-obscurity and topped a triumvirate that had begun ignominiously with Sigel and continued on much the same plane with Hunter. It had one more syllable than its predecessors and, no matter what that extra syllable was worth, something about the name and the man was expected to change the trend, bringing success out of failure, for the third time is by old wives' tale the charm. Over the wires it flashed from the headquarters of the Federal commander-in-chief: "I want Sheridan put in command of all the troops in the field, with instructions to put himself south of the enemy and follow him to the death." [1]

In this important message Grant revealed that he was still exercising the basilisk's gaze, staring into space and ignoring what was going on at his elbow, for the guerrillas, primed to the emergency, were prepared to sting as they had never stung before. McNeill and Mosby were daily engaged as independents, Gilmor had made plans to join them when he got back from Pennsylvania, and White would return to their peculiar branch of service before the year was over. A change of Union command in no way upset their mode of operation, and they were prepared to bear down as the plight of the South became more desperate.

Choice of Sheridan was an indication Grant had awakened to the fact that cavalry rather than infantry was what was needed to combat the Confederates in the Valley area. He had sent additional horse troops from Richmond before announcing the change, and more were to come. There would be three crack divisions, led by Torbert and headed individually by Merritt, Averell, and Wilson.

Sheridan's selection was in a way also one of desperation. He was Grant's favorite cavalry leader, and he was young—just thirty-three —so young it was feared Lincoln would raise an immediate objection, as Secretary of War Stanton had done earlier.[2]

Sheridan arrived in Washington August 4 and went into session with Halleck. When their conference ended, the chief of staff wired Grant a suggestion that the four departments of Washington, Maryland, Pennsylvania, and West Virginia be combined under one commander, something Grant had been trying to bring about since mid-July.[3]

After a few hours in Washington, Sheridan went on to Monocacy to join his troops. In the meantime Lincoln, constantly alarmed over the possible capture of the Union capital, entered the picture. He got a chance to see Grant's telegram about following the enemy to the death and he pounced on it immediately. Such a thing, he wired, would never be done "unless you watch it every day and hour and force it."[4] This kind of message was what it took to bring Grant up from Petersburg in person.[5]

Grant bypassed Washington, going directly to Monocacy, and got there ahead of Sheridan. Spread out in formidable array were the troops assigned to protect the capital. "Where's the enemy?" he asked Hunter, and that question brought a barrage of answers. Hunter finally admitted he didn't know, that he had been so embarrassed with orders from Washington, moving him "first to the right and then to the left, that he had lost trace of the enemy."[6] Grant immediately started the army in search of the foe, moving its base to Halltown, four miles from Harpers Ferry. He also announced that Sheridan was to have charge of the men in the field, and thereupon Hunter asked to be relieved, thus simplifying the matter of installing a new combat chief for the Army of the Shenandoah.

When Sheridan arrived, his orders were waiting—the same that had been drafted for Hunter. They were simple. Instead of swinging back and forth to guard Washington, the main object now would be to drive the enemy south, to follow him and attack him wherever found. More cavalry was on the way, it was announced, and with this new strength it was expected that "a sufficient force to look after the raiders and drive them back to their homes" could be detached.[7] But therein the commander-in-chief was underestimating the problem at hand. In his military career he had never been bothered with guerrillas as well organized as the bands now sweeping the Shenandoah Valley and dashing on occasion up to the outskirts of Washington. West Point had no textbooks on methods of coping with such fleeting and invisible bands, and Grant was too taxed with what seemed more serious problems to devise new procedure.

But in his instructions to Sheridan he did call for one performance designed to check the guerrillas and at the same time retard the progress of the regular army, one that the cavalry leader was able to execute to perfection: devastation of the Valley. "It is desirable," orders read, "that nothing should be left to invite the enemy to return. Take all provisions, forage and stock wanted for the use of your command; such as cannot be consumed destroy." [8]

For the people west of the Blue Ridge it thus was suddenly to be a terrible war, a war of horror. This abrupt swing to wholesale destruction of all but homes, a variation only in this exception from the penalty Hunter had applied at Lexington and McCausland had retaliated with at Chambersburg, was the infliction Grant knew must be brought to bear before the South would surrender. The Shenandoah Valley, breadbasket by which the Army of Northern Virginia had been feeding largely for the duration of the war, must be blanked out completely. All food, feedstuff, and animals must go.

In taking over the force at Halltown, Sheridan had a task on his hands not altogether pleasant. While turkey buzzards circled peacefully in the distance, reminding him of the guerrillas waiting to peck at his flanks and rear, he gave orders and took steps to get the army moving. Grant wanted speed, and that was what the new commander would try to give him. But, first, things must be got in better shape before any move southward could be started. There was the Sixth Corps, for instance, one of the best in the Army of the Potomac, and yet so badly demoralized through misuse that the rankest private could single out its faults. Its guns were dirty, camps disorderly, men disrespectful.[9] Not alone was this true of the Sixth. The entire Army of the Shenandoah lacked the belligerence of a winning combat force. A Rebel spy detected this situation and sent a message marked "official and reliable," saying that "the army above don't seem so full of fight; they seem jaded and tired." [10] These things the battered little cavalry leader with the strange felt hat of flat crown could see too, and he surveyed them without losing heart, barking orders by the hour. Some details connected with an army could be changed almost overnight.

But there were worries his military education had not fitted him for. Hourly scouts brought intelligence that could not be changed, by him or any of the force under his command, no matter how much they tried. Mosby had been found in the neighborhood of Leesburg with 500 to 600 Partisans, said to be from both his and White's commands, and right after that came a report from Berlin on the other side of the Potomac that he was in that vicinity with 400 to 500 men.

On the eighth Sheridan himself wired Augur that Mosby was at Point of Rocks with 200 cavalry. Then, while his message was still clicking over the wires, he got word that the Partisan leader had struck the Sixteenth New York Cavalry at Fairfax Station and executed another rout similar to that against Forbes near Aldie only a few weeks past. The report spoke of "disgraceful mismanagement," dozens of horses captured, a larger force demoralized by a smaller force. It was said the guerrilla chieftain had yelled, "Go through 'em, boys," and go through them they did. The body of the Union captain commanding was found by the roadside, stripped of much of its clothing, and was brought in and interred in the historic burial ground at Falls Church. This was different warfare from the fighting around Petersburg. The new commander was getting an early lesson.

By the ninth it was evident the troops under Sheridan were about to move. A Nineteenth Corps volunteer sat in his billet at Halltown and penned a note home that would go into the records: "We are going, and that soon, but where and when I cannot say. The officers' valises, the men's knapsacks and the spare camp kettles have all been sent for storage to Harpers Ferry. Everyone is stripped for the march, carrying his own blanket, shelter tent, haversack and canteen, whether he be captain or private. This prophesies lively traveling, probably in the direction of Lynchburg." [11]

At the close of this day the sun went down like a ball of fire, and then the night scenes became magnificent. It is a beautiful sight to see on a clear night an army of thousands of men, with all their innumerable campfires and illuminated tents, bedded down on a space only a few miles in circumference. Later in the evening heavy masses of clouds gathered in the north and west, and forked lightning began to dart out viciously from between them. But toward the southeast not a cloud was visible. From that way the moon and countless stars looked calmly down on the warlike scene below—thousands of blazes flickering in the night, hovered over by tired and hungry soldiers waiting for their coffee to boil. It was a contrast like that of the circling buzzards and the busy scenes at Sheridan's headquarters. Another note crept in later: thunder rumbled in the distance, hinting there might be rain before bedtime, but the storm never developed. Soldiers were able to go peacefully to their pallets for the last rest before starting a third great crusade up the Shenandoah Valley.

Sheridan took to his bed late at night, bunking down in an old hotel taken over as headquarters. Sometime during the hours he slept a small band of men walked inconspicuously and brazenly through the camp in the light of a moon in its first quarter, answering when hailed, "Hundred-sixth New York." Only an occasional fire burned by this time, most of them kept alive to heat coffee for the guard. Officers given to late-hour chatter under the stars had surrendered to wisdom long before and gone off to sleep, and the noises of an army at rest had fallen to a minimum, even off on the outskirts where the Rebel Partisans carried on their defiance.

At one point the little band, obviously fulfilling a mission, stopped long enough for one of its members, in stern voice, to dress down a sentinel: "What a hell of a way to stand on duty!" Then it went on, alert, quiet, business-like, moving with the smoothness and unison of soldiers well trained in military routines.

Three hundred yards from the building where the cavalry general with the queer flat hat slept, the band melted into the gloom, and there in the darkness of a ravine one member got his orders: go on alone and ascertain the strength of the guard protecting the head of this army soon to move against the South. He stole away—John Hearn of Mosby's band—picking the paths of faintest reflection from the campfires. Yards farther a rail fence loomed in front of him and, without hesitation, he took three quick steps and hopped over it in a manner designed to create the least suspicion. His estimate of the barrier was good. He cleared it without so much as a nick of wood and landed squarely on his feet, only to find himself in the midst of a group of sleeping men and inches away from a sentinel.

"Who're you?" asked the sentinel.

"Hundred-sixth New York," answered the fence-jumper, lunging for the guard's musket.

From the semi-darkness came sounds of a brief tussle, then cries of "Help! Murder!" and back to the ravine fled the Partisan carrying the sentinel's gun as the sole trophy of an expedition now definitely unsuccessful.

Next morning the camp stirred before dawn and men marched and wagons rolled in monotonous caravan. They went in three columns, along almost parallel roads, generally in the direction of Charles Town and Winchester, carrying ten days' rations. It was hot and dry and dusty.

The following day there was some skirmishing with the enemy near Newtown, but the advance continued. Around Strasburg the resistance stiffened. Early's army began to give signs it might be in mood for a drawn battle, so Sheridan took position along Cedar Creek, one of the finest battle lines in the Valley. He had 18,000 infantry and 3500 cavalry.[12] The enemy in front of him, he supposed, numbered at least 30,000.

At no time during the advance had Sheridan's troops been free of trouble from the guerrillas. Kelley, left at Cumberland guarding the B. & O., was bothered by McNeill's constant forays against him. He grumbled to Averell at Hancock, Maryland, that Sheridan did not understand "the importance of guarding the Cheat Mountain pass, or he would not have exposed the people of West Virginia to the incursions of guerrillas and robbers by ordering away the Eighth Ohio without giving me some troops to take their place."[13] Rebel independents centered their depredations in no particular area. The Star's correspondent messaged: "Mosby's guerrillas are hanging on the rear of our columns, and annoying us somewhat by picking up stragglers, and picking up information, and have picked up nearly 100 of our men."[14]

A rumor began to bother Sheridan. Scouts brought in reports of a column of the enemy moving up from Culpeper Court House and approaching Front Royal through Chester Gap. This might mean real trouble, the Union commander was aware. Such a force could get in his rear and rout his entire army. So he braced for the worst, and on the morning of the thirteenth a sizable portion of it came—from Mosby.

Sheridan was hauling supplies to his army by long wagon train from Martinsburg and other points along the B. & O., everything it needed—food, forage, ammunition. Near Berryville, Mosby, aided by a little mountain howitzer that threw holy terror into the 100-days men serving as a guard and the drivers of the wagons, tore into the reserve brigade's train and wrecked it.[15] In a style characteristic of this particular war the Union high command attempted to discount the damage done, but Sheridan himself set the records straight. Halleck prompted him to comment. The chief of staff was informed a Federal scout had got word of the raid from Mosby himself. "Mosby told him," Halleck related, "that he had captured one of your trains of 70 or 80 wagons, with 500 mules and horses. Is that true?"[16] Sheridan replied that it was true, that "it was said everything was recovered except six wagons, but this was not true."[17] One newspaper correspondent, in reporting the incident, intimated that it was a result of carelessness, and this infuriated the new commander. He summoned the reporters into his tent and lectured them sternly, after which he ordered them out of his department.[18]

The situation all at once took on more gravity. The brazenness of Mosby in striking the wagon train augured more audacity from the enemy than had been anticipated in the recent conferences with Grant.[19] Rumors of a Rebel force moving up by way of Culpeper continued, and Sheridan sent a brigade of cavalry to Front Royal to test the truth of the report. At the same time he moved the Sixth Corps south of Cedar Creek to occupy the heights above Strasburg. Then came a message from the adjutant general's office that said two divisions of Confederate infantry, some cavalry, and twenty pieces of artillery had been sent to the Valley.[20] "Early's force, with this increase," it said, "cannot exceed 40,000 men, but this is too much for Sheridan to attack." Instructions to the Army of the Shenandoah definitely were to "be cautious and act now on the defensive."[21]

Sheridan began to study the map of the Valley for a defensive line where "a smaller number of troops could hold a greater number"—actually where 20,000-odd men could safely face Early's fewer than 10,000—and the best spot seemed to be the one he had left on the tenth at Halltown.[22] This would solve another problem at the same time: he was aware he could not move farther and transport supplies to his army through the screen of guerrillas, and by moving back he would shorten his line of communications.[23] So he gave orders, while the Confederate regulars were shooting at him in front and the irregulars were nipping at him on the sides and at the rear, to turn around.[24]

There was more than appeared on the surface in this retrograde movement. Lincoln's influence was a dominating factor. He had pointed out to Grant that the Presidential election was coming in November with himself as a candidate, that there was a growing element in the North actively preaching that the war was a failure, and he made it plain that he wanted no serious defeat of a Federal army.

Military strategists have reasoned that there were other justifications for Sheridan's retirement. They point out that "it is not difficult to see that such manoeuvers were the best means to accomplish the purpose for which Grant had placed Sheridan at the mouth of the Valley," and then they go on to cite that it caused Lee to detach troops to aid Early and that it kept support from being sent to Hood facing Sherman at Atlanta.[25] Such argument is argument of convenience, without foundation of fact. Grant had directed both Sigel and Hunter to sweep up the Valley, wiping out the enemy along the way, and now he wanted Sheridan to do the same thing. Everything had gone well until the Valley commander found that, while fighting Early at the fore, the guerrillas were having a heyday at the rear.

As Sheridan moved back, his red and white headquarters flag with its twin stars showing in the van, he was largely out of touch with Washington and Petersburg. Scouts and couriers were finding it almost impossible to get through the cordon of guerrillas hovering on the outskirts of the Federal army.[26] An entire regiment of cavalry had been employed to bring from the adjutant general's office the message about the Rebel reinforcements.[27] The Valley commander was finding it necessary to act without sanction from his superiors. A period of five days, from the twelfth to the seventeenth, passed without word from Grant, and when dispatches did arrive from Petersburg they were concerned mostly with advice on how to get rid of the guerrillas.

The courier who got through on the seventeenth arrived at six-thirty o'clock in the morning. The message he brought opened with some unconfirmed information about the Confederate troops transferred to the Valley and advised against an attack on Early in an intrenched position. Next it instructed that the 100-days men, the recruits hastily signed up for the period it was estimated Grant would need to take Richmond, should be discharged at the expiration of their time unless immediate hostilities advised against it. The remainder concerned the guerrillas, and it revealed that Grant at last had awakened to the important role these scattered bands were playing against the Federal troops in the Valley. His words were shocking: "The families of most of Mosby's men are known, and can be collected. I think they should be taken and kept at Fort McHenry, or some secure place, as hostages for the good conduct of Mosby and his men. Where any of Mosby's men are caught hang them without trial." [28]

This message placed a new complexion on the conduct of the war, now well on its way into the fourth year. It completely violated the interpretation of Dr. Lieber, who had said guerrillas were legitimate soldiers as long as they were properly enrolled with the regular army, and it went a long step further than any other commander had gone in trying to stop the irregulars. In the past the private citizen had been made to pay for depredations of the independent bands in his vicinity; now the Partisans were to pay, and pay with their necks.

On the afternoon of the eighteenth another message arrived from Grant. It was brief: "If you can possibly spare a division of cavalry, send them through Loudoun County, to destroy and carry off the crops, animals, Negroes, and all men under 50 years of age capable of bearing arms. In this way you will get many of Mosby's men. All male citizens under 50 can fairly be held as prisoners of war, and not as citizen prisoners. If not already soldiers, they will be made so the moment the Rebel army gets hold of them." [29]

Grant had reason to be concerned. The country around Sheridan's army literally swarmed with guerrillas. Secretary of War Stanton was notified that no Federal party moved without trouble from the Partisans. And the independents appeared to be permeating the Union lines at will, and with a certain degree of intimacy. The Sixth Corps found that the movement published for a particular night was circulated among the men by Rebel intruders even before the order concerning it reached headquarters. [30]

The extreme measures Grant advised were quickly adopted by Sheridan. No matter to him if they violated the code of international warfare; that was Grant's worry. The day after the message about hangings without trial was received, this report went out from headquarters in the Valley: "Mosby has annoyed me and captured a few wagons. We hung one and shot six of his men yesterday. I have burned all wheat and hay, and brought off all stock, sheep, cattle, horses, etc., south of Winchester." [31]

During his march backward Sheridan destroyed as he went, carrying out his objective to make the Valley "as untenable as possible for a Rebel force to subsist." [32] Thus began the first wholesale destruction of one of the richest and most beautiful sections of Virginia. If natives had felt the enemy's heel before, they felt it worse now. On all sides their labor of months and even years went up in smoke, and away trotted their horses and livestock, herded by jeering Yankees.

A general cry of vengeance rose up in the Valley. It came from the man in gray uniform and the farmer in the rough denim of the furrow. And it was in the heart of the Partisan who one day stepped out of the bushes on the edge of a clearing in the vicinity of the scorched area and halted, surprised and stirred by what he saw. He reached for one of his revolvers, leveled it until a blue military cap hung in the sights at dead center, and slowly pulled the trigger. A profusion of smoke came out with the explosion, the echo cracking flatly in the trees at his back. The raider stalked across to the body of the Federal, sprawled across the carcass of a partly skinned ewe, and bent over and worked swiftly. When he straightened and turned away, the Union soldier's head was propped against the carcass, eyes staring blindly at the heavens. Out of the dead man's mouth protruded one of the ewe's feet, severed at the joint. To it was attached a torn bit of paper on which had been scribbled a note of triumph: "I reckon you got enough sheep now." [33]

The fierce violence Sheridan brought to the Valley could not upset the everyday tragedies, big and little, recognized as the hand of God. Thus it was that to a farmhouse in the path of the retreating army a death note was brought in the darkest hours of night. Reluctant bustle around the household, sleepy and confused, answered the predawn knock, and a lamp was lighted to read the contents of the message.[34] Shortly afterward a picket post of the Fifth Michigan Cavalry, one of Custer's regiments, was attacked by guerrillas and several members of the guard were killed or captured.

At dawn Custer was informed of the attack. Along with other details he was told that a light at a nearby farmhouse, the same struck to read the death note, had been the signal that drew the guerrillas.

In the young general there was no toleration for *petite guerre;* war in his camp was fought along the lines prescribed by the academies. So he promptly designated specific homes in the neighborhood that must be put to the torch, and ordered out two companies of the Michiganders to perform the task of retaliation.[35]

The house-burners split into groups and went about their task with luck against them. It was by coincidence that they fired the dwellings at a time when a band of Mosby's men was approaching from the east. They topped a ridge and looked down on the burning mansions, some of the most pretentious in the area, and they were stunned by what they saw. But the reaction was unanimous. Sinking spurs, they rode at mad gallop, splashing through the Shenandoah River at Castleman's Ferry and continuing with the speed of an Indian war party. At their head rode dashing young William Chapman, once a stalwart of the Dixie Artillery and someday to be a trusted employee of the United States Internal Revenue Bureau. But on this day there was murder in his heart and he cried out in a voice that spurred his men into a craze: "Wipe them from the face of the earth! No quarter! No quarter! Take no prisoners!" The cry was picked up by others as the maddened Rebels stormed down upon the unsuspecting Michiganders. Sight of women and children crying helplessly in the yards of the burning buildings inflamed tempers to the level of demons. "It was a sharp, quick and clean little fight; no prisoners," blandly wrote one of the participants.[36]

Unprepared for resistance, the Federals scattered while the cries of "No quarter!" goaded them into panic. One of the women of the neighborhood who stood by as an eyewitness recorded the sights she saw: "They hid behind the burning ruins, they crouched in the corners of fences, they begged for life, but their day of grace was past . . . Two came to us, the most pitiable objects you ever beheld, and we did what we could for them; for, after all, the men are not to blame half so much as the officers . . . These two wounded men . . . were removed that night . . . One man gruffly remarked: 'If we leave any of them with you all, Mosby will come and kill them over again.' We have since heard that those two men died that night."[37]

A Ranger returned to a Federal he had shot through the head earlier in the chase, and found his body lying in a scattering of papers. From pockets he pulled a handful of jewelry taken from the burning homes, and tied to the saddle of the dead man's horse waiting nearby were two bolts of cloth, lace curtains, women's clothing, blankets, sheets, and two bottles of wine. That night in going through the papers the Confederate found a letter from a girl. In it, along with the customary terms of endearment, was a request that she be sent some of the things her lover captured from the houses of Rebels he passed in his trek up the Valley.[38]

Riding up the slopes of the Blue Ridge as they hurried away from the smoking scene, the Rangers halted to look back, and it was then someone discovered that a solitary prisoner, saved by a softhearted Ranger, rode among them. Immediately a cry went up for him to be accorded the fate of his comrades. One member of the party wrote of the incident afterward: "It was a solemn spectacle to see this brave young soldier kneel in the solitude of the mountain and pour forth a fervent prayer to the Great Father to pardon his sins and forgive his own officer, whom he regarded, he said, as the true author of his death. The young man then rose slowly to his feet and, tearing open his shirt, with unquailing eye received the fatal shot." [39]

In the dark hours that night two regiments of Federal soldiers marched past the smoldering ruins of houses that had gone up in smoke as a result of Custer's order. They carried torches that marked their course to the frightened citizens of the countryside, and they drew up in front of a home that had been marked for burning but had escaped in the excitement of the Ranger attack. By dawn Custer's instructions had been executed to the last letter.

Mosby, who had been raiding near Charles Town while Chapman's party rode down the house-burners, disposed of the incident briefly in his next report: "Captain Chapman, coming upon a portion of the enemy's cavalry which was engaged in burning houses, attacked and routed them. Such was the indignation of our men at witnessing some of the finest residences in that portion of the state enveloped in flames that no quarter was shown, and about 25 of them were shot to death for their villainy. About 30 horses were brought off, but no prisoners." [40]

As Sheridan's army moved, there was fighting along the way. Custer, commanding one of the cavalry divisions, charged a Confederate brigade moving to aid Early and wound up with a small victory, taking two stands of colors and 300 prisoners. Next day Rebel cavalry struck a Union division at Winchester, defeated it, and chased it out of town.

Sheridan was back at Halltown by the twenty-second. Day by day the Rebels had fought him, looking past their foes at the billows of smoke rising into the sky with their token of doom for the house-holders in the Federals' path. The Valley commander sent off a report to Grant soon after returning to base. It told of his skirmishes and his successful withdrawal and wound up with an irrelevant sentence: "We have disposed of quite a number of Mosby's men." [41]

CHAPTER 5

August 22–October 5, 1864

NEVER UNDERESTIMATE THE POWER OF A GUERRILLA

Once back at Halltown, Sheridan's task was a matter of waiting, of holding his line in the hope that the army at Petersburg could stir up so much trouble Lee would be forced to recall the reinforcements sent to the Valley. In the meantime steps were taken to learn more precisely just what troops these were; reports so far—from Grant and other sources—had been conflicting. So detachments were ordered in all directions, to spy and to talk to citizens, and to round up captives for questioning. In the end it was concluded correctly that Early had been sent Kershaw's division of infantry and some of Fitz Lee's cavalry. These additions, it was assumed, just about wiped out the difference in strength between the opposing armies.

The first days after returning to Halltown went fast for Sheridan because the Rebels kept him busy. Daily until early September there was skirmishing of more or less degree, with the tide of war swinging back and forth from one side to the other. And then activity between lines gradually dropped to a minimum. This lull gave the Valley commander time to think of small details, and his attention turned more often to the guerrillas. To his way of thinking these irregulars still were a disposable enemy, and he planned sooner or later to prove it. Until a more formidable drive could be made, however, the Eighth Illinois Cavalry was dispatched to put an end to the hotbed of Mosby activities in Loudoun Valley. On a fine day these fighters galloped away, some of the best in the Union army, and a few hours later Sheridan wrote Halleck: "I hope the Eighth Illinois has cleaned out Loudoun Valley. I will do the same with this country before I am done with it." [1] But the task was far more formidable than the commander's message would indicate. When its enormity began to become evident a little later, the Loudoun Rangers, once more in passable standing at headquarters, were sent to aid with the undertaking and to frustrate themselves in the effort.

Varied reports of guerrilla activities were a constant menu these days. They came from widely scattered areas. One foggy morning Mosby posted two pieces of artillery just outside carbine range and for more than an hour blasted away at the stockade at Annandale, a Washington outpost just ten miles from where Lincoln slept. On the same day, miles westward at Huttonsville in McNeill's bailiwick, the irregulars surprised a camp of pickets and captured seventy horses with all accouterments, as well as seventy carbines. At this period McNeill had more freedom of operation than any of the Partisans. Halleck notified Sheridan that there was considerable panic in West Virginia from apprehended raids along the B. & O., that he had no troops in his department to help in this situation, and that the railroad's protection must be left entirely to the forces in the Valley. The chief of staff meantime had worries closer home. No forgiver of his panicky nature, the *Star* informed him that Mosby was boasting of a visit to Washington during which he had spent several hours in the city.[2]

As August advanced into its second half, a rainy spell of several days set in, and the Eighteenth Connecticut Volunteers, caught with marching orders that kept them outdoors during most of the storm, drew up finally at a camp near Charles Town. There they lay drying off while pesky Rebel Partisans persistently peppered them with potshots. This sniping got to be a serious matter, coming at all hours of day and night, so troublesome finally that a detail of twenty men was sent under cover of darkness to lie in wait behind entrenchments in the hope of dislodging the relentless Southerners. The detail moved out and lay still, ready to accomplish its objective. Presently the spurt of a gun flashed from the top of some tall trees, and the Federals, waiting with fixed finger, let loose a general barrage. Apparently their shot was wasted, for no answering cries of agony resulted. To their ears instead came a single voice, lonesome and pitched tauntingly high, "How are yuh, Horace Greeley? Does yo' mother know yer out tonight?" [3]

The Eighteenth Connecticut was not an exception. Any movement Sheridan's men made these days had to be executed with care. When guerrillas were not poised to snipe, Early's troops were waiting to skirmish. On the twenty-fifth the Confederates stole around the right of the Union army's fixed position, and there was general alarm. Rushed into the breech, defiant Federal cavalry charged up in complete confidence, to be met by some rough handling, Custer extricating his command only by making a wide circuit across the Potomac, cruelly staggering his ego.

With such developments Sheridan's worries were manifold. In addition to the matter of holding his own lines, there was the problem of keeping up with developments at Petersburg, and there, from what he could learn, successes were unpredictable. His intelligence from that quarter was none too reliable, and the guerrillas, constantly grabbing off couriers, made it worse. On one occasion Grant wrote he had "good reason" to believe Fitz Lee's cavalry had been ordered back to Richmond, and instructed: "Give the enemy no rest, and if it is possible to follow to the Virginia Central road, follow that far. Do all the damage to railroads and crops you can. Carry off stock of all descriptions, and Negroes, so as to prevent further planting. If the war is to last another year, we want the Shenandoah Valley to remain a barren waste." [4] This was the ninth time since taking command that Grant had expressed a desire for the army in the Valley to sweep up as far as Charlottesville. There would be others.

By the first of September it was reported from headquarters that all citizens of the country around Harpers Ferry and Washington under fifty years of age had been arrested, "even though there was no particular charge brought against them." [5] Thirty-two of these were conveyed to Washington in a single day and placed in Old Capitol Prison, among them two ministers.

At this same time another step was taken to combat the guerrillas. Orders were issued for all wagon-train guards to be armed with carbines, thus enabling them to shoot farther than with pistols. The Rebel irregulars meanwhile—and Mosby in particular—patted their revolvers appreciatively, admitting these lighter weapons might not have as great a range but maintaining that in the rattle-clatter of a cavalry fight they laid out more dead men than any other.

On the third of September, Atlanta fell, marking the development of an important segment of Grant's campaign for winding up the war.

There was more good news for the Unionists. Harry Gilmor was said to have been wounded in cavalry skirmishing around Darkesville, only twelve miles from Winchester. This report was true. Gilmor at the time was attached to Lomax's cavalry and was actually in command of the Eighteenth Virginia, as well as his own battalion. While he was directing an offensive, a bullet ripped into his shoulder, breaking the collarbone and putting an immediate end to his fighting. An ambulance jolted him into a hospital in Winchester where his wound was dressed and he was assigned to a bed in a room with several amputees. The groaning of these other unfortunates bothered the less-maimed Partisan so seriously that he finally managed to slip out and make his way to the home of Mrs. O'Bannon, a widow friend with ample facilities for his care. There, attended by her two nieces, he spent the next three weeks, a period he described as "among the happiest of my life." [6]

From the moment Sheridan took command of what was designated officially as the Middle Military Division, he was pestered with suggestions as to how to get rid of the guerrillas. In one instance, for what it was worth, a schoolmaster who had taught some of the boys fighting with Mosby was sent to headquarters.[7] There he cooled his heels in severe boredom, for his former pupils had to be caught before he could identify them.

Most of these proposals Sheridan ignored as of little value, but from Crook finally came one that had some promise of success. This general had in mind a task force especially assigned to the matter of getting rid of Mosby. It was to be a band of 100 picked men led by a personable individual named Captain Richard Blazer, experienced to some degree in fighting Indians in the West.[8] Such an individual, it was reasoned, would bring to the guerrillas a type of warfare akin to their own, thus applying the old principle of fighting fire with fire. But first there must be a Spencer repeating rifle for each man under Blazer's command, an idea acceptable to Sheridan, who promptly sent off an order for weapons of this type to be rounded up in Washington.[9] When they arrived, the outfit disappeared into the countryside, carrying the hopes of a troubled young Irish general who wore a funny hat.

Time would show that Blazer was a man of attractive personality, both to friend and foe; yet, as a fighter, he was equipped with more buildup than ability. Bit by bit reports of his band's activities would leak back, but it would not be until early September that anything remotely laudable would go into the records, and even this action could be termed largely a matter of coincidence. One day a number of Mosby's Rangers drew up unsuspectingly at a ford for a brief rest, most of them unsaddling their horses and stretching out relaxed on the ground. While they lolled, the rifle-toters, who happened to be nearby resting also, seized their opportunity and rushed in with such success that their leader later was able to wire Sheridan the rather unspecific message that the Partisans "fought with a will, but the seven-shooters proved too much for them." [10]

Sheridan also at this time organized a band of spies who earned almost as varied a reputation as the Jessie Scouts. They were paid from U. S. Secret Service funds and led by an enterprising officer from the Second Rhode Island Regiment, Major Henry K. Young, who as a captain had drawn attention to himself by volunteering to do a special chore behind the enemy lines soon after Sheridan took command.[11] Dressed in Confederate uniforms whenever necessary,[12] they were carefully selected men. Despite that they rode out under a cloud of suspicion, for it was said facetiously that scouts were plausible fellows who lay on the ground under a tree all night and then came back to headquarters in the morning with a detailed report about what the enemy was doing, fearing no contradiction. But an easy life was not meant for them so long as Young was their leader. He demanded results. Concealed by their gray uniforms, they rode among the friendly Valley people, drank their stirrup cups, talked freely, and stole back with what information they managed to gain. They also got a reputation as efficient rascals and in time, due to their looting, the sobriquet of "Sheridan's Robbers." The good they did failed to show up in the records. General Crook, writing of them in afteryears, said: "Just what they accomplished I don't know." [13] Certainly they were never able to determine, to any useful degree, the strength of the Rebel army under Early.

The same day Blazer was executing his surprise at the ford, six of Mosby's men stampeded Crook's ambulance train. It developed into a serious affair, most of the gravity centering on a larger wagon train that had gone into park a few hundred yards to the rear. Doctors and teamsters and even wounded men came dashing back from the ambulances in great alarm, spreading by voice and manner high havoc and general confusion. But the newspapers made more of a feat of it than it probably deserved, and Sheridan found it politic to hurry off a correction to Grant. Only one ambulance and thirteen horses were lost, he said, and added: "We have exterminated three officers and 27 of Mosby's gang in the last 12 days." [14]

Sheridan kept his army busy. Day after day details went out, some to burn flour mills, some to probe enemy lines, some to search for evidence that Early's reinforcements had been recalled to Richmond. These special detachments ran into a rash of trouble from the guerrillas, and the commander was made constantly aware of it. One day he took time out to write Augur at Washington about some of the problems the irregulars were bringing upon him, citing the retaliation his army had managed to inflict and winding up with evidence that he meant to take revenge: "As soon as I get time I will have a circular hunt for the whole gang. Many of these men are citizens who live in this vicinity, and have been selling produce to the government, and claim to be loyal on this account; they are getting loyalty now, with a prospect of poverty in the future." [15]

These days no one was more aware of Mosby's presence than Sheridan's young cavalry brigadier, George Custer, still enjoying the thrills of a newlywed. On one occasion he met his wife at Harpers Ferry for a day together and next morning wrote her from camp near Berryville: "Not even the supposed proximity of Mosby's gang could drive away my happy thoughts of you." [16]

On the fourteenth occurred news classified as especially good in Union ranks. Near Falls Church, Mosby stretched his luck too far in a running fight with a cavalry outfit and received a wound that put him on the inactive list. Before dawn he had stolen into a tent and captured a butcher, lying asleep near a beef he had slaughtered the night before—bringing off meat as well as prisoner. Successful in this escapade, he made plans to abscond with seventy-five horses quartered near, but the camp in some way was aroused and the Partisans had to flee. Later Mosby met a regiment of enemy horsemen and toyed with them, riding teasingly at their front and at one point underestimating the distance separating him from his pursuers. It was then the Federals, well aware of his identity from his fancy uniform and waving plume, fired shots that found their mark. A ball shattered the handle of one of his pistols and struck him in the groin, injuring him so badly that it was with difficulty he managed to remain in the saddle until he could make his escape.

On the night of the fifteenth Sheridan got reliable information that Kershaw's division was moving in the direction of Front Royal, and he misinterpreted the movement. Lee had written Early that Kershaw was needed at Richmond if he could be spared, but a specific recall was not included. So Jubal gave orders for the reinforcements to stand in readiness to return at a moment's notice, in the meantime, if possible, advancing eastward through Ashby's Gap to give the appearance of moving on Washington. When informed of this definite separation of forces, Sheridan assumed that the time had come for him to leave his fixed line, so without further delay he began timidly making plans for an attack.[17] While he pondered in uncertainty, a company of cavalry came flying down the pike from Harpers Ferry escorting General Grant.

The atmosphere around headquarters immediately became tense. Later in the day a private with time on his hands strolled near the camp of the Sixth Corps. His steps took him past a Vermont sergeant, standing idly for some purpose or other and possessing a bit of knowledge he was dying to spill.

As the private approached, the noncom called him to his side.

"See those two?" he whispered confidentially.

The private stared at him dumbly.

"Those two there, fool! Not me."

The private turned his head in the direction indicated. "Sure I see 'em."

"Know who they are?"

"Naw."

"That's Sheridan, the youngest of 'em. You know who the other is?"

The sergeant waited for an answer, but all he got was a dumb look.

"General Grant!"

The private's mind suddenly began to whirl and his eyes grew big.

But it was the sergeant's moment and he made the most of it. He wagged his head smugly, clucked once or twice with the air of a man to whom war can bring no new surprises, and then took a full step before kicking viciously at an imaginary pebble. "Hate to see that old cuss," he said, staring over his shoulder at Grant. "Whenever he's around there's sure to be a big fight on hand." [18]

From what happened in the next few hours it was no problem to guess what sort of conversation was going on between the two officers. Sheridan recorded for posterity that Grant told him to "go in." [19]

Jubal Early meanwhile was busy dividing his troops still further. Lee sent a message on the seventeenth that he was anxious to recall the reinforcements from the Valley, but that "a victory over Sheridan would be greatly advantageous to us." In view of which he revealed he had written Anderson to return with his staff and to leave Kershaw's division to come later. Kershaw was left in the hope that "Old Jube" could defeat the enemy if his strength was sufficient, and Lee suggested in this connection that such a thing might be done by throwing a body of troops behind Sheridan. [20]

But before Early could strike, Sheridan moved. The Union leader had it in mind to bring battle at Newtown, but on the afternoon of the eighteenth learned the army in his front had been further divided, two divisions going to Martinsburg and two remaining in the vicinity of Winchester. The Federal commander decided to attack them separately, beginning with the latter.

His army by this time had been increased to 45,000. It started moving in three separate columns at 3:00 A.M. on the nineteenth, and not long after daylight scouts brought in the upsetting information that Early's forces, with the exception of Kershaw's division, had got back together. To Sheridan's way of thinking this put a different complexion on the situation, for it meant he was facing almost everything the Confederacy had in the Valley. Actually he was opposed by only a pitiful little army of 8500 muskets and scattered bands of cavalry. [21] But such was not known to him at the time. The war would end before a comparison was made, and then it was shown that in this engagement Sheridan's cavalry alone outnumbered all of Early's infantry.

The battle lasted from dawn to late afternoon, and was fought at such a pace that Catherine Barbara Broun, miles away at Middleburg, wrote in her diary: "The cannonading has been terrible all day."[22]

While the fighting raged, so also raged Harry Gilmor, still abed at Mrs. O'Bannon's. He wanted his pants. It was bliss to be lying back on pillows with the two pretty young nieces of his hostess solicitous of his needs, but sound of the cannon reminded him that the Federals would like mighty well to have him in their clutches. Later in the day when the tide turned more sharply in favor of the Union and routed Rebels began fleeing through Winchester, the bedridden patient raised his voice to the shouting level in an empty house. Finally to his aid came one of the nieces. She had been off atop a fence on a ridge watching the battle through his fieldglasses. Quickly, in answer to his frantic pleas, she brought him his pants and then hurried in embarrassment to the porch, wondering how he would manage to get them on with one arm in a sling. But soon he appeared, wearing the pants, as well as his calico bed shirt, which had been split down the back by his nurses for purposes of convenience. And that was the extent of his wardrobe. He was shoeless and hatless, a condition that made no difference in the excitement of the moment. There he stood, unnoticed beside the throng of artillery wagons, horses, and men hurrying madly through the street, the worst of the wounded falling out one after another along the pavement. As luck would have it, the guerrilla chieftain had not long to wait. Soon he was recognized by one of his Rangers who chanced to pass at that strategic instant, and the obliging fellow promptly jumped down from his horse, hoisted his wounded leader into the saddle, and off they went, Gilmor holding on with his good arm, the reins clenched tightly in his teeth, and his bare feet dangling loose below the stirrups.[23]

On the twentieth Early took up a line on Fisher's Hill, a strong position overlooking a stream called Tumbling Run, and began building breastworks. While the Rebels worked frantically to throw up defenses, Sheridan laid plans for a turning movement, meanwhile sending Torbert, with Wilson and Merritt's divisions of horsemen, up Luray Valley in the hope that he could cross over to New Market and come in behind the Confederates.

The turning movement began spinning and was highly successful. There was desultory fighting during the first part of the day, but as the sun began sinking, Early's highly outnumbered army headed for the hills.

Over on the other side of Massanutten Mountain the Union cavalry was not faring so well. It had been confronted by Fitz Lee's cavalry and had chased after it until it reached the point at which Luray Valley narrows into a gorge at Milford and there the Gray horsemen whirled about and displayed great stubbornness. No concentration of effort would break their resistance, and the stand they thus put up no doubt saved the capture of a large part of the fleeing Confederate troops, for Early's men began forming their broken ranks into some sort of organization at New Market. After a few rounds of brisk fighting and futile charges, Torbert withdrew.

In falling back, Wilson's division proceeded toward Buckton Ford on the North Fork of the Shenandoah, while Merritt's troopers withdrew through Front Royal. As the Reserve Brigade's ambulance train neared the town, a band of Mosby's men under a ministerial student named Sam Chapman, brother of William and one day in another war to be sent to Cuba as a chaplain, attacked its cavalry escort. This was done without knowledge that Torbert was retreating and that there were large bodies of Union horse within supporting distance.

It was this attack by the Rebels that started the tragedy that marked the twenty-third of September, 1864, as a day some people would try for the rest of their lives to wipe from their memories. And it would bring in later years to the cemetery of this little Valley town a tall marble shaft in memory of six Confederates who were hanged and shot in the fashion of the Union commander-in-chief's directive. It also would bring there people who wanted to see with their own eyes the indictment in stone as proof that such a thing had happened.[24]

Chapman saw his mistake too late. Before he was aware of it, his retreat was blocked, and when the Rangers awoke to the emergency of fleeing they resorted to methods Mosby had taught them. They rode headlong into the Federals waiting in their path, shooting and shouting and creating general pandemonium. At this moment they were availing themselves, though unplanned, of a chance to test their revolvers against the more unwieldy carbines, and the lighter weapons won. At some stage in the brief melee, Union Lieutenant Charles McMaster fell, his body riddled. Fellow soldiers claimed his death came after he had tried to surrender, and there were later charges that several blue-clad fighters were seen lying on the side of the road with their throats cut, that McMaster's pockets were rifled, and that one Union combatant was found lurking in a barn stripped of his clothing, all implications involving feats that would seem scarcely possible in the heat and pressure of the moment.[25]

Not all of the Rangers escaped. When the dust of the wicked little spat cleared away, six remained behind as prisoners, one a teenaged boy who had borrowed a neighbor's horse that morning to ride with Mosby. They were the ones for whom the marble shaft was erected. Four were shot and two hanged, some of them after they had repeatedly refused to reveal Mosby's hideout. In late afternoon, as the sun went down behind the Alleghenies, the Nineteenth New York went straggling through town, and there on the far edge of the community still swung the bodies, a placard on one announcing: "This will be the fate of Mosby and all his men."

In these executions was posed a question for future generations to ponder: Who ordered the actual slaughter of these men? Custer was most generally blamed, and it would seem that he might have had ample reason to go to such an extreme.[26] The day before the affair at Front Royal, Mosby's irregulars had captured two couriers carrying dispatches to Custer. They also had picked up his orderly, who was caught in the act of lugging half a sheep, presumably for the general's mess. The brigadier was young and hotheaded and, in the slang of horse-and-buggy days, feeling his oats. He could not stand defeat, which was what the withdrawal from Milford implied. His letters to his wife revealed that the Rangers were prominently on his mind. All of this pointed accusingly in his direction.

But decades later some folks awakened to the fact that perhaps Torbert, who was chief of cavalry, had been instrumental in bringing about the killings. None of the official reports indicated who gave the order.[27] They spoke of the brush with Mosby's men and that some of the guerrillas were killed, but no mention was made of the manner in which they died. However, regardless of who was to blame, the action would certainly seem to bear the approval of the Union high command. Grant had wired: "When any of Mosby's men are caught, hang them without trial."

During all the furor and murder west of the Blue Ridge, Grant was hoping—and then requesting—that Sheridan would wipe out

"the stain the Valley of the Shenandoah has been to us heretofore."
When he was notified of the successes at Winchester and Fisher's
Hill, opening the way for the push toward Charlottesville, he immediately gave birth to an idea Sheridan later claimed he opposed
from the beginning. Due to the guerrillas the army in the Valley
was having severe supply problems. No train got through to it without a guard of several thousand men. This was a standing require-
ment. In view of which Grant now proposed that the Manassas Gap
Railroad running across the mountains to Strasburg be reopened.
Such a step, it was explained, would serve a double purpose: it
would provide a more direct line for supplies and it would enable
quicker transportation of men to protect Washington if needed.

While the idea was being batted around, Halleck and others in
Washington suddenly concluded some decision should be made as
to where Sheridan was going. If he kept on to Charlottesville, as
Grant so sincerely desired, then the Orange and Alexandria Railroad would be his most direct route of supply. On the other hand,
if he abandoned his triumphant march and retraced his steps, the
Manassas Gap line would more nearly meet his needs. The answer
in this case was left to Sheridan, and the young general, realizing
his problems more acutely than Grant, decided to reverse his steps
again, to wend his way back down the Valley and to operate from
Harpers Ferry.

Sheridan had very definite opinions as to why he should not continue up the Valley. In his victories to date he had pushed Early's
army aside with comparative ease, vastly outnumbered as it was, but
he had not been able to overcome a problem that was seriously
checking his progress: the matter of feeding his animals and men.
Destruction, as he understood his orders, was his first goal. To this
end he had had in mind that he would push up the Valley with a
certain amount of supplies, just how far was not determined in the
beginning, and then return, burning and pillaging as he moved in
each direction. These plans were made without consideration of
possible battles, and the two major engagements fought had taxed
his provisions heavily. On the twenty-fourth he wired Grant: "I am
now 80 miles from Martinsburg, and find it exceedingly difficult to
supply this army." [28] In reply he got a repetition of Grant's dream:
"If you can possibly subsist your army to the front for a few days
more, do it, and make a great effort to destroy the roads about
Charlottesville . . ." [29] Even in telegrams to Halleck the commander-

in-chief was driving hard on this idea that Sheridan should continue until he could destroy the Virginia Central Railroad, Lee's supply line.

As September expired, Sheridan got down as far as Harrisonburg, and from there he began to break it gently to Grant that his dream about the Army of the Shenandoah sweeping as far as Charlottesville and then turning toward Richmond would never happen in '64. His cavalry, he sent notice, had swept up as far as Staunton and Waynesboro, destroying as it went, and his infantry also was carrying out instructions to make the Valley "a barren waste." Two regiments alone, in traveling thirty miles, had destroyed ninety-three barns, eleven mills, one tannery, seventy-two stacks of hay and grain, one furnace, one foundry and one distillery, and had driven off 351 cattle and sixty-five sheep.[30]

But that was it as far as Sheridan was concerned. He announced to Grant: "It will be exceedingly difficult for me to carry the infantry over the mountains and strike at the Central road. I cannot accumulate sufficient stores to do so, and think it best to take some position near Front Royal, and operate with the cavalry and infantry."[31] He apparently had no worries about the Confederate army in the Valley, even though he was aware Kershaw's division and Anderson had rejoined it. The Union leader was under the impression that most of Early's men had fled eastward through the mountains at Brown's Gap and thus were entirely out of the Valley.

On the heels of his message to Grant, Sheridan wired Halleck that he strongly advised the campaign in the Valley be terminated and the Sixth and Nineteenth Corps returned to Petersburg. "This is my best judgment," he added.[32]

Some months after the war, in quieter surroundings, Sheridan gave a more deliberate explanation of why he was opposed to continuing the campaign. He explained that it would necessitate opening the Orange and Alexandria Railroad from Alexandria, "and to protect this road against the numerous guerrilla bands would have required a corps of infantry."[33] In addition, he would have to leave a force in the Valley, possibly the whole of Crook's command, to give security to the line of the Potomac. Remaining to him then would be only a small number of fighting men, too few in face of the constant threat that Lee might detach a force and move it rapidly by rail to overwhelm the Federals in the Valley, after which it would be returned quickly to Petersburg before Grant could take advantage of its absence.

Thus the thinking of a general facing a scattered foe. No mention is made of Early's troops, the twice-routed army that was supposed to be his Number 1 adversary. Instead, his fears were traced to the guerrillas and the potential threat of Lee's beleaguered army. At this time Sheridan actually had under his authority, subject to call, 173,264 men, of whom 94,026 were present for duty.[34] These included the troops at Washington, Baltimore, and Chambersburg and those in Crook's Army of West Virginia, all making up the Middle Military Division. Early's total before the two battles of September were fought was 8564, and these were encumbered with 2573 prisoners of war. The odds of their comparative strength on paper were better than five to one. But Sheridan considered—and later maintained in his memoirs[35]—that the Partisans in his rear compelled such heavy detachments to guard the border along the Potomac and his line of supplies that their actual strength was about equal.

In the end Sheridan's decision stood, and the work on the Manassas Gap line began. The Railroad Bureau in Washington estimated that the track could be put in running order in about a week, but that it would take somewhat longer to rebuild the bridges across the Shenandoah. Hoping to size up the task more exactly, Halleck ordered a cavalry detachment on a trip of examination along the road, at the same time expressing in a letter to Grant an awareness of some of the problems involved: "The country is wooded and full of guerrillas, and it will probably require a pretty large force to guard the road." [36]

But the problem would be found to be more basic than that. Experience along both the B. & O. and the O. & A. had shown that the men selected to do the spadework connected with this reconstruction project would go about their jobs timidly, spending much of the time looking over their shoulders in apprehension of guerrilla attacks. Even at that the work began at a rapid pace.

A construction party of 150 laborers, on a train drawn by two locomotives, started from Alexandria early one morning. With it went Richard Power, experienced telegrapher, and eighty soldiers under the veteran Colonel George B. Gallupe. They worked rapidly westward from Manassas, replacing rails and rotten ties, restoring the bedding wherever it had washed badly, building burned trestles and bridges, and restringing and patching telegraph wire. Speed was the order: Secretary of War Stanton had set the impossible goal of three days for the line to be reopened, pointing out that, since Sheridan had turned thumbs down on any further march up the Valley, the Sixth and Nineteenth Corps must be quickly moved over it on their way back to Petersburg. Summer had passed and now leaves were falling, and still Grant had not brought his campaign to a successful close. It was estimated Lee at most could have 50,000 men in the trenches around Richmond and Petersburg. The addition of some of Sheridan's 94,000-odd effectives should by rights be all that was needed to deliver the knockout punch.

The railroad party pushed on, keeping busy every daylight hour. It reached Thoroughfare Gap, worked through it, and stopped for the night near Broad Run. Before darkness closed in, Telegrapher Power opened an office on a barrelhead and clicked off an initial progress report. It went to M. J. McCrickett of Alexandria, assistant superintendent of the railroad, a young man of great capability. He had left Detroit originally to join the U. S. Military Telegraph Corps, but was too experienced a railroader to be wasted in such capacity.[37]

While the repair crew was summarizing its progress, Halleck was doing some serious thinking about the problem of maintaining the railroad once it was repaired. He wrote Grant a lengthy message on the subject, the most alarming part of which was embraced in these two sentences: "In order to keep up communication on this line to Manassas Gap and the Shenandoah Valley, it will be necessary to send south all Rebel inhabitants between that line and the Potomac, and also to completely clean out Mosby's gang of robbers who have so long infested that district of country, and I respectfully suggest that Sheridan's cavalry should be required to accomplish this object before it is sent elsewhere. The two small regiments under General Augur have been so often cut up by Mosby's band that they are cowed and useless for that purpose."[38]

Halleck's letter was written at a time when there were disturbing reports about Mosby. A few days earlier he had been seen at Culpeper hobbling around on a cane and boasting that he was on his way back to lead his men. Shortly afterward it was announced that he had rejoined his command and was accompanying it on raids in a buggy.[39]

298

Mosby lost no time in centering his attention on the Manassas Gap line once he was back with his Rangers. One day from a bivouac on the side of the Bull Run Mountains, he sent a scout, Tom Ogg, to reconnoiter and to report to him that night at Haymarket, a village on the railroad that so far had been left unoccupied by the Federals. In the hours of darkness Mosby set out for the rendezvous but was surprised to find on nearing the place a number of campfires. While he sat studying the Union soldiers who had suddenly decided to spend the night there, a different scene was taking place on the opposite side of the camp.

Over there, Ogg approached the fires in perfect bliss, confident he was approaching a camp set up by Mosby. When a picket hailed him with "Who comes there?", he replied with complete trust, "Tom Ogg!"

"Dismount and advance," ordered the picket.

This seemed like foolishness to Ogg, so he protested: "I'm Tom Ogg. You know me. I've been sent by the Colonel on a scout."

A bright thought suddenly came to Ogg. "What company do you belong to?" he shouted.

"Company E," replied the picket, "but what's that got to do with it?"

"That new company!" snorted Ogg. "That damned, green, new Company E."

The picket failed to catch the point. "Dismount and advance or I'll shoot!"

Ogg got down grumblingly in the dark and advanced. When he got close to the picket, he suddenly realized he was facing an enemy and that a hostile bayonet was close to his breast. Then the ability to think quickly that kept him alive as a scout came to his aid.

"I'm lame," he said. "Don't make me walk. Let me ride to see the Colonel."

The picket, now the unsuspecting one, consented, and Ogg climbed back into the saddle.

"Where's the Colonel now?" he asked. When the picket turned to point toward the campfires, the scout sank his spurs and darted off into the night. The shots fired after him caused Mosby to chuckle on the other side of camp. "Bet that's Tom Ogg now," he said.[40]

The railroad party soon heard more directly from Mosby. As it neared White Plains, two cannon balls were fired from the woods, one coming dangerously close to the bell of the front locomotive.

Colonel Gallupe was on the engine at the time, and while there was a general rush to get out of range of the artillery, he stole forward to reconnoiter, finding what looked like 150 Confederate horsemen waiting along the track ahead. The telegraph wires quickly were set abuzzing to call for reinforcements, and these soon came out along the winding rails from Manassas—200 men, certainly enough, aided by Gallupe's troops, to rout 150 guerrillas. Late in the day a charge was made against the Partisans, with surprising results. It was found that not all of the Rebels had been visible when the colonel was doing his reconnoitering, and the entire force of them struck back like a thunderbolt, routing the Union detail and capturing about fifty. The working crew managed to escape by hustling aboard the construction trains, backing up so hastily that baggage, camp equipage, and stores were left behind for the raiders.

But the railroader was undaunted. More reinforcements were sent, and as they approached, the construction crew moved back out, this time reaching White Plains. They kept on until they approached Salem, and there Mosby's guerrillas again threatened.

Halting to benefit from the earlier experience at the hands of the Partisans, a hurried call was made for a larger guard. This plea was heeded immediately, but more troops could not be sent until the engine Grapeshot and twelve cars, piled up in "a perfect wreck" in Thoroughfare Gap, could be cleared away. When the new reinforcements were able to push through, with them came McCrickett, riding out to his death, and General Augur, commanding troops at Washington, wired he too was on his way.

Next morning McCrickett and a party rode on a few miles to inspect the task ahead. As they knew one engine would be unable to override the bushes and weeds grown up along the track, two were used, and together they chugged along. Their progress was slow and steady and at first peaceful. It was not until they had got a mile and a half beyond White Plains that random shots suddenly were fired at them out of the woods, doing no damage but causing the engineers to open the throttles wide. Onward madly steamed the demons of the rail, rocking wildly back and forth with the roughness of the track. With cylinders hissing and smokestacks roaring, they rushed on, out of range of the guns in the trees, on toward a steep embankment and a curve. There was the trap, the trick so often executed by the guerrillas and later adopted by an outlaw named Jesse James. As the locomotives rounded the turn, a wire was drawn tight, displacing an outer rail. Wheels of the engines bumped with great noise along the ties, and then the giants rolled over and over down the embankment, tearing up the ground and spreading wreckage along the hillside. It would take days to clear up this mess. And at various intervals during the period the bodies of five men, one of them McCrickett, so badly mangled he could be recognized only by his clothing, would be removed.[41]

All at once the weather turned cold, and there was hail, snow, and wind, just as Augur was reaching Rectortown and setting up headquarters. From there he looked over the situation and soon was wiring that simply patrolling the track and guarding the bridges would not be sufficient, that the road must be literally guarded the whole way.[42] He made immediate plans to build small stockades so near each other that they would command the entire track. If that failed to provide protection, he had in mind forcing prominent Secessionists to accompany each train.[43]

Little had been heard from Sheridan, and now came a delayed message. He stated bluntly in it that he would not have advised opening the railroad. It was his reasoning that large guards would be required to protect it against a very small number of Partisan troops.[44] He also explained he had been unable to communicate more frequently on account of the operations of guerrillas in his rear. They had attacked every party he had sent out, he revealed, and for that reason he had forwarded as few dispatches as possible in order to economize on manpower.[45] From him a day or two later came another telegram that said among other things: "I would also advise that the repair on the Manassas railroad be stopped, and the disposal of the guard as you may think best." [46]

The stockades planned by Augur were hastily erected of logs along the track. Their effect was unnoticeable. The depredations continued without letup and, if anything with more flagrancy. Guards and workmen were sniped at out of the woods. An occasional engine or train was derailed. Rails were displaced and toted off into the woods when watchmen had their backs turned. Wires were torn down and piles of construction materials blazed up mysteriously.

Augur waited no longer to try his other ultimatum: prominent men known to be Southern in their sympathies were made to ride each train. After that the derailments stopped, but the other troubles continued.

It was at this point that Secretary of War Stanton stepped in with the most serious retaliation so far ordered in connection with the railroad. Every house within five miles of the tracks—"which is not required for our own purpose, or which is not occupied by persons known to be friendly"—was burned, and all timber and brush within musketry fire of the line cut down and destroyed. The area was completely depopulated of Southerners. Males suspected of aiding Mosby were arrested and imprisoned in Washington, and women and children were sent north or south. As a warning against their return, printed notices were circulated that any hostile person found within five miles of the road would be considered a robber and bushwhacker and treated as such. And as a final step inhabitants were notified that, if depredations continued, an additional strip on each side of the railroad would be laid in waste.[47]

While these drastic measures were being carried out, Halleck was converted and came over to Sheridan's way of thinking. It was easy now to recognize the futility of the move, for Mosby's men continued to heckle at almost every point along the railroad. Cannon balls came sailing through the air at unexpected moments. Bullets whined down upon the backs of guards and workmen, and trestles and bridges required strong guards in order to remain standing. But it was decided to continue the work—on a halfhearted basis,[48] pending the arrival of Sheridan in Washington for a conference.

As Stanton had threatened, the stretch on each side of the track laid in waste was increased to ten miles.[49] But the guerrillas had won their point. Sheridan showed up in Washington, and his appearance brought a change. It was only a matter of hours until Halleck was wiring Augur that the rails on the Manassas Gap line were to be taken up all the way back to Manassas Junction.

CHAPTER 6

October 6–19, 1864

OUT OF THE MIST CAME
HOSTILE MEN

For the second time in two months Sheridan turned back down the Shenandoah Valley—and this time he rode with sadness and murder in his heart. Dead lay his young friend and chief engineer, John R. Meigs, son of the Union Quartermaster General. His death had come from an enemy bullet that struck him down while he threaded the country near Harrisonburg after topographical information, and to Sheridan only one brand of enemy could have fired the gun—a guerrilla.

As a staff member Meigs had been particularly close to the Valley commander. When Sheridan took over in early August and moved to headquarters on the second floor of an old hotel at Harpers Ferry, one of his first steps was to send for the engineer. The new commander found him smart, neat, erect, and not much more than a beardless youth. It was soon evident that he had a high degree of intelligence. He was thoroughly familiar with the country through which they were operating and, what fitted him especially for his task, he was a rapid sketcher and could produce quickly the maps necessary to a battle or offensive. These were surprising qualities, for he was only a year out of West Point. However, he had finished at the head of his class. Going directly into the army, he performed such distinguished service that by the time of the '64 Valley campaign he was an ideal choice for chief engineer.[1]

Meigs' age may have been his undoing. Youth is impetuous, given to taking risks that maturity fears and evaluates with the wisdom of experience. Months earlier he had shown he had no patience for Partisans and their irregular warfare. When Hunter fled from Lynchburg, it was Meigs who went along the line of march talking with the men in an effort to organize a movement "to break up" the gang of guerrillas following in their rear.[2]

But it was not guerrillas who killed Meigs. The shot by which he died was fired by Private George W. Martin of the Fourth Virginia Cavalry, more familiarly known as the Black Horse.[3]

On the day of Meigs' death F. M. Campbell, Confederate private frequently sent on scouting duty, was ordered out again and, to accompany him, was allowed to select Martin and his first cousin, William L. Ficklin, also of the Fourth Virginia. It was a misty, raw morning, and they wore rubber coats, both as protection from the weather and to conceal their gray uniforms.[4] They stole behind the enemy lines, moving through the country with care, and while riding along a lane saw three horsemen approaching. Whispering discreetly, each selected a foe and, when the approaching riders came abreast, demanded a surrender. The Federals threw up their hands in answer, Martin facing Meigs, and were ordered to take off their arms. As the young engineer reached under his cape to loosen his holster, he fired, the bullet penetrating Martin's right lung. But the Confederate had his own pistol in hand and immediately pulled the trigger, shooting Meigs through the heart.[5]

This version of the killing Sheridan would never believe—if he ever heard it. The account he accepted was from one of Meigs' companions who managed to escape. A short time after the incident this man dashed into headquarters with the news, reporting that Meigs was "killed without resistance of any kind whatever, and without even the chance to give himself up."[6] The report was related with such coolness Sheridan was convinced beyond a doubt the details were correct. Under the impression guerrillas living in the neighborhood were to blame, he issued an order for all homes of Secessionists within an area of five miles of the killing to be burned.

Execution of the order was entrusted to Custer, already established as an officer with no mercy for guerrillas. He had just been assigned command of a division, and here was his chance to earn the new trust. Next morning his troops moved to carry out Sheridan's wishes. Within the radius to be scorched was the little village of Dayton, and its destruction fell to the One-Hundred-sixteenth Ohio Regiment under Lieutenant Colonel Thomas F. Wildes. Wildes was an experienced soldier, a veteran fighter known for his drive in battle and already cited for distinguished service, but when it came to converting an entire community into a pitiful conclave of weeping women, children, and old men, he rebelled, just as another officer had done at Newtown.[7] Without delay he forwarded to headquarters by courier a defense of the people involved and pleaded that their homes be spared. This was a brave step, especially in view of Sheridan's Irish temperament and his anger over Meig's death. Wildes knew it would not be gracefully received and he was right. He kept a record of the commander's reaction: "The general read the note and swore, read it again and swore, examined and cross-examined the messenger."[8]

Meantime a pitiful scene was developing at Dayton. Pending revocation of orders, the burning was set for noon. Soldiers helped the residents remove their most prized belongings, conveying them to a slight eminence overlooking the village. There the families sat among little piles of household effects and waited in misery, children and adults weeping in unison. Off on the horizon in all directions Sheridan's wrath was symbolized by columns of smoke rising furiously into the heavens. Minutes dragged with the slowness of hours. That night, the old folks knew, skies after sundown would be deeply colored with the flare of burning buildings and haystacks. So in their woe they sat and prayed, and the only solace they could lean upon was the resolute stubbornness of Wildes. Any minute he might have to fire the match that would consume their belongings, but in him they placed their trust, and it was trust well placed. Toward noon a horseman could be seen galloping from the direction of headquarters—and in time he rode up, the courier bringing reluctant word from Sheridan that Dayton might be spared.[9]

At this time sadness also crept into guerrilla ranks. McNeill, after a successful cattle raid through the West Virginia hills, decided to slip across the mountains into the Valley and attack Sheridan's supply line. There, in a predawn attack on a 100-man detail of Federals guarding a bridge across the Shenandoah near Mount Jackson, he was felled by a bullet supposedly from the gun of one of his own men.[10]

The Partisan leader, with sixty Rangers, had made a hurried ride from his native Hardy County. So badly was he wounded that he was lifted to the back of his horse, a little roan he had captured on his first raid around Moorefield, and held there by four men until he could be conveyed to the nearest home. This happened to be the domicile of a Methodist preacher, the Reverend Addison Weller. The minister's wife, Elizabeth, awakened by the firing at the bridge, described in later years the scene as McNeill was brought into her yard and laid on the grass, where "his noble form, writhing in agony," reminded her more of a wounded lion than a man. She noticed that his eyes still flashed with fire and heard him say, as his men bent over him with expressions of sympathy, "Goodby, boys. Go on and leave me. I've done all I can for my country."

His raiders, a picturesque band of young and old, hardened and suntanned, started away, leading sixty prisoners and horses. Before they had gone more than a couple of hundred yards, one of them, Nelson Kiracoffe, rushed back and knelt beside the victim for a last word of prayer. Hastily muttering the supplication, he leaped back upon his horse and hurried to overtake the others, the captain's eyes following them until the last one was out of sight. Then he exclaimed for the first time: "Oh, I am in such agony! Do something for me if you can!" [11]

Not much could be done. The Wellers vacated their bed for him, and as quickly as possible shaved off his beard and trimmed his hair closer than normal. This was a hasty effort to mislead the numerous scouting parties that soon came in search of the Partisan, for the Federals knew immediately of his wounding.[12] Two of these detachments visited the Weller home and stared at the victim in the minister's bed, but they could not be positive of his identification. Finally a captured Ranger was brought to the home. He was Simon Miller, a friend of the minister's family, and he caught a look in Elizabeth Weller's eyes at the front door and from then on steadfastly denied that he had ever seen the stricken man before.

Medical advice was sought. Dr. Leonidas Triplett of Mount Jackson, father of two of McNeill's Rangers, came to the bedside and conducted a thorough examination, leaving with a sad shake of his head: available to him was neither the power to aid a recovery nor the medicine to relieve the agony. A little later Mrs. McNeill arrived by horse, riding over fifty miles behind her son,

Jesse, without the benefit of a saddle. Then came Sheridan, to set up his headquarters temporarily near the Weller home.

After the customary chores of making camp, the general and several officers rode over to interview the wounded man, among them Sheridan. The visit brought results. The influence of Mrs. McNeill, a strong religionist, had been felt by her husband and, when he was asked his true identity, this time he admitted it. The Unionists, taking in the seriousness of his condition, agreed they would have to send a guard and an ambulance to convey him to a point where he could be held more closely in captivity.

Sheridan rode away and from his next camp wrote Grant: "McNeill was wounded and fell into our hands. This was fortunate, as he was the most daring and dangerous of all the bushwhackers in this section of the country." [13]

But McNeill was only temporarily in the hands of the Federals. By night his men stole in and whisked him away in a carriage supplied by none other than Jubal Early, who on one occasion had found an opportunity to visit the Partisan's bedside. Carefully and slowly the stricken leader was conveyed to Hill's Hotel in Harrisonburg, and there he died, five weeks and three days after his wounding. Burial followed in the local cemetery, with Masonic honors. But two months later, at a time when Sheridan's army was bogged down by winter, his body was taken up and moved to Cemetery Hill overlooking Moorefield. There it was laid in its final resting place, a spot where little more than a year prior he had made his moonlight attack on the First West Virginia Infantry. A later generation would erect a shaft near this grave—to commemorate the native son who had given his life for a cause, as well as the other Partisans, native and otherwise, who had fallen as members of his command—and on it inscribed in marble would be the explanation that they had fallen "in defense of constitutional liberty and our homes."

In the weeks McNeill lay waiting for death to claim him, his Rangers continued their activities, fighting now under the leadership of the son, Jesse, a twenty-three-year-old who had all the courage of the father but lacked the mature judgment of experience. After Hanse died, some of his men scattered to other commands, though a majority of them remained with Jesse. The son was an excellent shot with both pistol and rifle, a good rider and fighter, and he had learned from his sire that, in leading a raid, one should look first "to getting out before going in." Two traits he had that his followers did not admire in him: he was quick-tempered and he was impetuous.

But no matter who led them, the Rangers fought now with increasing personal danger. Sheridan's army, swarming back down the Valley, had lost its patience, and quick executions were more readily the order of the day. Rebels caught in pairs or small groups instantly were looked upon as bushwhackers and treated accordingly. And the guerrillas at this period were exceedingly active. Correspondent Francis Long of the New York *Herald* dutifully reported: "The intervening country between Harrisonburg and Winchester is literally swarming with guerrillas, and only a force of considerable strength can pass up and down the pike. It is difficult to get anything through in the way of news at a date early enough to be of general interest." [14]

Reports soon indicated that someone other than the person responsible for executing Mosby's men at Front Royal knew how to use the hangman's noose. A new brigadier had entered the field—William H. Powell, late successor to Averell, who had been cast aside after drawing upon himself the irate displeasure of Sheridan.

Newcomer Powell rode with vengeance in his eye. Small squads of guerrillas hovered around his command at all times, watching for opportunities to strike, and toward these bands lurking like predatory birds in the distance he had no mercy. In a report to headquarters a few days after taking command he revealed he had had two Confederates shot to death in retaliation for the murder of one of his soldiers, found with his throat cut from ear to ear.[15]

That was a start for the new brigadier. He would engineer other executions—and threaten even greater slaughter. Within a week, "though painful and repugnant" to his own feelings, three Rebel prisoners were shot in retaliation for two Union soldiers he charged guerrillas had slain. These executions were mentioned in a report to headquarters in which he explained he believed such measures to be the only means of protecting his soldiers against the operations of the irregular bands. His stern treatment of the enemy, he cited, had caused him to be threatened by the Richmond press, on which he commented: "But by this I cannot be intimidated in the discharge of my duties under orders. And I wish it distinctly understood by the Rebel authorities that if two to one is not sufficient I will increase it to 22 to one, and leave the consequences in the hands of my government."

Happenings like Meigs' death enabled Sheridan to put more emphasis on his relentless scourge of the Valley. He reported as he moved back toward the Potomac that he had made the whole country from the Blue Ridge to North Mountain untenable for a Rebel army. Up in smoke had gone more than 2000 barns filled with wheat, hay, and farming implements, as well as seventy mills filled with flour and wheat. In front of his army were herded 4000 head of stock and a great number of horses, all rounded up from neighboring farms. Also corraled were 3000 sheep, but these had been slaughtered and issued to the troops. When he finished, according to his plans, the ninety-two miles of rich farmland between Winchester and Staunton would have but little in it for man or beast.[16] A Confederate officer on the scene, writing in subsequent years, recorded: "I try to restrain my bitterness at the recollection of the dreadful scenes I witnessed. I rode down the Valley with the advance after Sheridan's retreating cavalry beneath great columns of smoke which almost shut out the sun by day, and in the red glare of bonfires, which, all across that Valley, poured out flames and sparks heavenward and crackled mockingly in the night air; and I saw mothers and maidens tearing their hair and shrieking to Heaven in their fright and despair, and little children, voiceless and tearless in their pitiable terror. I saw a beautiful girl, the daughter of a clergyman, standing in the front door of her home while its stable and outbuildings were burning, tearing the yellow tresses from her head, taking up and repeating the oaths of passing skirmishers and shrieking with wild laughter, for the horrors of the night had driven her mad." [17]

As Sheridan's army marched and spread destruction, his woes came in multiplied doses. Couriers were gobbled up. Supply trains were interrupted, even when escorted by thousands of both infantry and cavalry. And at his back constantly lurked a hounding force of Rebel horsemen, a mixture of guerrillas and Early's scattered troops. Day in and day out they dogged him, riders as ruthless and as vengeful as maddened bees.

By the time he reached Strasburg, the enemy at his rear took on some form of organization, raising a threat that grew in seriousness. Sheridan's scouts told him the cavalry thus assembled was led by

General Rosser, a dashing young fellow, but that it was unsupported by infantry. So Torbert was ordered to finish off this "New Savior of the Valley."[18] Next morning the Union horse moved out for an attack, Custer with the Third Division along one road and Merritt with the First on another. It was a pincers that met few obstacles in the face of the Southerners' great disparity of numbers. Rosser and his force were routed and chased twenty-six miles, dropping off in their rear eleven pieces of artillery, thirty-seven wagons and ambulances, including some belonging to the headquarters group, and 330 prisoners.[19]

This little cavalry chase provided the Federals with a bit of fireside humor. Rosser was leading the South's proud Laurel Brigade, Ashby's old outfit, long known for its battle stamina. But now it had been routed, and the Union boys, when they drew up at night after a day's march, got fun snickering over the thought that, since laurel was not a plant of the running variety, maybe the brigade name should be changed to Grapevine.[20] They also got a chuckle when Custer appeared wearing a fancy embroidered general's uniform captured the day before, an outfit gaudily set off by his red tie, broad-brimmed hat, and long hair.[21]

Grant in the meantime was wary about developments in the Valley. The sweep up to Charlottesville, with its corollary move on Richmond, had never been made, and now Sheridan was falling back, something the commander-in-chief had opposed even from the days of Sigel. Moreover, no less a journal than the New York *Herald* reported the Valley swarming with guerrillas. About thirty or forty of them had attacked the ambulance in which rode the Honorable F. W. Kellogg, congressman from Michigan, thus giving Corporal Reuben K. Hull of the Second Virginia (Union) Cavalry a chance for a little individual bravery. His horse was wounded as he sat astride it close to the statesman's vehicle, and it dropped so suddenly to the ground that he could not avoid its falling on his foot. "But," reported the *Herald*, "the corporal emptied his seven-shooter at the enemy and reloaded his piece before he stopped to look at it. By this time the 'Johnnies' had vamoosed, and Hull turned to Mr. Tom Wallis, who had been near him emptying his Colt's navy, saying, 'Mr. Wallis, I believe I am hurt.' And sure enough his foot was so swollen he could hardly walk."[22]

But such stories did not wipe out the threat of Rebel resistance in the Valley, and Grant took caution, notifying Halleck that

Sheridan had better retain the Nineteenth Corps and that the time for sending the Sixth Corps to Petersburg would have to be left to the Valley leader's judgment.[23]

It was two days before Sheridan received this message. By that time Rosser had been chased and the Union troops were north of Cedar Creek, on their way back. So the Sixth Corps was ordered toward Front Royal, in the direction of the transportation it was hoped soon would be made available via the Manassas Gap line. But that was the day the double-header was derailed and Mc-Crickett was killed, the big jolt that began to alter convictions about restoring this particular railroad.

Next day was a bad day for Sheridan. Though the weather was lovely and the Valley shone with the kaleidoscopic beauty of autumn, worries came to him aplenty. His chief quartermaster, Lieutenant Colonel Cornelius W. Tolles, and his medical inspector, Dr. Emil Ohlenschlager, met death at the hands of a band of guerrillas. Wagon trains, in several quarters, were attacked, and some of them badly broken up. From Petersburg, Grant got off another message keeping alive the idea of an advance on Charlottesville.[24] Powell was stringing up more Rebels, a pastime that in no way helped the progress of the Union army in the Valley. And newspapers were printing a dispatch written by a correspondent near Upperville: "From the 1st of January to the 1st of October, by a minute calculation, Mosby has killed and captured 69 Yankees for every man he has lost." [25]

Tolles and Ohlenschlager, it developed, had died victims of poor judgment. Riding along with an escort of twenty-five men and an ambulance loaded with mail, they were notified by the rear guard from time to time that guerrillas were forming behind them.[26] The lieutenant in charge of the escort wanted to turn and disperse them, but Tolles gave orders to keep moving in a steady trot.[27] This enabled the Partisans to get close enough for a charge, and when it came it was like an avalanche. Six of the Federals were killed, six wounded, and the ambulance captured.

In his practice of applying the hangman's noose, Powell was settling scores as Sheridan had done after the death of Meigs. Only a few hours had passed since the new cavalry brigadier had ridden past the body of a Union soldier allegedly killed by two of Mosby's Rangers, and his blood boiled. The victim he chose to die by the rope in retaliation happened to be a prisoner brought in by a detail sent to destroy a stillhouse, a nondescript individual they described as a Mosby man but who steadfastly maintained he was a Baptist minister and had had nothing to do with the Partisan leader.[28] Death was the sentence decreed by a drumhead court-martial, and on the limb of a tree he died. There he hung in the sunshine of a beautiful October day, his body turning monotonously back and forth as the life was choked out of it. After he quit kicking, to his clothing was pinned a card that explained: "A. C. Willis, member of Company C, Mosby's command, hanged by the neck in retaliation for the murder of a U. S. soldier by Messrs. Chancellor and Myers." [29] The alleged murderers had fled, but some personal revenge was possible. A detachment was ordered out to destroy the residence, barn, and all buildings and forage on the nearby farm of Chancellor.[30]

Willis was scarcely cold before Mosby's men came upon his body as it revolved slowly in the gentle breezes of the lovely autumn weather.[31] They took it down and buried it and then rode forth with vengeance in their heart. The first to come under their wrath was Francis Marion White of the Pennsylvania Ringgold Battalion. This unfortunate soldier was nabbed when he doubled back to pick up a sword he had left inadvertently at a home where he had stopped for dinner. The Rangers backed him up to a tree and were knotting the rope when some of McNeill's men arrived on the scene, in a friendly mood, ready to join forces temporarily with Mosby. But their attitude changed when they learned the man about to be hanged was a Ringgolder. For any member of this outfit they had a soft spot, so they argued long and loud that the man was entitled to go free, that members of his battalion treated Valley residents with respect and had even kept some of them from starving. Stoutly they gave voice in his defense, without indication of letup. The argument went back and forth, never waning, until finally the McNeill boys lost patience and backed up, guns drawn, to form a ring around the prisoner, announcing they were prepared to die with him. This put an entirely different slant on the matter and, after a few more futile words, the rope was removed from White's neck.[32]

That night when Sheridan drew up in camp, he sent off a troubled dispatch to Grant. In it he told of the death of Tolles and Ohlenschlager, charging they had been ambuscaded. Then he complained of the guerrilla parties which were becoming more formidable "and are annoying me very much," and concluded: "I know of no way to exterminate them except to burn out the whole country and let the people go North or South. If I attempt to capture them by sending out parties, they escape to the mountains on fleet horses." [33]

Next day he got the call to come to Washington for a consultation on several points, including the matter of the Manassas Gap Railroad. He also received a wire from Halleck informing him of Grant's desire that he take a position far enough south to serve as a base for future operations on Gordonsville and Charlottesville. These messages put a different complexion on his immediate activities, and he countermanded at once the order directing the Sixth Corps to start the move toward Petersburg.[34]

On the way to him within a few hours was another message, this one directly from Grant. It stated specifically: "What I want is for you to threaten the Virginia Central Railroad and canal in the manner your judgment tells you is best." [35] If that could not be done, the commander-in-chief said, the next best thing would be to make the enemy hold a force equal to the Army of the Shenandoah for the protection of these thoroughfares.

While these messages were moving in the direction of the Valley, there was tension in the air. For two days Mosby had not been heard from, and General Augur, over at Rectortown aiding with the railroad repair, commented on the fact to Halleck.[36] But before the day ended the situation had changed. Out of Martinsburg began to trickle details of a B. & O. train wreck and robbery two miles east of Kearneysville.

Bit by bit the telegraph brought a full report into Washington. It was a forerunner, this amazing incident, of the wild tales of Jesse James. Mosby, leading his band, had derailed the train at two-thirty in the morning, but without serious injury to anyone, burned it, and ridden away with two paymasters and their cache of 173,000 dollars.[37]

This was a definite change of pace. Until recently the wily Partisan had been concentrating on the Manassas Gap line. But pending Sheridan's arrival for a conference, the work on this railroad had been suspended, and the switch to the B. & O. was an indication the Confederate irregular knew as well what was going on as anyone in high Union circles.

The effect of the robbery was widespread. Paymasters throughout the area were panicked, and so was the top Federal command. Up and down the line went the word: not a single payroll was to be moved without a strong escort. The down express from Cumberland was held for twelve hours at Martinsburg.[38] From that point Paymaster Jonathan Ladd wired: "I have my funds in the parlor of the United States Hotel here, guarded by a regiment." [39] His guard was the Thirteenth Maine, kept on duty day and night, most of the time in the public square near the hotel.[40]

As newspapers picked up the incident, it was told that Mosby was seen limping around at the scene of the wreck on a cane. And he was said to have remarked rather nonchalantly to some of the protesting passengers that he was sorry to put them to inconvenience, but that he considered it a portion of his duty to teach Union officers how to guard their railway properly.[41] The New York *Herald* correspondent in his dispatch chirped smugly: "This was a timely rebuke, if he had said War Department instead of officers." [42]

On the fifteenth of October, Sheridan started for Washington. He was convinced that Early would not advance down the Valley and, as a result, determined to take Torbert and all of the cavalry with him, later pushing it through Chester Gap toward the railroad at Charlottesville.[43] Next day, at Front Royal, he was relayed a cipher message that had been copied from the Confederate signal station on the crest of Round Top Mountain.[44] As translated, it was signed by Longstreet and said: "Be ready to move as soon as my forces join you and we can crush Sheridan." The implication that reinforcements were on the way to Early from Richmond was contrary to information the Valley leader had been able to obtain, but it was disturbing in view of the fact that, just the day before, several cipher dispatches intended for him had been intercepted by guerrillas, possibly withholding from him intelligence that included reference to the Rebel movement.[45] His first thought was that it was a ruse, but after reflection he determined it was best to abandon the cavalry raid and to return Torbert to General Wright, commanding in his absence.[46]

Sheridan had assumed correctly that the message was a fake. It was a trick thought up by foxy old Jubal Early himself.[47]

On the morning of the seventeenth Sheridan reached Washington and went into conference.[48] Many things were talked over, but on the Manassas Gap line he had not yet made up his mind, and asked to be given a day or two longer, explaining that the message from Longstreet, fake or otherwise, and Grant's insistence on the advance toward Charlottesville were matters that precluded a definite answer. The meeting over, he immediately started his return to the Valley, arriving at Winchester the following evening. With him came two engineers Halleck had assigned to recommend a proper defense for the area west of Washington.

Back along Cedar Creek where Sheridan's army waited, the troops were in a joyous mood. They had just been paid, and some of them had sent off their absentee ballots to be cast in the Presidential elections.[49] Life was becoming brighter. A new supply of clothing and shoes had been issued, heavily guarded trains arrived with a large accumulation of mail from home, and the weather was perfect, warm in the daytime and cool enough at night to make a blanket welcome.

In the routine assignments Clinton Beckwith of the One-hundred-twenty-first New York was pegged for duty as corporal of the guard in one area of the camp. It was his responsibility to station three guards in each relief, one at the colonel's headquarters, one at the commissary, and one at the sutler's.

The first relief passed quickly, thanks to diversion supplied by a comrade who had just returned to the regiment and was in a mood to talk about his experiences while away. As a consequence so wide awake was the corporal when he was able to go off duty temporarily that he was in no mood for sleep. Out of the night came too much evidence of gaiety for him to think of going to his bed. Over at the headquarters of the Sixty-fifth New York a party was in progress, and it was known that the colonel of the One-hundred-twenty-first was among those taking part. So Beckwith forsook rest and settled down for a rough-and-rowdy game of penny-ante with some of the boys.

At 5:00 A.M. the corporal came back on duty, suffering a bit from lack of sleep. It was a beautiful night, illuminated by a moon three days past full, a moon that had come up at 8:25 P.M. and would not disappear until 8:45 A.M. In forty minutes it would be daylight, and at 6:14 A.M. the sun would rise.

The corporal drank in the scene. His regiment was camped to the right and rear of the remainder of the army, on a rise that permitted him to overlook the surroundings. Off toward Cedar Creek a bank of fog had risen and lay against the side of the

315

mountain like a streak of snow. This fog was bad on the pickets at that point, and he knew that some of them were standing duty on horseback out in the water, for General Wright was a careful soldier and wanted no surprises from the enemy.

A bit drowsy on his second relief, Beckwith was slow in turning out. The festivity, except for an occasional outburst of wild laughter from over at the headquarters of the Sixty-fifth, had ended and the camp was quiet now except for the snoring of the men. A fire burned near the kitchen tent, inviting the corporal, so he walked down for a little warmth before going to station the various pickets. While warming, he almost fell asleep and that frightened him, so he finally dragged himself away and went about his duty. Somewhere along the line he inquired about the officer of the day and the officer of the guard and was told they were over celebrating with the colonel. Then, his chores completed, he lit his pipe and went back to sit by the fire, having it in mind to walk over as soon as he got warm to see what stage the merriment had reached.

In a few minutes Beckwith found himself nodding again. He got up and stretched and it occurred to him that it must be all of half-past five o'clock. He was lonesome. As he yawned and his breath spread out a white mist in the morning air, he was aware he soon would be punished for loss of sleep, so he delayed no longer his trek in the direction of the merrymaking. But he had taken only a few steps before a spattering of shots sounded down to the left. Instantly through his mind flashed thought of the guerrillas constantly hounding their outskirts. Then came several more shots, and after that volley after volley. Fully alarmed, he ran to the nearest tents and kicked the feet of the sleepers. "Get up! Get up!" he shouted. "There's an attack on the line!"

Forty-four minutes later the sun rose on pandemonium. Early's troops, kissed off as too badly beaten ever to provide again a serious threat, suddenly had stolen in upon the sleeping Army of the Shenandoah. It was a great day for John B. Gordon, Jubal's brilliant assistant. Under cover of darkness and fog, he had led a part of the Confederate force single file along a narrow path between the creek and the mountain and had crept in upon the Union left. The first fire was the signal for a general attack, and by ten o'clock the Federals were fleeing in confusion.

Sheridan at Winchester heard the firing at an early hour, but it was not until after nine o'clock that he was awakened to the emergency at hand. It was then that he came flying up the Valley pike, slapping the flank of his horse with his ridiculous hat and shouting at his routed troops to turn back and fight. At first his efforts seemed wasted, but the nearer he got to the core of the fleeing army the more organization he was able to bring about.

The Confederates in the meantime had lost their drive. Sight of food in the deserted Union camps was too much temptation to starving men, and they forsook the battle to assuage their appetites. The organization they had had in the predawn went to pieces under daylight. From ten o'clock on they seemed to have no military objective, and by late afternoon the overpowering number of Federals were able to strike back with force. Early's army gave way and again fled toward Staunton.

But the daylight hours of October 19 had witnessed one of the great mass slayings of the war. Federals had died by the thousands—5565 killed and captured, according to official records. One of the participants on the Confederate side, Major Thomas G. Jones of Montgomery, Alabama, wrote his father: "The enemy's loss was very heavy. They were surprised in camp and slaughtered terribly. It has been my fortune to be on many battlefields of the war, but never have I observed one on which the dead were strewn at every step." [50]

Cedar Creek would be a field of death for days. Isaac O. Best of the One-hundred-twenty-first New York returned to his old camp after the Confederates had been routed and set up a desk for the A.A.G. Already the burial parties had moved through that particular area, so he was surprised to see a body lying only a short distance away. He walked over to investigate and caught the explanation at a glance: a bullet had torn off the top of the man's head, inflicting a wound that in time would be mortal. There the victim lay, breathing as quietly and as regularly as an infant. Next morning he was still breathing, but the following morning he was dead.

In his report of the battle Sheridan was jubilant. His officers informed him the enemy army he had dispersed with his three corps was made up of at least 25,000 infantry and an unknown number of cavalry.[51] This estimate would stand for years, and then Jubal Early, for the benefit of a later generation, would reveal that his entire force numbered scarcely a third that many—not as many as Sheridan had cavalry.

CHAPTER 7

October 20–November 10, 1864

REPULSIVE TO HUMANITY

The Eighteenth Connecticut Volunteers had a special reason for detesting Partisan warfare. Their lot it was, whenever the pesky Rebel irregulars caused an alarm in their area, to roll out at any hour of day or night and stand by for whatever service the emergency demanded. So often were they called on to do this that it came to be begrudgingly recognized as one of the penalties for the comparatively soft assignment of duty in the mountains along the B. & O. Such a summons sounded the morning of Mosby's big train robbery, and for much of the day the Vols stood in the middle of the road wondering what the commotion was all about. Ten days or so later they were hustled out by another alarm. It sounded early in the morning, while most of them were still asleep, and they fell over each other in confusion as they grabbed up arms and stood in line on the Winchester pike awaiting action that never came.[1]

The cause of this last emergency, they later learned, lay miles farther along the road. Before daylight a wagon train had pulled out of Winchester on its way back to Martinsburg. It was guarded by the veteran Lieutenant B. F. Hassan of the Twenty-second Pennsylvania Cavalry and fifty-five men, supported by a piece or two of artillery. Rolling along with the cumbersome vehicles, enjoying the protection of the guard, was a lighter conveyance, an ambulance, that frisked in and out of line at will, impatient to get ahead. Inside sat the dapper Frenchman, Cavalry General Alfred Nattie Duffie, twenty-nine-year-old graduate of Saint-Cyr, a man boasting the best military education Europe had to offer. He had fought over much of the world and been wounded several times, the war in the United States catching him at Saratoga, a resort to which he had gone for purposes of rectifying his health. A nervous man of medium height, dark-complexioned, he joined up first with a New Jersey outfit and then was transferred to the Harris Light Cavalry.[2] But no matter how complete his training, he was a thorn in the side of General B. F. Kelley. "Old Ben" looked upon Duffie's cavalry stationed at Cumberland as a Number 1 nuisance, and on occasion complained of it to headquarters. Its officers and men overran the town, he charged, drinking and fighting and paying no attention to one B.F.K. And on top of that their leader was absent much of the time, first to Charleston on an unexplained junket and then away in the opposite direction.[3]

The morning Duffie rode out of Winchester with the wagon train his nervousness got the better of him. He had chosen the ambulance for conveyance so he could rest and sleep while riding, but there was no sleeping in an atmosphere of lumbering wagon wheels and loud, profane teamsters. So a few miles out he got the idea of riding ahead, asking for a guard of ten men to accompany him. Hassan let him have them, no doubt in respect to his rank and more likely as a way to be rid of him.

Before the ambulance had rolled a mile in advance, guards who remained with the wagons watched Mosby and some of his band swoop down upon it, scatter the guard, and make away with the vehicle. This might have been anticipated, for ample warning had been given by the C.O. at Winchester that the Partisans were in the vicinity.[4]

In a matter of hours Sheridan was writing Halleck an ignominious finish to the Frenchman's career in the United States Army: "I respectfully request his dismissal from the service. I think him a trifling man and a poor soldier. He was captured by his own stupidity." [5]

Since the battle of Cedar Creek on the nineteenth, Sheridan had been seriously engaged in mopping-up operations. He had made demonstrations with his cavalry in all directions and had met no opposition except from a force of Rebel horsemen braced effectively in the same narrow gorge near Milford where Torbert had been stopped back in September. Convinced that Early's army was thoroughly scattered, he notified Halleck that these demonstrations, with others he would make, would secure Washington "against all but Mosby and the numerous robbers that now infest the country, and which one good regiment could clear out any time, if the regimental commander had spunk enough to try." [6]

But Sheridan had not yet appeased Grant, a man who yielded convictions reluctantly. While the accolades still were pouring in to the Valley leader, the commander-in-chief sent another message from Petersburg: "If it is possible to follow up your great victory until you can reach the Central road, do it, even if you have to live on half rations . . . If the army at Richmond could be cut off from Southwest Virginia it would be of great importance to us, but I know the difficulty of supplying so far from your base." [7]

For the fourteenth time—and the third during the month of October—Grant was repeating the plea he had been making for six months.

In reply Sheridan announced frankly he had found it impossible to move toward the Central road because of supplies and forage and because it would demoralize his troops. In further explanation he advanced the same reasoning he had given at the close of September: so many troops would have to be left behind for protection against the guerrillas that his army would be too small to operate successfully. But he revealed he was "meditating" cavalry operations against the railroad as soon as necessary preparations could be made. [8]

Meanwhile the two engineers who had accompanied him back to the Valley were ready to report. In their estimation a proper defense of the area west of Washington would require two armies of 10,000 each, one to be stationed near Winchester to guard the mountain gaps and the other near Manassas for the protection of the capital. Chief advantage of such a plan, they explained, would be shorter supply lines; in effect, much less temptation to the guerrillas.

On the strength of their advice steps were pushed to reopen the railroad between Harpers Ferry and Winchester, and rails for this purpose were brought from the abandoned Manassas Gap line. Sheridan had at last become convinced the guerrillas would not permit him to supply his army solely by wagon. [9]

At this time the Valley commander received some good advice, based on experience and straight thinking, from one of his subordinates. It was proffered by Brigadier General John D. Stevenson, commanding at Harpers Ferry, and was to the effect that the railroad construction party should be guarded at all times by a regiment of infantry and 500 cavalry. He also gave warning that, as the road progressed, it would have to be garrisoned to keep the guerrillas from tearing it up as fast as it was laid.[10]

The Harpers Ferry C.O. had other ideas. He reported Mosby's guerrillas "the only Rebels in force left in this end of the Valley" and gave the opinion that if he could remount the Maryland Home Brigade, deprived of its horses some months back, he could say that in sixty days he could "get rid of this quasi-military pest." [11] It was a proposal he repeated a day or two later, this time suggesting the Marylanders be given Spencer carbines and adding: "It is an experiment that I think it will pay to try." [12]

Stevenson was making Sheridan sick at the stomach. Along with all his other troubles, it was no joy to "Little Phil" to have a subordinate overly smug with knowledge, and the Valley commander became so fretted he complained to Halleck, saying he wanted the brigadier to have nothing to do with rebuilding the road. "Stevenson knows so much more about everything than I do myself, or than anybody else does," wrote Sheridan, "that it is getting to be very embarrassing to me." [13]

But a part of Stevenson's advice was accepted. Sheridan promptly sent a brigade of cavalry to cover the working party. And he also gave orders that, if the railroad or trains were interfered with by guerrillas, all male Secessionists in the adjacent country should be arrested, their stock confiscated, and every house and barn within a radius of five miles burned.[14] Posters to this effect were nailed to trees at numerous points along the line of the road.

With Early's army in the Valley scattered, guerrillas in the area in the future would find the war they were fighting one of extreme desperation. Sheridan now had more time to devote to them, and that would mean they would be forced to battle with their backs closer to the wall. In terrible suddenness, it seemed, every crossroad and doorstep took on an atmosphere of violence and rashness. A Union scout had found a black flag, emblem of no quarter, leaning against a tree between Harpers Ferry and Martinsburg, and knowledge of its capture brought bitterness and vile charges conducive to extremes. At the time the flag was presented to the City of Philadelphia as a prize taken from Mosby's Rangers, newspapers printed the story and stirred up a rash of public excitement. In black and white it was told that Rebel Partisans in the Valley of Virginia were fighting under the same code followed by pirates of the high seas. That was the report, and it was repeated. No matter if official records did establish that the piece of black cloth was left by two members of Early's army and that it had been found on August 1, before Sheridan arrived to tangle with the guerrillas, people of Union sympathy were in a mood to make the worst of anything.[15]

Since Mosby's capture of the 173,000-dollar payroll, weeks had passed and yet Martinsburg had never recovered from the alarm, nursing such fear of guerrillas that it remained constantly on edge. One night its alarm was particularly grave. Several paymasters were in town with their moneybags, too frightened to move out of the hotel. Moreover, a train loaded with supplies for Sheridan's army was parked on the outskirts awaiting such time as it could obtain sufficient guard to move to the front.

With these trusts at hand, the community became a potential target of the first order, a circumstance in no way relaxed by the fact it was an outpost surrounded by towering hills, any one of which might harbor a hostile band of Partisans. Under such circumstances the post commander ordered a full guard at all hours. Utmost vigilance must be the watchword, with no relaxation of the rule. Among regiments called out under this blanket direction was the Thirteenth Maine, a hearty band of fellows who at any other time would have had the privilege of taking things easy on Union Hill, a short hop to the southeast. In assignments made in connection with the tightened watch, half its members were quartered in the square, near the paymasters, and most of the others were placed on guard around the train or stationed farther out as pickets.

There was further cause for special alarm on this particular night: guerrillas had been seen lurking in the vicinity, staring silently from the hills as if busily mapping out their pattern of evil. But none of the basis for all this apprehension had been imparted to a naïve corporal of the Thirteenth Maine. He drew a station on the inner guard line, a young man serious in his duties but innocent in his thoughts. The war to him was a distant affair, so distant he could see little reason for keeping an all-night lookout for an enemy that weeks prior had been badly scattered by Sheridan at Cedar Creek.

Overhead from where he stood at his post stars glittered out of the black of the night, heavenly jewels reminiscent of a sparkle in the east that centuries agone had led wise men to a baby in a manger. It was a thought made incongruous by the gun at his side, but the corporal continued to stare above. For him romance was everywhere. He could hear no evil, see no evil, speak no evil. Off in some indiscriminate tent a harmonica picked up his mood and brought out the goose pimples. So thoroughly was he attuned to nature that he turned his face to the winds soughing moderately down from the hills and breathed deeply. To him they bore no tone of violence or threat of snow.

Thus it was only natural for him in such an oblivious mood to be off-guard when nine men in Federal uniform walked up to him in the still, predawn hours and asked to be passed. He presented arms and weighed their request routinely. Disposition to him was simple enough: he had no right to admit them, but he would gladly present the matter to the sergeant who made such decisions.

So complete was his guilelessness in the whole matter and so great his friendliness toward mankind that he asked only for the leader of the party to accompany him. This individual promptly moved forward, and the two of them started off, stepping side by side. But they had gone only a short distance before the corporal was shaken out of his lethargy by an order at gunpoint to surrender. It was a jolt to his senses, this sharp break from the ethereal, but he responded like a trooper. He attempted to fire, and that was as far as he got, for the pistol at his elbow blazed first, nipping him in the arm.

Under such odds the Federal fell out upon the ground, feigning death, and lay still while his pockets were searched. By that time the entire garrison was aroused. On all sides quickly arose a general hullabaloo, and up and down the line went the alarm. When the furor subsided, the intruders had disappeared, leaving no evidence of their visit other than the slight wound to the corporal. At daylight a giantic investigation got under way and pickets by the dozens were brought in for questioning. But it was never learned how nine strange men, supposedly unacquainted with the layout of such an important military outpost, could get so close to the paymasters without drawing special notice upon themselves.[16]

As it happened, the Thirteenth Maine, sometimes routed from their beds twice in one night, was not the only outfit forced by guerrillas to do extra and undesirable chores. At this very time no less a person than that astute New York lawyer, Colonel Henry Sanford Gansevoort, leader of the Thirteenth New York Cavalry, was writing: "I am wearied of the thankless task of fighting guerrillas—a task that, no matter how zealously performed, is but service ignored." [17]

Gansevoort felt he had ample reason to complain. A Rebel deserter a few days earlier had come into his camp and told him where Mosby's artillery was hidden on the summit of Little Cobbler Mountain, one of the peaks of the Blue Ridge about a mile high, and he had gone there and captured it—the entire cache of four pieces, complete with ammunition and harness. This he considered a great stroke, because he felt that the heavy guns, dreaded by all the Union posts that might come within their range, were the secret of Mosby's success. [18] With them, he estimated, the Partisan since spring "has done at least a million dollars of damage to us." To take them away, it was his feeling, deprived Mosby of his sting and thus was certainly a great break for the Federals west of Washington. But so far his deed had earned him little attention and no praise.

Guerrillas in these desperate days rarely restricted their activities. From Middletown the First New York Dragoons, moved by high hopes of bolstering the headquarters larder, sent a foraging expedition out the Front Royal road with the colonel's mess wagon. Soon the entire party came charging back without the wagon, which they reported had been deserted in the face of a band of Rebel irregulars that came bursting at them out of the woods. The colonel was furious, and possibly a bit hungry, so he hastily ordered out a squadron to rescue the vehicle. This detail in time came upon a group of what seemed to be about ninety men in Union overcoats loitering beside the road. Approaching within easy pistol range, the major in command inquired as to their identity and was informed by one of them that they were an independent company commanded by Captain Blazer. Reported the New York *Herald* correspondent, without enlargements: "The rascals succeeded in getting into the timber hard by before Major Smith discovered who they actually were." [19]

"Old Ben" Kelley got back into the picture at this period. His nemesis for years had been McNeill's command. He knew the leader of these Partisans was on his deathbed, and it was reported the

Rangers were assembled at Moorefield during his absence under the direction of a guerrilla named Blake L. Woodson. Kelley had a notion they would be an easy catch if properly surprised, so he instructed Colonel George R. Latham of the Fifth West Virginia Cavalry, who had seen duty in the mountain country from the very beginning of the war, to slip in and pull a coup. Latham set out with 225 men and one artillery piece and stole through the country, arriving at Moorefield at 5:00 A.M. The town was quietly surrounded without alarming a single inhabitant, after which the Federals sat by to wait for dawn to show them where McNeill had his camp. As the skies lightened the Union horsemen themselves were in for a surprise, for it was discovered they had drawn the trap too tight: the guerrillas were encamped outside the circle of Blue cavalry and were able to make a clean getaway. The best Latham could do was round up eight men of military age found sleeping in the village.

Since the execution of the six Rangers at Front Royal, nearly two months had passed without aftermath. During this period Mosby returned to active duty, first riding in a buggy, then moving about on a cane, and finally climbing to the saddle in his customary manner, a wiry little figure betopped by waving plume. As his recuperation advanced, he sent his adjutant to Richmond with a letter to General Lee. It was an important letter, for in it were recited the brutalities against citizens committed by the enemy in retaliation for the Partisan leader's efforts to prevent reconstruction of the Manassas Gap line. "As my command has done nothing contrary to the usages of war it seems to me that some attempt at least ought to be made to prevent a repetition of such barbarities," Mosby commented. Then he told of the death of his men at Front Royal—"by order and in the presence of General Custer"—and announced that it was his purpose to hang an equal number of Custer's men whenever he captured them. He was also disturbed by a bill of pains and penalties against guerrillas passed by the last U. S. Congress, saying he thought some understanding should be had with the enemy regarding it.

Lee immediately attached his indorsement to the Partisan's letter, with the statement: "I do not know how we can prevent the cruel conduct of the enemy toward our citizens. I have directed Colonel Mosby, through his adjutant, to hang an equal number of Custer's men in retaliation for those executed by him." [20] Days after the Federal soldiers who paid this penalty were in their graves, Secretary of War Seddon added his approval.

Fate has an uncanny faculty for concealing its intentions. At Winchester, Major Charles Brewster, commissary of subsistence, got a special order to come to cavalry headquarters at the front. The message indicated no special hurry was required, so he delayed, hoping he might be able to accompany some body of troops moving in that direction. However, after several days passed without such an opportunity, he decided to wait no longer and started up the Valley with four companions—an officer recently resigned from service, the saddler sergeant of the First Vermont Cavalry, and two privates. The morning was cloudy and damp and they wore overcoats and rubber ponchos. It was with some trepidation they rode, for they knew their course would take them through an area infiltrated by guerrillas. But in one respect they found consolation: their horses were of the best and should be able to pace or outdistance any and all they encountered.

The early part of their trip was more in the nature of a joyride. No disturbing element did they encounter until they reached a crossroads near Newtown. There they met a detachment of fifteen men dressed predominantly in blue. This blue was their undoing, lulling them into a false sense of security, and almost before they were aware of it they were prisoners. In short order they were rounded up and directed to the cover of a nearby hill, forced to dismount, and then informed they now were in the hands of Mosby.

A little later they were divided into two groups and started off in different directions, across fields, through streams and thickets, and along hidden paths and byways. As the day advanced, the sun grew warmer and the Rebels peeled off their blue overcoats, revealing gray uniforms of the Confederacy. The group in which rode Brewster reached the ford across the Shenandoah River leading to Ashby's Gap in the early afternoon. There a Rebel patrol appeared on the opposite bank and, after an exchange of signals, permitted the party to cross.

In Ashby's Gap the party drew up at a wayside house for provender for both riders and horses. While there a column of mounted men, all wearing blue overcoats, came suddenly around a turn in the road ahead. It passed without halting, and then into view a short distance to its rear appeared a wiry little man with a feather in his hat. He drew up to talk with the leader of the group, speaking in a tone too low for the prisoners to hear, and then turned to Brewster.

"What's your name?"

"Charles Brewster of the Michigan Cavalry Brigade."

"That's General Custer's Brigade?"

"It was until recently, when he took command of the Third Cavalry Division."

"Then you are one of General Custer's staff?"

"No, not since he went to the Third Division."

"Well, you were with him when he hung and shot some of my men at Front Royal."

"I was not there. I was with the supply train."

"Well, you were one of the officers at that time. I can't identify the particular men that put the ropes around the necks of my Rangers, but I have a little account to settle with General Custer anyway."

Mosby turned his horse and rode on after the column. As he started away, Brewster announced sharply, "I had nothing to do with it!" They were words wasted on the countryside.[21]

Shortly afterward another party of Rangers appeared with a number of prisoners. One of them, Private Prouty of the Seventh Michigan Cavalry, noticing Brewster's stripes, sidled up to him and muttered that Mosby had announced following his capture the day before that he was to be hanged. This was a blow to the major, but he smothered his feelings. He could tell from Prouty's behavior that he was in a highly distressed mental condition, so he ridiculed the idea of such a fate and tried to cheer the other out of his dejection.

When men and animals had been fed, the groups, now combined, rode through the gap and down to the little mountainside village of Paris. Arriving after dark, the prisoners were taken to a neighboring barn and put up for the night on beds of buckwheat straw. On duty throughout the night beside a lantern in the center of the barn stood a guard, silent and constantly alert.

Next morning the captives were moved to an empty storeroom in the village, along with other prisoners brought in during the night. It was a building to be remembered. Blinds covered the windows, and along each side of the room stood counters on which were blood-soaked pieces of clothing and rags that at some time or other had served as bandages. This was such a wretched place that the

Rangers on guard were moved to sympathize with the prisoners, promising deliverance from such surroundings as soon as Mosby returned.

That night the captives spent in a log cabin, and the next day they were conducted on foot to Rectortown. Along the entire length of the road as they marched they could see bloodstains and, when they showed interest, a guard informed them a wounded prisoner had been conveyed over the route in a cart some hours earlier.

At Rectortown, they were placed in a corncrib on a hill, from which they could look out over the countryside and see Mosby's men as they rode in from various directions. It was a scene that impressed Brewster, reminding him of "Sir Roderick Dhu's warriors arising as if from the earth."

After a time the door of the corncrib was opened and the prisoners were directed to form a line along the side of the building. About them as they walked into the open were a number of Rangers, most of them standing in the background and poised to watch the proceedings. Mosby was not to be seen.[22]

There were thirty of the Federals, a conglomerate group, some young, some old. Because of his rank Brewster was placed on the extreme right. At his left stood the only other commissioned officer of the group, First Lieutenant J. C. Disosway of the Fifth New York Heavy Artillery.

A Ranger now rode out before them and announced that from their number must be selected seven who were to be hanged in retaliation for the men executed by Custer. It was news to none of them. Since their capture they had been talking among themselves about the possibility of such a death.[23]

They were told they would decide by drawing marked ballots which of them were to die. Brewster glanced down the line. Almost without exception heads were bowed and lips moving in prayer. It was Sunday, November 6.

From behind the building suddenly appeared Partisans on horseback, one of them wearing a broad-brimmed affair that resembled a sombrero. This fellow rode up in front of Brewster, lifted the major's chapeau, and placed his own in its place. Behind him came three men on foot, the one in the middle, a tall man, holding a hat above the line of vision of the captives.

The drawing started at the lower end of the line. As each prisoner selected a slip of paper, it was examined by the two attendants and, if it bore a pencil mark, the drawer was ordered to the side and placed under a special guard, ruled over by a redheaded man with a bushy, untrimmed beard and wearing a Union infantry dress coat. He seemed to be enjoying the entire affair, as though it were some gathering of schoolboys merely choosing up sides. When a doomed man was assigned to his care, he patted him on the back and went through a routine of extending congratulations, uttering such cheering remarks as, "We'll give you a chance to stretch hemp," or "Now you can shake the dust off your feet."

Slowly the hat moved down the line. When it was extended to Disosway, he pulled a blank, and then Brewster reached. There were three slips left. These he ran through his fingers one at a time, praying for divine guidance in his selection.

"Hurry up!" ordered the tall man.

Brewster drew out a slip and held his breath while the attendants proceeded with their examination. It was blank.

Now followed a momentary lull as the conductors of the ceremony withdrew from the view of the prisoners. Only five men had drawn marked slips, so it was obvious a second drawing would be necessary.

Meantime off where the unfortunate five were gathered, one of them, a teen-aged boy, began to sob audibly, covering his face with his hands and stooping miserably with the simplicity of a child who has been denied privileges by its mother. Louder and louder grew his lamentations, and they were no consolation to the line of stern-faced men waiting with compressed lips for their fate to be decided. Suddenly, as the minutes dragged slowly by, a Ranger galloped up on a beautiful black horse and leaned over to confer with the red-bearded man in the Union dress coat. After a moment the guard caught the youth by the arm and directed that he be led away from the scene. This was no act of mystery, it developed. The rider was Guy Broadwater, Mosby's sergeant major, and he had ridden back to the spot where waited the Partisan leader, who frankly admitted he did not wish to witness the drawing, and reported to him that one of the condemned was a drummer boy. Mosby promptly ordered that the boy be withdrawn and an older prisoner substituted in his place.[24]

When preparations for a second drawing were completed, the

man with the hat and his two attendants returned. Again, following the same routine, they moved down the line. Two more men were drawn to the side. After that only four were left to decide upon the seventh doomed prisoner. The first two selected blanks. Now Disosway and Brewster were left. They looked at each other understandingly, as if to say, "One of us is it." The tall man holding the hat growled impatiently. Disosway felt for a slip. The attendants examined it and caught him by the arm. As they did so, he ran his hand across his forehead and muttered simply, "This is tough."

That evening the seven condemned men were led across the mountain by a party of Rangers instructed to hang them on the Berryville pike as near Sheridan's headquarters as possible. It was a black night, with rain. To prevent escape in the darkness a rope was stretched from the wrists of each prisoner and they were led along in single file. Somewhere along the last lap of the wearisome march Private George Soule of the Fifth Michigan Cavalry managed to slip his hands free and to fade away when they were crossing a depression. In a matter of hours he was at headquarters telling about his experience.

During the early dawn a citizen came upon the scene that told the fate of those unable to escape. Five bodies were there, three hanged, two shot. Attached to one was a note: "These men have been hung in retaliation for an equal number of Colonel Mosby's men hung by order of General Custer, at Front Royal. Measure for measure." [25] The sixth man had saved himself by feigning death after he had been shot in the head.

But nowhere was to be found Lieutenant Disosway. Years later it would be learned that this soldier, who afterward was commissioned in the regular army and died in 1889, had been saved by his membership in the secret order of Masons. Rangers, moved by a common tie through the bond of fellowship, somewhere along the route over the mountains had spirited him away and substituted in his place another Custer man held as a prisoner, one who was not so fortunate as to have been admitted to membership in a society distinguished by its association with King Solomon.[26]

But Mosby knew nothing of this substitution at the time and it is debatable what he would have done had the knowledge come to him. At the moment he was sick at heart over the retaliation, so upset that it was nearly a week before he dispatched his trusted scout, John Russell,[27] to Sheridan's headquarters with a message that told of the executions and concluded: "Hereafter any prisoners falling into my hands will be treated with the kindness due to their condition, unless some new act of barbarity shall compel me reluctantly to adopt a course of policy repulsive to humanity." [28]

CHAPTER 8

November 11–December 31, 1864

HISTORY BOWS TO A BULLET

Awareness that the constant war between Sheridan's army and the guerrillas had reached a stage of no quarter exerted a strange influence over the fighters on both sides. For a time it put an end to the old fraternization between pickets—swapping of coffee, tobacco, newspapers, and yarns—and soldiers in the Valley tensed their trigger fingers and centered attention on matters connected largely with the problem of self-preservation.

This desperate spirit had not yet reached the Rebel who one day, seated on a huge log, passed away his hours of guard duty by busying himself with the finishing touches to the head of a dummy he had fashioned out of a long-necked gourd. His figurine had several lifelike features, including a scragly mop of hair put together out of the trimmings from beef tails. When the artisan thus engaged looked up to spy a Federal sneaking Indian style through the woods a short distance away, he merely called, "Hello, Yank. Who you looking for?" The Unionist whirled, leapt behind a tree, and raised his single-shot rifle with such a display of belligerence that the picket, shocked into action, promptly fell backward over the log. There he lay in some degree of terror, frightened once more into a realistic world.

But his mind was equal to the test. Quietly he slipped his hat over the gourd and raised it slowly above the log. It remained there only a second before a blast shattered the silence of the glen and a bullet tore the dummy head into numerous pieces. Instantly the Rebel jumped up, gun in hand, and drew a bead on his enemy, now frantically trying to reload his weapon.

"I ought to kill ye," drawled the Southerner triumphantly. "But I won't, 'cause I wouldn't have no witness to what I just done. Come take a look."

The Federal dropped his rifle and walked over to peep at the shattered gourd behind the log. "Well, I be damned!" he muttered softly.

The Confederate made no effort to assume modesty. He smiled gloatingly at his prisoner and asked, "What's yo' name?"

"Hall," replied the Yankee.

"So's mine—George."

A light flashed suddenly in the eyes of the Federal. "Of Leesburg, Texas?" he asked.

"Yeah."

"Then you're my favorite cousin! Remember me—John Hall? We haven't seen each other in 20 years."

And thus it was—by chance in this instance—that kinfolk barely missed killing kinfolk.[1]

But the tenseness on the part of the pickets was in most cases only of a temporary nature. Mosby's letter to Sheridan, personally delivered by Scout John Russell, brought an abrupt end to retaliatory executions in the Valley and in time restored some of the unofficial amity between privates. The effect among officers was different. In them Mosby's message encouraged an all-out effort to exterminate the guerrillas once and for all, especially in the border area along the Potomac.

Planning the large-scale drive, Federal leaders were heavily taxed to discover effective measures. Almost every known method of stopping the irregulars had been tried, with no success. The most potent antidote was the order to hang them without trial, and this, due to the resourceful Mosby, suddenly had slapped back, showing it was procedure that could work both ways. For want of something more direct, it was decided to launch a campaign to starve out the bands of independent horsemen. Already the rich farming area of the lower Shenandoah had been scorched, and now Grant, from Petersburg, suggested that the same thing be done to Loudoun Valley, the little bowl east of the Blue Ridge where Mosby's men were most often seen. "There is no doubt," he said, "about the necessity of clearing out that country so that it will not support Mosby's gang." [2]

Though the Union focal point seemed to be Mosby, all the major Partisan outfits were in the field at the moment and creating plenty of trouble. Some of White's and Gilmor's men, for instance, came into Leesburg one day in such numbers as to give rise to a rumor that Rosser's cavalry was there, and large bodies of Federal horse were dispatched on a trail as cold as the November weather in which they trotted. A more persistent problem lay along the bed of the Winchester and Potomac Railroad. Construction crews refused to work unless they were amply guarded from guerrillas, and this became a major drain upon troops. Within a few days of each other a brigade each of infantry and cavalry was assigned to the task. Later another infantry brigade took up duty there. So did Stevenson's infantry force at Harpers Ferry. And at the same time four Pennsylvania regiments on their way to Philadelphia were ordered back and stationed at various points.

General Crook at Cumberland noticed the increased activity on the part of the guerrillas and urged that the blockhouses under construction along the line of the B. & O. be finished at once. Suddenly General Couch at Chambersburg joined the alarmists. He got a report that Rebel independents were planning a raid on the rich stores of feed and forage in the Susquehanna Valley north of the Potomac, and he hurried off a message to headquarters. Further excitement was caused one day by Gilmor who appeared at Shepherdstown with fifty men and moved down the river without leaving the slightest hint as to what he had in mind.

Union scouts noticed at this time that empty cars transferred to the Virginia Central Railroad by the Confederates were rolling westward from Richmond, a development that gave rise to a report Early's shattered troops were to be returned to Lee. Grant wired Sheridan that if he was satisfied such a thing was about to happen he might send the Sixth Corps back without delay. And he wound up the telegram with his pet obsession about breaking Lee's supply line: "If your cavalry can cut the Virginia Central road, now is the time to do it." [3] Next day there was a repeat on this, Grant suggesting that one division of cavalry be sent with the Sixth "unless they can get through to cut the Central road and canal." [4]

But Sheridan was cautious. Unable to determine definitely what Early was doing, he wanted to wait until his intelligence was more specific. Scouts sent out for this purpose failed to return, causing him to conclude that "they must have been captured."[5] And as for sending the cavalry, he had definite convictions along that line, explaining he thought cavalry of more importance "here on this long and sensitive frontier" than infantry.[6]

In time Sheridan learned that Kershaw's division, which he understood numbered 5000, had been returned to Richmond, while the remainder of Early's army was somewhere south of New Market. Even at that he was reluctant to send the Sixth Corps, advising Halleck that he thought it best to keep it in the Valley until the season was a little further advanced.

Grant meanwhile continued to ask for the return of the Sixth, saying he did not want to make the order imperative and yet that he would like to get the corps as soon as possible. But Sheridan delayed, for purposes of safety, and the Union high command at Washington supported his caution.

Toward the end of November, Grant made a hurried trip to the Federal capital. While there Halleck took occasion to corner him about the Sixth Corps and got assurance that the troops would not be moved as long as Sheridan thought they should remain in the Valley. The chief of staff conveyed this decision to the Army of the Shenandoah with the advice: "It seems to me that before any cavalry is sent away Mosby's band should be broken up, as he is continually threatening our lines."[7]

Sheridan may have been influenced in his reluctance about the Sixth Corps by the fact that his troubles with the guerrillas continued without abatement, and there was little hope for an immediate letup. Measures taken against them continued to be ineffective. Weeks had passed since Blazer's crack outfit, looked upon as proper cure for Mosby's command, had taken to the field and yet to date it could show virtually nothing for its efforts. In the waning days of November two of its members showed up suddenly at Harpers Ferry with a report that Mosby had attacked their force near Kabletown and either captured or killed everybody except themselves.[8]

This fight, it developed, was the aftermath of an engagement the day before in which Blazer had chased a part of Mosby's command into Loudoun Valley. There the Rangers gathered reinforcements and thus were able to strike back, capturing Blazer and sixty-odd of his men. When the skirmish was over and things once more were quiet at Kabletown, twenty-two of the men Sheridan had outfitted with special rifles lay dead, stretched out in a blacksmith shop in the heart of the village.[9]

As Thanksgiving neared, soldiers in the Army of the Shenandoah began to look forward to a very special dinner, an unexpected reward for their success against Early. Newspapers announced that certain states in the North were sending thousands of pounds of turkey to be divided among the fighters on this occasion, and word of the intended shipment in time reached the guerrillas, causing them also to anticipate its arrival. The Federals, expecting interference, strengthened guards on wagon trains scheduled to haul the poultry from the rail head at Martinsburg to the various troop centers, but this precaution was not completely effective. The Rebel irregulars, grabbing at every opportunity, managed in their apt and sly way to share in the special treat, causing a serious deficiency in some Union camps.[10]

Sheridan got madder and madder about the Rebel Partisans. As reports of their activities continued to pour in, he wired Stevenson at Harpers Ferry: "If the 12th Pennsylvania Cavalry cannot keep that country clear of guerrillas I will take the shoulder straps off of every officer belonging to the regiment and dismount the regiment in disgrace." [11] He also barked at Couch for anticipating a guerrilla raid in his direction and said there was no danger of such a thing. Then he instructed: "If you have arrested spies, hang them; if you are in doubt, hang them anyway. The sooner such characters are killed off the better it will be for the community." [12]

In as beautiful a piece of hypocrisy and face-saving as ever graced the pages of history, Sheridan, making a postwar report, admitted he was "at times annoyed by guerrilla bands," but explained he had constantly refused to operate against them because he believed they were "substantially a benefit to me, as they prevented straggling and kept my trains well closed up, and discharged such other duties as would have required a provost guard of at least two regiments of cavalry." [13]

This was distortion of fact, as borne out by Sheridan's own actions. Here he was, according to his statement, permitting the guerrillas to run wild against him because they meant a saving in personnel of two regiments of cavalry. He made no mention of the many detachments of several times that number he frequently sent through the country in an effort to break up the irregular horsemen. Also he took no account of the brigades of cavalry and infantry they forced him to place as guards along the railroads he was trying to rebuild. Nor did he acknowledge capture of hundreds of able-bodied soldiers by each of the Partisan bands, prisoners who if put together would have formed a sizable force, perhaps large enough to give Grant, through greater numerical superiority, the courage to capture Richmond during '64. Mosby alone estimated that he kept 30,000 of Sheridan's 94,026 Middle Military Division effectives tied up along the outposts and away from the battle front during the Valley campaign.

In that postwar report, dated February 3, 1866, Sheridan ignored action that he himself ordered, a fact that would remain buried to the public until the *Official Records* were published decades later. To carry out the drive against guerrillas desired by Grant, "Little Phil" directed that a sweep be made of the South Branch Valley west of the Shenandoah to break up McNeill and another east of the Blue Ridge, in snug little Loudoun Valley, to put a stop to Mosby and White and Gilmor and any other bands that habitually rendezvoused there.

The campaign in West Virginia was made the responsibility of Kelley, a man who by this time knew all the ins and outs of guerrilla warfare. But the outcome of his efforts brought this veteran leader a new burden of criticism for inertia similar to that heaped upon him by Milroy in '62. "Old Ben," first of all, issued a warning to the citizens, informing them that if they continued to harbor and feed McNeill's men the whole area "will be laid waste like the Shenandoah Valley."[14] This, as similar steps had done before, brought assurances of cooperation from the people, but experience might have warned the Union leader that most of the time these promises were hollow.

The actual expedition after the guerrillas in South Branch Valley was left to Colonel George R. Latham at New Creek, leader of the ineffectual raid against McNeill earlier in the month. This time he made some changes. To avoid drawing the trap too tight as he had done in the first instance, two separate detachments were ordered to Moorefield and directed to approach by separate routes, timing themselves so they could meet there for a daylight raid. As a further step to perfect the snare, a force of 150 troops was stationed to cut off escape via nearby gaps.

In carrying out orders Latham obviously was ignoring military precaution. He was aware that Confederate cavalry under Rosser was foraging in South Branch Valley, and yet he sent off the detachments as if there was no likelihood that they would meet any force except McNeill's small band.[15]

One of the detachments, under Lieutenant Colonel R. E. Fleming, was made up of 120 men and a single piece of artillery, while the other, commanded by Major P. J. Potts, consisted of 155 men unsupported by heavy guns. Fleming arrived on the edge of Moorefield the evening before the scheduled attack and sent his troops toward the town in skirmish-line formation to feel for information. Before they had moved more than a few hundred yards, Rebels by the score suddenly charged out of the woods and attacked front and rear, capturing a number of men, the single big gun, and an only wagon and ambulance. Next morning Potts arrived, unaware of what had happened the night before, and charged at sunrise, expecting Fleming to assist from the other side of the village. But when his troops were met by a superior force of the enemy and there was no responding fire at its rear, he immediately turned tail and fled by way of a mountain path, losing but a single man.

Acquainted with this turn of events, Kelley anticipated a follow-up on the part of the Confederates and wired Latham to prepare his post at New Creek for defense. Latham, commanding enough troops in Sheridan's opinion to stave off an attack by from 5000 to 7000 men, telegraphed back: "I am prepared for them." [16]

So it was with almost a complete degree of surprise that Kelley learned next day that New Creek, only station on the B. & O. west of Harpers Ferry where stores in considerable quantities were kept, had been taken by fewer than 800 Confederates without the slightest resistance—not even a shot from the garrison. The surprise came at about eleven-thirty in the morning. At the time pickets and patrols were out as far as eight miles from the post, and Latham was preparing a party of twenty mounted men to send in support of Burlington, twelve miles away. Without the slightest warning the Rebels stormed in, as quietly as if they were a regularly scheduled guard going on duty. Their advance, dressed in Federal overcoats, was mistaken for Potts' command returning and thus was able to capture the pickets without causing alarm.

During the next hour New Creek was wiped out as a military post. Buildings were burned—all but one dwelling, some reports said—and so were all stores that could not be transported. At nearby Piedmont the machine shops of the B. & O., repaired and

338

enlarged since their destruction by McNeill, were demolished, along with nine engines, a number of railroad cars, buildings, bridges, and some of the railroad track. In addition to conveyable stores the victorious Confederates took southward with them between 1200 and 1500 horses, as well as several hundred head of cattle, the latter much-needed food for Lee's army.

All of this the aftermath of Kelley's steps to break up McNeill's small guerrilla force—a raid Sheridan afterward termed "some Don Quixotic expedition." [17] Latham, acknowledging it as his "first disaster in over three years' active service," placed blame upon no one but himself and asked for an investigation.[18] He was quickly arrested and taken to Grafton to await court-martial, unaware that Secretary of War Stanton had said he should be shot if found guilty of cowardice.[19] His subsequent trial resulted in dismissal from the service, but this verdict later was set aside and he was honorably mustered out at his own request.

Sheridan, when he heard of the destruction at New Creek and Piedmont, was "very much chagrinned." [20] He telegraphed Washington that the expedition to Moorefield was "on the bragging system, which always embraced too many combinations, and turns out to be bad strategy after guerrillas in a mountainous country." [21] In fixing the blame for the capture of New Creek, where the colors of the Fifth and Sixth West Virginia Cavalry (Federal) were taken by the Fifth and Sixth Virginia Cavalry (Confederate), he said it was due to the cowardice of the officers in command, especially Latham. His ire also was turned upon Kelley. With more reserve than customary he wired Halleck: "I respectfully present the name of Brevet Major-General Kelley for being exceedingly cautious when there is no danger and not remarkably so when there is." [22] His Irish temper toward "Old Ben" later cooled, and he instructed Crook to tell Kelley not to take his dispatches too much to heart.

Over in Loudoun Valley the war against the guerrillas was aimed primarily at disposing of Mosby. Sheridan notified Halleck he was ready to go to work on this elusive Partisan, that heretofore he had made no attempt to break him up, for, in doing so, he would use ten men to his one. He felt he had made a scapegoat of the Rebel leader through the destruction of private rights, he said, adding: "Now, there is going to be an intense hatred of him in that portion of this Valley which is nearly a desert. I will soon commence on Loudoun County, and let them know there is a God in Israel." [23]

Sheridan admitted that Mosby had annoyed him considerably, but maintained the people were beginning to see the injury inflicted by the Partisan was not in proportion to the loss to them "of all they have spent their lives in accumulating." He looked upon the people around Harpers Ferry as the most villainous in the Valley and warned if the railroad were interfered with, he would make some of them poor.

The chore of scorching Loudoun Valley was left to Cavalry General Wesley Merritt. Sheridan's orders to the men who were to assist were specific: "Let them use every exertion to kill or capture any guerrillas that may be seen, by decoying them into ambush or in some other way." [24]

Even as Sheridan was writing his orders, he was looking for trouble from the guerrillas. At one point he turned aside to wire the commanding officer at Charles Town: "Look out for Mosby tonight. He is reported to be about." [25]

Merritt started out with two brigades of cavalry carrying five days' rations. The sweep of country he was to scourge was bounded on the south by the Manassas Gap Railroad, on the east by the Bull Run Mountains, on the west by the Shenandoah River, and on the north by the Potomac. His instructions directed him to consume and destroy all forage and subsistence, burn all barns and mills, and drive off all stock, but to burn no dwellings and to offer no personal violence to citizens. Orders from Sheridan in his saddlebags as the cavalry leader rode out to begin the pillaging informed him that the blame must rest upon the authorities at Richmond, "who have acknowledged the legitimacy of guerrilla bands." [26]

As Merritt rode through the country, Sheridan wired Stevenson at Harpers Ferry of the movement. He expected complaints to come in at that point from Loudoun County residents, so he instructed that in such cases they should be told that "they have furnished too many meals to guerrillas to expect much sympathy." [27] Sheridan meant business. He also notified Augur at Washington of what he was doing and concluded: "No dwelling houses are to be burned this time." [28]

But the dwellings were just about all that escaped. Catherine Barbara Broun, writing in her diary at Middleburg, gave a clear picture of Merritt's destruction on his second day out: "We have had a terrible day today. Expecting every moment to be burned up. The barns all around us are on fire. The Yankees are burning all the hay, corn and wheat, driving off all the cattle, sheep, hogs, etc. We put all of our valuables around us, packed trunks, etc. Four Yanks started here but turned back mercifully. We were not destroyed this time. Eight o'clock—the whole heavens are illumined by the fires burning and destroying as they go. Mr. Benton's mill and large barn filled with corn and hay looked terrific."

Merritt came back on the fifth day, leaving behind a trail of smoke that blanketed Loudoun Valley. He estimated he had done damage that ran into the millions. With him, according to his report, he brought 5000 to 6000 head of cattle, nearly 1000 hogs and from 500 to 700 horses. But he had bad news for Sheridan. This he conveyed in one sentence: "It was found next to impossible to come in contact with any guerrillas, as they avoided even the smallest portions of the command." [29] The Partisans themselves were able to explain their elusiveness. It was revealed in later years that they were kept busy after the first day running stock from the path of the enemy into areas already burned.

For weeks there had been talk of returning the Sixth Corps to Richmond, and once or twice this unit had started in that direction and had been called back. Early in December its transfer actually got under way, troops moving by foot and rail to Washington and there embarking on transports at the Seventh Street wharf. Even at that the movement was not complete. Sheridan at the last moment asked to keep Getty's division for purposes of security, promising to send it later. Grant concurred, but once more inquired if it was possible to send cavalry through to the Virginia Central road.[30]

Sheridan replied about the railroad promptly. He said he had contemplated such a cavalry raid and even intended to go himself when things were satisfactory in the lower part of the Valley, but he termed the move a waste of effort. His conclusion, he explained, was based on definite evidence that no supplies were transported over the line toward Richmond, that on the contrary the Rebels in the Shenandoah were drawing their needs from the Confederate capital. "I will make the raid soon, if it is made at all," he concluded, "and will only go myself if all affairs here are in a healthy condition." [31]

At this time the Federal high command got definite report through Harpers Ferry that Mosby had gone to Richmond.[32] A day or so later his trail was picked up at Gordonsville, where he was seen and personally identified by refugees. The word was spread to the outposts around Washington with the caution: "Do not on this account abate your vigilance in patrolling the country in front of your lines."

Mosby's junket to Richmond at this time was surrounded by mystery. And it was not without its worries for the Federal commanders in the area in which he operated. Still fresh in their minds were the details of his retaliation for the executions at Front Royal, and it was said he had been called to the capital to confer on proper vengeance for the destruction wrought by Merritt. It was also rumored he had gone to see about organizing a force to operate on the lower Potomac as an aid to smuggling near Port Tobacco. Officially at the moment the only evidence as to why he had made the visit was embraced in a written request he addressed to the Secretary of War asking permission to divide his command into two battalions, a step he said would result in greater efficiency. His explanation was that his duties were much broader than those of officers of the same rank in the regular service and thus that he had little time to attend to the details of organization and discipline.[33]

Further scare during Mosby's absence was caused by some refugees from Lynchburg who came into Fairfax Court House by way of Warrenton with a report the Partisan had been reinforced by two brigades of infantry. They were convinced this was correct, they said, because they had seen the campfires of these troops on the side of the Bull Run Mountains. Sheridan was alarmed and so was Augur. The refugees were called into Washington for questioning, and cavalry by divisions scoured the area for days before the rumor was satisfactorily blasted.

Mosby's absence from the Washington area brought no letup in the activities of the Partisans he had left behind. Even while he was en route to Richmond, a train was derailed near Duffield's Station by Rebels who had raised the track during the night. This interruption of traffic encouraged a policy decision by the B. & O. management. All manner of guards had seen service along the line of the road. Bridges were protected by forces ranging from a company to a regiment. Blockhouses were completed and others were under construction at strategic points. Now it was decided to establish a cordon of silent watchmen, with the thought in mind that, while perhaps unable to ward off the guerrillas, they could at least give timely warning of their presence.[34]

By mid-December, Virginia was buried under nearly a foot of

snow, and the weather became intensely cold. Union scouts brought reports that two divisions of Early's army had been returned to Lee and that the remainder were backed up to Staunton to go into winter quarters. In the face of these developments Sheridan was willing to batten down for the season himself. But not Grant. The commander-in-chief had learned that Richmond was supplied exclusively over the roads north of the James River, and he again broached the subject of an advance on the Virginia Central. Though convinced of the wisdom of such a move, he considerately asked the Valley commander for his views as to the best course by which to make the dash.[35]

Sheridan was cool to the idea. Again he assured that no supplies were coming to Richmond by way of the Central road. Furthermore, he said it would be impossible to make such a raid while the season of bad weather lasted, but that he would do so as soon as he could.

Grant was stubborn, and the Valley leader in the end begrudgingly bowed to his wishes. Sheridan waited a week, until the snow began thawing, aided by rain, and then sent off his cavalry, at the same time wiring Grant: "The weather is so very bad that I am not sanguine of success in getting to the railroad." [36]

The cavalry moved in separate detachments, two divisions under Torbert heading along the Blue Ridge for Charlottesville and one under Custer advancing up the Valley as a diversion, as well as in the hope of reaching the James River and crossing over to Lynchburg. They carried no artillery and no wagons, and Sheridan was convinced that only the weather could prevent good results. He was partially right. It was a war of mud and cold and slush, a period of suffering that went into personal records of the men as the worst in their lives.[37] But the weather, as it turned out, was not the sole obstacle to be met. At Gordonsville and at Harrisonburg, the enemy appeared in such force as to drive back the respective parties. Already disheartened owing to their punishment by the elements, they swung about and returned to the lower end of the Valley, their effort serving no purpose whatever.

With Christmas nearing, Augur dispatched a few troops of cavalry through Loudoun Valley to sweep up any guerrillas they encountered. The purpose was another all-out drive against the irregulars, similar to Merritt's campaign three weeks prior and yet hopeful of better results. They rode over a wide area of the country, here and there nabbing some careless Rebel, and still in no way accomplishing the object involved. At Rectortown a change of tactic was agreed upon, and the column was split thrice and directed along separate routes, all to come together at Middleburg that night.

One of these detachments, made up of the Thirteenth and Sixteenth New York Cavalry and commanded by Major Douglas Frazar, a soldier by compunction rather than training, was sent by way of Salem, known to be a gathering place for members of Mosby's band. On the edge of this little village along the Manassas Gap line seven Rangers brazenly confronted the two regiments, firing and yelling madly without thought of personal danger, and in the end they were surrounded and captured. Among them was a redheaded young man of twenty-three astride a mount that looked more like a pony than a horse. It was equipped with neither bridle nor saddle and was guided solely by a rope around its neck. A Union overcoat covered the rider, and at his sides hung brass-tipped pistol holsters, each snuggling a wicked-looking Colt. A Remington revolver was barely visible above the leg of his boot. As a final touch he wore a pair of spurs fashioned of old gold and set off by Mexican wheels an inch in diameter. Though no identification was demanded of him at the time, he was Hugh M. McIlhany, a Mosby first sergeant who would long outlive most of those present.[38] A close competitor for longevity honors was Union Captain Francis C. Brown, later of Chicago, who at the moment was having his hands full.[39]

Brown's worst problem was the major. The weather was terrible. There had been snow in the morning, and later in the day this turned to rain and sleet, whipped by a bitter wind. Frazar, as were other members of the outfit, was finding mental solace in the bottle and, of all the imbibers, was holding up worse than any. He rode noisily along, cursing and storming with or without reason.

When the seven Rangers were captured at Salem, Brown singled out the redheaded McIlhany.

"Johnny, what's your name?"

McIlhany mumbled something.

"Do you know the way to Middleburg?"

"Yes, sir. If you turn me loose I can go there, but I don't know the way well enough to take you and your command."

"You ride with me and I will see if you don't." [40]

McIlhany guided them to Rector's Cross Roads and there, as its name implied, he was confronted with a choice of routes.

"You can have your pick," he told Brown. "I don't know one route from another."

It was then nearly 9:00 P.M. and the Federal was in no mood for delay. Aided by the tracks in the snow barely visible in the night, he chose the road showing the most travel and ordered the advance to proceed in that direction.

Before the column had moved far along the new route, someone commented loudly that they were on the wrong road, and this brought a stream of curses from Frazar, whose words long ago had lost the sharpness of his rank. But Brown insisted they were traveling right and waved the advance ahead.

This advance was made up of a small band of men, one of whom was Corporal Kane, in a few minutes to change the course of history involving Confederate resistance. They trotted on barely a quarter of a mile from the crossroads, toward the lights of a home close to the road on the left, and as they approached they noticed in front of it two horses tied to a rack. Though the fittings of these animals were obscured by darkness, the Federals suspected they had come upon members of the enemy and quickly spread out to surround the building. Kane rode into the yard and approached a window through which shone the light. As he neared it, he noticed the light was quickly dimmed, and then he saw a figure in gray uniform slinking across the room from a doorway, a small man with sharp features faintly outlined by the reflection from a fireplace. Without hesitating, he raised his revolver and fired, the bullet cutting a neat hole through a bottom window pane and dropping the man on the inside.

By this time some of the main body of troops had arrived, and Kane and others stormed into the building. Behind them came Frazar, who had managed to struggle out of his saddle. He walked unsteadily across the lawn and pushed impatiently through several soldiers standing at the doorway. Inside the room with the fireplace he found two women and an elderly man seated at table and behind them a young Confederate soldier with his arms raised in surrender. The dishes before them were empty, indicating they were winding up a meal.

Frazar, accompanied by other officers, walked through the room to a bedchamber adjoining. There, by the light of a candle brought from the table, he saw a man lying on the floor, apparently in great agony. The victim was dressed in light blue cotton shirt and gray trousers with a yellow cord down the seam, but was hatless and bootless and shorn of every insignia of rank.

"Whash your name?" mumbled Frazar.

"Lieutenant Johnston—Sixth Virginia Cavalry," gasped the wounded man. His words were uttered with a gurgling sound, and as he spoke bloody saliva ran from the corners of his mouth.

"I mush shee your wound," Frazar said thickly, stooping and opening the man's pants. Had he turned his head slightly, he might have noticed beneath a washstand within arm's reach a uniform coat of gray cloth elaborately set off by gold buttons and the gold star and braid of a colonel.

But Frazar's mind, struggling to perform its function against an over-supply of intoxicant, was focused only on the wounded man. As the trousers were opened, he found where the bullet fired by Kane had entered the abdomen two inches below and to the left of the navel. The major took only a cursory look and was convinced the victim would die within twenty-four hours. This was enough for him. He knew his column was behind schedule, delayed by the skirmishing with guerrillas during the afternoon, and he immediately straightened and waved his fellow soldiers out of the chamber.

In the meantime other officers of the command had attended to necessary procedure in the adjoining room. The young Confederate beside the table was directed to put on his boots and coat, and was led out and lined up with the other prisoners. No one noticed when he sidled up to McIlhany in the dark and whispered, "The Colonel's been shot." It was not known by his captors that he was Tom Love, one of Mosby's favorite Rangers, or they might have denied him the privilege of leaving his watch and a picture of a young lady at a house farther along the road. Brown personally consented to the temporary halt for this purpose, unconsciously waiting at such a distance that it was impossible for him to hear what the Partisan whispered to the people in whose hands he placed his possessions.

When the New Yorkers arrived at Middleburg, it was dark and cold and Frazar was suffering from the alcoholic jitters. But fires soon were blazing, and these, coupled with another generous swig from the bottle, steadied the nerves of the major. As he stood with back to the fire, an orderly approached bearing a gray hat adorned with gold cord and star.[41]

"Where'd it come from?" asked Frazar.

"Back at that house where the wounded man lay. Somebody says it belongs to Mosby."

Frazar took the hat and went in among the prisoners.

"The man who wore this hat," he announced, "has been shot dead. Is it Mosby's or not?"

No one answered.

"There's no use to conceal it if it is," coaxed the major. "Whoever owned it is dead."

The prisoners stared at him silently, several shaking their heads in denial. Finally one of them spoke up with positive tone: "Mosby never had a hat like that."

But reports that the gray felt belonged to the Confederate leader continued to come in to Frazar, so next morning he doubled back on a cold trail. At the home where the wounded soldier had been left still remained the old man and the two women. They were identified now as Ludwell Lake, gentleman farmer, and his two daughters. A son was said to be off fighting with Mosby.

But not even the bloodstains remained to mark the spot where the man who identified himself as Lieutenant Johnston lay. Blue cavalry rode madly in all directions, assigned to a search that was to continue around the clock. Had they been expert at trailing a fugitive, they might have noticed the tracks of an oxcart leading away from the Lake home and toward the Quilly Glasscock residence a mile and a half away. And had they followed this trail they would have found the wounded Mosby, now desperately disabled. But this they did not do. There were other things to divert their attention, such as white flags wigwagging annoyingly from the top of distant hills. These they saw no matter through what area they moved.

On the last day of '64 Frazar returned to camp. Along the routes followed he had talked to people who admitted they had seen Mosby, and from some of them he learned the bullet had been extracted from the Partisan's body at the Glasscock home. It was said also that the guerrilla leader had been spirited away from Loudoun Valley and was now far enough south to be safe. Reported the major: "Several persons who saw him in the ambulance report his spitting blood, and it seems to be the general impression that he cannot live. There is no doubt in my mind but what he is yet in the country, concealed; seriously, if not mortally, wounded." [42]

As the last hours of '64 faded out, a new snowstorm swept the area, shutting off further military activity. In the dying moments of the most turbulent year of the war, Sheridan sent a telegram to General Emory that made no effort to conceal his relief: "I have no news today, except the death of Mosby. He died from his wounds at Charlottesville." [43]

Sheridan's intelligence, as so often the case with information involving the guerrillas, was erroneous. Before the first month of the new year ended, the public would be reading that the famed Rebel Partisan leader was a major attraction in the city of Richmond, that he was recovering rapidly from his wound, and that he had been invited to a privileged seat on the floor of the Confederate Congress.

But the change wrought by the bullet Corporal Kane fired through the window of the Lake home that night was not to be altered. A daring plan to carry on the battle for a cause already lost was completely upset by the wound that took Mosby, even though temporarily, out of the field of action. It was made public by Charles H. Farrell, veteran correspondent of the New York Herald.[44]

Farrell had been with Torbert on the recent cavalry raid toward Gordonsville and, while on the trip, made special inquiry as to the reason for Mosby's early-December junket to Richmond. Bit by bit he was able to piece together an enterprising story connected with the last-ditch fighting on the part of the South.

Of the troops now battling to save the Confederacy, he learned, only the guerrillas in the Eastern theater were conducting their activities with customary success. Suddenly these irregulars were seen to hold out promise to the losing cause, a promise that might have been recognized earlier as the possible answer to a desperate situation. So it was the Confederate government's top figure, Jeff Davis, who called Mosby to Richmond, reported Correspondent Farrell. There the Partisan leader sat in closed conference with civilian and military leaders and helped map out a master plan:

At the proper time Mosby was to be made a brigadier general and to gather around him in Loudoun Valley all the independent bands of the Eastern theater, to organize them into eight battalions of four companies each and to divide them into smaller detachments as the necessities of the service required. Picked men, with fleet horses, would be assigned to guard the gaps in surrounding mountains, to herald the approach of Union troops and to give the signal for a concentration of the independent bands. A mobile unit also would be formed, to move from point to point, gathering conscripts and arming old men as local guerrillas. An intricate system of mountain signal stations would flash messages back and forth. Headquarters of the bands would be located in mountain fastnesses, secure from surprise or attack by the enemy. And the watchword of every member of this irregular army was to be: "No quarter to the Yankees."

The correspondent wrote vindictively in conclusion that, whether Mosby recovered or died, "the facts I have related should command the attention of the military authorities . . . There is but one remedy where people have determined upon such diabolism, and that is to smoke them out and drive them with fire and sword until not a vestige of them or their places remains to blot the fair face of the earth."

The war had moved into the home stretch.

CHAPTER 9

January 1–February 25, 1865

GENERALS ARE HARD
TO KEEP

The year '65 opened with Union activities in the area west of Washington the deadest of any period of the war. Several inches of snow blanketed the ground in distinct layers, an accumulation since December 10, forcing organized military operations into a virtual standstill. Only beaten tracks cut zigzag lines through the white landscape, with here and there a dark blur in the beauty caused by the presence of a Federal outpost. At these centers of canvas-covered huts little more than the blue smoke of burning rails and logs, rising above crude, mud-chinked chimneys, told life was to be found inside. Soldiers, reading, playing cards, or talking, were satisfied to stay close to their bunks—and as near as possible to any source of heat. For some of them it was their fourth winter in Virginia, and by now they were well aware how severely the cold season clamped down, bogging traffic on highways and sometimes on railways, thus shutting off communication except by telegraph, a medium that even at best could be counted on only when Rebel guerrillas would permit the wires to stand.

Early's army had withdrawn to winter quarters at Staunton, leaving it up to the Partisans to heckle the outposts of northern Virginia during the season when the major battle was against nature's icy blasts. The largest of these Federal troop centers was at Stephenson's Depot, on the Winchester and Potomac Railroad, where most

of the Nineteenth Corps was gathered. At Summit Point lay a brigade, with another at Winchester, two at Clifton, and one at
Lovettsville. A division of cavalry was quartered out on the
Romney road west of Winchester. Another stood guard beside the
Berryville pike near the Opequon. To all intents and purposes they
were there to protect the Union, a purpose they were sworn to pursue every hour of day or night, but, no matter how sworn to duty
the personnel, camp chores and routines were cut to the barest
minimum. Every outpost was shut down as tightly as a logging
camp. Week after week life was the same. Men confined their interests and their activities to existence inside the accumulation of
huts, eating, sleeping, and, between times, searching for diversion to
help while away the dreary, monotonous hours. Meals were reduced
to two a day—breakfast at eight and dinner at three. Only pickets
on duty were denied the privilege of sleeping late. Each morning
ice in the water buckets had to be thawed for purposes of making
coffee and lathing the face and hands. Body baths were rare and
usually accompanied by agonizing howls as torturous cold liquid
made contact with human flesh. Even the spartan stamina of chap-
lains failed to provide them with complete ablution oftener than
once in two or three weeks. Retreat sounded at sunset, and from
then on it was every man to his own bed—when and if he liked.[1]

In this atmosphere John Lockra, servant to a lieutenant billeted
near Winchester, decided one night to hold a prayer meeting of the
colored fraternity responsible for the menial duties of the camp. It
was said of him that he was the regiment's most pious Negro, a
faithful who worked for the Lord as well as the lieutenant and an
individual very wise and very able when it came to expounding the
Scriptures. On this occasion Lockra opened his service in the hut
he shared with three other boys. Attendance at such a time when
men were in want of something to do was good, and the program
got off with a boat-rocking rendition of "I Want to Go," a blending
of bass and tenor more attuned to a week-end carousal in the mud
flats than a gathering dedicated to religion. Next came a long
prayer, another song more vocal than the first, and then John announced he would give "de sendoff," a short sermon. It lasted an
hour, after which the worshipers once more bowed their heads in
prayer. Midway of the supplication and while the brethren knelt
with their eyes closed and hands palm-together within an inch of
their flat noses, the chaplain's colored boy, not having the fear of

God anywhere in his copiously clothed soul, came thundering into the hut whistling a melody of "Yankee Doodle" and "Dixie." Lockra stopped praying, squinted through a frown fashioned of deep furrows across the wide sweep of his ebony brow, and shouted like a demon: "Wait, brudders, while I throws de chaplain's nigger fru de do'!" Turning, he grabbed the intruder and catapulted him out of the canvas-flap entrance to a sprawling position in the middle of the camp street. Then, brushing his hands together in token of a job well done, he steadied himself, straightened his clothes, and humbly bowed his head again. But the chaplain's servant was no crasher to be put out of action by a single encounter with so efficient a bouncer, not even when it meant a break in the worship of the Lord. Therefore and immediately he decided to become a more determined and drastic disturbing element. Lockra's voice still intoned pleas for mercy from Heaven over the bowed heads of the congregation when a handful of cartridges came rattling down the stubby, barrel-topped chimney, a moment later creating explosions that immediately caused the congregation to forsake religion and scatter in quest of safety and fresh air.[2]

Parson Lockra had a parallel in "Uncle Freeman," a Negro body servant attached to the Twenty-first Mississippi. While Freeman's outfit lay in camp around Richmond, he disappeared for several days. Later he turned up with positive proof he had earned, by performing odd jobs, money with which to buy food for the regimental mess. It was off to the left of the line that he first was noticed on his return, trudging along with a blue bucket of molasses on his head and a sack of baker's bread and bologna sausage in his hands. He walked up close to the huddle of soldiers and stopped, surveying the situation, and then, succumbing to curiosity and ignoring advice yelled in his direction, he walked toward the crown of a knoll, just as the sun was dropping behind the trees, to take a peep at the enemy. Owing to the bucket, which he forgot rose several inches above the top of his head, he was easily spotted by the Federals. Suddenly several guns opened across the way and shells tore up the ground in close proximity to the Negro, throwing dirt fifty feet into the air. When the dust settled enough to clear the view, Uncle Freeman was nowhere to be seen. But next day he showed up again, obviously changed into a profound Christian. Each night thereafter he held a prayer meeting and forced every Negro in the regiment to attend. While observing this unusual behavior with active interest, the soldiers in time got around to asking a question that had been bothering most all of them: what had become of the molasses, bread, and sausage? "God er mighty knows," said Freeman. "I ain't seed 'em since, an' I ain't lookin' fer 'em. I jis' gwine bless de Lord all de res' o' my life fo' sparin' me on dat occasion." [3]

While such incidents livened winter camp life for the soldiers from the North as well as the South, the Rebels, facing their darkest hour, were in the mood to grab at straws. The most substantial and promising of these appeared at the moment to be guerrilla warfare, the stratagem Jefferson Davis was reputed to have recognized, and there was growing sentiment for its widespread adoption. Newspapers came out openly in its support. An important South Carolina daily, citing the effective assaults made by Spanish guerrilla bands against the French armies earlier in the century, brazenly asserted: "It is as true today as if revealed by Heaven that, if our armies were disbanded and our people were still unalterably determined to resist Yankee rule over this land, such rule could not be maintained by 500,000 Yankee soldiers." [4]

But the needs of the moment called for more practical thinking than this sort of whistling in the dark. Peace efforts, extended by formal commission, were failing, and it was generally accepted on both sides of the Potomac that the end could not be far away. Lee's lines around Richmond still held, but outside the siege area there was little organization. Southern soldiers were ruled chiefly by a drastic shortage of food. Early had largely disbanded his army, allowing the men to go to their homes where they could be of help to their families in staving off starvation, and it was problematical how many of these would return. Guerrillas, too, had been forced to trim their activities. In Mosby's absence a part of his command was removed from its usual scene of operations and sent to the Northern Neck in hope of finding provender for themselves and their horses.

Out in South Branch Valley, McNeill's men still were heard from, but not with usual effectiveness. Jubal Early laid the blame for this drop in their activities on young Jesse's rashness, the trait that detracted from his men's confidence in him. Another detraction was the Partisan band fighting under Blake Woodson, fellow independent whose efforts frequently overlapped McNeill's, creating jealousy and confusion. It was to solve this predicament largely—and also in the hope that enough organization could be restored to the irregular bands to enable them to cut the B. & O. and thus stop the transfer of troops for the spring drive—that Early issued Special Order Number 137 dispatching Harry Gilmor to take command of all the Rangers in the area.

Gilmor, just back from a furlough during which he had traveled to South Carolina as escort to two young women refugees, immediately moved down the Valley as far as Harrisonburg with as many of his own men as he could summon together quickly, and at that point struck westward toward Moorefield. The trip was made in such freezing temperatures that even Sheridan was induced to comment he had scarcely ever felt so cold a spell. But the little band did not travel unnoticed by the Union general's scouts, for two of them trailed it every step of the way.[5]

At Moorefield, Gilmor failed to meet with a cordial welcome. Both McNeill and Woodson's men were reluctant to serve under him, some of them stubbornly refusing to recognize his authority. But he continued his efforts to restore order in the area, hoping in time to lead at least 300 men toward the railroad. The weather gave him an ideal excuse for delay; it was so cold that rivers and streams were frozen solid enough to bear the weight of wagon and team. Thus stymied and barred from immediate action, he laid out his plans: when the temperatures began to rise, he would go into camp; until then, the Partisans must arrange their own livelihood at friendly homes in the neighborhood.

It was this arrangement whereby every man had to look out for himself during moments of repose that took Gilmor out of the field of action for the remainder of the war. The two spies who trailed him to Moorefield returned bringing word of the Partisan leader's destination. They even knew at what home he had stopped. With this information Sheridan immediately dispatched Major Young and his gray-uniformed scouts, supported by a First Connecticut Cavalry colonel and about 300 men, to make the capture.

The Federals arrived at Moorefield during a heavy snow squall in the early dawn and halted until Young and a few men could steal into town to surprise Gilmor. But the Partisan had moved his sleeping quarters since the departure of the Union spies, and the scouts came back empty-handed. Disappointed but not disheartened, the expedition pursued the search down South Fork. As the column moved along, Rebel horsemen were noticed galloping across fields and hills on the right flank, and a lively race set in, some of the Blue riders stopping temporarily to search homes along the way. At the

Randolph residence three miles from town attention was drawn to a large number of horses in a barn near the road.

Major Young snooped about until he found a colored girl in the yard. "What soldiers are here?" he asked.

The girl was plainly frightened by his stern voice, but she answered promptly, "Major Gilmor is upstairs." [6]

When Young and four men burst into the Partisan's room a few minutes later, he was lying asleep with his cousin, Hoffman Gilmor. Beside the bed on a chair in easy reach lay his pistols, but the Federals had him covered before he could get his hands on them.

"Are you Major Gilmor?" Young asked.

Gilmor glanced about to see if there was a chance of escape before replying, "Yes, but who the devil are you?"

"Major Young of General Sheridan's staff."

The Partisan groaned and uttered an obvious presumption, "I suppose you want me to go with you."

"I shall be happy to have your company to Winchester." [7]

Gilmor was hustled out of bed and into his clothes. From his pockets were taken several papers, one of which was a letter that said Woodson's and McNeill's men were in a state of mutiny and had dispersed, that he had arrested one of the commanding officers, but that the arrest would not be recognized.[8]

As the Federals trotted back toward Moorefield with their important prisoner at the front of the column, Rebel horsemen gathered along the flanks, occasionally riding in closer and firing random shots. At each of these dashes they were cheered by Gilmor, who was confident he would be released.[9] Throughout the day the Confederates continued to trouble the column, but finally faded away as it neared Romney. Once along the way Young called a halt and glanced admiringly at the fine horse his prisoner was riding. "Colonel," he said, "I cannot trust you on such a splendid animal, for I know you will leave us if you get the smallest chance." So Gilmor was transferred to the saddle of a much more indifferent mount, and it was thus he next day was brought into Winchester, on his way to Fort Warren.

The McNeill Rangers now found themselves in serious disfavor with the Confederate leaders. Their refusal to accept Gilmor infuriated Early, and even before the Partisan's capture a letter asking that they be disbanded as an independent outfit was on its way to Richmond. In this message, while venting his ire chiefly on Mc-

Neill's men, Jubal made a blanket condemnation: "The fact is that all those independent organizations, not excepting Mosby's, are injurious to us, and the occasional dashes they make do not compensate for the disorganization and dissatisfaction produced among the other troops." [10]

Early's request was quickly indorsed by General Lee. Then it went on to the adjutant general's office where it wound up with an A.A.G.'s note of "no action," for McNeill's Rangers in the meantime had brought sudden and unparalleled acclaim upon themselves. They had captured two major generals on a single raid.

Back in December, Jesse McNeill was temporarily disabled by a fractured ankle, and for weeks he lay as a patient at the Felix B. Welton home four miles from Moorefield. This period of idleness gave him an opportunity to ponder over a matter that had been on his mind for a long while. His father had dreamed of capturing "Old Ben" Kelley in retaliation for the treatment the Union general had accorded Mrs. McNeill and children in '62. It was an idea that first had been proposed by one of his Rangers, Sergeant John B. Fay, native of Cumberland, the town along the B. & O. where Kelley had his headquarters, and from time to time it had been given serious consideration by the elder McNeill.

Jesse, as he lay thinking over the matter, decided no better tribute could be paid the memory of his father than to bring about this capture. But it was obvious careful planning would be necessary. Cumberland was a community of 8000 inhabitants, and it was guarded by as many or more soldiers. Notice had just been given officially that General Crook, in whose department it fell and who was quartered in a hotel near that in which Kelley slept, had enough troops to give ample protection to the entire line under his command.[11]

In early February, Ranger John Lynn sought permission to return to his home at Cumberland. Jesse granted the furlough and asked him, while there, to find out all he could regarding the possibilities of making the proposed raid. But Lynn was captured and never returned, so Jesse sent for Fay.[12] The sergeant readily accepted the hazards of going into Cumberland, only asking that he might be permitted to take with him a young Missourian, Ritcher Hallar, sixteen-year-old youth of courage and prudence. This was granted, and Fay was instructed to report to McNeill at the Hampshire County Poorhouse on the night of the nineteenth.

Jesse, moving about with the aid of a cane, arrived at the rendez-vous point with sixty-three men, fifteen of them temporarily on leave from Rosser's and other commands. The remainder of the Rangers had been left behind as a guard to watch for unexpected developments that might threaten the success of the undertaking.

Soon after dark Hallar slipped in out of a blinding snowstorm with a note from Fay. It reported that the sergeant had been into Cumberland, found the situation ideal for the raid, and was waiting at the Vance Herriott home six miles below Romney. Every detail had been given attention. Two residents of the town were to make a last-minute check to see that the generals were in their customary places and be waiting with a report.

Next day Jesse and his band rode carefully toward the Herriott place, taking every precaution to avoid being seen. They crossed the Northwestern Turnpike between New Creek and Winchester, steal-ing across at widely separated points to avoid creating an accumula-tion of hoofprints, realizing as they did so they were still twenty-six miles from their destination. Their greatest danger lay in the fact that strong Union outposts were at New Creek and Winchester and that troops from both of these places might be sent to intercept the raiding party even if it succeeded in getting away from Cumber-land.

After dark they arrived at the Herriott home and found Fay wait-ing. Now at last they were at the jumping-off point. Details were checked to make sure nothing had been forgotten. Horses were given a careful feeding, the last they would have before winding up the junket. And then Jesse gathered the men around him for a briefing on the purpose of the expedition. From there on, he an-nounced, they would proceed voluntarily, that anyone who desired had the privilege of dropping out free of censure. No one fell aside.

As they rode away, young McNeill was conscious of the responsi-bility now upon his shoulders, and he remembered the lecture about rashness his father had given him while on his deathbed.[13] Without halting, they continued along the Virginia side of the Poto-mac, keeping the column closed up as tightly as possible. Arriving at Knobly Mountain, the steepest barrier they would have to cross, they rode up through a gap and found the fields at the crest so deeply covered with snow that they had to dismount and lead their horses. The cold was intense. Men struggled along, occasionally fall-ing back to slide their numb fingers under the saddle blankets of their horses in search of warmth. The breath of the animals shot out in silky spurts on the still night air, a soft and consoling sound to the desperate riders.

As they descended the mountain they stopped at a friendly farmhouse to fill their canteens with bourbon as a protection against the weather. Then they crossed over the river into Maryland, worming their way through floating ice, and halted at the Sam Brady home for final instructions. There waiting for them was one of the two residents who had promised to watch for last-minute developments in Cumberland, an Irish Secessionist, George Stanton, and his news was good: both generals were in their beds and the town was closed up for the night.

At that point the Rangers were five miles from Cumberland, with two routes open to them. One of these, via Cresaptown and a narrow pass through Will's Mountain known as "The Narrows," would bring them into town from the northwest and would double the distance they would have to travel. The other would take them along the heavily guarded New Creek road but would bring them to their destination much sooner, provided they could escape capture. Because of the lateness of the hour Jesse decided to gamble time against safety, choosing the shorter route and lining up his men for final instructions. Hastily the column was divided into four parties, one to capture General Kelley, another to seize General Crook, a third to raid the stables for horses, and a fourth to destroy the telegraph office.

On leaving the Brady home McNeill took the lead. At his side rode Joe Kuykendall, whose task it was to search for Kelley. Three miles from Cumberland a voice suddenly rang out clearly in the frosty darkness, "Who comes there?" Jesse announced, "Friends and scouts from New Creek."

"One of you dismount, advance and give the countersign," ordered the guard.

Suddenly Jesse sank his spurs and dashed upon the vedette. Unable to check his speed, he went by him, firing a pistol in his face as he passed. The shot seemed to echo and re-echo through the hills, causing some of his men to wonder if here was an example of the rashness they feared in young McNeill as a leader. But there was no time to weigh such a possibility. They sped after him and gathered up the bewildered picket, who was baffled to the point of paralysis by the odd behavior of these "friends and scouts from New Creek."

358

A reserve of two guards, both Germans, were found nearby, and from one of them, after threatening him with hanging, was learned the countersign, "Bool's Kap," which was interpreted as Bull's Gap.

A mile farther along they saw a campfire and soon were challenged again. When told to dismount, advance, and give the countersign, Jesse replied that they did not have time to get down from their horses and, in the best imitation he could give of the German they had just threatened to hang, called out, "Bool's Kap."

"All right, come on," ordered the picket.

They rode up and formed a circle around the guard and his reserve, five men seated in a shedlike structure playing cards. Quickly ammunition and guns of the Federals were seized, after which the prisoners were told Cumberland had been surrounded, that they would be expected to remain at the post until they could be paroled in the morning.

This was the last barrier. Riding on, the column entered Cumberland from the west, passing a reserve picket without even hearing a challenge. Up Baltimore Street they went, whistling and chatting as though they had not a care in the world. When guards along the streets hailed them with a friendly "Whose command are you, boys?" they called back, "Scouts from New Creek." Between the two hotels where the generals they sought were quartered, the Barnum and the Revere House, they halted and divided into squads without so much as a whispered order. It was 3:00 A.M.

As the men climbed stiffly from their horses, a sentry walked back and forth in front of the Barnum only a few yards away, apparently accepting the newcomers as a scouting party returning from an expedition. Kuykendall's squad moved toward him, captured him without a disturbance, and entered the hotel. The first room on the second floor they invaded was that of Major Thayer Melvin, the adjutant general. When aroused and asked the whereabouts of Kelley, he pointed toward the partly open door to an adjoining room. Several men pushed into the chamber indicated, surrounded the general's bed, and, shaking him roughly, told him to get up and dress. "Old Ben" complied, though obviously with some nervousness.

While dressing he asked to whom he was surrendering, and Kuykendall replied, "To Captain McNeill, by order of General Rosser." Shortly afterward, fully clothed, he and Melvin were led down to the street and mounted on horses.

The squad sent to the Revere House meanwhile had been going

through a somewhat similar routine. Two of its members were thoroughly familiar with the scene to be invaded—Jacob Gassman, son of the owner of the hotel building, and Sergeant James Daily, the hotel proprietor's son and brother of the girl who afterward was to become the bride of the general it was their task to capture. This group also removed a sentry pacing in front, but they found the hotel locked and had to rap for entrance. Presently the door was opened by a small Negro boy who immediately suspected the intentions of the intruders. Asked if General Crook was upstairs, he flashed the whites of his eyes and stuttered, "Yas, s-s-suh—y-y-yas, suh, but don't you tell 'im I tole yuh."

Gassman, knowing the building, walked upstairs to Room 46 and rapped on the door, thinking it locked. A voice inside inquired sleepily, "Who's there."

"A friend," Gassman replied.

"Come in," said the voice.

Inside the general was found sitting up in bed.

"General Crook," said Joe Vandiver, leader of the squad who had entered the room behind Gassman, "you are my prisoner."

"What authority do you have for this?" asked the general.

"The authority of General Rosser of Fitzhugh Lee's division of cavalry."

"Is General Rosser here?"

"Yes," said Vandiver, "I am General Rosser. I have 2500 men, and we have surprised and captured the city."

Without comment Crook rolled slowly from the bed and began dressing. A few minutes later he took his place beside Kelley and Melvin.[14] In the street nearby were gathered headquarters flags and horses, among them "Philippi," Kelley's favorite charger named after the engagement near that community early in the war. At the time the animals were being rounded up from the stables, a town policeman on duty in the vicinity inquired the reason. "The Rebels are coming," he was told, "and we are moving these horses to keep them from being captured." The cop continued his beat, well satisfied with the answer.

On the way out of town twenty-five minutes after entering it, a picket at a bridge ordered the column to halt. When there was no evidence the speed of the horses had been checked, the guard was heard to ask, "Sergeant, shall I fire?" One of the Rangers in front yelled in answer, "If you do, I'll put you under arrest! This is General Crook's bodyguard and we have no time to waste! The Rebels are coming and we are going out to meet them!" That seemed to assure the picket, and they rode past without further challenge.

Four miles from Cumberland the Rangers suddenly heard the booming of artillery back in town and realized the post at last was fully awake. What they did not know at the time was that among the hotel occupants they had ignored were two future Presidents of the United States—Brigadier General James A. Garfield and Major William McKinley, the latter of Crook's staff.

The Federal pursuit, assembled from all directions, was futile. Fully an hour went by before telegraph wires could be repaired, and by that time the Partisans were well on their way. They had performed their task in such an orderly manner that Major Robert P. Kennedy, assistant adjutant general, in one of the first Federal reports of the affair to go out from Cumberland, stated: "It was done so quietly that others of us, who were sleeping in adjoining rooms to General Crook, were not disturbed." [15]

McNeill sent his prisoners toward Harrisonburg, along unbeaten paths and little-used routes. At one point, as they rested on the side of a mountain, down in the valley below a Federal column could be seen riding hard on their trail. While they stared at it, Crook was heard to remark, "So near and yet so far." [16] Next day, as they dismounted in Harrisonburg, the general spoke up again, "Gentlemen, this is the most brilliant exploit of the war."

The prisoners were taken the remainder of the distance to Staunton in an old stagecoach, climaxing a 154-mile trip made in three days, a difficult feat for even a skilled horseman in good physical condition. There they were turned over to Jubal Early, who wined and dined them in a manner befitting their rank, and the following day they were entrained under guard of their Partisan captors and headed for Richmond. Among the passengers as they climbed aboard was the wily independent, Mosby, now recovered from his wound and on the way back to his command. When he heard what had happened at Cumberland, a feat that overshadowed his enterprising invasion of Stoughton's headquarters at Fairfax in '63, he shook hands smilingly with McNeill's men and commented, "You boys have beaten me badly. The only way I can equal this will be to go into Washington and bring out Lincoln." [17]

Back at Cumberland, things quickly returned to normal. General Winifred S. Hancock was selected to replace Crook, guards were doubled to prevent his capture, and life in the town went on as usual. In a local theater on the second night after the capture an audience settled back to hear a program of entertainment that was to be highlighted by songs from the beautiful and talented Mary Clara Bruce, already recognized by townspeople as the future bride of "Old Ben" Kelley. She appeared on the stage, bowed amid heavy applause, and, when it died down sufficiently, announced her first song, "He Kissed Me When He Left." An unwise selection it proved to be, under the circumstances. The music struck up and, as she drew in her breath to begin the vocal, some irreverent individual at the rear of the hall, allegedly a soldier somewhat influenced by acohol, jumped to his feet and loudly exclaimed, "No, I'll be damned if he did! McNeill didn't give him time!" [18]

February 26–May 20, 1865

SOMETHING TO REMEMBER

Time was passing. In a few more weeks it would be a full year since Grant had launched his massive campaign to paralyze the South, and still the Rebels were unconquered. Frustrated over and over, the Union commander-in-chief was impatient. Early in February, even while winter's grip held military operations to a minimum, he wrote Sheridan of enemy troop movements from the Valley and wound up his message with a familiar refrain: "I believe there is no enemy now to prevent you from reaching the Virginia Central road, and possibly the canal, when the weather will permit you to move." [1] This was the last such plea from Grant. Nineteen times he had made it, first in a dispatch to poor, frustrated Franz Sigel on May 17, '64. [2]

Sheridan in reply promised action as soon as the weather would permit. He reported that at present twelve inches of snow lay on the ground, that it was extremely cold, and that many men had been frostbitten while chasing guerrillas. A few days later he backed up this excuse for delay with the statement "I have never experienced a colder or worse winter." [3]

Toward the end of February the situation in the Valley was such that Sheridan concluded the time was ripe for action. Rebel deserters were coming into Union lines by the dozens. The Confederate army shattered at Cedar Creek was still badly disorganized and there was no evidence that it could be braced to the point of making a formidable stand. But he got positive evidence that the next few weeks would bring stiffer resistance than he would encounter if he marched at once. Rosser, for instance, had ordered his disbanded forces to reassemble on March 1. And there were rumors that troops —White's battalion and men from the Sixth and Twelfth Virginia Cavalry—were assembling in Loudoun Valley, as if to put into effect the wholesale guerrilla warfare Mosby was reputed to have mapped out with Jefferson Davis and others at Richmond in December.[4] To counter this move Sheridan gave Merritt renewed instructions to clean out this snug little valley near Washington, and in the meantime began laying plans for his army to move.

But before he could get started, guerrillas again brought him embarrassment. A detachment of New York and Pennsylvania cavalry was sent out under the guidance of two Rebel deserters to search for Mosby's men and to seize certain property. Along the way a party of Rangers, using their revolvers effectively in a narrow defile, tore into the Federals and annihilated them. Secretary of War Stanton waited for days for Sheridan's report on the affair and, when it failed to come in, sent him a sharp message through the A.A.G., saying among other things: "The frequent disasters in your command have occasioned much regret in the department, as indicating a want of vigilance and discipline which, if not speedily cured, may occasion greater misfortune."[5] In answer Sheridan attempted to brush off the incident as another of the numerous attacks by guerrillas, most of them conducted after dark. But he admitted the Union party was stampeded and that the entire experience was badly managed.[6]

As February faded, Sheridan notified Grant that he was ready to start up the Valley and that he would leave behind 2000 men. A copy of this message reached the White House and elicited an immediate word of caution. Lincoln wired Grant to remind him of the possibility this movement might leave Maryland, Pennsylvania, and the B. & O. open to attack. In short order he was assured the advance would contribute decidedly toward their protection.

On the next to last day of the month Sheridan's troops began moving southward. Most of the infantry had been sent to Richmond weeks prior, leaving him with only 10,000 sabers—Custer's Third and Deven's First Divisions of cavalry and two sections of artillery. Before many hours had passed, guerrillas attacked outposts west of Washington, and Secretary of War Stanton immediately joined Lincoln in fearing for the safety of the capital. It took several messages from Grant to quiet him, dispatches that pointed out the city was protected by nearly 40,000 effectives in the Departments of Washington and West Virginia, not to mention a division of the Nineteenth Corps and the 2000 men left by Sheridan. One of these concluded: "On the whole, I think there is not the slightest need of apprehension, except from a dash of a few mounted men into Alexandria, and with proper watchfulness this ought not to occur." [7]

But the attack from the guerrillas was little more than a threat. As Sheridan moved up the Valley he found matters completely different from what they had been on his unsuccessful expeditions of the preceding summer and fall. The Partisans, shorn of three of their leaders, were not striking with their customary sting. Mc-Neill was dead, Gilmor in prision, and Mosby just now on the way back to his command.

Sheridan' army moved on schedule. Up the Valley it went, past the charred ruins of villages and fine estates put to the torch the year prior, and there was little to stop it. At Waynesboro the few hundred men still remaining in Early's army braced themselves, a pitiful handful backed against the headwaters of the Shenandoah, and there they were rounded up almost *in toto,* only their general and a minor part of his soldiers escaping. After that the Federals turned about and headed toward Richmond.

No doubt now that the enemy Grant had planned to paralyze the preceding summer was about to fold. Lee was asking for conferences to talk over the situation and Grant was refusing them, explaining such prerogatives were vested only in the President. Meanwhile the plight of the South grew more hopeless. In a message inspired by desperation the Confederate commander-in-chief instructed Mosby to collect his Partisans and protect the country from Gordonsville westward. "Your command is all now in that section," the dispatch read.[8]

Before the winds of March had ended, Sheridan brought his troopers to the outskirts of Petersburg, finally putting an end to the dream that had been turned into a nightmare by guerrillas. April came in with gentle rains, vegetation was advanced, and the grass was "growing finely." The grip on Lee tightened, while from the distance of northern Virginia came the faint echo of Partisan depredations. A B. & O. passenger train was stopped and robbed near Cumberland by remnants of White's and Gilmor's commands and a few from Mosby's. It was another narrow miss ruled over by fate, like that when Mosby had failed to intercept Grant at Warrenton Junction the preceding spring, for Vice-President Andrew Johnson would have been aboard had he not delayed his departure from Washington in the hope of seeing the President.[9] And farther west, McNeill's men, newly inspired since their capture of Crook and Kelley, derailed a mail train at Patterson's Run, robbed it, and escaped.

With Sheridan to support him, Grant began his grand assault on Petersburg, and the Confederate lines crumbled and doubled back. Lee sent his famous message of disaster to Jefferson Davis, reached while in church across the street from the Confederate capitol. It was the beginning of the end. Seven days later, on a quiet Palm Sunday when the song of new life was in the air and peach and apple trees were in bloom, the Gray horde from the South, now no more than a thin line, bowed in surrender to the Army of the Potomac—"greatest in the world save one, which modesty forbids me to mention," said a capitulator.[10]

But in the guerrilla area along the B. & O. there was still no peace. The Partisan bands that throughout the war had fought around the clock were still as sleepless as ever. Some of Mosby's men stole in upon the Loudoun Rangers and annihilated them, putting them out of action forever. Near Baltimore, Partisans appeared in the night and captured two Federal steamers, manning them and heading them out into the bay. At Fairfax Station, close to Washington, two companies of Rangers formed line and fought stubbornly against the Eighth Illinois Cavalry until driven off.[11] Others were reported on their way to Maryland to rob banks and to the Valley to intercept trains. One of Stevenson's couriers carrying messages westward from Harpers Ferry was taken in tow, along with the important dispatches he had in his pockets.

Hancock, who had assumed command of the area when Sheridan marched south, put it in the records that he would like nothing better than to wipe out these independents. As it turned out, he possessed the desire but not the cunning. Methods he proposed had been tried over and over by the leaders he succeeded. Grant suggested instead that he attempt to get the Partisans to surrender, offering them the same terms given Lee. This suggestion was a bit premature, for Chief of Staff Halleck was busy at the moment penning a message to Hancock that "the guerrilla chief Mosby will not be paroled." [12]

The surrender terms were made public, but all the answer that came back from the Partisans was defiance. Colonel Gamble, commanding at Fairfax, received a message from Mosby, however authentic or unauthentic it may have been, that he didn't "care a damn about the surrender of Lee, that he was determined to fight as long as he had a man left." The Washington *Star* reported the incident and commented: "He may fight his way to the gallows." [13]

Along the Potomac it was noticed that White's men had begun to disappear, and it was said they had taken to the mountains. A few Union soldiers managed to get within hailing distance of them and shouted that Lee had surrendered. There was a moment's silence from the mountain crags and than a lone voice hallooed back: "We know it! The Confederacy is played out, but our independent companies are not!" [14]

In the midst of efforts to get the guerrillas to stack arms Abraham Lincoln was shot in Ford's Theater by an unidentified assassin, and an immediate tenseness blanketed the land. Rumors flew thick and fast, some of them drawing Mosby into the act, but these quickly were discounted. In a matter of hours the assassin was cornered and shot in a Virginia barn between Washington and Richmond, and it was announced that he definitely was John Wilkes Booth, the actor. Mosby's name was drawn in possibly from the fact that one of his former Rangers, Louis Thornton Powell, for months a deserter, had cooperated in the threat against the United States government to the extent of stabbing bedridden Secretary of State Seward.

Hancock, somewhat new as a leader confronted by such guerrillas as those operating west of Washington, foolishly prepared to send Blue cavalry galloping through the area in search of men as elusive as raindrops. While he made his plans, a lean, tanned rider with a voice that in song could thrill the most backward girl rode up to his headquarters. This visitor was Lieutenant Colonel William Chapman, second in command to Mosby, and he had come to ask for a conference.[15] Hancock granted it and then sat down to read a message from Secretary of War Stanton that said: "In holding an interview with Mosby it may be needless to caution an old soldier like you to guard against surprise or danger to yourself; but the recent murders show such astounding wickedness that too much precaution cannot be taken." Without mentioning caution Grant advised haste in paroling the guerrillas. "My own views," he wrote, "are that it will be better to have Mosby's and White's men in Maryland as paroled prisoners of war then at large as guerrillas." [16]

More than a week had passed since Lee's surrender. When Hancock agreed to the conference, he also consented to a two-day truce, but there was no way to contact all the Partisans still in the field, and fighting broke out in some of the Maryland counties nearest the Potomac. A battalion of the veteran Eighth Illinois Cavalry was sent to quiet the disturbance.

The conference with Mosby was held on schedule, and the Partisan leader, speaking for most of the independents in the area, was calm in expressing his sentiments, even voicing regret over the death of Lincoln. He asked for an extension of the truce so he could have more time to learn the status of the army in the deep South led by Confederate General Joseph E. Johnston. But he made it clear, regardless of the resistance farther south, that he would not surrender his men, that he would disband them and let each pursue his own course. The truce he requested was granted—for two days.

When notified of the outcome of the meeting, Grant, in a brief telegram to Hancock, indicated he had no further patience for the Partisans: "If Mosby does not avail himself of the present truce, end it and hunt him and his men down. Guerrillas, after beating the armies of the enemy, will not be entitled to quarter." [17]

The second conference held with Mosby brought no better results. In the midst of it, thinking he had been tricked and was to be taken by force, he and the Rangers with him backed out of the meeting, jaws set, eyes flashing, and hands on their revolvers. Defiantly they climbed into their saddles and rode away, thus ending the last contact they would have with the United States government as a band of independent Partisan Rangers.

Next morning, a rainy morning, Mosby met the remnant of his band at the little village of Salem, a point where many times they had rendezvoused, and with a modicum of ceremony had his adjutant read to them his farewell address. It was brief and toned with sadness, the mood in which he rode away from the village a few minutes later.[18]

Nearly two weeks had passed since Lee and the Army of Northern

Virginia laid down their arms, and bands hostile to the United States still roamed the country. Gilmor's men, deprived of their leader, had scattered to other commands and were no longer an integral force, but Jesse McNeill was unparoled and asking for a truce so that he could have time to make up his mind as to what course to follow. Some of White's men were waiting on the side lines, too, delaying until they could determine the best and wisest procedure. But a vast majority of them had surrendered with Lee at Appomattox, where their colonel had commanded the famed Laurel Brigade in its dying moments.[19]

Official messages to the effect that "our cause is not dead" continued to make the rounds.[20] A pitifully few die-hard patriots still beat the tom-toms to stir sentiment for a continued fight. Jefferson Davis sent out a plea for Confederates to stay in the field. "There are more men at home today belonging to the Army of Northern Virginia than were surrendered at Appomattox," it was announced. "Let them rally to the call of our President . . ."[21] There was renewed talk of wholesale guerrilla warfare, a war of attrition, the worrying and wearying kind of fight the Spanish had used against the French, resistance that in time would cause even the best army to drop its guard.

But the Confederacy was licked, hungry, tired, and heartbroken, and the average Southerner had had quite, quite enough. One day General Grant, the victorious commander-in-chief of the Union army, was on his way by train from Appomattox to City Point near Richmond. Across the aisle sat a Confederate soldier, newly paroled, and beside him a citizen in knee boots and slouch hat. The Union general overheard some of their conversation.

"You shouldn't have surrendered," the citizen said. "You should have taken to the mountains and fought guerrilla warfare."

For a while the soldier took this sort of argument indulgently, and then he lost his patience and, raising his voice, faced the man seated beside him and said very firmly: "Look! I've been in 35 battles since this war started, and I'm plumb satisfied."[22]

And thus it was among the Partisans who lurked in the forests and mountains and the men of the ranks who stood for duty wherever their orders directed them. The war was over. For four long years some of the independents had been fighting, and they were as free today to carry on their activities as they had been in the past. But sentiment was against them, and this they knew. It was not long before Union dispatches were recording officially: "The race of guerrillas is rapidly returning to their former pursuits, the hatred of the Yankee invader not being such now as to excite a population to arms and individual desperation." From a more practical standpoint, it was said, "the desire is to have peace— with coffee, sugar, etc." [23]

May would come and advance into its third week before the curtain could be drawn finally on the Confederate guerrilla. Even as the days warmed with the positive assurance of approaching summer, his bullets would whine down from the hills toward the enemy who got too close. But one by one or in small groups these men who had fought alone and in bands, living the life of wild animals as they burrowed in freedom and sought food wherever it was available, faded out of the picture, some paroled, some never to be paroled, and some to reappear again in society as prominent citizens. The alternative left to them was no quarter—quick death by bullet or rope. It was July before guards were removed from the B. & O. and the same month before Harry Gilmor was given his freedom and released from prison.

The years ahead would be hard years for these free-riding and free-shooting men who had done their part for the South as guerrillas, waging a war that delayed for months the important surrender. In their active days in the saddle they had brought new esteem to their peculiar branch of the service, positive proof that it could figure in the outcome of an armed struggle and should be given study as a valuable weapon in future wars. This contribution they had made, and it was strong on their minds as they once more went about the routine of peaceful daily life. Represented among them were almost every profession and occupation of society— ministers, doctors, lawyers, writers, merchants, statesmen, diplomats —people recognized as the salt of the earth, the backbones of their respective communities. Back to their pursuits they went, no longer desperate, dogged warriors whose survival depended largely on their own cunning and caution. And in peace they hung their pistols on the walls above their heads and littered their desks with papers and instruments of personal business.

But always through the years of reconstruction and on into the century ahead, always until the earth shoveled to make their graves was banked above their still forms, there would be a bond between them. Never would they meet without an exciting subject of conversation, for only death could wipe away the thought that a guerrilla is a warrior ready to fight, to raid or pillage day or night, to sneak in where armies dare not tread, and to move without support, his life in his hands, upsetting enemy plans as the cause demands.

NOTES

PART ONE

CHAPTER 1

1 *Official Records of the Rebellion,* LI, Pt. II, 87. Referred to hereafter as *O.R.*

CHAPTER 2

1 From these two sources—Radford and the Richmond *Dispatch*—appears to have come the initial spark for large-scale guerrilla warfare in the South. Others followed, however, in rapid succession.
2 Baltimore *American and Commercial Advertiser,* April 22, 1861.
3 Letters and telegrams pertaining to the part played by the B. & O. during the war, from the papers of William Prescott Smith, master of transportation.
4 *O.R., LI,* Pt. II, 23.
5 While the call for guerrilla warfare was heard at first in spotted instances, the Confederate government recognized its potential at an early date and made provision for such an arm. In its regulations, drawn up and revised from the United States Army Code of 1857, instructions for the operation, composition, and purposes of a Partisan corps were included.
6 John W. Garrett, elected president of the B. & O. on November 17, 1858, had said of the railroad in a speech before a Baltimore audience soon after the John Brown raid at Harpers Ferry in 1859: "It is a Southern Line. And if ever necessity should require—which heaven forbid!—it will prove the great bulwark of the border, and a sure agency for home defense . . . During a period when agitation, alarm and uncertainty prevail is it not right, is it not becoming, that Baltimore should declare her position in 'the irrepressible' conflict threatened and urged by Northern fanaticism?"
7 Baltimore *American,* April 25, 1851.
8 Baltimore *American,* May 11, 1861.
9 *O.R.,* II, 825.
10 *Ibid.,* p. 841.
11 This remark about Kelley was made to Sergeant John W. Elwood of Coal Center, Pennsylvania, author of *Elwood's Stories of the Old Ringgold Cavalry* (privately printed, 1914), referred to hereafter as Elwood, by Major

George B. Davis, an army officer who assisted with the publication of the *Official Records*. (*Op. cit.*, p. 163.)

12 *O.R.*, II, 672.

13 *The Baltimore and Ohio in the Civil War* (New York, G. P. Putnam's Sons, 1939), by Festus P. Summers, p. 94. Referred to hereafter as Summers.

14 *O.R.*, Series 4, I, 395.

CHAPTER 3

1 *The Hero of Medfield; Containing the Journals and Letters of Allen Alonzo Kingsbury* (Boston, John M. Hewes, 1862). Referred to hereafter as Kingsbury.

2 *O.R.*, II, 703.

3 Scott to Patterson, *O.R.*, II, 694.

4 *O.R.*, II, 695.

5 *Ibid.*, p. 953.

6 Angus McDonald was sixty-two years old in 1861. He was a lawyer and had led an adventurous life, at one time living with the Indians. A graduate of West Point, he had specialized in artillery, but his greatest fame was derived from his work on the frontier, where he was a trusted friend of several Indian tribes. Shortly before the outbreak of war he returned from a junket to London in connection with the boundary dispute between Maryland and Virginia.

7 In his first report to headquarters, dated from Romney on June 25, 1861, Angus McDonald stated that his recruiting efforts had "met with success far beyond my most sanguine expectations, as this bids fair to become a popular arm of the service." (*O.R.*, II, 952.)

8 *Ibid.*, p. 953.

9 The date of McDonald's departure from Winchester seems to have been confused. Mrs. McDonald, in her recollections of the war, p. 21, says: "On the morning of the 17th of June the regiment marched away, with orders to move along the North Western turnpike and destroy the bridges of the Baltimore and Ohio Railroad over the Cheat River." But her husband, in his official report to the Secretary of War, dated June 26, 1861, says: ". . . I had ordered both of these troops (Ashby's and Gaither's) to march to this place (Romney), to leave Winchester in the afternoon. In the meantime I learned that General Johnston's command was drawn up in line of battle, expecting an attack. This induced me to countermand the orders which I had given to Captains Ashby and Gaither, that my men should have their part in the expected engagement. On the morning of the 18th, having learned enough of the enemy's position to convince me that there was no danger of an immediate attack, I ordered the above-named captains to move forward with their companies in this place." (*O.R.*, II, 952.)

10 *A Diary with Reminiscences of the War and Refugee Life in the Shenandoah Valley, 1860-1865* (Nashville, Tennessee, Cullom and Ghertner Company, 1935), by Mrs. Cornelia McDonald, p. 24. Referred to hereafter as McDonald.

11 *O.R.*, II, 239.
12 *Four Years in the Stonewall Brigade* (Guthrie, Oklahoma, State Capital Printing Company, 1893), by John O. Casler, referred to hereafter as Casler. According to this volume Richard Ashby was buried in the cemetery at Romney, West Virginia. Later his body and that of Turner were taken up and placed together in the Stonewall Cemetery at Winchester Virginia.

An eyewitness gave this description of Turner's behavior at the burial of his brother: "He stood over the grave, took his brother's sword, broke it and threw it into the opening; clasped his hands and looked upward as if in resignation; and then pressing his lips, as if in the bitterness of grief, while a tear rolled down his cheek, he turned without a word, mounted his horse and rode away."

13 *O.R.*, II, 196.
14 *Ibid.*
15 Letter of Charles W. Russell to Secretary of War Leroy Pope Walker, *O.R.*, II, 142.
16 *Ibid.*, p. 237.
17 *Ibid.*, p. 195.
18 The reconnaissance during the morning was directed by the engineer officer, Orlando M. Poe, who had been influential in bringing McClellan to command of the Ohio militia. In return McClellan, on his later transfer to Washington, took Poe with him, and the engineer moved up in rank rapidly. He it was who was largely responsible for the path of destruction laid down in 1864 by Sherman on his march to the sea.
19 Ohio troops passing through this area nearly a year later recorded that they were much impressed with the realities of war by what they saw on Rich Mountain. "The trees were marked with balls on every hand," wrote one of them, and they all sought souvenirs in memory of this first battlefield they had ever visited. See "Civil War Diary and Memoirs of Thomas Evans" (Unpublished, in Manuscript Division, Library of Congress).
20 *O.R.*, II, 287.
21 *The Story of a Regiment: A History of the Campaigns and Associations in the Field of the Sixth Regiment, Ohio Volunteer Infantry* (Cincinnati, Ohio, privately printed, 1868), by E. Hannaford, p. 83. Referred to hereafter as Hannaford.
22 *Ibid.*

CHAPTER 4

1 *O.R.*, II, 236.
2 *Ibid.*, p. 205.
3 *Ibid.*, p. 211.
4 *Memorial of Henry Sanford Gansevoort*, edited by J. C. Hoadley (Franklin Press: Rand, Avery & Co., Boston, Mass., 1875), p. 83. Referred to hereafter as Gansevoort.
5 *Ibid.*
6 *O.R.*, II, 299.
7 *Ibid.*, p. 743.

8 *Lamar Fontaine: My Life and Lectures* (New York, 1908), p. 69.

9 *O.R.*, II, 743.

10 *Ibid.*, p. 168.

11 Kingsbury.

12 Although young in appearance at First Bull Run, Andrew Clement got his share of war before 1865. The First Massachusetts Cavalry took him into its ranks, and by 1864 he had fought on a dozen battlefields. That summer he appeared around Richmond. He was wearing the stripes of a sergeant, fastened to a tight-buttoned blue jacket trimmed in yellow. Across his arm was a silver-bright carbine and at his side a curved Chicopee saber. Andrew had seen more war than most soldiers twice his age. (*Reveille in Washington* (New York, Harper and Brothers, 1941), by Margaret Leech, p. 346.)

13 Kingsbury.

14 *O.R.*, Series 4, I, 475, 505.

15 Brigadier General Henry R. Jackson, commanding at Monterey, to Colonel George Deas, assistant adjutant general at Richmond. *Ibid.*, LI, Pt. II, 188.

CHAPTER 5

1 "Recollections of Richard D. Rutherford" (unpublished), made available to the author by the late Forrest Rutherford, of Washington, D. C.

2 *O.R.*, II, 752.

3 *Ibid.*, 753.

4 *Ibid.*, 178.

5 On July 26, 1861, D. M. K. Campbell of Choctaw County, Alabama, wrote Secretary of War Leroy Pope Walker a letter in which he asked how the Confederate government felt about guerrilla warfare. He reported that "quite a number of men of undoubted respectability are anxious to serve the government on their own account." They wanted to organize companies, he explained, that would fight without restraint, under no orders, and would convert whatever property they captured to their own private use. They would take care of themselves, provided the governor of the state would not interfere with them or look upon them as unlawful bands. Within ten days Campbell received an official answer, prepared over the signature of A. T. Bledsoe, chief of the Bureau of War, to this effect:

The Confederate government preferred that these companies be armed and tendered for the war in the usual way. In order to have countenance and protection of the government, they would have to conform strictly to the laws and usages of civilized nations; they must be commissioned and paid by the government and in complete subordination to its authority. If they proceeded as proposed in the letter of inquiry, the government would have no right to interfere in their behalf and, if the enemy captured them, they would be subject to the same cruelties inflicted upon outlaws or pirates. (*Ibid.*, Series 4, I, 532.)

6 Report of John Henderson, captain of Virginia Rangers, dated from Charles Town July 31, 1861. *Ibid.*, LI, Pt. II, 205.

7 *Life and Letters of Wilder Dwight* (Boston, Ticknor and Fields, 1868),

a beautifully worded volume published as a memorial to him in 1868. Referred to hereafter as Dwight.

8 *Army Letters 1861-1865* (privately printed, 1903), by Oliver Willcox Norton, p. 46. Referred to hereafter as Norton.

9 *O.R.*, II, 907.

10 A member of the Sixth Ohio Volunteer Infantry, writing of his experiences in this phase of the war, said: "Thicker even than the bushwhackers they sheltered during the war are the laurel bushes that grow on every mountain side by every running stream throughout West Virginia." (Hannaford, p. 88.)

11 As an indication of the general thinking on the war, one participant later recorded: "I thought Virginia was to be the theater of war for six or eight weeks. We would have a battle in which one Southern man would whip five Yankees with cornstalks. England would intervene, peace would be declared, and we would return home finding all our servants smiling at our homecoming." *The Privations of a Private* (Nashville, Tennessee, Methodist Publishing House, 1907), by Marcus B. Toney, p. 13.

12 Norton, p. 24.

13 *Ibid.*, p. 26.

14 *Dictionary of American Biography* (New York, Charles Scribner's Sons, 1943).

15 According to an anonymous letter to the editor of the Baltimore *Sun*, dated December 22, 1929, a record of which now is on file in the Pratt Library at Baltimore, Howard and Arthur Gilmor were killed during the war.

16 After the war Harry Gilmor continued as a prominent citizen of Baltimore, where he died in 1883. For a time in the 70's he served as police commissioner of the city.

17 *Four Years in the Saddle* (New York, Harper and Brothers, 1866), by Colonel Harry Gilmor, p. 13, referred to hereafter as Gilmor. This is the Partisan's own account of his operations, a highly egotistical volume in which the author brazenly relates experiences that make him appear as a one-man army. On its title page appears the slogan: "I fight fairly and in good faith."

18 After the war, and until his death in 1907, White lived as a prominent citizen and businessman of Leesburg, Virginia. He helped found and was the second president of the People's National Bank there. He was a well-to-do merchant, a dealer in feed and grain, and he covered a wide circuit as a Hardshell Baptist preacher.

CHAPTER 6

1 Dwight, p. 111.

2 These scenes of camp life are taken largely from the letters of Wilder Dwight and Oliver Willcox Norton.

3 Confederate General John B. Floyd, writing from the headquarters of the Army of the Kanawha on September 27, 1861, said: "At this season of the year I do not remember to have seen such a storm in the mountains of Virginia. It has put an absolute stop to all locomotion." (*O.R.*, LI, Pt. II, 317.)

4 Dwight, p. 116.

5 Avirett to Secretary of War Benjamin, October 1, 1864. *O.R.,* LI, Pt. II, 329.

6 The New York *Herald,* October 3, 1861.

7 *O.R.,* V, 290.

8 Stone appears to have been in error concerning the number of companies he instructed Devens to take across with him. In his report dated October 29, 1861 (*Ibid.,* p. 294), Stone says he "sent orders to Colonel Devens to cross four companies." But Devens, in a report on October 23 (*Ibid.,* p. 208), puts the number at five. So also do the Confederate commander, Brigadier General Nathan G. Evans (*Ibid.,* p. 349), and the report of the Committee on the Conduct of the War.

9 Some of Baker's subordinates charged that he took no recognition of the terrain after crossing the Potomac, allowing the enemy to occupy the more advantageous position on the left. Stone later wrote in one of his reports: "That Colonel Baker was determined at all hazards to fight a battle is clear from the fact that he never crossed to examine the field, never gave an order to the troops in advance, and never sent forward to ascertain their position until he had ordered over his force and passed over a considerable portion of it." (*Ibid.,* p. 301.)

10 In the ensuing congressional investigation of the battle at Ball's Bluff, this order became the subject of controversy. It was charged in the press that Baker had been directed by Stone to attack Leesburg on the twentieth. Stone claimed that this was absurd, that Baker got no order at all from him on the twentieth, and that the one found on the senator's body did not reach him until 2:00 A.M. on the twenty-first. And even then, clarified Stone, it in no manner informed him of the object of the movement, but merely directed him to go to Conrad's Ferry. The order found in Baker's hat, he said, had been "somewhat altered" either by the bloodstains or by " 'friendly' hands, which may easily happen in a pencil order." (*Ibid.*)

11 Writing of the battle of Ball's Bluff years later in a pamphlet published to raise money for a Confederate monument at Leesburg, Virginia, Colonel Elijah V. White identified this mysterious Rebel as Lieutenant Charles B. Wildman of General Evans' staff and said he, "mistaking a part of the Federal line for our people, galloped to the front of the Tammany Regiment, and in the most peremptory and commanding manner ordered them to 'charge the enemy,' which they promptly did."

12 Colonel Charles Devens of the Fifteenth Massachusetts said in his report: "It was impossible longer to resist, and I should have had no doubt, if we had been contending with the troops of a foreign nation, in justice to the lives of men, it would have been our duty to surrender; but it was impossible to do this to rebels and traitors." (*O.R.,* V, 311.)

13 Dwight, p. 122.

CHAPTER 7

1 A portion of these losses was attributed largely to Southern marksmanship. A few days afterward the Wheeling *Intelligencer,* in reporting that a "dozen noted Kentucky shots" had offered their services to the Union,

said: "It is thought that out of this offer and its acceptance will grow a fine corps of men used to border life and good shooting, whose business it will be to harass the enemy by picking off his officers. It is evident that the Rebels at Ball's Bluff had numbers of sharpshooters, and that Colonel Baker and other officers were shot down by them."

2 General Stone was arrested and placed in Fort Lafayette. It was understood by General in Chief H. W. Halleck that this was done "by the orders of the President." (*O.R.*, V, 344.) Later the prisoner was transferred to Fort Hamilton in New York Harbor. On August 16, 1862, after 189 days of confinement, he was released. During this period, he revealed, he never once was informed of the charges against him.

But the man on the street and the soldier in the ranks took no notice of the fact that the over-all command of the Federal forces involved in this disaster rested with Stone at Edwards Ferry, if such was the case. The more astute and discerning, it would seem, thought in terms of Baker, the officer who had led the troops to the crest of Ball's Bluff. Observed one of them: "The violation of every rule and maxim of war, the exaction of the extreme penalty therefor. Such is the summing up of the massacre near Leesburg. Does it awaken you to the fact that politicians are not generals?" (Dwight, p. 120.) And again: "There does not seem to be a single redeeming feature in the whole business. They went on a fool's errand— went without means, and then persisted in their folly after it became clear." A Rebel officer, speaking to a Federal burial party sent out from Harrison's Island under flag of truce the day following the battle, put it more bluntly: "The officer who brought you here ought to be hung."

3 Dwight, p. 118.
4 *History of the Battle of Ball's Bluff* (Leesburg, Virginia, The Washingtonian Print, 1900), by Colonel E. V. White.
5 Throughout the war White carried at all times an early-model Colt revolver captured from a Yankee lieutenant at Ball's Bluff and a knife equipped with a blade, spoon, and fork. These now are in the possession of his granddaughter, Miss Elizabeth White, at Leesburg, Virginia.
6 Letter of Confederate Congressman A. R. Boteler to Secretary of State R. M. T. Hunter, dated Charles Town, Virginia, October 24, 1861.
7 *Report of the Joint Committee on the Conduct of the War*, I, 6.
8 *O.R.*, V, 937.
9 Dwight, p. 159.
10 Wheeling *Intelligencer*, November 24, 1861.

CHAPTER 8

1 Norton, p. 34.
2 Oliver Willcox Norton of the Eighty-third Pennsylvania Volunteers, who was stationed around Washington during the winter of '61-'62, wrote his sister a letter on February 21 in which he said: ". . . today's Press says that they [the Confederates] are leaving Centreville and Manassas to protect Richmond. If this is true, we may be following them up in a very short time and completely whip them by the middle of March. Things certainly look brighter every day . . . All the regiments in the vicinity have the

same orders, and last night the cook-fires on all the hills in sight were spluttering in the rain all night, cooking the rations." (Norton, p. 52.)

3 This ravine now has been officially identified, largely through the efforts and initiative of Frank B. Sarles, Jr., formerly park historian at the Manassas National Battlefield Park. The spot where the graves were found is three tenths of a mile south of Sudley Church, a short distance east of the Sudley road, and just north of the wartime Newman house, now, in 1956, the Lindsay home.

Eyewitnesses at the exhumings testified that the body of Major Ballou was burned thirty or forty yards downstream from the graves, in an area marked by "large pines and oaks." Trees of these species still are there, easily distinguished from the smaller pines and cedars in the surrounding fields.

4 This girl is mentioned in virtually all accounts of the exhumings, including *Sabres and Spurs* (privately printed, 1876), by the Reverend Frederic Denison, referred to hereafter as Denison; Moore's *The Rebellion Record* (New York, G. P. Putnam, 1863), IV, 343, Document 104; *The Second Rhode Island Regiment: A Narrative of Military Operations* (Providence, Rhode Island, Valpey, Angell and Company, 1875), by Augustus Woodbury; and in the testimony before the congressional committee.

5 The exhuming of these bodies came at a time when charges and countercharges about the atrocities committed by soldiers of both armies were rampant. One accusation made against the North was that prisoners captured during the battle along Bull Run were handcuffed and shackled. Many years later the widow of a Confederate veteran, Mrs. E. A. Meriwether of St. Louis, Missouri, referring to an article on the subject, wrote: "Some years ago my husband's cousin, Captain Robert Walker Lewis of Albemarle, Virginia, wrote to him of being in that First Manassas battle, and that he and his men captured a wagon loaded with handcuffs and shackles. Some of the Union prisoners captured at the same time stated that these instruments were intended to be used on the Rebels they expected to make prisoners, and intended to march them into Washington in that shackled condition. I now have hanging in my hall one of these shackles. It is made of two strong iron rings, with lock and key, to be fastened on the ankles. These rings are fastened together by a strong iron chain 17 inches long." (*Confederate Veteran*, XIV, 304.)

George C. Bryson, who took part in the battle, wrote for public print that he saw handcuffs in barrels on "the slope of the hill between the Henry house and the spring." (*Ibid.*)

6 In a letter in which he tried to impress Confederate Secretary of War Leroy Pope Walker with the fact that he had stayed behind to nurse the wounded after the rout along Bull Run, John F. Mines, chaplain of the Second Maine Volunteer Regiment, who was taken prisoner, said: "At Manassas I sought to comfort the wounded and dying. I soothed the last hours of Major Ballou." (*O.R.*, Series 2, II, 1509.)

7 In his testimony April 2 before the Joint Committee on the Conduct of the War, shortly after his return from the grave-hunting expedition, Chaplain Frederic Denison said: "In regard to the mistaking of the body of

Major Ballou for that of Colonel Slocum by the Georgians, it resulted from this, I have no doubt: Colonel Slocum was buried in an oblong box—a square box; Major Ballou was buried in a coffin, or a box which was coffin-shaped; and it is supposed—of course we know nothing about that—that they had taken the body of Major Ballou. Rumor accordingly stated that they had taken the body of Colonel Slocum. But his body was found. It was the body of Major Ballou that they took."

8 During the congressional investigation of the incident Governor Sprague was asked whether he was satisfied Tower and the other men in this grave were intentionally buried face downward. He replied: "Undoubtedly! Beyond all controversy! It was done as a mark of indignity."

He had a somewhat similar reply when asked about the object of the Georgians in digging up what they thought was Slocum's body: "Sheer brutality, and nothing else. They did it on account of his courage and chivalry in forcing his regiment fearlessly and bravely upon them. He destroyed about one-half of that Georgia regiment, which was made up of their best citizens."

When the author visited the scene of these exhumings, he was accompanied by a veteran of World War II who had fought against the Japs in the Pacific. Thoroughly acquainted with the history connected with the Bull Run battlefield, he commented voluntarily as we drove away: "Such horror stories as this concerning Slocum and Ballou happen pretty often in war these days. We called it souvenir hunting. Whenever a Jap fell, there was a race to see who got there first. Many a time I've run my hand in a dead man's pocket for souvenirs and brought it out covered with blood. We didn't look upon it as bad. We knew somebody else would rifle his pockets if we didn't. And what we found there certainly wasn't going to do him any more good."

Looting of bodies seems to have been a common practice throughout the Civil War. Reporter Edwin S. Barrett, who covered the battle of Bull Run from the top of a persimmon tree (*The Civil War in Song and Story* (privately printed, 1889), p. 256) recalled: "I also saw one of our soldiers take $60 from the body of a dead Georgian, and their knives and revolvers were appropriated in the same way. This I looked upon as legitimate plunder for the soldiers, but as a citizen I forbore to take anything from the field."

9 Denison, p. 51.

CHAPTER 9

1 *Letters Written During the Civil War*, by Charles Fessenden Morse (privately printed, 1898), referred to hereafter as Morse.

2 Elwood, p. 101.

3 Charles D. Rhodes in *The Photographic History of the Civil War* (New York, The Review of Reviews Company, 1911), IV, 170.

4 *O.R.*, V, 1090. Johnston to President Davis, March 5, 1862. By this letter Johnston became the first high-ranking Confederate officer to cite a threat that later became serious—the tendency of the soldiers in the regular ranks to desert and join the independent bands. Some of the Partisan leaders,

Mosby and White particularly, refused to accept deserters on their rolls. But the danger of sapping the strength of the main armies remained, and the Confederate War Department finally took what it thought would be remedial action. In General Orders Number 53, issued at Richmond July 31, 1862, it decreed: "Persons who are liable to conscription under the act of April 16, 1862, will not be taken to serve as Partisan Rangers. Such as may be engaged for that branch of service must be over 35 years of age." (*Ibid.*, Series 4, II, 26.) But this order was notoriously disobeyed. Most of the Ranger outfits boasted of the fighting ability of their more youthful members, and Mosby in later years gave the younger members of his command major credit for his success.

5 *Ibid.*, LI, Pt. II, 334.

6 *Ibid.*, V, 898.

7 William Elsey Connelley, who made perhaps the greatest contribution to Quantrill's biography (*Quantrill and the Border Wars* (Cedar Rapids, Iowa, The Torch Press, 1910)), says the outlaw voluntarily "imposed himself on the South." He describes his subject as "a fiend wasteful and reckless of human life," and adds: "Somewhere of old his ancestors ate the sour grapes which set his teeth on edge . . . Because of him, widows wailed, orphans cried, maidens wept, as they lifted the lifeless forms of loved ones from bloody fields and bore them reeking to untimely graves." Perhaps the greatest condemnation of Quantrill lies in the charge that on occasion he turned on his own men to protect himself.

General Halleck, commanding the Department of the Mississippi early in the war, issued an order outlawing Quantrill and his band. So did General Totten, in charge of Jefferson City, Missouri.

Quantrill once made a trip to Richmond to confer with the Confederate authorities. It was his hope to enlist a regiment under the Partisan Ranger Act so that he could serve as its colonel. But the officials in power at the Rebel capital wanted no part of him. The plight of the South was desperate, yet they looked upon the future as not so hopeless that they must give license to an outlaw.

8 Dwight, p. 221.

9 *Ibid.*

10 Henry Kyd Douglas, who served on Jackson's staff, was an eyewitness to this affair and tells about it in his book, *I Rode with Stonewall* (Chapel Hill, North Carolina, University of North Carolina Press, 1940), p. 40. Referred to hereafter as Douglas. He said the horse was wounded in the stomach during a fight on a bridge, but carried its master to safety before sinking to the ground. Ashby bent over the animal and stroked its mane until it died. "Thus," concluded Douglas, "the most splendid horseman I ever knew lost the most beautiful war-horse I ever saw."

11 *O.R.*, XII, Pt. III, 50, 52.

12 *Ibid.*, p. 75.

13 *A Rebel Cavalryman* (Chicago, W. B. Conkey Company, 1899), by John N. Opie, p. 234. This author states: "When a Rebel was captured, his furlough or pass was taken from him, and also his outer garments. A soldier was then found who resembled him in size, age and general appear-

ance. The Rebel's uniform, from hat to boots, was put upon this man, who assumed the name of the prisoner, and the Federal left camp, a soldier of the Confederacy."

14 *The Civil War in Song and Story* (New York, P. F. Collier, 1882), by Frank Moore, p. 45. Moore visited Carpenter and spent a few hours with him after the latter was wounded in an affair with a woman at Cumberland.
15 Wheeling *Intelligencer*, July 10, 1862.
16 *O.R.*, LI, Pt. I, 591.
17 *Ibid.*, XII, Pt. III, 131.
18 *Ibid.*, p. 136.
19 Richmond *Dispatch*, May 8, 1862.
20 Wheeling *Intelligencer*, May 21, 1862.
21 *O.R.*, LI, Pt. I, 617.
22 *Ibid.*, XII, Pt. III, 169.
23 *Ibid.*, p. 175.
24 *Ibid.*, p. 193.
25 *Ibid.*, p. 259.
26 *Ibid.*, Series 2, IV, 506.
27 Wheeling *Intelligencer*, June 2, 1862.
28 *The Comanches* (Baltimore, Kelly, Piet and Company, 1871), by Frank M. Myers, pp. 45, 71.
29 *O.R.*, XII, Pt. I, 32.
30 Douglas, p. 74.
31 *Ibid.*, p. 79.
32 Henry Kyd Douglas says this was the same horse Stonewall was riding at the time he was wounded in the hand at First Bull Run. Regardless of its identity, its description varied widely among contemporary writers. Some confused it with the white horse shot under Ashby at Mount Jackson. Others pictured it as a black, a bay, or a sorrel.
33 The veterans who took part in this skirmish became confused in their memory in later years concerning the exact type of weather at the time of Ashby's death. The prevailing opinion seems to have been that it was rainy and foggy, the tail end of the storm that had continued for days.
34 *The Memoirs of General Turner Ashby and His Compeers* (Baltimore, Selby and Dulaney, 1867), by the Reverend James B. Avirett. This author quotes Major Goldsborough of the First Maryland Infantry, who took part in the battle and, during a portion of the day, was near Ashby, under whom he had served at Point of Rocks. According to Goldsborough, "no dying words issued from his (Ashby's) lips, and the last command he was heard to give was, 'Forward, my brave men!' "
35 From the recollections of James Baumgardner, Jr., of Staunton, Virginia, published in the *Confederate Veteran*, XXIII, 72.
36 *Ibid.*
37 *Recollections of a Maryland Confederate Soldier and Staff Officer* (Baltimore, Williams and Wilkins Company, 1914), by McHenry Howard, p. 119.
38 *Battles and Leaders* (New York, The Century Company, 1887), II, 292.

1 One of the most natural weapons used against the Partisans was to call them by names that placed them in disrepute. Bushwhacker and guerrilla were the terms most generally employed for this purpose. Throughout the war any small group of the enemy, whether near the Federal lines or off in some isolated area, promptly were tagged either as bushwhackers or guerrillas, and this was taken by the friendly public to mean that they were operating outside the realm of civilized warfare. In many cases this was an injustice, for the men referred to were as properly enrolled in the military service of the Confederate States as were the members of the regular army.

2 *O.R.*, Series 2, IV, 97.

3 *Ibid.*, Series 2, III, 885.

4 *Ibid.*, Series 4, II, 45.

5 *Ibid.*, Series 2, IV, 49.

6 *Ibid.*, Series 2, p. 334.

7 *Ibid.*, Series 2, p. 47.

8 *Ibid.*, Series 2, p. 86.

9 *Ibid.*, LI, Pt. II, 601.

10 *Ibid.*, Series 2, IV, 394.

11 Wheeling *Intelligencer,* June 6, 1864.

12 *O.R.*, Series 2, IV, 422.

13 *Ibid.*, Series 2, p. 907.

14 *Ibid.*, Series 2, p. 601.

15 Parkersburg, W. Va., *Gazette,* June 5, 1862.

16 *O.R.*, Series 2, IV, 913.

17 *Ibid.*, Series 2, p. 621.

18 *O.R.*, Series 3, II, 301.

19 In compiling this volume about guerrilla warfare, the author has tried diligently to distinguish in meaning between the term guerrilla and other terms closely allied with it in usage. The line of demarcation is delicate.

   Webster's Dictionary describes a guerrilla as "one who carries on, or assists in, an irregular war, or engages in irregular, though often legitimate, warfare in connection with a regular war; especially a member of an independent band engaged in predatory excursions in wartime." This definition would apply correctly to any of the men who fought on detached duty during the war.

   Here are other definitions applicable to the independents:

   Irregular: "not belonging to the regular army organization but raised for a special purpose."

   Partisan: "a member of a body of detached light troops."

   Ranger: "one of a body of mounted troops who range over a region."

   Raider: "one who participates in a hostile or predatory incursion."

   Bushwhacker: "one accustomed to beat about through bushes. Hence, a guerrilla; originally, as used by the Federal troops, a Confederate guerrilla in the Civil War."

   Any of these terms were acceptable to the independents except the last.

Mosby, for example, was willing to be classified as a guerrilla. He wrote after the war: "Although I have never adopted it, I have never resented as an insult the term 'guerrilla' when applied to me." So he had no reaction when his men were thus called. But he had violent resentment if they were termed bushwhackers. That word to him seemed to connote murder, to arouse visions of a stealthy enemy lurking under cover to fire a death-dealing charge on the approach of some unsuspecting victim. "The bush-whackers had the long guns, my men the short ones," Mosby explained in driving home the point that his Rangers fought hand to hand rather than as pot-shotters.

The most evident difference between a bushwhacker, accepted as con-trary to the rules of legitimate warfare, and the other independents seemed to lie in their individual methods of operation. A bushwhacker band had about it little if any organization and fought irrespective of the operations of the regular army. The independents, rangers, or irregulars, on the other hand, were properly enrolled in the Confederate service and were or-ganized to some degree, at times carrying on their activities in close co-operation with the regular army.

This was the basic difference between legitimate warfare and illegitimate warfare as applied to irregular service eventually by both governments. Even as Dr. Lieber was preparing his letter giving this interpretation, a Confederate aide-de-camp at Richmond was writing a group of Gloucester County citizens: "The advantage of such a corps (Partisan) is that the members are regularly in service and entitled to be treated as prisoners of war and have the benefit of exchange, which is not the case with un-organized volunteers." (*O.R.*, Series 2, IV, 842.)

20 *Ibid.*, Series 2, p. 739.
21 *Ibid.*, Series 2, V, 289, 326.

CHAPTER 11

1 See *Ranger Mosby*, by Virgil Carrington Jones (University of North Caro-lina Press, 1944) for the career of John Singleton Mosby.
2 *Lee's Lieutenants* (New York, Charles Scribner's Sons, 1942), by Douglas Southall Freeman, I, 279.
3 Richmond *Dispatch*, June 25, 1862.
4 Baltimore *American*, June 30, 1862.
5 *The Comanches*, p. 80.
6 *O.R.*, XII, Pt. III, 474.
7 Officers as well as privates had been convinced McClellan was the man who would lead the Union army to victory. On March 17, 1862, General George A. Custer wrote his parents from Fairfax, Virginia: "I have more confidence in General McClellan than in any man living. I would forsake everything and follow him to the ends of the earth. I would lay down my life for him . . . Every officer and private worships him. I would fight anyone who would say a word against him." (*The Custer Story* (New York, The Devin-Adair Company, 1950), by Marguerite Merington, p. 27.)
8 *O.R.*, XII, Pt. II, 51.
9 *Ibid.*, p. 52.

10 *Ibid.*, Pt. III, p. 487.

11 *Ibid.*, p. 490.

12 *Three Years in the Federal Cavalry* (New York, R. H. Ferguson and Company, 1874), by Captain Willard Glazier, p. 73.

13 R. H. Ferguson, who was a member of the Harris Light Cavalry, told in a book published in 1892 of his imprisonment at Andersonville Prison and of meeting while there the Methodist enthusiast, Boston Corbett, of the Sixteenth New York, whom he had known at Dismounted Camp at Washington, D.C., and who later killed the assassin, John Wilkes Booth. Corbett had been sent to Andersonville following his capture by Mosby, and he related the experience to Ferguson, who recorded that "I also gave him the account of my capture of Mosby, assisted by Gallagher, of Company E, Second New York Cavalry, at Beaver Dam Station, in July, 1862." (See *History of the Ninth New York Cavalry 1861-1865* (New York, D. Appleton and Company, 1892), by Noble D. Preston, p. 616.)

14 This letter later was deposited in the Confederate Museum at Richmond. There also was placed the volume of Napoleon's *Maxims* Stuart had sent Jackson. It was found in Stonewall's haversack after his death.

15 *The Rebellion Record,* Document 66, p. 362.

16 Mosby was married to Pauline Clarke, daughter of Beverly J. Clarke of Franklin, Kentucky, member of Congress and later minister to Guatemala, on December 30, 1857.

17 The Federals appear to have been completely baffled about Mosby's identity. When the adjutant general's office at Washington released the names of officers involved in this exchange, he was listed as "aide to General "Stevens" instead of Stuart. *O.R.,* Series 2, Pt. IV, p. 442.

18 Wheeling *Intelligencer,* May 17, 1862.

19 *Ibid.,* July 29, 1862.

20 *Ibid.,* July 21, 1862.

21 *Ibid.,* July 30, 1862.

22 Morse, p. 74.

23 Dwight, p. 244.

24 Gilmor, p. 53.

25 *O.R.,* XII, Pt. III, 939.

26 *Ibid.,* LI, Pt. II, 609.

27 *Ibid.,* Series 4, IV, 303.

28 *Ibid.,* XII, Pt. III, 574.

29 *Ibid.,* p. 653.

30 *Ibid.,* LI, Pt. I, 764.

31 The letter in which the Leesburg women expressed their thanks to White for "delivering us from our oppressions and restoring us again to our beloved Confederacy" now hangs framed in the home of his granddaughter, Miss Elizabeth White, near Leesburg.

32 *O.R.,* LI, Pt. I, 766.

33 *Ibid.,* XII, Pt. III, 738.

34 *Ibid.,* LI, Pt. I, 772.

35 *Ibid.,* XII, Pt. II, 549.

36 *Ibid.,* p. 781.

37 This account is taken from *The Comanches*. Its author, Captain Frank Myers, was first assistant to White. Before it was published in 1871, its statements were carefully checked for accuracy by White himself and by other officers of his command.

38 Dwight, p. 287.

39 One soldier who took part in the Seven Days battles wrote his sister of the fall-back from Richmond: "I would not, if I could, tell you how we have suffered on this march. Eating raw beef without salt and drinking water from mud holes were done more than once. I have marched 46 miles on nothing but raw beef and ditch water, and yet I have held out to the end. Now I am worn out, and can neither write nor do anything else until I am some rested." (Norton, p. 118.)

40 *O.R.*, XIX, Pt. II, 219.

41 For a list of the Partisan Ranger commands existing at this time under authority of the resolution of the Confederate House of Representatives, see *O.R.*, Series 4, II, 82.

42 Gilmor, p. 57.

43 Miss Elizabeth White of Leesburg, Virginia.

CHAPTER 12

1 For an account of the feat of logistics involved in the movement of these troops, see Summers, p. 162.

2 Copied from *Boots and Saddles* (Harrisburg, Pennsylvania, Patriot Publishing Company, 1879), a history of the First New York Cavalry, written some years after the war by James H. Stevenson and referred to hereafter as Stevenson.

CHAPTER 13

1 *O.R.*, XIX, Pt. II, 24.

2 According to the records of the Adjutant General's Office, U.S.A., no charges were filed against the officers of Company B. Captain Hite and Lieutenant Baer resigned in 1864, and Lieutenant Cole, by then a captain, was mustered out at the end of his term of service the same year. (*Ibid.*, XII, Pt. II, 21.)

3 Wheeling *Intelligencer*.

4 The shortage of winter clothing in the Southern army had begun to be felt at this time to such a degree that a clamor against it already was beginning to be heard in Federal circles. Brigadier General John W. Geary, writing to the Twelfth Army Corps assistant adjutant general about a fight he had had with some of White's guerrillas led by Captain R. B. Grubb, commented: "The Rebel captain and some of his men were clothed in our uniform, a growing practice, so reprehensible that it should meet with condign punishment, as the deception engendered is always apt to cost lives and disasters." (*O.R.*, XIX, Pt. II, 100.)

In the spring of '63 orders were issued that any officer or soldier of the Confederate States found wearing any article of clothing or accouterments belonging to the Federal uniform should be treated as a spy. The South promptly replied in general orders that such items were considered legitimate objects of capture under the rules of war, to be used by the captors at their pleasure for the equipment of their troops, and that steps would be taken to repress any attempt to treat them as spies. (*Ibid.*, Series 2, V, 733.)

5   Taken from "Border Raids into Pennsylvania During the Civil War," a thesis prepared by J. Melchior Sheads of Gettysburg, Pennsylvania, and submitted in partial fulfillment of his history requirements at Gettysburg College. This was placed at the use of the author through the kindness of Dr. Frederick Tilberg, veteran historian of the National Park Service.

6   *O.R.*, XIX, Pt. I, 13.

7   *Ibid.*, pp. 14, 16.

8   *Ibid.*, Pt. II, p. 485.

9   *Ibid.*, p. 675.

10 *Reminiscences of General Herman Haupt*, p. 254.

11 *O.R.*, Series 3, II, p. 944.

12 *Ibid.*, Series 2, III, p. 11.

13 *Ibid.*, Series 2, p. 15.

14 *Ibid.*, XIX, Pt. II, 158.

15 *Ibid.*, p. 159.

16 *Ibid.*, p. 587.

17 *History of the Sixth New York Cavalry* (Worcester, Massachusetts, The Blanchard Press, 1908).

18 References to Redmond Burke are taken from *O.R.*, vols. V, XI, XII, and XXI; *Jeb Stuart* (New York, Charles Scribner's Sons, 1930), by John W. Thomason, p. 348; *War Years with Jeb Stuart* (New York, Charles Scribner's Sons, 1945), by W. W. Blackford, p. 91; and *War Letters of John Chipman Gray* (Boston, Houghton Mifflin Company, 1927), referred to hereafter as Gray, p. 32.

19 Gray, p. 39.

20 For a most gruesome description of the horrors of the battle of Fredericksburg, consult *Four Brothers in Blue* (Washington, Press of Gibson Brothers, Inc., 1913), by Captain Robert G. Carter.

21 New York *Herald*, September 29, 1862.

22 *Army Life in Virginia* (Burlington, Vermont, Free Press Association, 1895), a compilation of letters written to the Burlington, Vermont, *Free Press* by its junior editor, George Grenville Benedict, p. 98. Referred to hereafter as Benedict.

23 Wheeling *Intelligencer*, December 16, 1862.

24 *O.R.*, XXI, 1076.

25 *The Comanches*, p. 148.

26 Oddly enough, just at the time Mosby was beginning the independent operations that were to bring renown, esteem, and respect to this arm of the service, Secretary of War Seddon was penning his annual message to President Davis in which he said "the policy of organizing corps of Partisan Rangers has not been approved by experience." He added that they were not useful as guerrillas and that their independence and peculiar rewards for capture induced "much license and many irregularities." They excited

more odium and did more damage to friends than to enemies, he alleged, and added that the War Department, while reluctant to disband them, avoided raising any more of them. (*O.R.*, Series 4, II, 289.)

PART TWO

CHAPTER 1

1 *O.R.*, Series 4, II, 336.
2 *Ibid.*, XXI, 947.
3 *The National Cyclopædia of American Biography* (New York, J. T. White and Company, 1893-, IV, 218) says that the order issued by Milroy levying damages against citizens, on threat of death if they did not pay, "at once put an effective end to the guerrilla warfare." The record proves this assertion to be untrue. Guerrilla warfare continued to thrive unabated, in West Virginia and elsewhere, and, if anything, was conducted with greater zeal after Milroy announced his harsh policy.
4 In his message to the Confederate Congress, Jefferson Davis said of Milroy: "Recently I have received apparently authentic intelligence of another general by the name of Milroy, who has issued orders in Western Virginia for the payment of money to him by the inhabitants, accompanied by the most savage threats of shooting every recusant, besides burning his house, and threatening similar atrocities against any of our citizens who shall fail to betray their country by giving him prompt notice of the approach of any of our forces, and this subject has also been submitted to the superior military authorities of the United States with but faint hope that they will evince any disapprobation of the act." (*O.R.*, Series 4, II, 345.)
   Throughout the war, Milroy's men suffered from the retaliation of the Southerners. The Indiana general's name was anathema in Dixie and brought quick reaction. His soldiers, officers and privates alike, when captured, were given special treatment. In Libby Prison at Richmond, in the fall of '63, for instance, inmates with money, except those of Milroy's command, were permitted to supplement their starvation diet by sending someone to purchase items from the markets of the city. (*Ibid.*, Series 2, VI, 302.)
5 McDonald, p. 168.
6 *Reminiscences of the Civil War* (privately printed, 1911), by Emma Cassandra Riely Macon and Reuben Conway Macon, p. 67.
7 *A History of the Laurel Brigade* (privately printed, 1907), by Captain William N. McDonald.
8 McDonald, p. 127.
9 *O.R.*, XXVII, Pt. II, 41.
10 Richmond *Dispatch*, January 10, 1863.
11 *Record of the 116th Regiment Ohio Infantry Volunteers in the War of the Rebellion* (Sandusky, Ohio, I. F. Mack and Brother, 1884), by Thomas Francis Wildes, referred to hereafter as Wildes, p. 33.

12   *Ibid.,* p. 42.

13   *Ibid.,* p. 44.

14   *O.R.,* XXV, Pt. II, 642, 649.

15   Wheeling *Intelligencer,* January 31, 1863.

16   *O.R.,* XXV, Pt. II, 49.

17   *Diary of Catherine Barbara Broun* (unpublished). This diary is now in the possession of Miss Nannie Fred of Middleburg, Virginia. It was called to the attention of the author through the kind thoughtfulness of Mr. and Mrs. Henry B. Weaver of Aldie, Virginia, two history-conscious friends whose ears remain tuned for hidden lore that will help retell the war.

18   Throughout his career in the war Milroy lacked the confidence of his superior officers. He soon was shackled with a reputation as a stampeder. (*O.R.,* XXV, Pt. II, 127.) When he wired while at Winchester that a large cavalry force was collecting in front of him, Hooker scoffed at the report confidently, and Halleck messaged Schenck at Baltimore: "General Milroy seems to be a very unreliable man, and hardly fit for such a position. Can you not make a better position for him?"

Milroy wanted to reopen the railroad from Harpers Ferry to Winchester and to make the latter place a permanent base of supplies and operations for an advance up the Valley, but Halleck described the plan as contrary to every military rule, explaining that to move up the Shenandoah while the main army was near Fredericksburg would be "to repeat the same old error of distant parallel lines, with the enemy between them, ready to concentrate upon and crush our divided forces."

19   *Ibid.,* p. 64.

20   *Ibid.*

21   Milroy's animosity was reciprocated by B. & O. officials. They constantly represented to Washington that the railroad was unsafe under Milroy's protection and clamored for a more competent officer at Winchester.

22   *Ibid.,* p. 82.

23   *Ibid.,* p. 108.

CHAPTER 2

1   There seems to be some discrepancy in the records as to Stoughton's age. The confusion is noticeable in General Cullum's *Biographical Register of the Officers and Graduates of the U.S. Military Academy* (New York, J. Miller, 1879), II, 327, recognized as an authoritative publication. It lists Stoughton as "born in Vermont in 1841" and then says he "died December 25, 1868, at Boston, Mass., aged 31," which would have fixed the year of his birth as 1837. The muster roll records in the U. S. Department of Archives list him as twenty-three on September 21, 1861. But the Baltimore *American* of March 11, 1863, says: "General Stoughton . . . is the youngest general in the service, being but 21 years of age."

2   Reference made to Stoughton by Brigadier General W. T. H. Brooks in his report on the siege of Yorktown in *O.R.,* XI, Pt. I, 373. Stoughton was graduated from West Point in 1859, finishing seventeenth in a class of twenty-two. It was a somewhat undistinguished group. Of his classmates,

perhaps Joseph Wheeler, Jr., who finished nineteenth and later became a lieutenant general in the Confederate army, was the most outstanding. After graduating, Stoughton served as a second lieutenant in the Fourth U. S. Infantry, resigning in the spring of '61.

3   Stoughton had only one blur on his military record up to the time he went to Fairfax. In January, '62, he was placed under arrest and confined to his camp after he was found guilty of making a trip to Washington, D.C., without a pass, a violation of orders. Then a colonel in the Fourth Vermont, Smith's division, he was charged with disobedience of orders and tried by court-martial. He was ultimately sentenced to be privately reprimanded by his division commander after being found guilty of neglect of duty. Stoughton appealed the finding of the court on the ground that he had never been faced with this modified charge and therefore had had no opportunity to defend himself, but he was overruled.

4   In the late summer of '62 Stoughton went home on leave of absence suffering from general debility as a result of battle fatigue and exposure. Before his return in early November he was assigned to the governor of Vermont to assist in organizing and drilling state militia.

5   *O.R.*, LI, Pt. I, 975.

6   This home still stands, now as the Episcopal rectory, occupied by the Reverend Raymond W. Davis, rector of the Truro Church. Around the turn of the century it was enlarged and the part to the right of the porch, facing the building, was added. During the war it was abandoned by the Gunnell family, which moved first to Fauquier County and then took up residence in Waco, Texas.

7   The drunkenness of Provost Marshal O'Connor was later denied by Moses Sweetser, the Union sutler at Fairfax, in a letter published in the Washington *Star* of March 18, 1863.

8   *Spies, Traitors and Conspirators of the Late Civil War* (Philadelphia, John E. Potter and Company, 1894), by General Lafayette C. Baker, p. 239. Referred to hereafter as Baker.

9   From the report of Stoughton's capture, published in the Washington *Star* of March 10, 1863.

10   *O.R.*, XXV, Pt. II, 114.

11   Statement of Moses Sweetser, in a letter published in the Washington *Star* of March 18, 1863.

12   *History of the United States Secret Service* (privately printed, 1867), by General Lafayette C. Baker, p. 170.

13   *History of the 18th Regiment of Cavalry, Pennsylvania Volunteers, 1862-1865* (New York, privately printed, 1909).

14   Baker, p. 173.

15   *O.R.*, XXV, Pt. I, 5.

16   Washington *Star*, March 2, 1863.

17   *O.R.*, XXV, Pt. II, 114. The identity of this spy apparently was never known. It may have been Mosby, although it is likely that, had it been, some mention would have been made in his later writings on his operations. It also may have been a deserter from Wyndham's cavalry, James F. (Big Yankee) Ames, who quit the Union ranks because of Lincoln's Emancipa-

tion Proclamation. Mosby leaned heavily upon him for intelligence concerning the Federal troops in and around Fairfax.

18 *The Military Telegraph During the Civil War* (Chicago, Jansen, McClurg and Company, 1882), by William B. Plum, I, 360.

19 The Washington *Star*, March 16, 1863. According to *Army Life in Virginia*, a compilation of the letters of George Grenville Benedict, this letter later led to an interesting dispute. In a communication to the New York *Times* the Reverend George B. Spaulding of Vergennes, Vermont, said that Stoughton's capture had been predicted in a letter from Fairfax Court House. Stoughton's uncle, the Honorable E. W. Stoughton of New York, afterward United States Minister to Russia, avowing disbelief in the statement, offered to give 250 dollars to the New England Soldiers' Relief Association for the name and address of any person who had received a letter containing such a prediction. These were furnished him and he paid the sum to the Association.

20 This was the figure used by Mosby in his account of the affair. (*O.R.*, XXV, Pt. I, 1121.) The Federal report, prepared by Colonel Robert Johnstone, commanding the cavalry at Fairfax Court House, makes no mention of the number in the group gathered at the mill.

21 Washington *Star*, March 2, 1863.

22 Mosby had planned to enter the town of Fairfax around midnight, in which case he would have caught Stoughton's party in full sway. But the column of raiders got separated in the dark, causing valuable time to be lost before it got back together. This separation of the Partisans took place between Chantilly and the point where they crossed the highway between Fairfax and Centreville. They had started from Dover beyond Aldie in the late afternoon, swung to the west before reaching Chantilly, on a circuit that took them through the picket line and brought them eventually to the road between the Court House and Fairfax Station. Along the way they encountered one vedette and captured him without creating a disturbance.

23 This version of the conversation between Mosby and Stoughton in the latter's bedroom that night was checked for accuracy by the guerrilla leader himself in later years and is given here as he approved it.

24 Stoughton and Confederate General Fitzhugh Lee, nephew of General Robert E. Lee, had attended West Point Military Academy at the same time, although as members of different classes.

25 These prisoners were turned over to Fitz Lee at Warrenton and by him forwarded to Richmond, which they reached at 7:30 P.M. March 11. When they arrived at the military prison there, a roll of them was called and four were found missing. These were Stoughton, Captain Barker, Private B. F. Pratt, and Baron Wardener. Upon inquiry it was learned they had been put up at the Ballard Hotel, through special disposition by Fitz Lee as a favor to his friend of West Point days, and were there under guard. Prison rules allowed no such favoritism, so request was sent for them to be transferred behind bars with the other prisoners. When this failed to get results, Captain T. P. Turner, commanding at the prison, went to the hotel himself shortly after midnight and, following a parley of

nearly an hour, succeeded in bringing the quartet back with him. (*O.R.,* Series 2, V, 847.)

26 The gist of Colonel Johnstone's cries that night is gathered from *The Military Telegraph During the Civil War,* p. 360.

27 The nature of this outhouse is variously described, depending upon the allegiance of the author. Some say it was a privy, while others identify it as a stable. Whichever it was, it is supposed to have stood behind the present Walter Oliver home.

28 *O.R.,* XXV, Pt. I, 43.

29 *History of the United States Secret Service.*

30 Washington *Star,* March 18, 1863.

31 No record of any reply to this request has been found. But Mosby later wrote in his memoirs that he had no communication with anyone in Fairfax prior to the raid. During or immediately after the war he told Author John Esten Cooke, close friend of Antonia, that she had not supplied him with information concerning the Union forces in Fairfax, that he gained his knowledge through his own scouts. This is in direct contradiction to the statement allegedly made to the Secret Service by the girl, and may have been a continued effort on the Ranger leader's part to cover up for her.

Details of the raid are confused in many respects. Mrs. John S. Barbour, present resident of Fairfax, commented on this once to Colonel Mosby and asked which version was correct. An old man at the time, he replied, "Take your pick."

32 Antonia was buried in Oak Hill Cemetery in Georgetown, now a part of Washington, D.C. She was survived by one son, Joseph E. Willard, one-time lieutenant governor of Virginia and from 1913 to 1921 American Minister to Spain. A granddaughter, Belle Willard, is the widow of Kermit Roosevelt, son of President Theodore Roosevelt.

33 Editor George Grenville Benedict, in a footnote to his collection of letters compiled under the title *Army Life in Virginia,* says that Stoughton's appointment as brigadier general was withdrawn by President Lincoln. His name was sent up for a brigadiership on November 5, 1862, and expired by constitutional limitation when it failed to receive confirmation before the 37th Congress adjourned on March 3, 1863, less than a week before his capture. It could have been presented again when the next Congress convened the following December, but it is more than likely that Stoughton returned to private life because he was aware that his promotion would never be confirmed in view of what had happened at Fairfax.

CHAPTER 3

1 *O.R.,* XXV, Pt. II, 656.

2 *Ibid.*

3 *Ibid.,* p. 660.

4 *Ibid.,* p. 689.

5 *The Baltimore and Ohio* (privately printed, 1951), by Carroll Bateman, p. 15.

6 The quotation is from General W. E. Jones' report of the expedition, as reproduced in *O.R.*, XXV, Pt. I, 120.

7 "Diary of Jasper Hawse," unpublished and made available to the author through the kindness of Mr. Lewis H. Riffles of Drexel Hill, Pennsylvania, and Colonel R. H. Hannum of Washington, D.C.

8 *O.R.*, XXV, Pt. II, 295.

9 *History of the Bucktails* (Philadelphia, Electric Printing Company, 1906), by O. R. Howard Thompson, p. 246.

10 Numerous stories about Union efforts to snare Mosby were circulated during and after the war. One of these came from Author John Esten Cooke, who served on Jeb Stuart's staff. It was included in an unfinished manuscript of his that came to light in recent years in letters of the Cooke family held by an antique dealer at Front Royal, Virginia, and called to the attention of the author by Miss Laura Virginia Hale, local historian.

Cooke recorded the story at his home at Millwood, Virginia, on May 28, 1866. According to this account, which the author said he would "vouch for," a Union cavalry detail riding along a road came upon a Negro woman standing in front of her cabin, and asked if anybody was inside. "Ain't nobody in dere but Mosby," she replied. That was all the blue-clad riders needed to know at the moment. They immediately fanned out and approached the cabin from all sides with drawn guns. Finally they burst into the little hut, but all they found inside was a Negro baby sucking his thumb in a cradle. "Where's Mosby?" they asked. "Dere he," said the woman, pointing to the child. "We sometime calls him Cunnel Mosby."

Cooke added: "The incident escaped the newspaper correspondents, and but for the present historian would be forever buried. I have rescued it from oblivion. I vouch for it. I knew the 'parties'—the mother of 'Colonel Mosby' (Black and Junion) was a servant in this establishment and, I will do her the justice to say, was a very worthless one."

11 *The Civil War Diary of General Josiah Gorgas* (University, Alabama, The University of Alabama Press, 1947), p. 158.

12 *O.R.*, XXV, Pt. II, 667.

13 *Ibid.*

14 Benedict.

15 *O.R.*, XXV, Pt. I, 1107.

16 *Confederate Veteran*, XIII, 211.

17 When organized, this command was identified officially as the Second Maryland Cavalry.

18 *The First New York (Lincoln) Cavalry* (New York, privately printed, 1902), by William H. Beach, p. 222. Referred to hereafter as Beach.

CHAPTER 4

1 *O.R.*, XXV, Pt. II, 499.

2 Beach, p. 272. This incident also is described by James H. Stevenson in *Boots and Saddles*, p. 218.

3 *O.R.*, LI, Pt. I, 1043.

4   Havens, later promoted to lieutenant, wrote an eyewitness account of the train raid at Catlett Station under the title "How Mosby Destroyed Our Train." This is included in a history of the Seventh Michigan Volunteer Cavalry compiled by William O. Lee.

5   *O.R.*, XVV, Pt. II, 172.

6   *Stuart's Cavalry in the Gettysburg Campaign* (New York, Moffat, Yard and Company, 1908), by John S. Mosby, p. 7. Other members of the command fixed the number at forty-eight.

7   *Historic Records of the Fifth New York Cavalry* (Albany, New York, J. Munsell, 1868), by the Reverend Louis N. Boudrye, p. 62.

8   Gilmor, p. 71.

9   Now Marshall in Fauquier County, Virginia.

10 *O.R.*, XXVII, Pt. II, 160.

11 At her husband's direction (this correspondence is included in a letter dated March 16, 1863, the original of which now is in the possession of the author), Mrs. Mosby had come up to northern Virginia in March. This she did after he had made arrangements for her to stay at the Hathaway home near the scene of his operations so he could slip in to see her at times. She was conveyed there in a buggy by an escort of Confederates in uniform, a courtesy of Jeb Stuart.

12 Reference to this incident is found in Mosby's own account of his operations, in the Washington *Star* of June 12, 1863; in Beach, p. 228; and in Stevenson, p. 180.

    Hathaway descendants in recent years have disputed the accuracy of the incident on the grounds that there was no tree near enough to the house for Mosby to have climbed to from a window. But this does not conform to the experience of the present owner of the home, Mr. Robert B. Young. When he moved there in the 1930's, he informed the author, the limb of an old walnut tree that still stands in the side yard was rubbing so dangerously against the house near a window of the room in which Mosby is reputed to have stayed that he had it removed by a tree surgeon. While engaged in this work, the surgeon found in a hollow of the tree an old vanilla bottle dated many years prior to the Civil War.

13 Now Atoka in Fauquier County, Virginia. This was Mosby's favorite meeting place for his command because of the numerous roads coming into it from various directions, a factor he recognized would make it easier for his men to escape if surprised while there.

14 *O.R.*, XXVII, Pt. III, 72.

15 For discussion of this phase of the Gettysburg campaign, see *Battles and Leaders*, III, 251; *R. E. Lee* (New York, Charles Scribner's Sons, 1934), III, 547; and *Lee's Lieutenants*, III, 35 n.; 58, 61, 63, and 208 n., both by Douglas Southall Freeman; *Stuart's Cavalry in the Gettysburg Campaign*, by John S. Mosby; *The Life and Campaigns of Major-General J. E. B. Stuart* (Boston, Houghton, Mifflin and Company, 1885), by H. B. McClellan.

16 *O.R.*, XXVII, Pt. III, 525.

17 *Ibid.*, Pt. II, p. 26.

18 *Ibid.*, Pt. III, p. 194.
19 *Reports of the Baltimore and Ohio Railroad,* IX, 49, and *Civil War Papers of the B. & O.*
20 *O.R.*, XXVII, Pt. II, 124.
21 McDonald, p. 175.
22 *O.R.*, XXVII, Pt. I, 31.
23 *Ibid.*, p. 35.
24 *Ibid.*, p. 39.
25 *Ibid.*, Pt. II, p. 213.

CHAPTER 5

1 Stevenson, p. 218.
2 Now The Plains, Virginia.
3 Norton, p. 24.
4 Gansevoort, p. 48.
5 See correspondence between Halleck and Meade in *O.R.*, XXVII, Pt. I, 99, 100, and 108.
6 Wheeling *Intelligencer,* July 24, 1863.
7 Haupt was forty-six years old, a native of Philadelphia. He attended West Point in the class with George G. Meade and afterward became a designer and builder of roads and bridges. In '62, when called to Washington to serve as chief of the Bureau of United States Military Railroads, he was general superintendent of the Pennsylvania Railroad, which he had helped build. The speed with which he was able to reconstruct bridges and repair other damage caused by the Confederates set a new record in the history of such matters.
8 *O.R.*, XXVII, Pt. III, 755.
9 *Ibid.*, p. 770.
10 *Ibid.*, p. 774.
11 *Ibid.*, Pt. I, p. 102.
12 *Ibid.*, Pt. III, p. 790.
13 Washington *Star,* August 4, 1863.
14 Baltimore *American,* August 10, 1863.
15 *Ibid.*, August 25, 1863.
16 *Field, Camp, Hospital and Prison, 1861-1865* (Boston, Press of George H. Ellis Company, 1918), by Charles A. Humphreys, p. 371.
17 *O.R.*, XXIX, Pt. II, 77.
18 *Ibid.*, Pt. I, p. 90.

CHAPTER 6

1 *O.R.*, XXIX, Pt. I, 102.
2 John B. Fay, member of McNeill's Rangers, as told in an article in the *Confederate Veteran,* XV, 408.
3 *Ibid.*
4 *Walter S. Newhall, A Memoir* (Philadelphia, 1864), p. 115.
5 *O.R.*, LI, Pt. I, 1092.
6 Baltimore *American,* October 31, 1863.
7 New York *Herald,* September 24, 1863.

8 Washington *Star*, September 21, 1863.

9 *O.R.*, XXIX, Pt. II, 766.

10 Letter written by Mosby to his wife dated October 1, 1863, and reproduced in his *Memoirs* (Boston, Little, Brown and Company, 1917), p. 263.

11 This son was French Dulaney, killed while serving with Mosby in 1864.

12 *O.R.*, XXIX, Pt. II, 346.

13 *Your Soldier Boy Samuel*, by Charles Sterling Underhill (privately printed,
1929).

14 "Diary of Major John Chester White," p. 22, in Manuscript Division of the
Library of Congress. White was never an admirer of Mosby, during or
after the war. Writing in later years, at a time when the Partisan leader
was receiving considerable attention in New England and other areas, he
charged the ex-raider with "violation of the rules of war," and observed:
"To one who was personally cognizant of these outrages the lionizing of
Mosby . . . has evoked anything but his sympathy, and can scarcely be
necessary for the 'harmonizing of sections' or for peaceful assimilation, as
claimed by political claptrap."

15 "Diary of Major John Chester White," p. 27.

16 The date of this expedition is in dispute. Some diarists describe it as taking place on Christmas Eve, while the *Official Records*, XXIX, Pt. II, 585,
indicate it was on Christmas Day.

17 "Diary of Lieutenant Rawle Brooke," as reproduced in *History of the
Third Pennsylvania Cavalry* (Philadelphia, Franklin Printing Company,
1905), p. 384.

CHAPTER 7

1 Wheeling *Intelligencer*, January 19, 1864.

2 *The Rebellion Record*, Document 329.

3 Christopher Armour Newcomer, author of *Cole's Cavalry: or Three Years
in the Saddle in the Shenandoah Valley* (Baltimore, Cushing and Company,
1895), says a stable guard, posted for duty only a few minutes earlier,
fired the shot that alarmed the camp.

4 *Rebellion Record*, Document 329.

5 *O.R.*, XXXIII, 1081.

6 Paragraph 2 of General Order Number 6, that which specifically prescribed
hanging for Rebels clothed in the Federal uniform, lasted only a few
weeks. By April so many Southerners were found to be dressed in blue as
the sole expediency to freezing that the drastic measure was rescinded.
(*Ibid.*, p. 806.)

7 *Ibid.*, p. 1140.

8 Gilmor, p. 140.

9 *Ibid.*, p. 143.

10 *Reports of the Baltimore and Ohio Railroad*, February 12, 1864.

11 The Wheeling *Intelligencer* of February 16, 1864, reported: "Mr. Tshude,
the agent, sort of concealed himself under some mail bags. The safe con-
tained $4,000 in money."

12 Gilmor, p. 143.

13 Testimony of Sergeant Levy of Company B, Gilmor's command, as reported in *O.R.*, XXXIII, 154.

14 *Ibid.*, p. 223.

15 In the fall of 1904 the skeleton of a soldier was unearthed near the schoolhouse at Vienna, Virginia. A flare of correspondence immediately burst forth in an effort to determine the identity. At first it was thought to be the remains of Ormsby, but, on the basis of a diary kept by Colonel E. Mason Kline, first lieutenant and adjutant of the Second Massachusetts Cavalry at the time of the execution, this identity later was discounted. But one factor remained as a puzzle: no uniform buttons were found in the grave, and it was recalled that Ormsby's clothing had been trimmed of buttons before he was shot.

CHAPTER 8

1 Wheeling *Intelligencer*, April 14, 1864.

2 *Ibid.*, June 8, 1864.

PART THREE

CHAPTER 1

1 Private Marcus B. Toney, who had come up from Tennessee to fight with the Forty-fourth Virginia Infantry, went into camp along the Rapidan in March, 1864. In his account of the war, *The Privations of a Private*, p. 70, he says: "When I reached the camp, rations consisted of middling meat and corn bread, without any salt . . . By the first day of May the meat was gone, and many of the soldiers were without shoes. When the meat gave out, we resorted to wild onions, which were plentiful in that section, but hard to dig up. They were about the size of shallots, but very deep rooted, and we had to dig pretty deep with bayonets to get them up. These onions and corn bread without salt did very well toward appeasing the appetite of hungry soldiers."

2 *The Custer Story*, p. 86.

3 *The History of the Civil War in America* (Springfield, Massachusetts, Gordon Bill, 1866), by John S. C. Abbott, II, 384.

4 *The Campaign of 1864 in the Valley of Virginia* (New York, National Americana Society, 1925), by Henry Algernon Du Pont, referred to hereafter as Du Pont, p. 33.

5 Wheeling *Intelligencer*, March 31, 1864.

6 "I Goes to Fight Mit Sigel" was the title of a poem that became the war song of the Germans fighting with the Union army. The composer of its ringing lines, having the swing of a polka, is unidentified. (*The Photographic History of the Civil War*, IX, 348.)

7 *A Stillness at Appomattox* (New York, Doubleday and Company, Inc., 1953), by Bruce Catton, p. 177.

8 *O.R.*, XXXIII, 765.

9 *Ibid.*, p. 306.

10 *The Custer Story*, p. 94.

11 *Recollections of War and Peace 1861-1868* (New York, G. P. Putnam's Sons, 1938), by Anna Pierpont Siviter, p. 128. In her account Mrs. Siviter says Mosby sent her father this message: "You did not see the farmer who rode by your hotel on a hay wagon yesterday, did you, Governor? My driver pointed out your window, and I marked it plain. It's just over the bay, and I'll get you some night, mighty easy."

Although the wordage of the message lacked the dignity of Mosby's customary writing, the daughter says her father laughed at the insolence of it. But he heeded the warning it brought. She relates that it was one of the factors that induced him to establish his family for the summer of 1864 at Laurel, Maryland.

In another account of this incident, Charles Henry Ambler, biographer of Pierpont, says the family summered at Washington, Pennsylvania.

12 *Personal Recollections and Civil War Diary 1864* (Burlington, Vermont, Free Press Printing Company, 1908), by Lemuel Abijah Abbott, p. 39.

13 *O.R.*, LI, Pt. II, 878. In this report to Stuart, Mosby places himself one mile from Centreville.

14 *Personal Memoirs of U. S. Grant* (New York, Charles L. Webster and Company, 1885), II, 141.

15 Mrs. Custer wrote her parents, Mr. and Mrs. Daniel Stanton Bacon, of the incident, saying: "Do you know Autie [her pet name for her husband] was on that car that was so nearly captured by Mosby? They made their dash too soon, as the cars were about an hour behind time. Autie never told me a word about it, but Mr. Ferry, agent for the Gettysburg cemetery, told me." *The Custer Story*, p. 90.

16 *O.R.*, LI, Pt. II, 880.

17 Grant actually had planned his campaign for early April, but was delayed by spring rains and bottomless roads. Sigel, however, was ordered to move off first to divert attention from southwest Virginia, where Crook was expected to strike. (*Battles and Leaders*, IV, 487.)

18 *Ibid.*, p. 488.

19 *Ibid.*, p. 480.

20 *O.R.*, XXVII, Pt. I, 2.

21 "The McNeill Rangers: A Study in Confederate Guerrilla Warfare," an unpublished thesis submitted at the University of West Virginia by Simeon Miller Bright.

22 *Ibid.*

23 *O.R.*, XXXVII, Pt. I, 383.

24 *Ibid.*, p. 68.

25 *Ibid.*, p. 69.

26 *Ibid.*, p. 391.

27 A letter complaining of the part played by this unidentified horseman was written to the Baltimore *American and Commercial Advertiser* by a person who described himself as "a delayed passenger" and used the pseudonym "Alpha."

28 Now the Western Maryland Railroad.

29 *Reports of the Baltimore and Ohio Railroad*, vol. IX.

30 An account of the ruse employed at Bloomington was prepared by Peerce
    himself some years after the war and appeared in *Southern Bivouac*, II,
    352-355.
31 Leonora W. Wood, in her account of the raid on Piedmont, said Captain
    Peerce announced that "no lady need feel the slightest alarm."
32 *O.R.*, XXXVII, Pt. I, 392.
33 This was among the charges made against Mosby in a volume entitled
    Sufferings Endured for a Free Government (Philadelphia, Smith and
    Peters, 1864), written by Thomas L. Wilson. One chapter of it was headed
    "Outrages Committed by Mosby," a part of it stating (p. 120): "This is
    only one of the many thousands of the damnable outrages that have been
    committed by this Rebel fiend within a few miles of the capital of our
    nation."
34 *The Bivouac and the Battlefield* (New York, Harper and Brothers, 1863),
    by George F. Noyes, p. 102.
35 *O.R.*, XXXVII, Pt. I, 416.
36 *Ibid.*, p. 422.
37 *Ibid.*, p. 414.
38 *Battles and Leaders*, IV, 181. In his account Imboden fixes the date of
    the start of this flank movement as "Sunday, the 8th of May." This ob-
    viously is an error. The particular Sunday referred to was May 9.
39 *Ibid.*, p. 488. Sigel, in writing of this episode after the war, mentioned
    specifically that the party sent into Luray Valley went there "especially
    against Mosby." Its strength was placed at 300, while the force moving
    westward was fixed at 500.
40 *O.R.*, XXXVII, Pt. I, 421.
41 *Ibid.*, p. 427.
42 Wildes, p. 86.
43 *O.R.*, XXVII, Pt. I, 73. In his subsequent account of this affair, written
    for *Battles and Leaders*, Imboden said he captured 464 men. Sigel, writ-
    ing for the same publication, placed his loss at 125 men and 200 horses.
44 *The 22nd Pennsylvania Cavalry and the Ringgold Battalion* (privately
    printed, N.D.), by Samuel Clarke Farrar, p. 216.
45 *O.R.*, XXXVII, Pt. I, 87.
46 Regiments of infantry with Sigel consisted of the Eighteenth Connecticut,
    Twenty-eighth Ohio, One Hundred Sixteenth Ohio, One Hundred Twenty-
    third Ohio, organized as the First Brigade, and the First West Virginia,
    Twelfth West Virginia, Thirty-fourth Massachusetts, and Fifty-fourth
    Pennsylvania, as the Second Brigade. His cavalry was the First New York,
    First Maryland Potomac Home Brigade, Twenty-first New York and Four-
    teenth Pennsylvania, and detachments of the Fifteenth New York, Twen-
    tieth Pennsylvania, and Twenty-second Pennsylvania.
47 This explanation of Sigel's defeat was given by him in reports to the War
    Department immediately after the battle. It was reviewed by Secretary
    of War Stanton in a letter to Major General Dix, dated May 17, 1864, and
    reproduced subsequently in the New York *Herald*.

CHAPTER 2

1   *O.R.*, XXXVII, Pt. I, 479.
2   *Ibid.*, p. 475.
3   *Ibid.*, XXXVI, Pt. II, 840.
4   *Ibid.*, XXXVI, Pt. I, 485.
5   *Ibid.*, p. 492.
6   A fellow officer writing of Hunter in later years said: "Unfortunately, his mentality was largely dominated by prejudices and antipathies so intense and so violent as to render him at times quite incapable of taking a fair and unbiased view of many military and political situations." Du Pont, p. 37.
7   *The Civil War Diary of Charles H. Lynch* (privately printed, 1915).
8   Mosby is the authority for the report that only one Federal wagon train went up the Valley after his attack at Strasburg. (*O.R.*, XXXVII, Pt. I, 3.) This he unquestionably should have known beyond dispute, for his Rangers were patrolling every highway in the area.
9   *Ibid.*, p. 416.
10 *Ibid.*
11 For an account of the fight between McNeill and Hart, see *Ibid.*, pp. 567, 578, 603, 605, and 607.
12 *Ibid.*, Pt. II, p. 340.
13 *Ibid.*, Pt. I, p. 516.
14 General Orders Number 29, published in *Ibid.*, p. 517.
15 The order of march was outlined in a special circular prepared in the field near Cedar Creek. See *Ibid.*, p. 537.
16 *Ibid.*, pp. 521, 532.
17 *Ibid.*, p. 429.
18 Baltimore *American*, June 2, 1864.
19 *Bull Run to Bull Run* (Richmond, Virginia, B. F. Johnson Publishing Company, 1900), by George Baylor, p. 121.
20 Wheeling *Intelligencer*, May 25, 1864.
21 *Life with the 34th Massachusetts Infantry in the War of the Rebellion* (Worcester, Massachusetts, Press of Noyes, Snow and Company, 1879), by William S. Lincoln, p. 29.
22 Beach, p. 343.
23 *O.R.*, XXXVII, Pt. I, 548.
24 *Ibid.*
25 For evidence of the confusion in high ranks caused by the guerrillas, all one needs do is consult *Ibid.*, Series 1, vol. XXXVII, Pt. I. Successive messages reveal the alarm of Kelley, Weber, Sigel, and even Hunter. Their greatest problem was to keep track of the Rebel Partisans. McNeill repeatedly was said to be active on both sides of the Alleghenies, and Mosby was seen throughout northern Virginia and southern Maryland, areas so widely separated that it was obvious certain of the reports were false. But which?
26 It was reported in some quarters that the attack at Newtown was conducted by Mosby's Rangers. Farrar, in his *The 22nd Pennsylvania Cavalry and*

the *Ringgold Battalion 1861-1865*, p. 233, explains that this false information was brought by Gil Holmes, wagon master of the First West Virginia
Infantry, who fled the scene on foot and walked thirty miles before he
reached a friendly camp.

27 *O.R.*, XXXVII, Pt. I, 578.
28 *The Civil War Diary of Charles H. Lynch.*
29 *Forty Years of Active Service* (New York, The Neale Publishing Company,
    1904), by Charles T. O'Ferrall, pp. 101-104.
30 *O.R.*, XXXVII, Pt. I, 618.
31 *Ibid.*, pp. 162, 619, 620, 621, 622, 623, and 625.
32 *The Civil War Diary of Charles H. Lynch.*
33 *Ibid.*
34 *O.R.*, XXXVII, Pt. I, 763.
35 *Ibid.*, p. 769.
36 *Ibid.*, p. 645.
37 *Ibid.*, p. 651.
38 These are the figures given by General Early in his account of the Lynch-
    burg campaign published in *Battles and Leaders*, IV, 492.
39 "Diary of William B. Stark, 34th Massachusetts Volunteers," published in
    The Atlantic Monthly.
40 *Ibid.*
41 *I Rode with Stonewall*, by Douglas, p. 290.
42 *O.R.*, XXXVII, Pt. I, 683.
43 *Reminiscences of the Civil War* (New York, Charles Scribner's Sons, 1904),
    by General John Brown Gordon, p. 301.
44 *O.R.*, XXXVII, Pt. I, 657.
45 *Ibid.*, p. 667.

CHAPTER 3

1   *O.R.*, XXXVII, Pt. I, 660.
2   *Ibid.*, p. 681.
3   *Ibid.*, p. 683.
4   Wheeling *Intelligencer*, June 19, 1864.
5   *O.R.*, XXXVII, Pt. II, 6.
6   *Ibid.*, p. 4.
7   Gilmor, p. 171.
8   *O.R.*, Series 3, IV, 505.
9   *Ibid.*, XXXVIII, Pt. II, 15.
10 *Ibid.*, XXXVII, Pt. II, 79.
11 Sigel was severely criticized for surrendering the stores at Martinsburg
    without making any defense. He was accused of having no scouts out and
    to have guessed wildly at the size of the force advancing on him. (See
    Ibid.)
12 The matter of Mosby's cooperation with Early in the advance on Wash-
    ington was the subject of a rhubarb between the two in later years. They
    avowedly disliked each other, and this dislike may have stemmed from the
    experience back in '64. Early wrote Mosby a letter in 1867 asking him
    whether he had crossed the Potomac as requested by messenger, and the

guerrilla chief replied that he very definitely had crossed and had "hundreds of witnesses" to the fact. Despite this assurance Early wrote in his autobiography that Mosby "had not crossed the river, and I had received no information from him."

13 *Ibid.*, p. 74.
14 *Ibid.*, p. 55.
15 This is Mount Zion Church, a structure standing on the south side of Highway Route 50 one and a half miles east of Aldie.
16 *Ibid.*, Pt. I, p. 358.
17 More than thirty years later the Reverend Charles A. Humphreys went to Tremont Temple in Boston, Massachusetts, to hear Mosby lecture. After the program was over, the minister was introduced to the speaker as the chaplain of the Second Massachusetts Cavalry and asked, "Do you remember me?" Mosby shook his head: "No, but I remember your horse." The reference was to the roan the chaplain had been riding the day of the fight at Mount Zion Church and on which he managed to escape from the Rangers. It was the next day, while digging a grave for one of the Union troopers killed in the conflict, that he was surprised and captured. See *Field, Camp, Hospital and Prison in the Civil War, 1863-1865,* by Humphreys, p. 108.
18 *O.R.,* XXXVII, Pt. I, 4.
19 Elwood, p. 215.
20 *O.R.,* XXXVII, Pt. II, 79.
21 Washington *Star,* July 9, 1864.
22 *O.R.,* XXXVII, Pt. II, 173.
23 Gilmor's account of this raid is reproduced in the magazine of the Maryland Historical Society of September, 1952, p. 234.
24 This incident is related in Gilmor's own account of his activities, *Four Years in the Saddle.*
25 *Ibid.*
26 *O.R.,* XXXVII, Pt. II, 300.
27 *Ibid.*, p. 302.
28 *Ibid.*, p. 301.
29 Gansevoort, p. 162.
30 *O.R.,* XXXVII, Pt. II, 332.
31 *Ibid.*
32 *Ibid.*, p. 340.
33 *Ibid.*, p. 366.
34 *Ibid.*, p. 364.
35 *Ibid.*, p. 366.
36 *Ibid.*, p. 374.
37 *Ibid.*, p. 384.
38 *Ibid.*, p. 426.
39 *Ibid.*
40 Gilmor, p. 209.

CHAPTER 4

1   *O.R.,* XXXVII, Pt. II, 558.
2   *Personal Memoirs of U. S. Grant,* p. 317.
3   *O.R.,* XXXVII, Pt. II, 374, 400.
4   *Ibid.,* p. 582.
5   In his memoirs, p. 318, General Grant describes this telegram as a "very characteristic dispatch" from the President.
6   This language is reported by Grant in his memoirs, p. 319.
7   *O.R.,* XLIII, Pt. I, 57.
8   *Ibid.*
9   *A Volunteer's Adventures* (New Haven, Connecticut, Yale University Press, 1946), by John William DeForest, p. 165.
10 *O.R.,* XLIII, Pt. I, 993.
11 *A Volunteer's Adventures,* p. 164.
12 *O.R.,* XLIII, Pt. I, 42.
13 *Ibid.,* p. 771.
14 Washington *Star,* August 13, 1864.
15 For a detailed account of this wagon-train raid, see *Ranger Mosby,* by V. C. Jones. References to it also can be found in *O.R.,* XLIII, Pt. I, 484, 489, 633, 782, 823, 836, 841, and 842.
16 *Ibid.,* p. 841.
17 *Ibid.,* p. 842.
18 Beach, p. 413.
19 A Board of Inquiry to investigate this wagon-train raid was convened at Harpers Ferry September 8, 1864. After days of testimony it concluded the blame could be fixed upon no individual, that the guard attached to the train—3000 men—was not strong enough.
20 The basis of the rumor seems to have been the dispatch from Lee's army of Kershaw's division of infantry and Fitz Lee's cavalry under command of General R. H. Anderson, bringing Early's strength roughly to 12,400.
21 *O.R.,* XLIII, Pt. I, 43.
22 *Ibid.*
23 *Ibid.,* p. 792.
24 James H. Stevenson, who wrote of Sheridan's fall-back in his book, *Boots and Saddles,* p. 301, attributes the retreat to Mosby's attack on the wagon train near Berryville. He says: "General Sheridan was not yet acquainted with Mosby's strength and tactics, and he deemed it prudent to fall back, temporarily, from his advanced position, to avoid a repetition of the raid upon his trains."
     This explanation for the retirement also is given by Dr. Harris H. Beecher in his *Record of the 114th Regiment, New York State Volunteers* (Norwich, New York, J. F. Hubbard, Junior, 1866), p. 402. He comments: "In the meantime the wily Mosby was making sad havoc with its communications. His operations at length compelled General Sheridan to fall back."
     Again he says: "It was at this place [Berryville] that 25 or 30 wagons of a supply train had been captured by Mosby . . . It seemed strange, indeed, that so short a line of communication as 20 miles could not be kept

open. But Mosby was indefatigable as well as venturesome, and his raids were so well planned and executed that he held the entire army at bay."

The same theory is advanced by Alfred S. Roe in *The Ninth New York Heavy Artillery* (privately printed, 1899), p. 143. As he explains it: "Mosby was active near Berryville, hence the necessity of a reverse movement."

Mosby himself thought he had caused the fall-back. In a letter to his scout, John Russell, in 1899, he opened with the sentence: "I have mailed you a set of photographs of the Berryville raid that made Sheridan retreat 50 miles down the Valley to the place where he started from."

25 *The History of the Civil War in America,* by Abbott, p. 548.
26 *O.R.,* XLIII, Pt. I, 798, 805.
27 *Ibid.,* p. 43.
28 *Ibid.,* p. 811.
29 *Ibid.*
30 *Ibid.,* p. 814.
31 *Ibid.,* p. 822.
32 *Ibid.,* p. 792.
33 This incident was related to the author by the late H. I. Hutton, prominent businessman of Warrenton, Virginia. He identified the man who fired the shot as Joseph H. Nelson of Mosby's command, later mayor of Warrenton.
34 *Diary of a Southern Refugee* (New York, E. J. Hale and Son, 1868), by Judith White McGuire, p. 293.
35 Letters from relatives in the Valley to Judith McGuire, she relates in *Diary of a Southern Refugee,* reported that Custer ordered three houses burned. However, a correspondent for the New York *Times,* who was on the scene at the time, said in his dispatch, dated from Berryville August 21, 1864, that the order applied to four residences. John W. Scott, whose account of Mosby's operations, *Partisan Life With Mosby* (New York, Harper and Brothers, 1867), was published in 1866, immediately after the war, placed the number at five.
36 W. W. Patterson of Manteo, Virginia, whose horse was shot from under him during the affray, wrote thusly in the *Confederate Veteran,* XII, 472.
37 In 1939 the author, in company with the late Mrs. Stuart Mosby Coleman, daughter of Colonel John Singleton Mosby, visited the last survivor of the band of Rangers who took part in the attack on the house-burners. He was Mason Lawrence of Amissville, Virginia, then nearing ninety-five. Though bedridden and close to his death, he remembered over a period of seventy-five years that ringing cry of "Take no prisoners!" It was the most vivid recollection that came from his fading mind. At the time of the attack in '64 he was new to Partisan life, having as a nineteen-year-old boy joined Mosby the preceding spring, at a time when the guerrilla chieftain was hiding out in the bushes near Salem, and he was afraid such a cry would bring vengeance upon them from the enemy.

As he recalled, only two prisoners were brought away, both by a "chick-enhearted" member of Mosby's command, and these later were shot.
38 W. W. Patterson in the *Confederate Veteran.*
39 *Partisan Life with Mosby,* by Scott, p. 282.

40 *O.R.*, XLIII, Pt. I, 634.

41 *Ibid.*, Pt. II, p. 880. By this period of the war Mosby's name had become so prominent in Federal circles that all guerrillas in the Eastern theater, with the possible exception of McNeill's, were referred to as members of his command. Occasional reference was made to White's men, but usually they were said to be fighting with Mosby, although this was not always the case. White and Gilmor still were operating independently, when not attached to regular troops for some special assignment, as in the case of the latter during the Chambersburg raid.

CHAPTER 5

1 *O.R.*, XLIII, Pt. I, 898.

2 Washington *Star*, August 27, 1864.

3 *The Civil War Diary of Charles H. Lynch.*

4 *O.R.*, XLIII, Pt. I, 917.

5 *Ibid.*, Pt. II, p. 11.

6 Gilmor, p. 271.

7 This man's name was John McGinn of the One Hundred Sixteenth Pennsylvania Volunteers. He had taught at an academy at Upperville. He was sent to assist in finding Mosby, as revealed by a letter in the Sheridan Papers now in the Manuscript Division of the Library of Congress, by General Grant.

8 *General George Crook, His Autobiography*, p. 135.

9 *O.R.*, XLIII, Pt. I, 860.

10 *Ibid.*, p. 615.

11 *The Second Rhode Island Regiment*, by Augustus Woodbury, p. 308.

12 Sheridan's *Memoirs*, II, 2.

13 Crook's *Autobiography* (University of Oklahoma Press, 1946), p. 135. In this statement regarding the Young Scouts, Crook was obviously biased. In the same paragraph he claimed much more credit for Blazer's command, which he had originated, than it deserved, and blamed its failure to do greater things on the fact it was not increased to proper size to cope with Mosby's outfit.

14 *O.R.*, XLIII, Pt. II, 69. In 1869 Mosby wrote a long letter to his scout, John Russell, in which he said: "Sheridan's dispatches in the War Records about the men he hung were not even a revelation to me—they revealed nothing. They were simply spectres of imagination, like the dagger in the air that Macbeth saw."

15 *Ibid.*, p. 64.

16 *The Custer Story*, p. 119.

17 The word "timidly" is taken by the author in this instance from Sheridan's own account of his activities at the time. (See *O.R.*, XLIII, Pt. I, 46.)

18 *A Volunteer's Adventures*, p. 172.

19 This conference between the two generals was held in the parlor of the Richard D. Rutherford home. A table was cleared of books and other objects, and they sat around it for more than two hours. As they emerged, General Grant thanked the householder and made some complimentary

remarks about the surrounding country. ("Recollections of Richard D. Rutherford.")

20 *O.R.*, XLIII, Pt. II, 873.

21 *Battles and Leaders*, IV, 524.

22 "Diary of Catherine Barbara Broun."

23 *Reminiscences of the Civil War*, by Macon, p. 92.

24 *Confederate Veteran*, XVI, 392.

25 *Sabres and Spurs*, p. 390. The vilest of the charges against the Rangers came from the author of this volume, the Reverend Frederic Denison, whose bitterness may have stemmed from his witnessing of the exhumings of the Rhode Island veterans' bodies near Bull Run in the spring of '62. Throughout his book he is venomous in his comments.

With reference to McMaster's death, one of Mosby's men, James J. Williamson, writing in later years, said: "Lieutenant McMaster was killed in the excitement of a fight, by men who were seeking to escape from a superior force and who were fighting for their lives. It is hardly possible at such a time to say whether he had an opportunity of surrendering, for the affair was only of a few moments' duration."

26 Throughout his life Mosby, as well as a majority of his men, blamed Custer for the deed. In 1869, during postwar rule in Virginia, according to the *Southern Historical Society Papers*, XXVII 214-22 (referred to hereafter as *S.H.S.P.*), Mosby answered charges made against him in the New York *Sun* of hanging five stragglers at Berryville by saying: "In September, 1864, General Custer captured and hanged seven of my men in the streets of Front Royal, Va." No denial of this was ever made publicly by Custer, who was alive at the time. Nor did Torbert or Merritt ever make comment in public print.

At the time of the unveiling of the monument at Front Royal, the principal address was delivered by Adolphus E. Richards, one of Mosby's principal officers. It was his conclusion that the Ranger attack had been made upon the ambulance train of the Reserve Brigade, commanded by Colonel C. R. Lowell, Jr., and that "we may reasonably conclude that it was under his immediate supervision, and not Custer's, that our men were executed." But it would seem in this instance that Richards was grabbing at straws. Lowell was to die in the fighting soon to take place along Cedar Creek, leaving behind a letter he had written to his wife, one sentence of which stated: "Mosby is an honorable foe, and should be treated as such." Mosby openly disagreed with the ideas presented by Richards.

27 Referring to the fact that Torbert, Merritt, and Custer failed to make official report of the hanging of his men, Mosby afterward commented: "It was their duty to report the fact, and, if justifiable, to report the circumstances that justified it; but none of them were willing to assume the responsibility, and admit or to go on record about the hanging. No matter whether they were active or merely passive in the business, this silence gives it a dark complexion." This appeared first in the Richmond *Times* and later was published in the *Confederate Veteran*, VII, 388.

28 *O.R.*, XLIII, Pt. I, 28.

29 *Ibid.*, Pt. II, p. 177.

30 *History of the Sixth New York Cavalry,* p. 228.
31 *O.R.,* XLIII, Pt. I, 29. Repeated in *Ibid.,* Pt. II, p. 209.
32 *Ibid.,* p. 250.
33 *Ibid.,* Pt. I, p. 50.
34 *Ibid.,* p. 974.
35 *S.H.S.P.,* XXVII, 314.
36 *O.R.,* XLIII, Pt. II, 151.
37 *The Military Telegraph During the Civil War,* by Plum, II, 272-274.
38 *O.R.,* XLIII, Pt. II, 272.
39 *Ibid.,* pp. 290, 314.
40 Mosby's *Memoirs,* p. 328.
41 *The Military Telegraph During the Civil War.*
42 *O.R.,* XLIII, Pt. II, 335.
43 *Ibid.,* p. 334.
44 *Ibid.,* Pt. I, p. 31.
45 *Ibid.,* Pt. II, p. 309.
46 *Ibid.,* p. 340.
47 *Ibid.,* p. 348.
48 For days, sometimes two in a row, laborers along the railroad were completely idle, waiting for orders.
49 *Ibid.,* p. 415.

CHAPTER 6

1 *The 22nd Pennsylvania Cavalry and the Ringgold Battalion,* by Farrar, p. 326.
2 *The Civil War Diary of Charles H. Lynch.*
3 J. K. Taliaferro of Remington, Virginia, in *Confederate Veteran,* XXII, 128.
4 As late as 1954 an article appeared in a metropolitan newspaper to the effect that the men who killed Meigs were dressed in Federal uniforms. This was vehemently denied by J. D. Ficklin of Bealeton, Virginia, who often had heard his father say their uniforms were gray and were concealed by raincoats.
5 Martin was one of three brothers from Warrenton who fought in the Confederate army and set an enviable record. George, who survived the war by many years, suffered until his death from the wound he had received at the hands of Meigs. Shortly after the war ended, Quartermaster General Meigs offered 1000 dollars for delivery to him of the Rebel who had killed his son. This caused Martin to move to a secluded section of Missouri where he remained until the war excitement subsided. (J. K. Taliaferro in *Confederate Veteran,* XXII, 128.)
6 Sheridan's *Memoirs,* II, 50.
7 Many of the Federal soldiers who participated in the burning of the Valley wrote in afteryears of their distaste for such recrimination. One of them, recording his experiences at Dayton, said: "This was the most heart-sickening duty we had ever performed . . . The execution of such orders, however just and right, has a very demoralizing effect upon the men." (*Historic Records of the Fifth New York Cavalry,* by Boudrye, p. 176.)

8 *Record of the 116th Regiment Ohio Infantry Volunteers in the War of the Rebellion,* by Wildes.

9 In his report (*O.R.,* XLIII, Pt. I, 30) Sheridan makes no mention of the leniency shown in the case of Dayton. Nor does General Early, writing years later in *Battles and Leaders,* IV, 525 .

10 The best account of this incident is given by the Reverend J. W. Duffey, D.D., who fought under McNeill and participated in the affair near Mount Jackson. His story was published in a pamphlet entitled *McNeill's Last Charge* by the Moorefield *Examiner* in 1912.

In *West Virginia, a Guide to the Mountain State,* a volume compiled by the Writers' Program of the Works Progress Administration, p. 337, the statement is made: "After he had ordered his men to cease firing, McNeill was mortally wounded by George Valentine, a member of the Rangers whom he had severely reprimanded for stealing chickens from a farmer who lived near a cave used by the Rangers for a hideout."

11 Moorefield *Examiner,* August 23, 1895, as referred to in "The McNeill Rangers: A Study in Confederate Guerrilla Warfare," by Bright.

12 *O.R.,* XLIII, Pt. II, 272.

13 *Ibid.,* p. 308. Up to the time he was wounded, according to the Reverend J. W. Duffey, D.D., who wrote as a participant, McNeill had captured 2600 prisoners, or about forty to each Ranger.

14 New York *Herald,* October 9, 1864.

15 *O.R.,* XLIII, Pt. I, 518.

16 *Ibid.,* p. 31.

17 *I Rode with Stonewall,* p. 315.

18 This was the sobriquet used in referring to Rosser by Custer and others who had been at West Point with him.

19 Sheridan's report, recorded in *O.R.,* XLIII, Pt. II, 327.

20 *History of the Sixth New York Cavalry.*

21 *History of the 18th Regiment of Cavalry, Pennsylvania Volunteers, 1862-1865.*

22 New York *Herald,* October 9, 1864.

23 *O.R.,* XLIII, Pt. II, 327.

24 *Ibid.,* p. 339.

25 Dated October 11, 1864, for the Richmond *Enquirer* and reprinted in the New York *Herald.*

26 According to a dispatch from the New York *Herald's* correspondent, Finley Anderson, who wrote from near Strasburg, these guerrillas were from White's battalion, now back in the field of independent activity. See the *Herald* of October 13, 1864.

27 *O.R.,* XLIII, Pt. II, 374.

28 *Elwood's Stories of the Old Ringgold Cavalry,* p. 267.

29 *The 22nd Pennsylvania Cavalry and the Ringgold Battalion 1861-1865,* by Farrar, p. 404. Also *O.R.,* XLIII, Pt. I, 509.

30 Writing from San Francisco in 1899 (*S.H.S.P.,* XXVII, 320), Mosby gave this version of the incidents leading up to the hanging:

A man in citizens' clothing came to the home of a Fauquier County farmer named Myers, who had never been a member of Mosby's command, and asked for work, explaining he was a deserter from Sheridan's army. Myers suspected he was a spy, and, when his neighbor, Chancellor, on furlough, passed by en route back to the army, asked him to turn the fellow over to the provost marshal at Gordonsville. Chancellor agreed. Before they had ridden far, the prisoner tried to escape. Chancellor warned him the next attempt would be his last. It was.

31 Willis joined Mosby on November 1, 1863. He was hanged in Rappahannock County, on a graded road leading to Chester Gap in the Blue Ridge Mountains.

32 In the summer of 1901 members of the Ringgold Battalion were invited to participate in a gathering of McNeill's Rangers at Moorefield. Nearly thirty accepted, and assembled in the little hill town to fight over their battles with the Southerners, this time verbally. Next year the Rangers were invited to Pennsylvania for a reunion with the Ringgolds.

33 *O.R.*, XLIII, Pt. I, 32.

34 *Ibid.*, Pt. II, p. 355.

35 *Ibid.*, p. 363.

36 *Ibid.*, p. 364.

37 This money was divided equally among the Rangers taking part in the raid, giving each of them about 2100 dollars. Following a rule adhered to throughout the war, Mosby refused to share in the spoils.

38 New York *Herald*, October 17, 1864.

39 *O.R.*, XLIII, Pt. II, 373.

40 *History of the 13th Maine Regiment* (Bridgton, Maine, H. A. Shorey and Son, 1898), by Edwin B. Lufkin.

41 It was also reported that passengers on the train were robbed, but this Mosby steadfastly denied in a report to General Lee: "I hope you will not believe the accounts published in the Northern papers and copied in ours of my robbery of the passengers on the railroad train I captured. So far from that, I strictly enjoined my officers and men that nothing of the kind would be permitted. That a great many of the passengers lost their baggage is true, because the proximity of a considerable force of the enemy allowed us no time to save it, but I explained to the passengers that persons traveling on a military road subjected themselves to the incidents of war." (*O.R.*, XLIII, Pt. II, 918.)

42 New York *Herald*, October 17, 1864.

43 *O.R.*, XLIII, Pt. I, 51. Also *Ibid.*, Pt. II, p. 346.

44 Some accounts refer to this station as being on Three Top Mountains. It is believed, on a basis of Early and Wright's recollections in later years, that the report originated on Round Top and was repeated by the station on Three Top.

45 *Ibid.*, p. 386.

46 *Ibid.*, Pt. I, p. 52.

47 *History of the 19th Army Corps* (New York, G. P. Putnam Sons, 1892), by Richard B. Irwin. Writing on November 6, 1890, General Early related: "I went to the signal station just in rear for the purpose of examining the position, and I found the officer in charge of the station reading some signals that were being sent by the Federal signal agents. I then asked

him if the other side could read his signals and he told me that they had discovered the key to the signals formerly used, but that a change had been made. I then wrote the message purporting to be from Longstreet and had it signaled in full view of the Federal signal men . . ."

48 *O.R.*, XLIII, Pt. I, 51.
49 *History of the 121st New York State Infantry* (Chicago, J. H. Smith, 1921), by Isaac O. Best, p. 189.
50 The original of Major Jones' letter is on file at the Alabama Department of Archives in Montgomery. A copy is among miscellaneous personal papers in the Manuscript Division of the Library of Congress.
51 *O.R.*, XLIII, Pt. II, 465.

CHAPTER 7

1 *The Civil War Diary of Charles H. Lynch.*
2 Denison, p. 103.
3 *O.R.*, XLIII, Pt. II, 382.
4 *Ibid.*, Pt. I, p. 453.
5 Sheridan Papers in the Manuscript Division of the Library of Congress, vol. IV.
6 *O.R.*, XLIII, Pt. II, 475.
7 *Ibid.*, p. 436.
8 *Ibid.*, p. 464.
9 *Ibid.*, p. 487.
10 *Ibid.*, p. 529.
11 *Ibid.*, p. 453.
12 *Ibid.*, p. 530.
13 *Ibid.*, p. 483.
14 *Ibid.*, p. 565.
15 Some years after the war Senator George Graham Vest of Missouri charged that Mosby's command fought under the black flag and was not recognized by the Confederate government. Taking exception to this, Colonel Mosby stated in a letter, now in the William H. Chapman collection of material on Mosby: "No man who had the courage to face us in a fight, or whom the fortunes of war made a prisoner in our hands, has ever made such an accusation against us. It is true that my notions of war were not sentimental and that I did not look upon it as a tournament or pastime, but as one of the most practical of human undertakings; I learned the maxims on which I conducted it from Napoleon and not from Walter Scott."
16 *History of the 13th Maine Regiment,* by Lufkin.
17 Gansevoort, p. 185.
18 *Ibid.*
19 New York *Herald*, November 7, 1864.
20 *O.R.*, XLIII, Pt. II, 910.
21 This personal account of the meeting with Mosby was written by Major Brewster and compiled in *War Papers and Personal Reminiscences, 1861-1865* (St. Louis, Becktoll and Company, 1892), a collection of war experiences read before the Commandery of the State of Missouri, Military Order

of the Loyal Legion. It appears in the published version in the first volume, page 74.

22 At the time of the unveiling of the monument at Front Royal to the Rangers executed there, Mosby wrote a special article on the subject for the Richmond *Times*. In this he expressed his feelings regarding the retaliation: "I determined to demand and enforce every belligerent right to which the soldiers of a great military power were entitled by the laws of war, but I resolved to do it in a humane manner and in a calm and judicial spirit. I felt in doing it all the pangs of the weeping jailer when he handed the cup of hemlock to the great Athenian martyr. It was not an act of revenge, but a sentence—not only to save the lives of my own men, but the lives of the enemy." (Parts of this article were republished in *Confederate Veteran*, VII, 388.)

23 Personal account of Major Charles Brewster, p. 88.

24 Some weeks later, while in Richmond recuperating from a wound, Mosby was invited to go down the James River on a boat conveying a number of prisoners to be exchanged. Among them was the drummer boy, and he rushed up to Mosby and embraced him. An account of this was written by the Partisan leader in a letter dated from San Francisco in 1899 and published in *S.H.S.P.*, vol. XXVII.

25 *O.R.*, XLIII, Pt. II, 566.

26 Brewster's personal account, p. 95. Also see the Richmond *Dispatch* of December 1, 1864, for an article republished from the New York *Herald*.

27 For a personal account of Russell's visit to Sheridan's headquarters, see the Washington *Star* of July 2, 1922.

28 *O.R.*, XLIII, Pt. II, 920.

CHAPTER 8

1 The incident between John Hall of Columbus, Ohio, and George Hall of Texas is related in *Confederate Veteran*, I, 239.

2 *O.R.*, XLIII, Pt. II, 581.

3 *Ibid.*, p. 645.

4 *Ibid.*, p. 648.

5 *Ibid.*, p. 653.

6 *Ibid.*, p. 654.

7 *Ibid.*, p. 671.

8 *Ibid.*, p. 648.

9 These Union casualties were viewed by John N. Opie of the Confederate cavalry who came upon the scene soon after the fight had ended. He tells of the experience in his book *A Rebel Cavalryman*, p. 277.

10 *The 116th Regiment of New York State Volunteers* (Buffalo, New York, Printing House of Matthews and Warren, 1868), by Orton S. Clark, p. 211.

11 *O.R.*, XLIII, Pt. II, 665.

12 *Ibid.*, p. 682.

13 *Ibid.*, Pt. I, p. 55.

14 *Ibid.*, p. 658.

15 *Ibid.*, p. 668.

16 *Ibid.*, p. 659.

17 *Ibid.*, Pt. II, p. 746.
18 *Ibid.*, Pt. I, p. 661.
19 *Ibid.*, Pt. II, p. 746.
20 Sheridan's own account in *Ibid.*, p. 742.
21 *Ibid.*, Pt. I, p. 654.
22 *Ibid.*, Pt. II, p. 696.
23 *Ibid.*, p. 671.
24 *Ibid.*, p. 685.
25 *Ibid.*, p. 675.
26 *Ibid.*, p. 679.
27 *Ibid.*, p. 687.
28 *Ibid.*, p. 709.
29 *Ibid.*, p. 730.
30 *Ibid.*, p. 740.
31 *Ibid.*, p. 744.
32 *Ibid.*, p. 758.
33 *Ibid.*, p. 937.
34 *Reports of the Baltimore and Ohio Railroad*, vol. IX.
35 *O.R.*, XLIII, Pt. II, 778.
36 *Ibid.*, p. 804.
37 *Field, Camp, Hospital and Prison, 1863-1865*, by Humphreys, pp. 194, 419. This excellent volume gives a vivid description of the rigors of the march and the horrors of trying to sleep in freezing weather, sometimes on snow so crusted over as to bear the weight of horses.
38 McIlhany had been thrown from his horse in a fight with Union cavalry earlier in the day and the animal had chased after other Rebel riders, leaving its master without a steed until he came upon the pony-like creature on the side of the road.
39 After the turn of the century Brown and McIlhany became friends and carried on an extended correspondence over a period of years. Some of the letters thus prepared were made available to the author by Captain Brown's daughter, Mrs. Elizabeth B. Rutter of Princeton, N. J., through the kind intercession of Francis F. Wilshin, present superintendent of the Manassas National Battlefield Park.
40 This conversation was recalled by McIlhany in a letter he wrote Brown from Staunton, Virginia, on December 21, 1907. Said the ex-Confederate: "I had never been on that road in my life, but I do not think you believed me."
41 *O.R.*, XLIII, Pt. II, 843. Forty years after this incident Mosby's hat taken from a corner of the home in which he lay wounded was returned to him by Sarah Coles T. Halstead of Central Park, N. Y., daughter of a Thirteenth New York Cavalry officer. A few days after it arrived, newspapers told that the ex-Partisan appeared at the White House to present it to the President. It now is on display in the Smithsonian Institution in Washington.
42 *O.R.*, XLIII, Pt. II, 844.
43 *Ibid.*
44 See the New York *Herald* of January 8, 1865.

CHAPTER 9

1 *Field, Camp, Hospital and Prison in the Civil War, 1863-1865,* by Humphreys.
2 *Sabres and Spurs,* by Denison, p. 431.
3 *James Dinkins: Personal Recollections and Experiences in the Confederate Army,* (privately printed, 1897).
4 Editorial from the Charleston (S.C.) *Courier,* republished in the New York *Herald* of January 25, 1865.
5 *The 22nd Pennsylvania Cavalry and the Ringgold Battalion, 1861-1865,* by Farrar, p. 442.
6 *O.R.,* XLVI, Pt. I, 456.
7 This conversation is taken from Gilmor's own account of his capture as told in *Four Years in the Saddle,* p. 276.
8 *O.R.,* XLVI, Pt. II, 469.
9 Gilmor, p. 276, and *O.R.,* XLVI, Pt. I, 455.
10 *O.R.,* LI, Pt. II, 1061. This letter no doubt was one of a combination of things that led to an intense dislike on the part of Mosby for General Early following the war. There was at times sharp correspondence between them, and Mosby frequently commented that he stayed away from Confederate reunions because Early tried to hog all the glory.
11 *Ibid.,* XLVI, Pt. II, 504. Estimates on the number of Union troops stationed at Cumberland in February, '65, ranged from 3500 to 10,000. Sheridan placed the total at 3500 to 4000.
12 Plans for the raid were outlined by Jesse McNeill in a personal account published in the *Confederate Veteran,* XIV 410.
13 *Ibid.,* XV, 410.
14 This account of the entrance to General Crook's bedroom is given by John B. Fay, one of the participating Rangers, and quoted in *Ibid.,* XXXIII, 420.
15 *O.R.,* XLVI, Pt. II, 621.
16 *Confederate Veteran,* XXXIII, 422.
17 *Ibid.*
18 *Ibid.*

CHAPTER 10

1 *O.R.,* XLVI, Pt. II, 495.
2 For these nineteen separate messages, see *Ibid.,* XXXVII, Pt. I, 475, 500, 593, and 683; and Pt. II, 79, 300, 422, and 426. XLVII, Pt. I, 917; and Pt. II, 177, 187, 338, 363, 436, 645, 648, 740, and 778. XLVI, Pt. II, 495.
3 *Ibid.,* XLVI, Pt. II, 496, 595.
4 *Ibid.,* p. 621.
5 *Ibid.,* p. 683.
6 *Ibid.,* p. 702.
7 *Ibid.,* pp. 781, 782.
8 *Ibid.,* Pt. III, p. 1359.
9 Baltimore *American,* April 3, 1865.
10 These words were attributed to his father, a member of the Army of North-

ern Virginia, by the late Dr. Douglas Southall Freeman, eminent historian and authority on the Civil War, in an address before the Civil War Round Table of the District of Columbia only a few weeks before his death.

11 This engagement, one of the last of the war, took place at "Brimstone Hill," then the residence of the Arundel family and now the home of Judge and Mrs. Paul E. Brown.

12 *O.R.*, XLIII, Pt. III, 699.

13 Washington *Star*, April 13, 1865.

14 Baltimore *American*, April 13, 1865.

15 For many years after the war Colonel Chapman was a prominent official of the U.S. Internal Revenue Bureau.

16 *O.R.*, XLVI, Pt. III, 818.

17 *Ibid.*, p. 839. It is odd that this drastic message should concern two men who afterward became firm friends. Mosby often visited Grant at the White House and, when he made his round-the-world junket in the 1880's, one of the former President's stopping-off points was Hong Kong, where he went to visit the ex-Rebel guerrilla leader, serving there in the post of American consul. In the memoirs Grant wrote shortly before his death, he said of Mosby: "He is a different man entirely from what I expected . . . He is able, and thoroughly honest and truthful. There were probably but few men in the South who could have commanded successfully a separate detachment in the rear of an opposing army, and so near the border of hostilities, as long as he did without losing his entire command." (II, 142.)

18 This address was printed in the *Official Records* as the last entry in vol. XLVI, Pt. III. Owing to a later effort to trim out some of its verbosity, the version represented is different in a few respects from copies on file at the Confederate Museum in Richmond and elsewhere.

19 Until his death Colonel White carried in his wallet a copy of General Lee's Order Number 9, in which the surrender was announced.

20 *O.R.*, XLVI, Pt. III, 1395.

21 *Ibid.*

22 This incident was repeated to the author by Major General U. S. Grant, 3rd, in the presence of members of the Civil War Round Table of the District of Columbia, at the Army and Navy Club on the night of January 11, 1955. The general, a distinguished gentleman and student of Civil War history, explained that he was too young to get the story directly from his famous soldier grandfather before the latter's death, but that over a period of years he often heard his grandmother relate it.

23 *O.R.*, XLVI, Pt. III, 1308.

Index

ment, 10; watches Union advance, 17; confident, 43; frowns on guerrilla warfare, 76; recognizes need for "local service," 76; authorizes Partisan Rangers, 80; fights audacious warfare, 96; abolishes Partisan corps, 214

Cooke, John Esten: 158

Couch, Gen. D. N.: 184

Coyle, James: 192

Crocker, G. A.: 132

Crook, Gen. George: advance from W. Va., 228; joins Hunter, 251; assures supplies waiting, 254; heads Department of W. Va., 266; begins moving back, 267; routed by Early, 268; sends Blazer, 287; ambulance train stampeded, 289; urges completing blockhouses, 334; captured, 356-362

Cumberland, Md.: left unprotected, 228; capture of generals, 356-362

Curtis, Sam: 256

Custer, Gen. George Armstrong: bothered by guerrillas, 189; misses capture by Mosby, 232; orders homes burned, 280; forced across Potomac, 286; aware of Mosby, 289; hangs Mosby's men, 294; ordered to avenge Meigs' death, 304; wears captured uniform, 310; Mosby retaliates against, 325

Custer, Mrs. George A.: 230

Daily, James: 360

Dana, C. A.: 266

Davis, B. F.: 111

Davis, Jefferson: disagrees with Johnston, 19; changes opinion, 20; commissions McDonald, 24; holds council of war, 52; criticized, 75; pursues report about Milroy, 129; accuses North of atrocities, 139; urges destruction of Cheat River bridge, 162; considers wholesale guerrilla warfare, 348; asks men to stay in field, 369

Dayton, Va.: 305

Denison, Rev. Frederic: 66-73

Dent, Alf: 103

Deven, T. C.: 132

Devens, Charles: sent to destroy camp, 54

Devereaux, J. H.: 190; complains about guerrillas, 191

"Devil's Hole" Pass: 239

Dietrick, Charles W.: 145

Disosway, J. C.: captured by Mosby, 328; saved from hanging, 330

Donnelly, Patrick: 173

Douglas, Henry Kyd: 253

Downs, George: 103

Dranesville, Va.: Mosby attacks at, 166

Duffie, Gen. Alfred Nattie: 319

Duffield's Station, Va.: Mosby attacks at, 257; train derailed at, 342

Dulaney, D. H.: 205

Duncan, D. G.: 8

Dusky, Andy: 103

Dusky, Dan: indicted for treason, 77; 103; release asked, 139; held as hostage, 140; gun displayed, 246

Dusky, George: organizes guerrilla company, 77; falls in love, 221

Dusky, Sallie: captured by Kelley, 103; 139, 221

Dwight, Wilder: in Md. camp, 41; deplores Northern strategy, 113; death, 114

Early, Gen. Jubal A.: 10; sent after cattle, 210; goes on second raid, 214; moves to meet Hunter, 252; reaches Lynchburg, 252; starts up Valley, 256; move northward a surprise, 258; advances into Md., 259; gets guerrilla support, 260; demands ransom of Frederick, 262; on outskirts of Washington, 262; pursued by Wright, 264; whirls about, 268; writes terms for Chambersburg, 269; faces Sheridan, 276; actual strength, 291; occupies Fisher's Hill, 292; greatly outnumbered, 297; supplies carriage for McNeill, 307; sends fake message, 314; reveals strength, 317; withdraws to Staunton, 350; sends Gilmor to W. Va., 353; urges disbanding guerrillas, 355; receives captured generals, 361; routed at Waynesboro, 365

Echols, John: drawn into W. Va. raid, 161

Eighth Illinois Cavalry: assigned to

orders Nineteenth Corps to Washington, 262; urges Hunter to follow Early, 264; wants Valley cleaned, 265; renews plea for Valley to be made desert, 266; suggests merging departments, 266; asks 300,000 new recruits, 267; wants Wright and Hunter to continue south, 267; calls for Sheridan, 271; sees need for cavalry, 272; visits Washington, 272; relieves Hunter, 272; underestimates guerrillas, 272; prescribes war of horror, 273; cautions against defeat, 278; orders Mosby's men hanged without trial, 279; orders raid after guerrillas, 279; urges army to move up Valley, 286; visits Sheridan, 290; orders advance, 291; proposes reopening Manassas Gap Railroad, 295; acts cautiously, 310; orders Sheridan to move base, 313; wants Virginia Central threatened, 313, 334; repeats request for march up Valley, 320; suggests scorching Loudoun Valley, 333; visits Washington, 335; insists on Virginia Central raid, 343; last plea for advance, 363; lists troops around Washington, 365; refuses to confer with Lee, 365; urges getting Partisans to surrender, 366; urges paroling Mosby, White, 368; no quarter for guerrillas, 368; overhears conversation, 369

Gray, John Chipman: 133

Greeley, Surgeon James B.: 66-73

Green, Mary Jane: 84

Gregg, Maxcy: 23

Guerrillas: capture Yankee knapsacks, 84; get credit for ride around McClellan, 98; Kelley reports them driven out, 103; wreck train, 108; threaten railroads, 109; renew activity, 127; trouble pickets, 134; face busiest years, 167; busy following Gettysburg campaign, 188; Sargent's formula for eliminating, 196; criticized by Rosser, 213; close in on Sigel, 232; block ammunition, 250; Tyler prescribes only interment for, 260; ignored in official correspondence, 265; annoy Sheridan, 276; efforts to erase, 287; influence

Sheridan's turning back, 296; cause heavy detachments, 297; interfere with railroad workers, 297; Sheridan threatens to burn entire country to stop, 312; prevent Sheridan's march, 320; share in Thanksgiving turkey, 336; Early urges disbanding, 355; without leaders, 365; continue depredations, 366; defiant, 367; disperse, 370

Guerrilla warfare: 4; effect of, 8, 10, 12; proposed, 11; invited by Federal government, 12; topography at Manassas favors, 17; approved by Confederacy, 21; McClellan issues proclamation against, 26; McClellan reports guerrillas have disappeared, 32; "the only way," 38; on increase, 41, 63; Ashby sets example for, 74; demand for, 75; frowned on, 76; Frémont learns about, 79; Milroy inquires about punishment for, 80; grows in popularity, 82; Letcher threatens retaliation, 90; recrimination against varies, 91, 95; Lieber gives views on, 94; encouraged by Pope; drive against tightened, 191; criticized by Rosser, 213; quicker punishment for, 259; wholesale plan bared, 348; wholesale plan indorsed, 353

Halleck, Gen. Henry W.: asks Lieber's views on guerrilla warfare, 93; tables White's suggestion, 107; wires Pope for information, 109, 110; asks probe of Milroy report, 129; blames Schenck for Cheat River raid, 165; angered by guerrillas, 189; warns citizens about O. & A., 191; irritates Meade, 206; no faith in Sigel, 242; guerrillas bar information, 255, 259; urges caution against guerrillas, 261; warns of retaliation, 267; urges merging departments, 272; 296; warns of guerrillas along railroad, 297; wants Mosby driven out, 298; changes mind about railroad, 302; wants Mosby broken up, 335; refuses parole to Mosby, 367

Halltown, Va.: Grant moves base to, 272; Sheridan moves back to, 277

Leopole, Andrew T.: 246
Letcher, Governor John: troubled by
  W. Va., 11; worried over B. & O.,
  12; authorized to issue Ranger commissions, 77; acts to protect guerrillas, 90; asks Dan Dusky's release,
  139; home burned, 251
Lieber, Dr. Francis: Halleck asks
  views on guerrilla warfare, 93; interpretation violated, 279
Lincoln, Abraham: calls for action,
  33; upset by Baker's death, 60;
  forces McClellan to divide army,
  62; favors advance by Manassas,
  78; delays guerrilla punishment, 89;
  ousts McClellan, 99; issues Emancipation Proclamation, 116; criticized by Hite, 122; heckles McClellan, 126; Proclamation angers people, 139; quips about generals, 157;
  Mosby sends lock of hair, 230;
  agrees to Hunter, 243; fears for
  safety of Washington, 267; brings
  Grant up in person, 272; warns
  against defeat, 278; 361; fears for
  Washington and vicinity, 364;
  assassinated, 367
Little Cacapon, W. Va.: Imboden attacks, 122
Long, Francis: 308
Longstreet, Gen. James: reported near
  Salem, 111; reported sent to Valley,
  268; fake message concerning, 314
Loring, Alonzo: 15
Loring, W. W.: resents Lee's pres-
  ence, 61
Loudoun Heights: Mosby attacks on,
  211
Loudoun Rangers: guilty of misdo-
  ings, 109; sent to help erase guer-
  rillas, 285; annihilated, 366
Loudoun Valley: scorched, 333, 339,
  340; troops assembling in, 364
Louisville *Courier:* 52
Louisville *Journal:* 52
Lowe, C. W.: 215
Lowell, Charles R.: 218; sent after
  Mosby, 230; reports "perfect rout,"
  261
Lowell, James Russell: 218
Lynchburg, Va.: Early sent toward,
  252; Hunter retreats from, 253
Lynn, John: 356-362

McCall, George A.: 53
McCarthy, John: 195
McCausland, Gen. John: drawn into
  Cheat River bridge raid, 161; gets
  ransom at Hagerstown, 261; con-
  verges on Chambersburg, 269
McClellan, Gen. George B.: ordered
  to Grafton, 17; leaves Ohio, 18;
  pokes along, 23; crosses to Parkersburg, 26; unsure of enemy strength,
  28; decides to break up guerrillas,
  281; congratulates men, 32; ordered
  to Washington, 40; building army,
  43; spirit spreads, 44; visits soldiers,
  45; takes his time, 49; approves
  reconnaissance, 53; visits Ball's
  Bluff, 57; succeeds Scott, 61; moves
  to Fort Monroe, 78; warns Lee
  against retaliating, 90; Seven Days
  battles, 98; ousted, 99; returned
  to command, 114; starts moving
  army, 127; ousted for Burnside, 127
McCrickett, M. J.: 298; visits railroad,
  300; killed, 301
McDonald, Angus: offers services, 24;
  wants Ashby commissioned, 25
McDonald, Cornelia: remembered
  Ashbys, 25; visits Milroy, 141; does
  no rejoicing over Milroy's fate, 183
McDowell, Gen. Irvin: discounts
  alarm, 23; leads advance, 34; army
  in retreat, 40; bothered by guerrillas, 83
McIlhany, Hugh M.: 344
McKinley, William: 361
McMaster, Charles: 293
McNeil, John: 140
McNeill, George: 47
McNeill, Jesse: 47; named lieutenant,
  112; escorts mother, 307; takes over
  command, 307; plans capture of
  Kelley, 356; captures Kelley and
  Crook, 356-362; asks truce, 369
McNeill, John Hanson: thinks of guerrilla warfare, 47; arrives in East,
  112; captures New Yorkers, 117;
  force reduced, 137; draws attention
  to parole racket, 143; praised for
  raid, 144; plans destruction of
  Cheat River bridge, 160; cooperates in raid, 165; drive to catch,
  170; captures Romney, 177; cooperates in Gettysburg advance, 182;

424

wife, children arrested, 196; attacks camp at Moorefield, 198; grazed by bullet, 202; denied authority to increase command, 202; captures wagon train, 207; aids Early, 210; passes up wagon train, 210; crosses Rosser, 213; goes on second Early raid, 214; second run-in with Rosser, 215; with Imboden, 232; ordered to attack B. & O., 233; court-martialed, 233; helps rout Sigel troops, 239; eludes Hart, 245; on Hunter's trail, 247; captures bathers, 257; attacks at Huttonsville, 286; mortally wounded, 305; wife attends bedside, 306; admits identity, 307; death, 307; men save White, 312; South Branch Valley raid, 337; Rangers in disfavor, 353-355

McNeill, William: 47

McNeill's Rangers: organized, 112; cooperate with Jones, 143

Magnolia Station: 263

Manassas Gap Railroad: condition bad, 84; Union to operate, 188; Grant proposes reopening, 295; work begins, 297; Halleck warns guerrillas present, 297; citizens made to ride trains, 301; homes near tracks burned, 302; burning increased, 302; rails to be taken up, 302

Manassas, Va.: occupied by Rebels, 16, 17; Johnston ordered to, 35; Rebels fall back, 67; Jackson destroys supplies at, 111

Marion, Francis: 48

Martin, George W.: 304

Martinsburg, W. Va.: Sigel concentrating at, 232; 233; panicked by guerrillas, 238, 322; Early captures, 260

Matthews, Andrew W.: 122

Maulsby, William P.: 246

Meade, Gen. George G.: misses chances to catch Mosby, 181; reported sending troops to Burnside, 204; backs up, 206; irritated by Halleck, 206; angered by soldiers, 210; advance on Richmond, 228

Means, Samuel C.: leads Loudoun Rangers, 93; attacked by White,

109; calls for help, 110; routed by Munford, 112

Meigs, John R.: killed, 303; no patience for Partisans, 304

Meigs, M. C.: ordered to reopen Manassas Gap line, 189; son killed, 303

Melvin, Thayer.: 359

Merritt, Gen. Wesley: heads cavalry division, 272; heads Loudoun Valley raid, 340; ordered on new drive, 364

Middleburg, Va.: citizens protest, 166

Miles, D. S.: 109

Miller, Simon: 306

Milroy, Gen. R. H.: impatient for action, 79; slurs at Pierpont, 80; wants to hang Chewning, 89; heads for Virginia Central Railroad, 128; defies government, 130; engenders hatred, 140; wants guerrillas broken up, 143; says $100,000 offered for his head, 144; aspires to capture Jones, 144; asks permission to break up Imboden, 145; bluffed by enemy, 172; chased out of Winchester, 183

Moorefield, W. Va.: McNeill attacks camp at, 198; raid after McNeill's men, 338

Morris, T. A.: 28

Mosby, John Singleton: dreams of guerrilla warfare, 48; outlines plan for encircling McClellan, 96; cited as hero, 97; captured, 101; seeks independent service, 101; sent to Jackson, 102; exchanged for Lieut. Bayard, 102; informs Lee Pope to be reinforced, 102; joins guerrillas, 137; busy around Middleburg, 145; centers attention on Fairfax, 149; notifies Stuart about Union cavalry at Fairfax, 151; attacks Union party at Aldie, 152; captures Stoughton, 156; drive to catch, 165, 170; attacks at Herndon Station, 166; citizens punished, 166; praised and promoted, 166; asked to scout railroad, 167; attacks at Warrenton Junction, 168; trap set for him, 170; busy around Washington, 172; visits wounded Yankee, 173; destroys train at Catlett Station, 174; captures Stahel's reserves, 177; escapes to limb of tree, 178; horse captured, 179; organizes command, 179; attacks at Seneca, 179; bribe proposed, 180; captures Hooker's dispatches, 180; proposes Stuart route, 180; Meade tries to capture, 181; prisoners describe Rangers, 191; censured by Lee, 192; torpedoes to be sent, 193; wounded near Gooding's Tavern, 194; death announced, 195; reported at parents' home, 196; returns to command, 204; captures Dulaney, 205; Christmas party raided, 208; Loudoun Heights attack, 211; Stuart defends, 214; reconnoiters enemy on his trail, 230; lock of hair, 230; tries to capture Pierpont, 231; misses capturing Grant, 231; enters Martinsburg, 232; strikes toward Grant's communications, 233; Partisan most feared, 237; cuts off Hunter's supplies, 244; reported in several places simultaneously, 248; gathers men to attack ammunition train, 254; gobbles up cherry-pickers, 256; attacks at Duffield Station, 257; doom prescribed by Ringgold cavalry, 261; men surprise picnickers, 262; heckles Washington outposts, 265; notifies Early of Crook's withdrawal, 267; worries Sheridan, 274; Berryville wagon train raid, 276; Grant orders Rangers hanged without trial, 279; men slay house-burners, 281; attacks at Annandale, 285; Blazer on trail, 287; stampedes Crook's train, 289; wounded near Falls Church, 289; men hanged by Custer, 294; reported riding on raids in buggy, 298; concentrates on railroad, 299; blocks railroad repair, 302; odds reported 69 to 1, 311; wrecks B. & O. train, 313; captures Duffie, 319; accused of fighting under black flag, 322; artillery captured, 324; asks authority to retaliate, 325; saves drummer boy, 329; hangs Custer's men, 325-331; sends Sheridan message about hangings, 331; routs Blazer, 335; junket to Richmond, 341; wounded at Lake home, 343-348; wholesale

guerrilla warfare, 348; congratulates McNeill's men, 361; routs raiding parties, 364; asked to protect country west of Gordonsville, 365; annihilates Loudoun Rangers, 366; refused parole, 367; defiant, 367; drawn into Lincoln assassination, 367; asks conference, 367; extension of truce, 368; leaves conference, 368; disbands, 368

191; trains interrupted, 205; Burnside to guard, 228

Ormsby, William E. (Pony): deserts, 218; executed, 219

Ould, Robert: complains about guerrilla treatment, 92; pursues report about Milroy, 129; protests Mrs. McNeill's arrest, 196

Parkersburg, W. Va.: troops to rendezvous at, 15; McClellan crosses to, 26; alarmed by guerrillas, 84, 105; George Dusky brought to, 221

Parkersburg Gazette: 93

Parsons, Abraham: 129

Parsons, Job: 128

Partisan Rangers: approved by Confederacy, 21; Va. authorizes, 76; authorized by Confederacy, 80; hard to combat, 80; advertisements for, 82; ordered exchanged, 95; criticized by Randolph, 107; Stuart advises against term, 167; criticized by Rosser, 213; cause Sigel to divide forces, 241

Patterson, Gen. Robert: ordered to Harpers Ferry, 17; leaves Philadelphia, 19; urges advance, 23; eluded by Johnston, 35

Peerce, John T.: 234

Pegram, Gen. John: 28

Pelham, John: 150; death, 178

Pendleton, Alexander S.: 85

Pennsylvania Bucktails: set trap for Mosby, 166

Philadelphia, Pa.: presented black flag, 321

Pickett, Gen. George E.: 259

Piedmont, W. Va.: residents forbidden to use lights, 210; McNeill on way to, 234; captured, 235; damage, 235

Pierce, R. Butler: 152

Pierpont, Francis H.: advises McClellan, 26; library destroyed, 164; 205; sent message by Mosby, 231

Pleasanton, Gen. Alfred: inquires about bribing Mosby, 179; ousted by Grant, 228

Point of Rocks, Md.: inspections at, 15; rock on railroad at, 18

Poolesville, Md.: home of "Lige" White, 46; raided by White, 132

Pope, Gen. John: encourages guerrilla warfare, 99; holds public responsible, 100; reviews army, 105; relieved of command, 114

Porterfield, Gen. George A.: sent to Grafton, 16; destroys B. & O. bridges, 17; meets resistance at Grafton, 18; escapes trap at Philippi, 19; reports Secessionists mistreated, 19

Potomac Home Brigade: Loudoun Heights attack, 211

Potomac River: Union troops cross, 17; open to crossings, 109

Potts, P. J.: 338

Powell, Louis Thornton: 367

Powell, Gen. William H.: orders hangings, 308; hangs Willis, 312

Power, Richard: 297; opens telegraph office, 298

Price, Gen. Sterling: 47

Proclamations: McClellan issues, 26; Beauregard issues, 43

Quantrill, William Clarke: 76

Radford, R. C. W.: proposes guerrilla warfare, 10

Randolph, George W.: cites faults of Confederate army, 106

Ranger service: proposed, 10, 11; authorized by Virginia, 76

Reed, Maggie: 189

Reid, John Whitelaw: 30

Richardson, Josiah W.: 66-73

Richmond, Va.: excitement at, 11; attention focuses on, 96; battles around, 98; Grant's strategy for surrender, 228; Sheridan ordered away, 250

Richmond Dispatch: urges guerrilla warfare, 10, 11; publishes guerrilla advertisements, 82; praises guerrilla warfare, 83

Ringgold Cavalry: moves to Greenland Gap, 64; chases Ashby, 74-75; surprised by Mosby, 261; defended by McNeill's men, 312

St. George, W. Va.: captured by Imboden, 130

Salem, Va.: Mosby party raided at, 208; Mosby disbands at, 368
Sargent, Horace Binney: 196
Sayles, Lieutenant Colonel: 66-73
Schenck, Gen. Robert C.: notifies railroad reconstructed, 139; blamed for Cheat River raid, 165; daughters on captured train, 236
Scott, John: 82
Scott, Gen. Winfield: directs arming of Washington, 11; fretted by Butler, 16; orders McClellan to Grafton, 17; has trouble with Union generals, 23; accuses Patterson, 35; acts after Bull Run, 39; retires, 61
Second Massachusetts Cavalry Volunteers: Ormsby deserts, 218; routed by Mosby, 260
Second Massachusetts Infantry: cotton in ears, 106
Seddon, Secretary of War James A.: approves Cheat River bridge raid, 160; approves Mosby's retaliation, 326
Sedgewick, Gen. John: 207
Seventh Michigan Cavalry: chases Mosby, 176
Sharpsburg, Md.: fighting at, 114
Shenandoah Valley: Davis wants to hold, 19; military objective, 63; abandoned to Rebels, 188; to be blanked out, 273; destruction in, 309
Sheridan, Gen. Philip Henry: replaces Pleasanton, 228; ordered westward, 250; blocked, 251; called for by Grant, 271; Grant's favorite cavalry leader, 272; arrives in Washington, 272; goes to Monocacy, 272; told to follow enemy south, 272; forced to reorganize, 273; bothered by Mosby, 274; effort to capture fails, 274-276; starts moving, 276; faced by Early, 276; annoyed by guerrillas, 276; Rebel column reported on way, 276; Mosby wrecks wagon train, 276; moves back to Halltown, 277; couriers blocked, 278; reports execution of Mosby's men, 280; destroys Valley, 280; back at Halltown, 283; imprisons citizens, 286; plans circular hunt for guerrillas,

289; army moves again, 291; orders cavalry on flank movement, 292; decides to return to Harpers Ferry, 295; bothered by supply problems, 295; reaches Harrisonburg, 296; cavalry sweeps to Staunton, 296; advises ending Valley campaign, 296; reasons for turning back, 296; strength vastly superior, 297; messages blocked by guerrillas, 301; advises work on railroad be stopped, 301; attends Washington conference, 302; turns back, 303; avenges Meigs' death, 304; visits wounded McNeill, 307; estimate of McNeill, 307; tightens down on guerrillas, 308; destruction in Valley, 308; enemy forms in rear, 309; officers killed by guerrillas, 311; threatens to burn widely, 312; called to Washington, 313; gets fake message, 314; reaches Washington, 315; saves victory at Cedar Creek, 316; reports country clear of all but guerrillas, 320; says guerrillas held him back, 320; engineers outline defense, 320; flares at Stevenson, 321; gets madder about guerrillas, 336; ignores facts in postwar report, 337; orders raids after McNeill and Mosby, 337; criticizes Latham and Kelley, 339; threatens vengeance on Mosby, 339, 340; raid on Virginia Central, 343; orders new drive on Loudoun, 364; Stanton censures, 364; starts up Valley, 364; routs Early, 365; reaches Petersburg, 365
Sherman, Gen. William Tecumseh: to storm Atlanta, 228
Shields, Gen. James: fights Jackson, 77; contact severed, 82; transferred, 85
Sigel, Gen. Franz: ordered up Valley, 228; heads Department of W. Va., 228; troops ordered from B. & O., 230; troops concentrate, 232; orders strong escorts, 233; troubled by guerrillas, 237; divides forces, 238; appears at New Market, 240; defeat attributable to guerrillas, 241; blames defeat on

Virginia: Union invades, 17; Mc-Clellan occupies, 20; takes lead in guerrilla warfare, 76
Virginia Central Railroad: Pope strikes at, 100
Virginia Military Institute: cadets aid Imboden, 240; damaged by Hunter, 251

Walker, Leroy Pope: 8, 27
Wallace, Gen. Lew: reports fight with Ashby, 25; wife on captured train, 236; disturbed over raid, 237; witnesses execution, 246; says B. & O. infested with guerrillas, 250; meets Early, 262
Wallis, Tom: 310
Wardener, Baron R. B.: 154
Warrenton, Va.: Mosby visits, 167
Warrenton Junction, Va.: Mosby attacks at, 168
Washington, D. C.: armed, 11, 12; Kingsbury arrives in, 22; a madhouse, 33; Union troops move from, 34; Sixth Corps ordered to, 261
Washington, George: 25
Washington Star: criticizes Union cavalry, 153; reports guerrillas ordered close to main army, 205; reports Mosby sending. lock of hair, 231; Falls Church picnic, 262; Mosby visits Washington, 286; warns Mosby of gallows, 367
Watson, P. H.: orders guerrillas shot, 83, 84
Waynesboro, Va.: Sheridan's cavalry reaches, 296; Early routed at, 365
Weber, Gen. Max: wants cavalry sent after guerrillas, 244; subordinate to Sigel, 245; plans trap for Mosby, 257
Weller, Elizabeth: 306
Weller, Rev. Addison: 306
Welton, Felix B.: 356
West: guerrillas take field in, 76
West Virginia: would sustain Letcher, 12; citizens describe situation, 27; guerrillas increasing, 63; new state, 136; Early's cattle raid, 210; Hunter retreats toward, 253
Westbrook, Ulysses: 107

Wheeling, W. Va.: guerrillas active near, 63; Mary Jane Green returns, 85
Wheeling Intelligencer: predicts destructive guerrilla warfare, 44; reports guerrillas increasing, 63; heckles authorities, 79; reports on Jessie Scouts, 81; describes Mary Jane Green, 84; reports guerrillas driven out, 103; accuses McNeill, 210; reports on George Dusky, 221-225; scores Hunter, 253
White, Elijah V.: leads Gilmor on first scout, 46; joins Ashby, 47; cited at Ball's Bluff, 60; calls command "The Comanches," 61; wounded, 85; cooperates with Ewell, 99; ordered back by Stuart, 112; wounded, but forgives foe, 114; increases activity, wounded, 132; attached to Jackson, 137; cooperates in Cheat River raid, 165; drive to catch, 170; fights at Brandy Station, 177; takes lead on Gettysburg advance, 182; goes on second Early raid, 214; men disperse, 367
White, Francis Marion: 312
White, John Chester: fooled by baby cries, 207; describes Christmas celebration, 208
White, Julius: urges dismissal of Westbrook, 108; tries ruse against guerrillas, 111; flees Washington, 111
White Plains, Va.: Mosby attacks train at, 299; work crew reaches, 300
Wildes, Thomas F.: 305
Willard, Joseph C.: 158
Willis, A. C.: 312
Wilson, Gen. James H.: 272
Winchester, Va.: Jackson commands at, 62; Jackson strikes at, 84; Milroy commands at, 140; Crook routed at, 268; battle of, 291
Winchester and Potomac Railroad: to be reopened, 320; work crews guarded, 334
Winder, Gen. Charles S.: 101
Witcher, V. A.: 107
Woodson, Blake L.: leads McNeill's men, 326